Bernard Hamilton

Crusaders, Cathars and the Holy Places

Ashgate
VARIORUM

Aldershot · Brookfield USA · Singapore · Sydney

This edition copyright © 1999 by Bernard Hamilton.

Published in the Variorum Collected Studies Series by

Ashgate Publishing Limited
Gower House, Croft Road,
Aldershot, Hampshire GU11 3HR
Great Britain

Ashgate Publishing Company
Old Post Road,
Brookfield, Vermont 05036–9704
USA

Ashgate Website: http://www.ashgate.com

ISBN 0–86078–785–0

British Library Cataloguing-in-Publication Data
Hamilton, Bernard, 1932–
    Crusaders, Cathars and the Holy Places. (Variorum Collected Studies Series: CS656).
    1. Christianity – Europe, Western – Relations. 2. Crusades. 3. Europe, Western –
    Church History.
    I. Title.
    274'.05

US Library of Congress Cataloging-in-Publication Data
Bernard Hamilton, 1932–
    Crusaders, Cathars and the Holy Places / Bernard Hamilton.
        p.   cm. – (Variorum Collected Studies Series: CS656).
    1. Church History – Middle Ages, 600–1500. 2. Crusades. 3. Albigenses.
    4. Christian Shrines. 5. Latin Orient – Church History I. Title. II. Series:
    Collected Studies: CS656.
    BR270.H36   2000   99–042636
    270.421– dc21   CIP

The paper used in this publication meets the minimum requirements of the
    American National Standard for Information Sciences – Permanence of
    Paper for Printed Library Materials, ANSI Z39.48–1984.   ™

Printed by WBC Book Manufacturers Limited, Bridgend

VARIORUM COLLECTED STUDIES SERIES CS656

HELEN NICHOLSON
The Military Orders: Welfare and Warfare

MALCOLM BARBER
The Military Orders: Fighting for the Faith and Caring for the Sick

BENJAMIN Z. KEDAR, JOHNATHAN RILEY-SMITH and RUDOLF HIESTAND
Montjoie: Studies in Crusade History in Honour of Hand Eberhard Mayer

NICHOLAS COUREAS
The Latin Church in Cyprus 1195–1312

JOHN FRANCE and WILLIAM G. ZAJAC
The Crusades and their Sources

in the series Crusade Texts in Translation

PETER W. EDBURY
The Conquest of Jerusalem and the Third Crusade: Sources in Translation

JANET SHIRLEY
The Song of the Cathar Wars: A History of the Albingensian Crusade

HELEN NICHOLSON
The Chronicle of the Third Crusade: The *Itinerarium Peregrinorum et Gesta Regis Ricardi*

JANET SHIRLEY
Crusader Syria in the Thirteenth Century: The *Rothelin* Continuation of William of Tyre

and in the Collected Studies Series

PETER W. EDBURY
Kingdoms of the Crusaders: From Jerusalem to Cyprus

H.E.J. COWDREY
The Crusades and Latin Monasticism, 11th–12th Centuries

ANTHONY LUTTRELL
The Hospitaller State on Rhodes and its Western Provinces, 1306–1462

Professor Bernard Hamilton

VARIORUM COLLECTED STUDIES SERIES

Crusaders, Cathars and
the Holy Places

CONTENTS

This volume contains xii + 336 pages

ACKNOWLEDGEMENTS

I should like to thank the following for allowing my articles to be reproduced in this volume: Dr. Robert Swanson and The Ecclesiastical History Society (I and X); Professor H-E. Mayer, Dr. E. Müller-Luckner and the Historische Kolleg of Munich (II); Professor B.Z. Kedar (III); Dr. P.W. Edbury (IV); Miss Julian Chrysostomides and Porphyrogenitus Limited (V); Frank Cass Publishers (VI); Professor M.C.E. Jones and the Board of *Nottingham Medieval Studies* (VII); Dr. E. Rozanne Elder and Cistercian Publications Inc.(VIII); Victoria van Aalst and the A.A. Bredius Foundation of Kasteel Hernen, and the Peeters Press of Leuven (IX); Dr. David Morgan and the Royal Asiatic Society (XI); Adolf M. Hakkert (XII); Cambridge University Press (XIII); Revd. Mgr. Robert Trisco and *The Catholic Historical Review* (XV); Professor Edward Ingram and *The International History Review* (XVI); and Professor Mark Millington and *Renaissance and Modern Studies* (XVII).

PREFACE

The studies in this volume all deal with relations between Western Europe and the neighbouring civilizations in the Eastern Mediterranean. They fall into three main groups. The first is concerned with the settlement of westerners in the Crusader States in the twelfth and thirteenth centuries. Three of these essays are about the role of women in crusading society, which has hitherto received comparatively little attention. Yet because the states of the Latin East were almost permanently at war considerable powers often had to be delegated to women. Four essays deal with the Church in the Crusader Kingdom. Although the Catholic Church was established there, western Christians were always in a minority, and I have examined some of the ways in which Latin churchmen came to terms with this. My researches have shown that they were remarkably tolerant of eastern Christianity in its various forms. No attempt was made to convert members of other churches to Catholicism, but cordial relations were fostered between the Latins and some of the non-Chalcedonian Christians with the result that some oriental churches, notably the Maronites, were drawn into corporate union with the papacy. The Franks in the east also had many dealings with Muslims, as serfs and merchants and diplomats, as well as enemies on the battlefield. In essay XI I have considered how the Franks came to view their Muslim neighbours and whether they had any real understanding of the Islamic faith.

The second group of essays deals with the impact of eastern dualist heresy on western society, and the origins of Catharism. Because Christianity is a religion rooted in history, all churches have had to offer proofs of their descent from the Apostolic Church, and in essay XII I have tried to reconstruct what the Cathar Church's proofs may have been. When writing about the reaction of the Catholic Church to dualist heresy it is important to bear in mind that the authorities did not necessarily know nearly as much about it as modern scholars do. In essay XIV I have looked at one aspect of that problem and tried to estimate how much the Western Church authorities knew about the eastern dissident groups to whom the Cathars were affiliated.

The third group of essays is concerned with the Holy Places. The Crusade movement was launched, partly at least, in order to restore the Holy Land to Christian rule, and 1 have examined the way in which after the conquest the

Franks turned the shrine churches of the Holy Land, particularly those in Jerusalem, into Catholic Holy Places, and have tried to assess the impact which this had on the thousands of western pilgrims who visited them each year and how in the long-term this affected western piety. The final essay, on the shrine or Loreto, considers one way in which devotion to the Holy Places developed in Western Europe in the centuries after they had come once again under Muslim political control.

Many of these essays were first given as conference papers, and 1 should like to thank the sponsors who stimulated my research in that way: the Ecclesiastical History Society(I and X); the Society for the Study of the Crusades and the Latin East (III, IV, and XVI); the A.A. Bredius Foundation (IX); the Society for the Promotion of Byzantine Studies (XII); the School of Slavonic and East European Studies (XIV); and Professor Patrick O'Brien who invited me to address the 65th Anglo-American Conference of Historians, held at the Institute of Historical Research in London in 1996, on the theme of essay XI. A great deal has been written since I first published some of these essays and in the Addenda at the end of this volume I have given details of the more important new contributions, and have noted the cases in which authors have challenged my opinions or led me to change them. I have also taken the opportunity to correct inadvertent mistakes in my texts: these are indicated by asterisks in the margin of the essays and the corrections appear at the end of the relevant text.

I should like to express my thanks to Mrs Janice Avery for preparing the previously unpublished text of essay XIV for this volume; and to thank John Smedley and Ruth Peters for all the encouragement and practical help they have given me.

Looking back over the twenty years during which these articles were written, I am reminded of how much I owe to the advice of friends and colleagues in producing them. My special thanks are due to my undergraduate pupils on whom I first tried out many of the ideas expressed in these papers, and who often pointed out flaws in my arguments and suggested new lines of inquiry. I am also very grateful to the help which I have received from my postgraduate students and from my medieval colleagues in the History Department of the University of Nottingham. The Society for the Study of the Crusades and the Latin East was founded in 1980, and I have found it immensely helpful in my work on crusading history and should like to express my warmest thanks to its members for their advice and support. There is no parallel body in this country to coordinate the activities of those working on heresy, but I should like to give special thanks for help in that field to Malcolm Barber and Peter Biller, whose wise advice I have very much appreciated. Finally, I want to thank my wife Janet for the sustained practical help and the intellectual stimulus she has given me, particularly in my work on dualist heresy; and my daughters, Sarah and Alice, who have always been willing to make space in their busy lives to talk to me about my work. I very much appreciate that.

Nottingham, 1999   BERNARD HAMILTON

PUBLISHER'S NOTE

The articles in this volume, as in all others in the Collected Studies Series, have not been given a new, continuous pagination. In order to avoid confusion, and to facilitate their use where these same studies have been referred to elsewhere, the original pagination has been maintained wherever possible.

Each article has been given a Roman numeral in order of appearance, as listed in the Contents. This number is repeated on each page and quoted in the index entries.

I

WOMEN IN THE CRUSADER STATES: THE QUEENS OF JERUSALEM (1100–1190)

HE important part played by women in the history of the
crusader states has been obscured by their exclusion from the
battle-field. Since scarcely a year passed in the Frankish east
which was free from some major military campaign it is natural that
the interest of historians should have centred on the men responsible
for the defence of the kingdom. Yet in any society at war considerable
power has to be delegated to women while their menfolk are on active
service, and the crusader states were no exception to this general rule.
Moreover, because the survival rate among girl-children born to
Frankish settlers was higher than that among boys, women often
provided continuity to the society of Outremer, by inheriting their
fathers' fiefs and transmitting them to husbands many of whom came
from the west.

The queens of Jerusalem are the best documented group of women in
the Frankish east and form an obvious starting-point for any study of
the role of women there. There is abundant evidence for most of them
in a wide range of sources, comprising not only crusader chronicles
and documents, but also western, Byzantine, Syriac and Armenian
writers. Arab sources very seldom mentioned them: the moslem world
was clearly shocked by the degree of social freedom which western
women enjoyed[1] and reacted to women with political power much as
misogynist dons did to the first generation of women undergraduates,
by affecting not to notice them. Despite the fulness of the evidence there
is, so far as I am aware, no detailed study of any of the twelfth century
queens of Jerusalem with the notable exception of Mayer's article on
Melisende.[2] For reasons of brevity only the queens of the first kingdom
will be considered here.

Godfrey of Bouillon, the first Frankish ruler, was a bachelor and no
woman occupied a central position in the state until his brother,

---

[1] *The Autobiography of Ousâma,* trans G. R. Potter, (London 1929) p 177.
[2] [H. E.] Mayer, ['Studies in the History of Queen Melisende of Jerusalem',] *DOP* 26 (1972) pp 93–183.

Baldwin I, count of Edessa, succeeded him in 1100. Baldwin's wife, Godvera, had accompanied him on crusade, but had died at Marasch in October 1097.[3] Soon after this Baldwin married the daughter of the Armenian prince Thoros, brother of Constantine the Roupenian. Paoli called her Arda, and it is convenient to use this name, although it is given in no source known to me.[4] She was an only child, and potentially a great heiress[5] and was promised a dowry of 60,000 bezants which her impoverished husband sorely needed to raise troops to defend his county, while he also benefitted from the advice and alliance of his father-in-law.[6]

When he was summoned to Jerusalem in 1100 Baldwin travelled there by the hazardous land-route, but his wife and her ladies waited at Antioch for a ship to take them south.[7] Possibly the queen did not make the journey that winter: she would have needed a strong naval escort, since most of the coastal cities were still held by the moslems. Certainly she does not seem to have been present at Bethlehem when Baldwin was crowned there on Christmas day. By 1101 Arda had reached Jaffa, possibly escorted by a Genoese fleet which had wintered at Laodicea.[8] When the battle of Ramleh was fought in September 1101 she was still at Jaffa, and when a false rumour reached the garrison that the king had been killed she took charge and sent a message by sea to Antioch asking Tancred for help.[9]

Nothing more is known about her until the king repudiated her. William of Tyre implies that this happened before 1105, but Guibert of Nogent, a contemporary source, places it more exactly immediately after Arda's arrival in the kingdom. He tells a romantic story of how the king put away his wife because she had been raped by pirates on the

---

[3] A[lbert of] A[ix, *Historia Hierosolymitana*,] bk 3, cap 27, *RHC Occ* 4, p 358; H. Hagenmeyer, *Chronologie de la première Croisade (1094–1100)* (Paris 1902) no 196, pp 101–2. compare Orderic [Vitalis, *Historia Ecclesiastica*,] bk 5, cap 13, ed A. Le Prévost, L. Delisle, 5 vols (Paris 1838–55) 2, p 404.

[4] C. [du Fresne] Du Cange, [*Les Familles d'Outremer*, ed E. G. Rey] (Paris 1869) p 11.

[5] W. H. Rüdt-Collenberg, *The Rupenides, Hethumides and Lusignans. The Structure of the Armeno-Cilician Dynasties,* Calouste Gulbenkian Foundation Armenian Library (Paris 1963) table 1 and p 50 no 7.

[6] AA bk 3, cap 31, *RHC Occ* 4, p 361 places the marriage before Baldwin reached Edessa in March 1098; W[illiam of] T[yre, *Historia rerum in partibus transmarinis gestarum*,] bk 10, cap 1, *RHC Occ* 1, p 402 places it after he came to Edessa.

[7] WT bk 10, cap 5, *RHC Occ* 1, p 407; Guibert [of Nogent, *Gesta Dei per Francos*,] bk 7, cap 48, *RHC Occ* 4, p 259.

[8] F[ulcher of] C[hartres, *Historia Hierosolymitana (1095–1127)*,] bk 2, cap 8, [ed H. Hagenmeyer] (Heidelberg 1913) pp 393–4.

[9] *Ibid* bk 2, cap 14, p 421.

Queens of Jerusalem

voyage south.[10] William of Tyre is more cautious: some people, he says, believed that the queen had been unfaithful, but others supposed that the king wished to make a more advantageous marriage. Fulcher of Chartres who, as Baldwin's chaplain, was in a unique position to know the truth about the separation, is totally silent. This suggests that the rumours about the queen's unfaithfulness were not true, since if they had been the king's repudiation of his wife would have met with general sympathy. Fulcher's silence implies that the king's action was criticised, and circumstantial evidence suggests that Baldwin's motives were political rather than moral: the marriage to a Roupenian princess which had been politically advantageous to him as count of Edessa was valueless to him as king of Jerusalem; the bride's father had only paid a fraction of the dowry;[11] and the queen was still childless after several years of marriage.[12] All these factors suggest that Baldwin's chief concern was to marry a richer wife who would bear him an heir. The marriage was not annulled. William of Tyre states that the separation took place 'without due process of law', and the queen was forced to take the veil at Saint Anne's Jerusalem.[13] She lived as a nun for some years and then asked permission to visit her kin in Constantinople on a fund-raising mission. Once there she abandoned the religious habit and, according to William of Tyre, lived promiscuously,[14] though this may be doubted since the king later professed his readiness to take her back.

A suitably rich replacement for Arda was not immediately available, and Jerusalem was without a queen for some years. Then in 1112 the patriarch Arnulf persuaded Baldwin to seek the hand of Adelaide, countess dowager of Sicily, who must have been in her late thirties.[15] Since the death of her husband, Roger I, in 1101, she had acted as regent of Sicily until Roger II came of age in 1112.[16] An alliance with

[10] Guibert, bk 7, cap 48, *RHCOcc* 4, p 259.
[11] 7,000 of the promised 60,000 bezants, AA bk 3, cap 31. *RHC Occ* 4, p 361.
[12] Orderic bk 9, cap 11, 3, p 570.
[13] Although this was later a Latin convent it may have been an eastern rite community at this time, since Arda was an Armenian Christian. B. Hamilton, 'Rebuilding Zion: the Holy Places of Jerusalem in the twelfth century', *SCH* 14 (1977) p 111.
[14] WT bk 11, cap 1, *RHC Occ* 1, pp 451–2.
[15] She married Roger I in 1089 as a young woman and had probably been born in *c*1074. Her marriage settlement shows that she was not considered to be above the age of child-bearing in 1113 and there seems no reason for crediting Orderic Vitalis's report that she was a wrinkled old hag when she married Baldwin, Orderic bk 13, cap 15, 5, p 36.
[16] For an account of her regency see J. J. Norwich, *The Normans in the South* (London 1967) pp 280–9.

Sicily, the nearest western power to the crusader states, and one which had a strong navy, was attractive to Baldwin, and so was the countess's wealth, of which his penurious kingdom stood in great need. He therefore instructed his envoys to agree to any conditions which the Sicilian court might make: these were onerous, for it was required that not only should any child born of the marriage be heir to the kingdom, but also that if the union were childless Roger II of Sicily should succeed Baldwin. The countess reached Acre in August 1113 with a large dowry[17] and also, according to Albert of Aix, with a thousand men-at-arms in her suite and a company of Saracen archers. It is a matter of conjecture whether her ship-of-state was so ornate as Albert reports, since he was writing from hearsay.[18]

Initially the countess's money eased the financial problems of the state, but she failed to produce the heir that the king needed.[19] The prospect of the succession of the count of Sicily, which became more likely as the countess passed the age of childbearing, was not viewed with enthusiasm by some of the Jerusalem baronage. They attacked the marriage-settlement indirectly through the patriarch. Arnulf was very vulnerable: he was accused of simony and concubinage, and was also denounced for solemnising a bigamous marriage between Baldwin and Adelaide while the king's first wife was still alive at Constantinople. The case finally went to Rome where, as his opponents had perhaps correctly calculated, Arnulf was able to clear himself of all the charges made against him except that relating to the Sicilian marriage where the facts were beyond dispute. In July 1116 Paschal II re-instated him as patriarch[20] on condition that he secured the separation of Baldwin and Adelaide.[21] That proved easy, because in the winter of that year Baldwin fell gravely ill and was persuaded by his clergy that he had contracted a bigamous marriage. He therefore vowed to dismiss Adelaide and recall Arda, a decision which seems to have been motivated solely by religious conviction, since he would have gained nothing from a reconciliation with his long-estranged wife.[22]

Life in the royal household must have been strained in the Lent of

[17] WT bk 11, cap 21, RHC Occ 1, pp 487–9; FC bk 2, cap 51, pp 575–7 relates her arrival but says nothing about her dowry.
[18] AA bk 12, cap 13, RHC Occ 4, pp 696–7.
[19] WT bk 11, cap 21, RHC Occ 1, p 489.
[20] FC bk 2, cap 54, p 591; WT bk 11, cap 26, RHC Occ 1, p 499; Paschal II's bull of 19 July 1116 in [E.] de Rozière, [Cartulaire de l'Église du Saint-Sépulchre de Jérusalem], Collection des documents inédits sur l'histoire de France, 1 ser, 5 (Paris 1849) no 11, pp 11–13.
[21] AA bk 12, cap 24, RHC Occ 4, p 704.
[22] FC bk 2, cap 59, p 601; WT bk 11, cap 29, RHC Occ 1, p 506.

Queens of Jerusalem

1117. The queen was highly indignant at the treatment she had received, and had to undergo the further humiliation of having her marriage annulled by a church synod at Acre.[23] Moreover, though she lost her husband and her royal status she did not recover her dowry, which had been spent. On Saint Mark's day 1117 she finally sailed to Sicily,[24] vowing to build churches to Saint Anne and the Blessed Virgin if she made the journey in safety. She fulfilled this vow,[25] but she did not long enjoy the peace of Sicily, where she died on 16 April 1118.[26] The ill-treatment accorded to her was not only inhumane, it was also politically ill-advised. Her son never forgave the insult to his mother or the disregard of his own rights of succession under the terms of her marriage settlement. Writing some fifty years later William of Tyre laments that the rulers of Sicily, alone of all the kings of the West, had never sent help to Jerusalem.[27]

Queen Arda did not return to her husband after Adelaide's departure, and when Baldwin I died in 1118 there was no queen in Jerusalem. He was succeeded by his cousin, Baldwin II, count of Edessa, who had come to Jerusalem on pilgrimage and arrived there by chance in time for his predecessor's funeral.[28] Baldwin II had also married an Armenian wife after he became count of Edessa, probably in 1100. She was Morphia, daughter of Gabriel of Melitene who, though an Armenian, was Orthodox in religion. The alliance of Gabriel was initially valuable to Baldwin, as, no doubt, was the large dowry which his wife brought him.[29] Unlike his royal cousin, Baldwin II was happily married; it was as well for Morphia that this was so, since she signally failed to meet two of the chief requirements in the wife of any medieval ruler: her father's principality was conquered by the Turks soon after her marriage, so that no long-term political advantage accrued to her husband from the match; and she failed to produce a male heir. When Baldwin became king the couple had three daughters, Melisende, Alice and Hodierna, and the queen subsequently gave birth to a fourth girl,

[23] AA bk 12, cap 24, *RHC Occ* 4, p 704.
[24] FC bk 2, cap 60, p 602.
[25] [H. F.] Delaborde, [*Chartes de la Terre Sainte provenant de l'abbaye de Notre-Dame de Josaphat,*] B[*ibliothèque des*] É[*coles*] F[*rançaises d'*] A[*thènes et de*] R[*ome*], 19 (Paris 1880) no 20, pp 38–40.
[26] FC bk 2, cap 63, p 608 and n 14.
[27] WT bk 12, cap 29, *RHC Occ* 1, p 506.
[28] *Ibid* bk 12, cap 2, *RHC Occ* 1, pp 512–13; FC bk 3, cap 1, p 616.
[29] WT bk 10, cap 24, *RHC Occ* 1, p 437, places this marriage before the arrival of Jocelyn Courtenay in the east with the crusade of 1101.

I

Yveta.[30] Matthew of Edessa remarks that Baldwin was devoted to his wife[31] and this is borne out by the fact that he delayed his coronation for almost eighteen months, until Christmas day 1119, so that she could travel to Jersualem and be crowned with him.[32]

Perhaps as a result of the oriental environment in which she had grown up the queen took no part in the public life of the kingdom: her name is never associated with Baldwin's in any of his acts. Nevertheless, she was capable of taking the initiative in political affairs when necessary. When the king was captured by Nur-ad-Dualah Balak in 1123 Morphia is alleged to have hired Armenians who disguised themselves as Turks and infiltrated the garrison of Kharpart where the king was held.[33] She certainly took a central part in the negotiations leading to Baldwin's release in 1124, travelling to north Syria, and handing over her youngest daughter, Yveta, as a hostage to stand surety for the payment of the king's ransom.[34] Paradoxically, although the exact day of Morphia's death is known—it was 1 October—[35] the year is not, although it took place before 1129. She was buried in the shrine church of our Lady of Josaphat at Jerusalem.[36]

Neither Morphia nor either of the wives of Baldwin I had taken any public part in the government of the kingdom, but because Baldwin II had no sons he recognised his eldest daughter, Melisende, as his heir, and towards the end of his reign she began to be associated with him in official documents. In March 1129 she witnessed a grant which the king made to the Holy Sepulchre and took precedence over all the clergy,[37] while in another document from about the same period she

[30] Ibid bk 12, cap 4, RHC Occ I, p 517.
[31] M[atthew of] E[dessa, Chronique d'Arménie,] cap 76, Armenian text with French translation, RHC Arm I, p 119.
[32] FC bk 3, cap 7, p 635.
[33] Armenian infiltrators certainly played some part in Baldwin's escape attempt. WT bk 12, cap 18, RHC Occ I, pp 538–9; Morphia's involvement is recorded by Orderic, bk 11, cap 26, 4, pp 250–1.
[34] ME cap 91, RHC Arm I, p 139.
[35] Entry in the calendar of queen Melisande's psalter, ed [H.] Buchtal, [Miniature Painting in the Latin Kingdom of Jerusalem] with liturgical and palaeographical chapters by F. Wormald (Oxford 1957) pp 124–6.
[36] [C.] Kohler, ['Chartes de l'abbaye de Notre-Dame de la vallée de Josaphat en Terre Sainte (1108–1291). Analyse et extraits'], R[evue de l'] O[rient] L[atin], 7 (Paris 1899) no 21, p 128, which was drawn up before Melisende's marriage in June 1129. Compare de Rozière no 46, pp 85–6, in which Baldwin II remits some customs charges on pilgrims in the port of Acre for the repose of Morphia's soul.
[37] de Rozière no 44, pp 81–3. This is dated the fourth indiction, March 1128. The indiction has certainly been wrongly transcribed. As the patriarch Stephen was present on this occasion, and only took office in 1128, it seems likely that the new year

Queens of Jerusalem

styled herself *filia regis et regni Jerosolimitani haeres*.[38] She married count Fulk V of Anjou, an experienced ruler, and a widower with grown sons who had been chosen as her husband by Louis VI of France. The wedding took place at whitsuntide 1129. Mayer argues that Baldwin II had originally promised Fulk sole right of succession, implying that Melisende was only to be queen-consort, but that on his deathbed he altered the terms of the settlement and associated Melisende and the infant Baldwin III with Fulk as joint-heirs, fearing lest after his death Fulk should repudiate Melisende and make one of the sons of his first marriage his heir. This is not convincing, since the accounts which William of Tyre gives of the terms of the marriage settlement and of the king's dying wishes are not incompatible: in the account of the marriage settlement there is nothing to suggest that Baldwin was intending to exclude Melisende from power. An important indication of Baldwin's intentions in the matter of the succession is the grant which he made to the Holy Sepulchre in 1130-1, in which he associated both Fulk and Melisende with him, which implies that from the time of the marriage he treated them as joint-heirs of the kingdom.[39] In 1130 Melisende gave birth to the future Baldwin III, and thus the succession was assured before the death of her father on 21 August 1131. On Holy Cross Day, 14 September, an important feast in the crusader kingdom, Fulk and Melisende were crowned in the church of the Holy Sepulchre.[40]

After her father's death Melisende did not enjoy the power which she had previously possessed: she is not associated with Fulk in any public act in the first five years of his reign. The revolt of Hugh II of Le Puiset, count of Jaffa, which Mayer convincingly argues took place in 1134, happened in this period. The facts of this *cause célèbre* are known only through William of Tyre. The king took a strong dislike to Hugh who was thought to be having a liaison with the queen. Some time later Hugh's stepson accused him of treason in the curia regis, and Hugh retired to Jaffa, allied with the moslems of Ascalon and defied the royal army which was sent against him. Peace was mediated by the patriarch, who obtained lenient terms from the king: the rebels were to be exiled

---

reckoning employed began on March 25 and that in modern style the document should be dated March 1129.

[38] Kohler, *ROL* 7, no 21, p 128.

[39] de Rozière no 43, pp 80–1. The marriage settlement is in WT bk 13, cap 24, *RHC Occ* 1, p 594: the account of the dying king's wishes *ibid* bk 13, cap 28, *RHC Occ* 1 pp 601–2. See Mayer, *DOP* 26, pp 99–102.

[40] WT bk 14, cap 2, *RHC Occ* 1, pp 608–9.

for three years, but at the end of that time they might return and resume their fiefs. But before Hugh left, an unsuccessful assassination attempt was made on him, which was commonly supposed to have been instigated by the king, although his collusion was never proved. Hugh then went to Apulia, where he died before his sentence had run its term, but the queen bitterly resented the way Hugh had been treated and the slight on her own honour. As a result, the king's supporters went in terror of their lives, and even the king himself did not feel safe among the queen's suite. Finally peace was mediated between Fulk and Melisende and, concludes William of Tyre, the king 'did not attempt to take the initiative, even in trivial matters, without her knowledge'.[41]

Mayer is undoubtedly correct in discounting the love element in this story: if Fulk had been a wronged husband a strong section of public opinion, led by the church, would have sided with him, not, as it did, with the queen, in a matter which might concern the royal succession. Mayer rightly sees the conflict as a dispute between the king's supporters, and those whose loyalties lay with the queen as Baldwin II's daughter. Hugh of Le Puiset, who was Melisende's second cousin, and the only great nobleman of the blood royal in the kingdom, was the natural leader of the queen's party.[42] There was evidently widespread resentment among some sections of the nobility and the church about the way in which the queen was being treated. I am not convinced by Mayer's argument that Fulk was trying to implement the terms of his marriage settlement and set aside the dying wishes of the old king, since I would suggest that the two settlements did not differ; but whichever interpretation is correct, the consequence was the same: Fulk excluded Melisende from power.[43] This was not simply a matter of protocol, but also one of patronage: unless the queen had some effective share in the affairs of state she could not reward her supporters with appointments and land. Hugh's revolt failed because he made the tactical error of allying with the saracens, thereby alienating many of his own supporters, but at this point Melisende first

---

[41] *Ibid* bk 14, caps 15–18, *RHC Occ* 1, pp 627–33; on the dating see Mayer, *DOP* 26, pp 104–6.

[42] In *c*1129 Hugh of Le Puiset witnessed a charter of Baldwin II immediately after the princess Melisende, Kohler, *ROL* 7, no 21, p 128.

[43] Mayer *DOP* 26, pp 102–13. I can find no evidence to support Mayer's view that Fulk may have wished to repudiate Melisende and set aside the claims of Baldwin III in favour of Elias, the younger son of his first marriage. He seems only to have wished to reduce Melisende to the status of a consort.

Queens of Jerusalem

showed her considerable powers of initiative. She rallied her supporters, particularly the churchmen, obtained lenient terms for the
rebel count, and, when an attempt was made to infringe this settlement,
made life so unpleasant for the king that he was forced to recognise
that he could only continue to rule with her co-operation.

The reconciliation of Fulk and Melisende took place before 1136
when their younger son, Amalric, was born.[44] Thereafter the queen
was regularly associated with her husband in official documents
relating to the kingdom of Jeruselam.[45] The scale on which she was
able to dispense patronage in those years was expressed in a spectacular
way in 1138. Of her three sisters, Alice had been married to
Bohemond II of Antioch in her father's lifetime, and Hodierna to
Raymond II of Tripoli earlier in Fulk's reign, but her youngest sister,
Yveta, had become a nun at Saint Anne's. Melisende, who did not
consider it fitting that a king's daughter should be a simple choir-sister,
founded a convent at Bethany so that when she was old enough her
sister could become abbess there.[46] Recent excavations have revealed
the extensive scale of the building operations at Bethany [47] and the
house received endowments commensurate with its status as a royal
abbey, including the fertile plain of Jericho. The queen also supplied
rich furnishings and liturgical vessels to the house, wishing 'that it
should not be inferior to any community of men or women in the
kingdom in wordly wealth.'[48]

In the later years of Fulk's life Melisende might justly be described as
co-ruler, and from 1138 the child Baldwin III was associated with his
parents in some of their acts.[49] No woman had previously enjoyed
such power in the kingdom, but it was to grow greater. In 1143 Fulk

[44] Amalric was seven when Fulk died in 1143, WT bk 15, cap 27, *RHC Occ* I, p 702,
[45] The first of these relates to the gift of Bethgibelin to the Hospital in 1136.
C[artulaire] G[énérale de l'] O[rdre des] H[ospitaliers de St.-Jean de Jérualem (1100–1310).
ed J. Delaville Le Roulx], 4 vols (Paris 1894–1906) I, no 116. As Mayer points out,
Melisende is not associated with Fulk in documents which he issued as administrator
of Antioch, *DOP* 26, pp 109–10.
[46] de Rozière no 33, pp 60–5. Bethany belonged to the canons of the Holy Sepulchre,
who were given Thecua in exchange. As Yveta was only about eighteen in 1138 an
elderly abbess was appointed on the understanding that the princess would succeed
her.
[47] S. J. Saller, *Excavations at Bethany (1949–1953), Publications of the Studium Biblicum
Franciscanum* 12 (Jerusalem 1957).
[48] WT bk 15, cap 26, *RHC Occ* I, pp 699–700.
[49] For example, de Rozière no 32, pp 58–60; [A.] de Marsy, ['Fragment d'un cartulaire
de l'Ordre de St.-Lazare en Terre Sainte',] A[rchives de l'] O[rient] L[atin], 2 vols
(Paris 1884) 2, no 2, p 124.

was killed in a hunting accident: Melisende made the public demonstration of grief which her position as chief mourner required; then she took over the government. Baldwin III was only thirteen, and Melisende is commonly said to have acted as regent for him. This is not what she considered her position to be, nor is it what William of Tyre believed her to have done: he writes, *reseditque regni potestas penes dominam Melisendem, Deo amabilem reginam, cui jure hereditario competebat.*[50] Melisende was not a regent, but the queen regnant.

Baldwin III and Melisende were crowned on Christmas day 1143.[51] The association of the boy Baldwin with his mother shows the strength of feeling in this feudal society that there should be a male head of state, but while Baldwin was under age all power was in the hands of the queen. By reason of her sex she could not command the army, so she appointed Manasses of Hierges, her cousin, who had only recently arrived from the west, as constable of the kingdom, the officer who deputised for the king in military affairs.[52] In this way she avoided giving too much power to one of her subjects, which might have weakened the royal authority. As co-ruler with a thirteen year old child Melisende had no alternative but to take the measures she did: what surprised her contemporaries was that she showed no signs of relinquishing power to him when he came of age in 1145, an occasion which was marked by no public solemnity.

It would be otiose to describe the build-up of tension between Baldwin and Melisende since Mayer has discussed the evidence so thoroughly.[53] A breach had clearly occurred between them by 1150, when Melisende began to issue documents in her own name without reference to Baldwin.[54] No complaint was made about the quality of the queen's government: she seems to have been a good administrator and to have ruled wisely; but Baldwin and his supporters resented the fact that he had no share in power and was not allowed to make independent decisions. The king blamed the constable Manasses for alienating his mother from him, and matters reached a crisis in 1152

[50] WT bk 15, cap 27, *RHC Occ* I, p 702 dates Fulk's death 1142, but since he also states that Baldwin III was then thirteen Fulk must have died in 1143. Melisende and Fulk were not married until Pentecost 1129 (Whitsun fell on June 2 in that year), so Baldwin cannot have been born before March 1130.
[51] WT bk 16, cap 3, *RHC Occ* I, p 707.
[52] He was in office by 1144 when he led the royal relief force to Edessa, *ibid* bk 16, cap 4, *RHC Occ* I, p 710.
[53] Mayer *DOP* 26, pp 114–66.
[54] de Marsy, *AOL* 2, no 8, p 129, no 10, pp 130–1; de Rozière no 49, pp 90–2, no 48, pp 87–9.

I

Queens of Jerusalem

when Baldwin demanded to be crowned in the Holy Sepulchre on easter day without his mother's being present. The patriarch Fulcher refused to agree to this, so on easter Monday, 31 March, the king staged a solemn procession through Jerusalem, wearing a laurel wreath as a symbol of royal power, presumably because the patriarch refused to let him use the crown jewels.[55]

Baldwin then summoned the high court and demanded that the kingdom should be divided between his mother and himself. The request was criminally irresponsible, for the small kingdom could only maintain its defences satisfactorily if its military resources were under a unified command. Melisende agreed, presumably because she thought that such a solution would be less dangerous to the state than a civil war: she kept Samaria and Judaea while Baldwin held the north.[56] Melisende has often been criticised for not resigning power gracefully to her son at this time: it is difficult to see what justification she would have felt for doing so; she obviously had the support of the church and of most of the southern lords; she was not a regent clinging tenaciously to power after the heir had reached his majority, but the acknowledged co-ruler of the kingdom; she had governed well, but her son was in-experienced and had shown little capacity for government hitherto. The most important need of the kingdom was to avert a civil war, so she acquiesced in the demands of Baldwin and the northern baronage who supported him.

Mayer is surely right in asserting that this situation lasted only for a few weeks.[57] The king retired to the north, raised an army and invaded his mother's half of the kingdom. He defeated and deposed the constable, siezed Nablus, and was admitted to Jerusalem by the citizens. Melisende was deserted by many of her vassals, perhaps because the king had now proved himself to be a competent general, which the state needed, and they feared to prolong the civil war in case their enemies took advantage of it. But some of her followers remained loyal to the queen, notably Rohard the Old, castellan of Jerusalem, Philip of Nablus, and her younger son, Amalric, count of Jaffa. The queen and her supporters fortified themselves in the tower of David, to which Baldwin III laid siege. This unedifying spectacle of son fighting mother and brother was brought to an end by the intervention of some unnamed peacemakers, perhaps churchmen. It might have been

[55] WT bk 17, cap 13, *RHC Occ* I, p 781.
[56] *Ibid* bk 17, cap 14, *RHC Occ* I, p 781.
[57] *DOP* 16, pp 166–71.

153

I

expected that Melisende, who had no hope of winning against such unequal odds, would have been allowed to retire with dignity to live with her sister in the convent of Bethany, but she held out for better terms: the city of Nablus and its adjacent lands were granted to her for life and the king swore a solemn oath that he would not disturb her peace.[58] This shows that although the queen had lost the war she still had powerful allies, for sixteen years of authority had enabled her to exercise a great deal of patronage. The patriarch and the church as a whole took her side and so did her younger son, Amalric, who was now sixteen and heir-presumptive to the throne.

The queen's initiative was not exhausted as she showed soon after this. The king was anxious about the government of north Syria where the power of Nureddin was growing. Antioch was ruled by his cousin Constance, a widow since the death of Raymond of Poitiers in 1149, and he wanted her to re-marry in order to provide the state with a new military leader. This need was all the more pressing now that he had sole charge of the kingdom of Jerusalem and could less easily absent himself than he had formerly done to deal with trouble in the north. He therefore summoned a general assembly of the crusader states to meet at Tripoli in the early summer of 1152.[59] This was attended by the princess of Antioch and the chief clergy and barons of her state, the high court of Tripoli, and the chief vassals of the king. Queen Melisende also came to Tripoli. The ostensible reason for her visit was to straighten out the marital difficulties of her sister, the countess Hodierna, and Raymond II of Tripoli. It was an astute move, since the queen could not be prevented from paying a visit to her sister, yet when she was there she had to be invited to the assembly since the chief business on the agenda was the marriage of her niece, Constance of Antioch. Neither the assembly nor the royal aunts, Melisende and Hodierna, could persuade Constance to choose a new husband, and Melisende was unsuccessful in

[58] WT bk 17, cap 14, RHC Occ 1, pp 781-3.
[59] Ibid bk 17, cap 18, RHC Occ 1, p 790, places this event after his account of the deposition of Melisende, but gives no date. It is in a section of his work which relates to events in north Syria, some of which occurred before 1152. Some scholars have therefore placed the assembly of Tripoli before the civil war, for example, [S.] Runciman, [A History of the Crusades], 3 vols (Cambridge 1951-4) 2, p 333. I accept the date given by Mayer, because the reasons he gives are convincing in the light of a piece of evidence recently discovered, J. Riley-Smith, 'The Templars and the Castle of Tortosa in Syria: an unknown document concerning the acquisition of the fortress', EHR 84 (1969) pp 278-88. Mayer's date is also convincing because Baldwin would have been in no position to summon a general assembly unless he had been sole ruler, DOP 26, p 160.

her attempts to reconcile the count of Tripoli and his wife. Soon after the council the count was murdered by members of the sect of the assassins, and Hodierna became regent of Tripoli for her young son, Raymond III. After the count's funeral Baldwin III escorted his mother home. By attending the council Melisende had asserted the strength of her influence in north Syria. Henceforth, if the king wished to preserve some measure of control over Tripoli and Antioch, which the rising power of Nureddin and the absence of an adult male ruler in the Christian states of the north made desirable, he would have to treat his mother with outward respect, since the regent of Tripoli was her sister and the regent of Antioch her niece, and any harsh treatment of Melisende by Baldwin might cause tension between the king and the northern states.[60]

Indeed, as Mayer has shown, the king continued to pay his mother every sign of outward respect. There was a short period of coolness between them, which is scarcely surprising in view of the recent civil war, and during this time the king asserted his sole authority. But once he had established his position as a military leader by conquering Ascalon in 1153 he made peace with his mother. From 1154 onwards she was associated with him in many of his public acts, and he also ratified the grants which she had made by her sole authority during the time of their estrangement.[61] Melisende's involvement in state affairs after her retirement to Nablus was not always confined to internal matters, such as the transference of land. In 1156, for example, the king made peace with the merchants of Pisa *concessione Melisendis reginae, matris . . . meae*.[62] In 1157 when Baldwin was campaigning in Antioch Melisende took a military initiative. According to William of Tyre, the important cave-fortress of el-Hablis, which controlled the lands of Gilead beyond the Jordan, was recovered from the moslems 'through the planning and zeal of Melisende the queen'.[63] In the same year the patriarch Fulcher of Jerusalem died, and the appointment of his successor, Amalric of Nesle, was thought to have been due to the intervention of the king's half-sister, Sybil, countess of Flanders, and one of his aunts, perhaps the abbess of Bethany. Again it is significant

[60] WT bk 17, caps 18, 19, *RHC Occ* 1, pp 789–92.
[61] *DOP* 26, pp 172–5.
[62] *Documenti sulle relazioni delle città toscane coll'Oriente cristiano e coi Turchi fino all'anno 1531*, ed G. Müller, *Documenti degli archivi toscani* 3 (Florence 1879) no 5, pp 6–7.
[63] WT bk 18, cap 19, *RHC Occ* 1, p 851.

that this important appointment was decided in the circle of the queen, not by the king.[64]

On 30 November 1160 Melisende gave her assent to a gift made by her son Amalric to the Holy Sepulchre.[65] Soon after this she had what appears to have been a stroke: her memory was impaired and she could take no further part in the affairs of state. Her sisters, the countess of Tripoli and the abbess of Bethany, nursed her for several months. She died on 11 September 1161 and was buried, like her mother, in the shrine of our Lady of Josaphat.[66] Among her bequests, as befitted the daughter of queen Morphia, she left property to the Orthodox monastery of Saint Saba.[67]

Throughout her life she had been a great benefactor of the church. In addition to founding the convent of Bethany she had also given endowments to the Holy Sepulchre, our Lady of Josaphat, the *Templum Domini*, the order of the Hospital, the leper hospital of Saint Lazarus, and the Praemonstratensians of Saint Samuel's, Mountjoy.[68] It is not to be wondered at that a good churchman like William of Tyre considered that the eternal salvation of this pious queen was assured.[69] Her contemporaries do not remark on it, but she was evidently a cultured as well as a devout woman. The psalter which bears her name and which is now in the British Museum is evidence of her interest in the fine arts. Buchtal, who argues that it was executed for the queen in the lifetime of Fulk, has detected the presence of Byzantine, western and south Italian traditions in the illuminations, and concludes: 'Jerusalem during the second quarter of the twelfth century possessed a flourishing and well-established scriptorium which could, without difficulty, undertake a commission for a royal manuscript *de grand luxe*.'[70] Melisende must be given credit for being an important patron of the artists of the young Latin kingdom.

[64] *Ibid* bk 18, cap 20, *RHC Occ* I, p 854; the king's aunt who is mentioned could also have been Hodierna of Tripoli.
[65] de Rozière no 58, pp 115–17. [66] WT bk 18, caps 27, 32, *RHC Occ* I, pp 867, 877.
[67] de Rozière nos 140, 144, pp 256, 262–8.
[68] Holy Sepulchre: de Rozière nos 32, 48, pp 58–60, 87–9; Josaphat: Delaborde, nos 33, 34, 36, pp 80–4; *Templum Domini*: F. Chalandon, 'Un diplôme inédit d'Amaury I roi de Jérusalem en faveur de l'Abbaye du Temple-Notre-Seigneur', *ROL* 8 (1900–1) pp 311–17; Hospital: *CGOH* I, nos 175, 191, 244; Saint Lazarus: de Marsy, *AOL* 2, nos 10, 16, pp 130–1, 135; Saint Samuel's: H. E. Mayer, 'Sankt Samuel auf dem Freudenberge und sein besitz nach einem unbekannten diplom König Balduins V', *QFIAB* 44 (1964) pp 35–71.
[69] 'Sepulta est autem inclytae recordationis domina Milissendis, angelorum choris inferenda, in valle Josaphat', WT bk 18, cap 32, *RHC Occ* I, p 877.
[70] Buchtal p 14.

Queens of Jerusalem

She was a truly remarkable woman who for over thirty years exercised considerable power in a kingdom where there was no previous tradition of any woman holding public office. William of Tyre's comment, that 'she was a very wise woman, fully experienced in almost all spheres of state business, who had completely triumphed over the handicap of her sex so that she could take charge of important affairs', has a patronising ring to a twentieth-century ear. Few, however, would disagree with his judgement that, 'striving to emulate the glory of the best princes . . . she ruled the kingdom with such ability that she was rightly considered to have equalled her predecessors in that regard'.[71]

When she died there was already another queen in Jerusalem. In 1157 the high court had debated the king's marriage, and had finally decided to seek a Byzantine bride. It was hoped that Manuel Comnenus would provide a large dowry, and Jerusalem was extremely short of money; but it was also hoped that he might give the crusaders military help against Nureddin.[72] Baldwin III's envoys were kept waiting in Constantinople for months. The Byzantine emperor was less wealthy than the crusaders supposed: the marriage which they proposed would involve the emperor in great expense and it would be of no value to him unless he could follow it up with a military campaign. In 1157 he could not take his armies to the east because he feared an attack from the Normans of Sicily, but the situation changed in 1158 when the Sicilians made a thirty years truce with Byzantium against their common enemy, Frederick Barbarossa.[73] Negotiations with Baldwin III's ambassadors then went ahead smoothly. The bride chosen was the emperor's niece Theodora, daughter of the sebastocrator Isaac, who left Constantinople in the late summer of 1158.[74] The marriage fulfilled all the Franks' hopes: the emperor brought his army to north Syria to fight Nureddin;[75] the bride was given a dowry of 100,000 gold *hypereroi*, a trousseau worth a further 14,000, and 10,000 *hypereroi* to defray the expenses of the wedding. There was also the uncovenanted bonus

[71] WT bk 16, cap 3, *RHC Occ* I, p 707.
[72] *Ibid* bk 18, cap 16, *RHC Occ* I, p 846.
[73] [F.] Chalandon, [*Les Comnènes. Études sur l'empire byzantin au XIe et XIIe siècle. I. Essai sur le règne d'Alexis Ier Comnène (1081–1118). II. Jean II Comnène (1118–43) et Manuel Ier Comnène (1143–80)*] (Paris 1912) 2, pp 380–1.
[74] She reached Tyre in September 1158, WT bk 18, cap 22, *RHC Occ* I, pp 857–8; Chalandon 2, p 441.
[75] Gregory the Priest, *Continuation of the Chronicle of Matthew of Edessa*, cap 123, *RHC Arm* I, p 186.

I

that Theodora, who was twelve, was exceptionally beautiful. The emperor, of course, also made conditions: the bride should receive as her dowry from Baldwin Acre, the greatest city in the kingdom, to hold for life if she were widowed;[76] and the king solemnly vowed to secure the recognition of Byzantine overlordship in the principality of Antioch.[77] On her arrival the queen was taken to Jerusalem where she was solemnly anointed and crowned before being married to the king. Baldwin, whose life-style had previously been a cause of scandal to his more staid subjects, became a reformed character, and the marriage seems to have been a happy one.[78]

The alliance between the crusaders and Byzantium achieved what both sides had hoped it would do: Manuel by a show of military force restrained the aggression of Nureddin, and Antioch acknowledged Byzantine overlordship. Yet although she was so politically important as the chief link in this alliance, Theodora enjoyed no public exercise of power in the crusader kingdom. She was not normally associated with the king in his public acts, and it is arguable that the forceful character of queen Melisende made her sons reluctant to give any share in state affairs to their wives. The two documents in which Theodora is associated with the king are exceptional: one relates to sugar plantations at Acre and was made with the queen's assent presumably because Acre was her dower-fief;[79] the other was the charter of 31 July 1161 in which the king arranged with Philip of Milly to exchange his lands at Nablus for the great fief of Outre-Jordan. This was agreed to by all the members of the royal family, the queen, the king's brother, Amalric, his aunt, Hodierna, countess of Tripoli, and her children, Raymond III and Melisende, which indicates how important the transaction was considered to be. Queen Melisende was dying: her lands at Nablus would revert to the crown, and if the other great landowner there were bought out the whole of Samaria would become part of the royal domain.[80] Theodora seems to have enjoyed complete freedom in disposing of her

[76] WT bk 18, cap 22, *RHC Occ* I, p 858.
[77] This is not recorded by William of Tyre but is in Gregory the Priest, cap 125, *RHC Arm* I, p 189.
[78] WT bk 18, cap 22, *RHC Occ* I, p 858.
[79] S. Pauli, *Codice diplomatico del sacro militare ordine Gerosolimitano, oggi di Malta*, 2 vols (Lucca 1733–7) I, no 50, pp 50–1.
[80] [E.] Strehlke, [*Tabulae Ordinis Theutonici*] (Berlin 1869) no 3, pp 3–5. Mayer *DOP* 26, pp 179–80, argues that Baldwin III was punishing Philip for his support of Melisende in 1152. This is not convincing: the fief of Outre-Jordan was greater than Philip's fief at Nablus. The exchange was to Philip's advantage and was only of benefit to the king because he could integrate Philip's lands with his mother's lands.

Queens of Jerusalem

own lands: in 1161 she granted a house in Acre to her usher, Richard the Englishman, without reference to her husband.[81]

Theodora brought her husband money, prestige, political security and a happy marriage but, perhaps on account of her youth, she bore him no children. When he died on 10 February 1163[82] his widow was only seventeen. She retired to Acre and became the first dowager queen of Jerusalem; and for some years she remained the only queen.

Baldwin III was succeeded by his brother Amalric who had in 1157 married his third cousin, Agnes of Courtenay, daughter of Jocelyn II of Edessa.[83] Agnes was a widow: her first husband, Reynald of Marasch, had been killed in battle alongside Raymond of Antioch in 1149.[84] It is not known how old Agnes then was, but since the canonical age of marriage for girls was twelve, she may have been born in c1136 and therefore have been the same age as Amalric. After the loss of western Edessa in 1150 she and her mother came to live in Jerusalem, but when Amalric wished to marry her the patriarch Fulcher objected that they were related within the prohibited degrees and the couple seem to have waited to be married until after the patriarch's death in 1157.[85] No objection was made by anybody else, including Amalric's mother, the pious queen Melisende. It must have appeared a most suitable marriage; Agnes, it is true, had no dowry, since her family had lost all their lands, but there was no woman of better birth in the kingdom. She bore her husband a daughter, Sibylla, and then, in 1161, a son, the future Baldwin IV, to whom Baldwin III stood godfather.[86]

In 1163 the high court refused to recognise Amalric as king unless his marriage was annulled. It is difficult to establish the true reasons behind this request, which would be unusual in any age, since all three accounts of it are hostile to Agnes: William of Tyre never forgave her for preventing him from becoming patriarch; the thirteenth century *Estoire d'Eracles* is heavily dependent on William of Tyre for its early

---

[81] de Marsy, *AOL* 2, no 20, pp 138–9. Two Greeks are among the witnesses: Michael Grifo, *panetarius*, and Dionisius *miles*, who was presumably a member of Theodora's bodyguard.

[82] William of Tyre dates this 10 February 1162, 'regni ejus anno vicesimo . . . aetatis vero tricesimo tertio', bk 18, cap 34, *RHC Occ* 1, p 880. The twentieth year of Baldwin's reign would not have begun until 25 December 1162, his thirty-third birthday cannot have been earlier than March 1163 (see note 50 above). It is therefore generally agreed that he died on 10 February 1163.

[83] *Chronicles of the Reigns of Stephen, Henry II and Richard I, 4, The Chronicle of Robert of Torigni*, ed R. Howlett, *RS* 82, 4 (1889) p 194.

[84] WT bk 17, cap 9, *RHC Occ* 1, p 775.

[85] *Ibid* bk 19, cap 4, *RHC Occ* 1, p 889.

[86] *Ibid* bk 18, cap 29, *RHC Occ* 1, p 871.

material; while the chronicle of Ernoul was written by a supporter of the Ibelins[87] who held Agnes responsible for excluding them from the royal succession. William of Tyre and the *Eracles* give substantially the same account of the annulment: that the patriarch refused to crown the king because his marriage contravened canon law.[88] William adds that the annulment was made by a papal legate, but that the children of the marriage were declared legitimate.[89] The chronicle of Ernoul, however, gives what purports to be the objection raised by the lay members of the high court: *Car telle n'est que roine doie iestre di si haute cite comme de Jherusalem.*[90] This implies a slight on Agnes's moral character, but this can only be substantiated by instances which this same biased source gives of her lapses from virtue. Although the marriage was annulled on grounds of consanguinity, it is difficult to credit that this was the real reason for objecting to it: the relationship between Agnes and Amalric was such a distant one that William of Tyre, who had been studying overseas when the annulment took place, had to ask the abbess of Sainte Marie-la-Grande to explain the grounds for it to him.[91] There are two possible reasons why Agnes was unacceptable to the high court: they may have thought that the king could make a more politically and financially advantageous marriage, as he ultimately did; or they may have suspected that Agnes, like queen Melisende, would try to take too active a part in state affairs, as she was later to do.

Agnes kept the title of countess which she had held when Amalric was count of Jaffa and Ascalon. Almost immediately after the annulment she married Hugh of Ramleh, the eldest of the three ambitious Ibelin brothers, a marriage which may, as Ernoul relates, have been arranged by the king himself:[92] it certainly relieved him from the duty of making provision for his penniless ex-wife. Although she was never a crowned queen of Jerusalem, Agnes of Courtenay was the wife, mother, mother-in-law and grandmother of kings, and an influential person in the state for twenty years, and must therefore be included in this study.

---

[87] M. R. Morgan, *The Chronicle of Ernoul and the Continuations of William of Tyre,* Oxford Historical Monographs, (Oxford 1973) pp 41–6.
[88] [*L'Estoire d'*] *Eracles* [*Empereur et la Conqueste de la Terre d'Outremer*], bk 23, cap 3 *RHC Occ* 2, p 5.
[89] WT bk 19, cap 4, *RHC Occ* 1, p 889.
[90] [*La Chronique d'*] *Ernoul* [*et de Bernard le Trésorier,* ed L. de Mas Latrie] (Paris 1871) p 17.
[91] WT bk 19, cap 4, *RHC Occ* 1, pp 889–90.
[92] Ernoul p 17; *Eracles* bk 23, cap 3, *RHC Occ* 2, p 5; WT bk 19, cap 4, *RHC Occ* 1, p 890.

Queens of Jerusalem

It was not until 1165 that Amalric began negotiations for a second marriage. The chief aim of his foreign policy at that time was to prevent the weakened Fatimid caliphate of Egypt from falling under the control of Nureddin, and to achieve this he needed Byzantine military and financial help. On the advice of the high court he therefore sent an embassy to Constantinople to seek a bride from Manuel Comnenus.[93] The discussions dragged on for two years because, as Byzantine sources make clear, Amalric wished the emperor to relinquish his claims to sovereignty over Antioch. Amalric eventually gave way about this[94] and the emperor's great-niece Maria, daughter of the protosebastos John, came to Syria and married the king at Tyre on 29 August 1167.[95] From the vagueness of Frankish sources it may be inferred that her dowry was not so great as that of her cousin Theodora had been, while the silence even of her supporters about her beauty is equally suggestive.

At the time of Amalric's marriage to Maria the dowager queen Theodora was still living in retirement at Acre. She had not remarried: she could only do so with the king's consent, and Amalric was unlikely to give this, since he would not wish Acre, the greatest city in the kingdom, to pass into other hands, whereas if Theodora remained a widow it would revert to the crown at her death. Her life must have been very boring: she was cut off by background and language from the Frankish nobility among whom she lived, and such ceremonial precedence as she had enjoyed would come to an end with the king's remarriage. In the winter of 1166-7, when Theodora was twenty-one, there came to the kingdom a distant kinsman of hers, Andronicus Comenus, the emperor Manuel's first cousin. He was an unusual figure in the hieratic court of Byzantium, an adventurer, who would have been temperamentally more at home as a freelance knight in the feudal world of western Europe. His early life had been a series of political and amorous scandals, but in 1166 the emperor had appointed him governor of Cilicia. He soon became bored by his official duties and went to Antioch where he seduced the princess Philippa, a tactless choice, since she was the emperor's sister-in-law, and the resulting scandal was so great that he was forced to leave in haste.[96] Armed with

[93] Ernoul pp 17–18.
[94] [John] Cinnamus, [Epitome Historiarum], bk 5, cap 13, CHSByz (Bonn 1836) pp 237–8.
[95] WT bk 20, cap 1, RHC Occ 1, pp 942–3; Ernoul p 18.
[96] For Andronicus's early life see [C.] Diehl, ['Les romanesques aventures d'Andronic Comnène, Figures byzantines], (5 ed Paris 1918) pp 86–106.

the revenues of Cyprus and Cilicia, which he had had the forethought to collect,[97] he went to Jerusalem. The king was absent on campaign in Egypt, but, as courtesy demanded, Andronicus called on his kinswoman, the dowager queen. Despite the great disparity in their ages, (Andronicus was in his late forties) Theodora was attracted to him and they became lovers. When Amalric returned from Egypt he was impressed by this distinguished and seemingly rich visitor, who had great charm, and bestowed the fief of Beirut on him. But, in the delightful phrase of William of Tyre, Andronicus behaved to the king 'like a mouse in a wallet' (*more muris in pera*): for he invited Theodora to visit him in Beirut and, while she was travelling there, abducted her and carried her off to the court of Nureddin at Damascus.[98]

The Franks did not know the reason for this extraordinary behaviour, but an explanation is given by the Byzantine writer, Nicetas Choniates. The emperor Manuel, who had learned of Andronicus's intrigue with Theodora, presumably from one of the noblemen who had escorted queen Maria to Syria, feared that this scandal might jeopardise his carefully constructed Syrian policy. There was no hope of regularising the liaison, for Andronicus had a wife in Constantinople. The emperor therefore sent orders to his agents in Syria to blind Andronicus, which he hoped would satisfy the Franks that he took this slight on the honour of their royal house seriously, but a copy of his letter was seen by Theodora, who informed Andronicus of his danger, and he persuaded her to elope with him.[99] The defection of a first cousin of the Byzantine emperor and a dowager queen of Jerusalem to moslem Damascus was, as may be imagined, very welcome to the entire islamic world. The couple were received with enthusiasm throughout the moslem near east, and appear to have lived happily together, having two children, a son, Alexis, and a daughter, Irene. Their subsequent adventures are not relevant to this paper, but Theodora, it would seem, died before 1182 when Andronicus made himself Byzantine emperor.[100] Contrary to Manuel Comnenus's fears the crusader states do not seem to have paid very much attention to this scandal: the Byzantine alliance was assured through Amalric's marriage to Maria, and, as a result of Theodora's elopement, the dower lands of Acre could revert to the crown.[101]

[97] Cinnamus bk 6, cap 1, p 250. [98] WT bk 20, cap 2, *RHC Occ* 1, pp 943–4.
[99] Nicetas Choniates, *Historia, De Manuele Comneno*, bk 4, cap 5, *CHSByz* (Bonn 1835) p 185.
[100] For Andronicus's subsequent career see Diehl, pp 107–33.
[101] Ernoul p 15.

Queens of Jerusalem

Maria Comnena took no part in affairs of state during her husband's lifetime. In this regard Amalric followed the example of his elder brother and, like him, had no wish to allow a new queen Melisende to contest his authority. Maria bore the king two daughters, Isabella, who was born in 1172, and another girl who died in infancy.[102] The lack of a male child was a misfortune not only for the queen, who proved to be a most ambitious woman, but also for the kingdom. For Baldwin, the son of the king's first marriage, had leprosy, and there seems little doubt that had Maria borne the king a son he would have succeeded to the throne. As it was, when Amalric died in 1174 the thirteen year old leper child became king Baldwin IV.

On his deathbed the king granted Maria his mother's former lands of Nablus as a dower fief.[103] She and her daughter Isabella withdrew from public life, because the unusual situation existed in the new reign that the dowager queen was not the king's mother and had no natural place at court because Baldwin IV's own mother, the countess Agnes, was still living. In 1169 Agnes's third husband, Hugh of Ibelin, had died.[104] The marriage was childless, and she subsequently married Reynald, son of Gerald, lord of Sidon: William of Tyre places this event in king Amalric's lifetime. A mystery surrounds Agnes's fourth marriage: William of Tyre relates that Gerald of Sidon solemnly swore that the couple were related within the prohibited degrees (he carefully does not specify how), and that the marriage was consequently annulled.[105] Gerald may have objected to Agnes on moral grounds as a daughter-in-law since, with or without foundation, rumours were certainly circulating about her indiscretions.[106] William's account makes it plain that the annulment occurred while Gerald was still alive. This must have been before 1173, for in that year Reynald first appears in charters as lord of Sidon, which shows that his father had died.[107] Yet when William of Tyre describes the release of Jocelyn of Courtenay from prison in 1175–6 he attributes this to the efforts of 'the countess Agnes, wife of Reynald of Sidon'.[108] Moreover, the list of witnesses to a charter issued in 1179 by Agnes's daughter, Sibylla

---

[102] *Itinerarium [peregrinorum et gesta regis Ricardi I*, ed W. Stubbs], bk 1, cap 46, *Chronicles and Memorials of the reign of Richard I*, 1, RS 38,1 (1864) p 97.
[103] Ernoul p 31.
[104] Hugh is last mentioned in a document of 1169 (together with Agnes), de Marsy, *AOL* 2, no 25, pp 142–3.
[105] WT bk 19, cap 4, *RHC Occ* 1, p 890.
[106] Ernoul pp 59, 82.
[107] *CGOH* 1, no 551.
[108] WT bk 21, cap 11, *RHC Occ* 1, p 1023.

countess of Jaffa, is headed by *domina magna comitissa Sagite* and *dominus Reinaudus Sagite*.[109] Although the lady of Sidon is not given a Christian name in this document it clearly refers to Agnes, for she was the only wife of a lord of Sidon who was entitled to be styled countess: it was, moreover, natural that as Sibylla's mother she should have taken precedence over all the other witnesses. From this it must be concluded that if the annulment was ever granted it was reversed on appeal after Gerald of Sidon's death, and that Agnes remained the wife of Reynald of Sidon probably until her death, but certainly until 1179. It is equally clear that William of Tyre did not regard the marriage as valid, and this may account for the disfavour with which Agnes regarded him.

Up to the time of Amalric's death Agnes had little contact with her children: Baldwin IV had grown up at his father's court and Sibylla was brought up in the convent of Bethany by her great-aunt Yveta, queen Melisende's sister.[110] Nor does Agnes seem to have had any *entrée* to the court during her son's minority, which ended in 1176, during which Raymond III of Tripoli was regent. The regent's chief concern was to find a suitable husband for Sibylla, who could take over the government in the event of the king's death or incapacity, since it was evident that, because of his leprosy, the king could not himself marry and beget an heir. The man chosen for the princess was William Longsword of Montferrat, who married Sibylla in the autumn of 1176 and was created count of Jaffa and Ascalon. He died in the following June, leaving his wife pregnant with the future Baldwin V, and countess of Jaffa and Ascalon in her own right.[111]

Agnes seems to have taken no part in the negotiations for the Montferrat marriage, but she was clearly anxious to obtain power at court. Her first step was to arrange for the ransom of her brother, Jocelyn III, titular count of Edessa, who was a prisoner-of-war at Aleppo, for which purpose she raised the considerable sum of 60,000 dinars.[112] The sick young king came of age in 1176 and Raymond of Tripoli's regency ended, but Baldwin IV had a great shortage of male kin to whom power could be delegated. Jocelyn III was his uncle, and

[109] J. Delaville Le Roulx, *Les archives, le bibliothèque et le trésor de l'Ordre de Saint-Jean de Jérusalem à Malte, BEFAR* 32 (1883) no 53, pp 144–5.
[110] WT bk 21, cap 2, *RHC Occ* I, p 1006.
[111] *Ibid* bk 21, cap 13, *RHC Occ* I, pp 1025–6.
[112] *Ibid* bk 21, cap 11, *RHC Occ* I, p 1023; details of the ransom in *Chronique de Michel le Syrien, patriarche jacobite d'Antioche (1166–99)*, bk 20, cap 3, ed with French translation, J. B. Chabot, 4 vols (Paris 1899–1924) 3, pp 365–6.

Queens of Jerusalem

when he arrived at Jerusalem he was given the important office of seneschal of the realm.[113]

Shortly after William of Montferrat's death count Philip of Flanders, the king's cousin, came to Jerusalem on crusade and claimed the right to arrange marriages for both the king's sisters to his own vassals. The high court refused to agree to this, and Baldwin of Ibelin publicly insulted the count, who was offended and left the kingdom to campaign in Antioch.[114] Ernoul says that Baldwin acted in this way because he wished to marry Sibylla himself, and this may well be true although Ernoul's chronology is very confused at this point in his narrative.[115] The Ibelin brothers were certainly very ambitious: in the autumn of 1177 the king gave his consent for the queen dowager, Maria Comnena, to marry the youngest Ibelin brother, Balian, who thus carried on the family tradition of marrying king Amalric's former wives.[116] By this marriage the Ibelins gained control of the dower-fief of Nablus and custody of the king's younger sister, Isabella. An English source, admittedly one which is very hostile to Maria, gives an unflattering portrait of this marriage: the queen found in Balian, the writer says, 'a husband whose character matched her own . . . where he was savage, she was godless; where he was shallow-minded she was fickle; where he was treacherous she was scheming'.[117]

The Ibelin marriage excluded the possibility that Maria could, as the king's stepmother, fulfill the duties of queen at Baldwin IV's court. This function was performed by the countess Agnes, whose influence over both her children grew more marked in the following years. When the constable of the kingdom, Humphrey II of Toron, was killed in battle in 1179 Agnes secured the appointment of Amalric of Lusignan as his successor. In Ibelin circles it was rumoured that he was her lover, but, whether this was true or not, he was clearly not chosen simply for that reason, for he was an extremely able man who was later to become an outstanding king both of Jerusalem and Cyprus.[118] But

[113] He held that office by 1176, CGOH I, no 496; R. L. Nicholson, Joscelyn III and the Fall of the Crusader States (1134–1199) (Leiden 1973) p 73, n 173.
[114] WT bk 21, caps 14, 15, 18, RHC Occ I, pp 1027–30, 1034–5; Ernoul p 33.
[115] Ernoul p 33 places Philip of Flanders's arrival before Sibylla's marriage to William of Montferrat instead of after William's death: this is certainly wrong. He adds that Baldwin had separated from his first wife in order to be free to marry Sibylla, but that when she married William he married the widow of the lord of Caesaraea, pp 47–8. This also is wrong, since Baldwin had married that lady by 1175, CGOH I, no 470; Du Cange p 365.
[116] WT bk 21, cap 18, RHC Occ I, p 1035.
[117] Itinerarium bk 1, cap 63, p 121. [118] Ernoul p 59.

the Ibelins hated Agnes and the Lusignans, whom they held responsible for thwarting Baldwin of Ibelin's plans to become king. It is difficult to establish the truth about this, because the Ibelin assertion rests on the uncorroborated and highly romanticised story told by Ernoul. He relates that Baldwin of Ibelin was captured in battle by Saladin in 1179 and that while he was a prisoner-of-war the princess Sibylla wrote to him suggesting that he should marry her when he was released. Baldwin was at that time a widower, and therefore free to contract a new marriage, and, as the events of 1177 had showed, he had already aspired to Sibylla's hand. Moreover, Saladin, according to Ernoul, demanded a king's ransom of 200,000 bezants for him, which adds colour to the story. Baldwin was released on security, but since he would have been ruined if he had attempted to pay the ransom himself, he went to Constantinople to ask the help of the emperor Manuel. It may be supposed that Maria Comnena, who was Baldwin's sister-in-law and the emperor's kinswoman, was behind these negotiations, and that she informed Manuel that Baldwin had every prospect of becoming king of Jerusalem. The emperor, who had always had a strong interest in the crusader states, paid the ransom without raising any difficulty, presumably because he regarded the goodwill of the future king as a sound long-term investment.[119] The improbable element in this story is the account of Sibylla's indiscretion in writing to Baldwin while he was in prison: possibly Baldwin had previously reached some understanding with her, which was generally known, and which would explain both the size of the ransom which Saladin demanded and Manuel's readiness to pay it.

The weakness of Ernoul's account is that it treats the whole matter in terms of personal relationships, whereas the marriage of the king's sister and heir was a matter of state. Sibylla was not free to marry whom she chose: the final decision rested with the king and his advisers, and no source suggests that any formal marriage contract had been made between the princess and Baldwin of Ibelin. In fact Baldwin's hopes were frustrated, but for reasons which had nothing to do with Courtenay antipathy towards the Ibelins. The ascendancy of the king's mother and of his uncle, Jocelyn of Courtenay, was challenged by the only other members of the royal house in Syria. The king's health was known to be deteriorating, and at Easter 1180 his cousins, Raymond III of Tripoli and Bohemond III of Antioch, entered the kingdom, it was

[119] Maria Comnena's influence is implied by Ernoul who relates that Manuel offered to pay Baldwin's ransom *pour l'amour de Balyan son frere*, p 58. See Ernoul pp 56–60.

believed with the intention of choosing a husband for Sibylla, and thus of choosing the next king. Faced by this possible *coup d'état* the king, acting on his mother's advice, used his prerogative and arranged for Sibylla to be married to the constable's brother, Guy of Lusignan, who had recently arrived from the west. Contemporaries considered that this marriage took place with indecent haste, but it served its purpose by rendering any attempt at intervention by Raymond III and Bohemond III futile. But when, later that year, Baldwin of Ibelin returned from Constantinople, he found that Sibylla was already married.[120]   *

The Ibelins were angered by this, and do not seem to have considered that if Sibylla had not married Guy she would have been forced to marry somebody other than the absent Baldwin of Ibelin by Raymond III and Bohemond III. Their chief grievance was that they had lost a claim to the throne, and their chances of exercising even indirect power at court became even more remote when the king made formal arrangements for the marriage of his younger sister Isabella, Balian of Ibelin's stepdaughter. She was only eight years old, and therefore below the age for canonical marriage, but a marriage contract was drawn up in October 1180 between her and Humphrey IV of Toron, stepson of Reynald of Châtillon, lord of Outre-Jordan, who was a firm adherent of the Courtenays and the Lusignans.[121] Runciman sees in this a conciliatory gesture on the part of the king, intended to heal the division between the Ibelins and the Courtenays,[122] but it is arguable that it was, on the contrary, designed to deprive the Ibelins of the right to choose a husband for this alternative heir to the throne in the event of the king's death. This marriage too, like that of Sibylla, was almost certainly arranged by Agnes of Courtenay who was the chief immediate beneficiary, for by the terms of the marriage settlement Humphrey surrendered to the king the fiefs of Toron and Chastel-neuf which he had inherited from his grandfather[123] and Baldwin IV gave them, either then or later, to his mother.[124] For the first time in her life the king's mother became a great landowner in her own right. William of Tyre's judgement that she was 'a woman who was hateful to God and a shameless money-grabber' therefore seems unduly harsh.[125]

[120] WT bk 22, cap 1, *RHC Occ* I, pp 1062–3.
[121] *Ibid* bk 22, cap 5, *RHC Occ* I, pp 1068–9.
[122] Runciman 2, p 424.
[123] WT bk 22, cap 5, *RHC Occ* I, p 1069.
[124] [*The travels of*] *Ibn Jubayr*, [trans R. J. C. Broadhurst] (London 1952) p 316.
[125] WT bk 22, cap 9, *RHC Occ* I, p 1078.

I

But William had reason to hate her, for when the patriarch Amalric died in October 1180 and the canons of the Holy Sepulchre met to choose a successor and submitted two names to the king, Agnes persuaded her son to choose Heraclius, archbishop of Caesaraea, in preference to William of Tyre.[126] Predictably both Ernoul and the *Eracles* attribute Heraclius's success to his having slept with Agnes, but since the *Eracles* places the beginnings of this affair in king Amalric's reign, and attributes Heraclius's first major appointment, that of archdeacon of Jerusalem, to Agnes's favours, the story must be viewed with some mistrust, since the king would surely have been reluctant to bestow office on his former wife's lover. [127] It is simpler to suppose that Agnes as the king's mother, like queen Melisende before her, was merely exercising rights of church patronage in the patriarchal election, and a reason has already been suggested for her dislike of William of Tyre.

Agnes was clearly a remarkably clever woman. Starting from a position of no power at king Amalric's death, she had secured the appointment of her nominees to the chief lay and ecclesiastical offices in the kingdom by 1180: those of seneschal, constable and patriarch; and had arranged the marriages of both the king's sisters to husbands of her own choosing. The territorial power which she and her supporters commanded was equally great: the king held the great cities, Jerusalem, Acre and Tyre; Sibylla and Guy held the counties of Jaffa and Ascalon; Agnes's supporter, Reynald of Châtillon was lord of Outre-Jordan and Hebron; her husband was lord of Sidon; and she held Toron and Chastel-neuf in her own right. Her opponents could not move against her, and when Raymond of Tripoli wished to see the king in 1182 Agnes was powerful enough to refuse to allow him to enter the kingdom.[128]

Her influence was greatest while Baldwin IV was well enough to rule in person, for she was then virtually uncrowned queen. When the king's health grew worse in the summer of 1183 and he appointed Guy of Lusignan as regent Agnes's ascendancy was not threatened, for Sibylla was under her influence and Guy owed his advancement to Agnes. That autumn the princess Isabella, who was now fully of

[126] *Ibid* bk 22, cap 4, *RHC Occ* 1, p 1068, reports the election without comment. Full detail in *Eracles* bk 23, cap 38, *RHC Occ* 2, pp 58–9; Ernoul pp 82–4.
[127] *Eracles* bk 23, cap 39, *RHC Occ* 2, pp 59–60; Ernoul p 82. Heraclius is first mentioned as archdeacon of Jerusalem in a document of 1169, de Rozière no 167, pp 301–5.
[128] She later relented under pressure from members of the high court, WT bk 22, cap 9, *RHC Occ* 1, pp 1077–9.

168

marriageable age, was sent to Kerak of Moab to be married canonically as well as legally to Humphrey of Toron. The festivities were, however, marred by the arrival of Saladin's army, which laid siege to the castle while the wedding-breakfast was in progress.[129] Baldwin IV meanwhile had been offended by the conduct of Guy of Lusignan as regent and chose the occasion of mustering his host to march to the relief of Kerak to depose Guy from the regency. This was the opportunity for which Agnes's opponents had been waiting, since the king was evidently too ill to live much longer, and as Guy had been excluded the only other serious contender for the regency was Agnes's enemy, the count of Tripoli. With great presence of mind, Agnes advanced a compromise solution which met with general approval. The king should not appoint another regent, but should hold power directly himself: this guaranteed the continuance of Agnes's own ascendancy. But the king should also designate his heir, and exclude Guy of Lusignan from the succession: this conciliated the barons who were hostile to Guy. The heir she suggested was the child Baldwin, whom Sibylla had borne to William of Montferrat: his claim to the throne was impeccable, for he was the king's nephew, but he was also Agnes's grandson, and if he became sole king her position at court would still be assured. The child Baldwin V was duly crowned and the baron-age did homage to him.[130] As a final act of humiliation to the boy's stepfather, Guy of Lusignan, and as a conciliatory gesture to the Ibelins, which cost nothing, the boy was carried in the coronation procession by Balian of Ibelin, who was the tallest member of the high court.[131] Only when this was done did the royal army march to the relief of the wedding party at Kerak of Moab.[132]

Agnes's opponents therefore gained no immediate advantage from the disgrace of Guy of Lusignan. The leper king ruled in person for the last years of his reign despite his ill-health; while the Ibelins lost any influence which they may formerly have had over the princess Isabella since Humphry of Toron, acting on his mother's advice, refused to allow his young wife to visit her mother, Maria Comnena.[133] Agnes

---

[129] Ernoul p 103; WT bk 22, cap 28, *RHC Occ* 1, pp 1124–5.
[130] WT bk 22, cap 29, *RHC Occ* 1, pp 1127–8.
[131] *Les Gestes des Chiprois*, cap 38, *RHC Arm* 2, p 658, which wrongly date this event 1181.
[132] I propose to publish elsewhere my reasons for supposing that the relief of Kerak was delayed by the deposition of Guy de Lusignan. It is implicit in William of Tyre's account, bk 22, caps 28–30, *RHC Occ* 1, pp 1124–30.
[133] *Eracles* bk 25, cap 11, *RHC Occ* 2, p 152.

I

could not prevent the king from pursuing his vendetta against Guy: he sought, with the help of the patriarch, to have Sibylla's marriage annulled, but Guy and Sibylla foiled this attempt by shutting themselves in Ascalon and refusing to leave even when the king summoned them in person. Since proceedings in a matrimonial case could not be heard in the absence of the contracting parties the case was abandoned.[134] This happened in the early months of 1184. The countess Agnes did not intervene, although she was still alive then, for when Ibn Jubayr, secretary of the moorish governor of Granada, passed near Toron in September of that year he remarked with the tolerant courtesy which characterises moslem writings about Christians in that period: Toron 'belongs to the sow known as queen who is the mother of the pig who is lord of Acre—may God destroy it.'[135]

It is not known whether Agnes was still alive when Baldwin IV died in 1185 and Baldwin V became sole king under the regency of her chief enemy, Raymond of Tripoli. If she was, her influence, although diminished, would not have been at an end, since her brother Jocelyn was the personal guardian of the young king. Her death occurred before the late summer of 1186, for she took no part in the succession crisis which arose then, and on 21 October king Guy acknowledged that count Jocelyn, who was her executor, had satisfactorily discharged the provisions of her will.[136] Agnes was, in many ways, a worthy daughter-in-law of queen Melisende. She lacked, it would seem, her mother-in-law's piety, but she shared her desire for political power and had a more decisive influence on the history of the first kingdom than any other woman except Melisende herself. It was her misfortune to have bad relations with the press: all contemporary sources are hostile to her, but they are not unprejudiced and it is arguable that her influence was not as baneful as the Ibelins and the archbishop of Tyre would like posterity to suppose.

Any hope that the coronation of Baldwin V would resolve the tensions of the kingdom was rendered ineffectual by the young king's death in the late summer of 1186. Raymond of Tripoli had only consented to be regent on the understanding that should Baldwin V die a minor the chief rulers of the west should be asked to adjudicate between the claims of his two sisters to the succession.[137] Accordingly

[134] WT bk 23, cap 1, RHC Occ 1, p 1133.
[135] Ibn Jubayr p 316.
[136] Strehlke no 32, p 20.
[137] Ernoul pp 116–17; Eracles bk 23, cap 4, RHC Occ 2, pp 6–7.

170

Queens of Jerusalem

when Baldwin V died Raymond summoned the high court to Nablus to discuss the succession, while Jocelyn of Courtenay, as the dead king's guardian, made arrangements for his burial in Jerusalem. Guy and Sibylla attended the funeral with a strong armed escort with which they garrisoned the city. It is too well-known to need repeating here, how Sibylla, with the help of her supporters, who were, for the most part, the old supporters of Agnes of Courtenay, stole a march on the high court of Nablus and was crowned queen. Two points are worth emphasising: first Reynald of Châtillon gained popular support for Sibylla by affirming that she was *li plus apareissanz et li plus dreis heirs dou roiaume*; secondly that the patriarch crowned Sibylla alone, and that she conferred the crown on Guy. There was no real doubt, following the precedent of Melisende, that Sibylla, as the elder daughter of king Amalric, had the best claim to the throne; equally, there could be no doubt after the ceremony that Guy only held the crown matrimonial.[138]

Humphrey of Toron and the princess Isabella were present at Nablus, and when news reached the high court there of the coronation of Sibylla and Guy the barons wished to crown Humphrey and Isabella in opposition to them. Humphrey wrecked this plan by going to Jerusalem and taking the oath of fealty to Sibylla: he had never liked the Ibelins and, it may be argued, had no wish, in the event of a civil war, to fight against his mother and stepfather, both of whom supported Guy. Once they were deprived of an alternative candidate most of the barons at Nablus made their submission to Sibylla and Guy.[139] But Maria Comnena never forgave her son-in-law for depriving her daughter of the chance to be queen, a chance which would have led to the restoration of Maria herself to a position of power.[140]

Had Sibylla lived in more peaceful times she could have exercised a great deal of power since her husband's authority so patently derived from her. In the first few months of the reign, indeed, she was associated with Guy in some of his acts.[141] But the conquest of Saladin, which occurred within a year of the coronation, brought Guy and Sibylla's joint rule to a speedy end. When Guy was taken prisoner at Hattin, Sibylla was in Jerusalem, where she was joined by her stepmother,

[138] Ernoul pp 130–4; *Eracles* bk 23, cap 17, *RHC Occ* 2, pp 26–9.
[139] *Eracles* bk 23, caps 18–21, *RHC Occ* 2, pp 30–3; Ernoul pp 134–9.
[140] *Eracles* bk 25, cap 11, *RHC Occ* 2, p 152.
[141] Strehlke nos 20, 21, pp 18–19.

Maria Comnena. Both ladies were treated courteously by Saladin: Sibylla was allowed to join her husband, who was in detention at Nablus,[142] and Maria Comnena and her children were allowed to go to Tripoli, despite the fact that Balian of Ibelin failed to keep the oath which he had sworn to the sultan not to take up arms against him when Saladin gave him permission to go to Jerusalem to escort his wife to safety.[143] After Jerusalem had fallen Guy was taken to Damascus, but Sibylla was allowed to join queen Maria in Tripoli.

She stayed there until she was joined by Guy on his release from captivity in 1188.[144] The only city in the kingdom of Jerusalem which remained in Christian hands was Tyre, but when Guy and Sibylla marched there in 1189 they were refused entrance by Conrad of Montferrat, who had taken charge of its defence. After some months spent outside the walls, Guy led the vanguard of the third crusade, newly arrived in Syria, to lay siege to Acre,[145] and among those who followed him there were Humphrey of Toron and the princess Isabella, and Balian of Ibelin and Maria Comnena. It seemed as though former differences had vanished in the face of a common disaster. How illusory this unity was became apparent when Sibylla died of an epidemic in the camp at Acre on 25 July 1190, together with her two little daughters, Alice and Maria.[146]

Guy's enemies, and there were many who blamed him for the defeat of Hattin, claimed that as he only had the crown matrimonial his kingship ended with the death of his wife. The only other candidate for the throne was the princess Isabella, but her husband Humphrey was a friend of Guy's and unwilling to set himself up as king in opposition to him. Conrad of Montferrat, hero of the defence of Tyre, was an ambitious man who wanted to become king, and who found a ready ally in Maria Comnena. She deposed before the archbishop of Pisa, the pope's legate, and the bishop of Beauvais, that her daughter's marriage was invalid because she had only been eight when it was contracted, and had been forced into it by Baldwin IV against her wishes. Isabella, who was happily married and had no wish to be separated from her husband, was browbeaten into agreeing with this

[142] Ernoul p 185.
[143] Ibid pp 186–7; Eracles bk 23, cap 46, RHC Occ 2, pp 68–71.
[144] Ernoul p 252; Eracles bk 24, cap 11, RHC Occ 2, pp 120–1.
[145] Eracles bk 24, caps 13, 14, RHC Occ 2, pp 123–5; Ernoul pp 256–7.
[146] Sibylla had borne Guy four daughters. It is not clear whether they all died at the same time as their mother or whether two had predeceased her: Ernoul p 267; Eracles bk 25, cap 10, and see also variant readings C and G, RHC Occ 2, pp 151, 154.

statement by her strong-willed mother. The legate annulled the marriage; Isabella was then crowned, and immediately restored to Humphrey his fiefs of Toron and Chaste-neuf (an academic piece of justice since they were in enemy occupied territory); then she was married to Conrad.[147] Maria Comnena had had to wait for sixteen years to see her daughter made queen, but her patience was finally rewarded. As her conduct in the matter of the annulment shows, there was some truth in her opponents' view that she was a ruthless and scheming woman.[148]

Maria bore Balian of Ibelin four children: John, who became the 'old lord' of Beirut; Philip of Ibelin, who later became *bailli* of Cyprus; Margaret, who married successively Hugh of Tiberias, and Walter III of Caesaraea; and Helvis, who, ironically, married Reynald of Sidon, former husband of the queen's old rival, Agnes of Courtenay. When Balian died in about 1194[149] Maria did not remarry. She continued to take an active part in forwarding the interests of her family: in 1208 she helped to arrange the marriage of her grand-daughter Alice to king Hugh I of Cyprus.[150] She apparently died in the summer of 1217, for in October of that year Hugh I of Cyprus confirmed the endowment made by her son, Philip of Ibelin, for masses to be said in Nicosia cathedral for the repose of the soul of his mother *inclite recordationis*.[151] She had lived to see her great-grand-daughter, Isabella II, become queen of Jerusalem, and all the kings of Jerusalem and Cyprus, together with many of the higher nobility in both states in the thirteenth century, were descended from her.[152] By the time of her death she was the sole survivor of any consequence from the first kingdom of Jerusalem. She had occupied a central position in the state for twenty years before its fall. Perhaps the reputation which her son, the 'old lord' of Beirut, acquired as a repository of knowledge about the laws and customs of the first kingdom owed much to the memory of his long-lived mother.

[147] *Eracles* bk 25, caps 11, 12, *RHC Occ* 2, pp 151–4; *Itinerarium* bk 1, cap 63, pp 119–22; Ernoul pp 267–8 does not mention Maria's involvement.
[148] See note 115 above.
[149] He is last recorded in a document of that year, *CGOH* 1, no 954.
[150] Alice was the daughter of Maria's eldest child, queen Isabella, by her marriage to count Henry of Troyes. G. Hill, *A History of Cyprus*, 4 vols (Cambridge 1940–52). 2, p 75.
[151] L. de Mas Latrie, *Histoire de l'Ile de Chypre sous le règne des princes de la Maison de Lusignan*, 3 vols (Paris 1852–61) 3, pp 608–9.
[152] See the genealogical table at the end of Runciman 3.

Maria Comnena had great resilience and considerable powers of adaptation. She became queen of Jerusalem because that state needed the alliance of the powerful Byzantine empire. After 1180 Byzantium had ceased to be a world power, and before her death it had almost ceased to exist at all as a result of the fourth crusade. The kingdom of Jerusalem likewise had dwindled into the kingdom of Acre, yet Maria's influence increased rather than diminished under these adverse conditions. Like Agnes of Courtenay and queen Melisende, Maria Comnena had a central interest in power, though she was more concerned with the realities and less with the external trappings of power than they had been, and in consequence was more devious in her methods of attaining it.

All eight queens who reigned in the first kingdom made a serious impact on its development: this is true even of those of them who were a-political, like Theodora, whose dowry strengthened the inadequate finances of the state, and who was the personal link by which the Byzantine alliance was forged, which held the threat of Nureddin in check. Further investigation would probably show that women were equally influential at other social levels in this outwardly male-dominated feudal state.

Addenda

p. 167, Baldwin of Ibelin was in Jerusalem when Sibyl and Guy were married and only went to Constantinople later that year: *CGOH*, n. 582; WT, 22 cap. 5.

King Consorts of Jerusalem and their Entourages from the West from 1186 to 1250

Between 1186 and 1228 the crown of Jerusalem was held by women: Sibyl, Isabella I, Maria, and Isabella II. None of them had a strong political drive: they all married, in Isabella I's case four times, and they devolved power to their husbands. Jerusalem was therefore governed by a series of king consorts, none of whom had been born in the East and each of whom had his own entourage. I use that term in the following sense: first there were the members of his own household: knights, chaplains and professional servants; secondly there were his kindred who came from the West to join him; thirdly there were the members of noble families from his own part of Europe who took service with him. All these men might hope to enjoy the patronage of the king consort, and the native Franks feared that this would be achieved at their expense.

When Guy of Lusignan became king in 1186 his entourage is said to have roamed the streets of Jerusalem chanting

Maugre li Polein

Avrons nous roi poitevin[1].

Guy had been living in the Holy Land for six years and had had time to build up a Poitevin following. The descendants of Hugh Martin and Massé de Gaurèle, for example, later claimed that they had come to the East with him[2], and his brother Aimery had been in the kingdom since c.1170 and had been constable since c.1181. During the brief period when he was regent for the Leper King in 1183, Guy had made enemies by boasting about his powers of patronage[3]. In the few months that he held the crown in 1186–7 he attempted to consolidate the fortunes of his family by arranging the betrothal of the two daughters of Joscelin of Courtenay, heirs to their father's considerable estates, to his brother, William of Valence and an un-

---

[1] La continuation de Guillaume de Tyre, c. 41, ed. *Margaret R. Morgan* (Académie des Inscriptions et Belles-Lettres, Documents relatifs à l'histoire des Croisades, XIV [Paris 1982]) 53.

[2] Les Lignages d'Outremer, cc. xl, xli, RHC Lois, II, 472f.

[3] *William of Tyre*, Chronicon, XXII, 26, ed. *Robert B. C. Huygens* (Corpus Christianorum, Continuatio Mediaevalis, LXIII, LXIIIA [Turnholt 1986] 472f.).

specified Lusignan nephew[4]. The fears of the Jerusalem nobility that they would be inundated by Poitevins did not seem unreasonable.

Although Guy's ambitions were interrupted by the loss of the kingdom in 1187, he continued the same policy after he was released by Saladin. When his eldest brother, Geoffrey of Lusignan, came on crusade he enfeoffed him with the county of Jaffa and Ascalon still in Muslim hands[5]. Guy's brother Aimery remained constable of the kingdom, and when Guy lost the support of the marshal Walter Durus, he appointed the Poitevin Hugh Martin in his place[6]. But Guy was unpopular because he was blamed for the defeat of Hattin, and after the death of Queen Sibyl and her daughters in 1190, his kingship was contested. In 1192 he renounced the crown and became lord of Cyprus. This decision was important in two ways: it gave the Lusignans a secure power base; and it also created a constitutional precedent. Henceforth it was axiomatic that any ruler who held the crown matrimonial was only a king consort whose power would normally come to an end should his wife predecease him.

In 1192 it was intended that the new king of Jerusalem should be Conrad of Montferrat who had married Sibyl's sister Isabella in 1190 after the annulment of her marriage to Humphrey of Toron. The Montferrats were not newcomers to the kingdom, for Conrad's elder brother, William Longsword, had been Queen Sibyl's first husband and the father of the child-king, Baldwin V. Conrad had brought with him to Tyre in 1187 a household which included a seneschal and a chamberlain, and as his power increased he promoted his secretary to be his chancellor[7]. It looked as though once he became king he would give most of the great offices of state to his Italian followers, but that did not happen because he was assassinated in 1192 before he had been crowned. Although his household returned to Italy, the house of Montferrat's interest in the Holy Land did not end at that point because the crown later passed to Conrad's daughter Maria and her descendants.

Within a week of his death the queen was married to Henry II of Troyes, count of Champagne, nephew of the kings of England and France, who had accompanied Philip Augustus on the Third Crusade. He postponed his coronation, hoping

---

[4] *Ernest Strehlke,* Tabulae Ordinis Theutonici, no. 23 (Berlin 1869, reprinted with preface by *Hans E. Mayer,* Toronto 1975) 21.

[5] Geoffrey heads the witness list as Count of Jaffa in a diploma of Guy of Lusignan issued on 31 January 1192, *Reinhold Röhricht,* Regesta Regni Hierosolymitani (MXCVII-MCCXCI), no. 698 (Innsbruck 1893–1904) I, 186.

[6] Walter Durus had been marshal of the kingdom in 1185, *Strehlke,* 17 f., nos. 18, 19. In a charter of Conrad of Montferrat of April 1192 he appears as 'Gualterius Durus, marescalcus', *Röhricht,* no. 704, I, 188. Hugh Martin is named marshal in a diploma of Guy's dated 10 February 1192, *Röhricht,* no. 701, I. 187.

[7] In October 1187 three charters of Conrad were witnessed by 'Ubertus Nepos, senescalcus marchionis' and 'Datum per manum Bandini, domini marchionis scribae.' *Röhricht,* nos. 665, 667–8, I, 177 f.; Bandinus also appears in no. 666. By September 1188 Bandinus was styled 'cancellarium et secretarium', ibid. no. 676, I, 181. In May 1191 Bandinus is styled chancellor, and Henricus de Cannelli 'camerarius marchionis', ibid. no. 705, I, 188 f.

that a new crusade would recover Jerusalem and that it could take place there. He ruled over a diminished kingdom, consisting principally of the royal cities of Acre and Tyre, and the lordships of Jaffa, Arsuf, Caesarea and Cayphas. He did not attempt to concentrate power in the hands of his own entourage, although some members of his household, like Milo Breban of Provins, the marshal of Champagne[8], and his jester, Escarlate[9], remained with him in the Holy Land, while other Champenois, like Vilain of Aulnay, later joined him there[10].

He faced opposition from the Lusignans. Guy bitterly resented the loss of his kingdom, and his brother Aimery, who remained constable of Jerusalem, supported the revolt of the Pisans against Henry in 1193[11]. But when this was suppressed and Aimery had fled to Cyprus, Henry appointed his own young brother-in-law as new constable. This was John of Ibelin, who can only have been sixteen[12] and whose family, which had been one of the greatest in the last days of the First Kingdom, had lost almost all their lands to Saladin. Henry sought to share power with the native baronage by making Ralph of Tiberias seneschal of the kingdom[13]. But he also used his patronage to encourage new men to settle there, some of whom may have been crusaders who had remained in the East after 1192. One was Thierry of Tenremonde in Flanders, who may have accompanied Philip of Flanders on crusade, and who married Agnes, the heiress of Adelon[14]; another was Thierry of Orgue, who married Melisende, the lady of Arsuf[15]; while a third was Adémar of Lairon, who married Juliana, the widowed Lady of Caesarea[16]. Henry must have arranged the two latter marriages himself, and perhaps per-

---

[8] Milo Breban witnessed Henry of Troyes' first diploma as ruler of Jerusalem in 1192, and subsequently others, *Röhricht*, nos. 707, 710, 713, 716, 720, I, 189–93; *Theodore Evergates, Feudal Society in the Bailliage of Troyes* ... (1152–1284) (Baltimore 1975) 10, 47.
[9] Continuation, c. 179, 189 and n. 2.
[10] Aulnay was a lordship in the county of Champagne. Villanus de Alneto first appears as a witness in a diploma of 19 October 1197, *Röhricht*, no. 735, I, 196.
[11] Continuation, c. 147, 159ff.; *Marie-Luise Favreau-Lilie*, Die Italiener im Heiligen Land ... (1098–1197) (Amsterdam 1989) 312–15.
[12] John's parents married in 1177, and he cannot have been born before 1178, *William of Tyre*, XXI, 17, II, 986. The Old French Continuation dates the gift of Beirut to 1194, c. 147, 161.
[13] He first appears with this title in a diploma of 5 January 1194, *Röhricht*, no. 717, I, 192.
[14] Thierry first appears in Henry's entourage in January 1193, *Röhricht*, no. 709, I, 190, and often thereafter. His marriage is recorded in Lignages, c. 35, RHC Lois, II, 469. Adelon was a rear-fief of Sidon and the marriage must have received the consent of Reynald of Sidon. Cf. *C. du Fresne Ducange*, ed. *E. G. Rey*, Les familles d'Outremer (Paris 1869) 169f.
[15] He appears as a witness in Henry of Troyes' diplomas from January 1194, *Röhricht*, nos. 717, 720, 722, 724, I, 192ff. For his marriage, *Ducange*, 222.
[16] Juliana inherited Caesarea from her brother Walter II who died at the siege of Acre. By her first husband, Guy 'de Beritho', she had Walter III, still a child at the time of her marriage to Adémar of Lairon who first appears as lord of Caesarea in January 1193 ('Azemarus, Caesariensis dominus'), *Röhricht*, no. 709, I, 190. *John L. LaMonte*, The Lords of Caesarea in the period of the Crusades, in: Speculum 22 (1947) 152ff. See also *Peter Jackson*, The End of Hohenstaufen Rule in Syria in: Bulletin of the Institute of Historical Research 59 (1986) 31, no. 68.

suaded Reynald of Sidon to give Thierry of Tenremonde the hand of the lady of Adelon, and all three new vassals became important members of his court. The number of heiresses available no doubt reflected the high mortality rate among Frankish noblemen in the years following Hattin, but it benefited Henry by extending his powers of patronage in a very small kingdom.

Guy of Lusignan died in 1194 and the lordship of Cyprus passed to his brother Aimery, who later made peace with Henry, and proposed that when they were old enough his sons should marry Henry's daughters. As part of the marriage settlement Henry and Isabella promised to restore Jaffa to the Lusignans[17]. Henry's reign ended tragically when he fell to his death from a window in the palace of Acre in 1197. His reputation stood high in the Frankish East partly because he had drawn on the revenues of Champagne very extensively to meet the needs of the Holy Land[18]. He left two young daugthers in Acre, Alice and Philippa, but his brother, Thibaut III, succeeded him as count of Champagne. He died in 1201, leaving his widow pregnant with the future Thibaut IV who did not come of age until 1222 and during those years the house of Champagne was in no position to intervene in the affairs of Jerusalem[19].

In 1197 Aimery of Lusignan was crowned king of Cyprus by Conrad of Hildesheim, the imperial chancellor who led the vanguard of Henry VI's crusade, and it was at his suggestion that Aimery, who had recently become a widower, married Isabella of Jerusalem. Unlike Henry he was crowned king of Jerusalem and, as the Eracles comments of Isabella, 'lors a primes fu ele reine'[20]. Aimery's court in Cyprus contained former members of his brother Guy's entourage, men like Hugh Martin, Walter Lo Bel (whom Guy had made viscount of Acre), Rainier of Gibelet and Gawain of Cheneché, some of whom were Poitevins[21]. That element had been strengthened by other Poitevins who had come to Cyprus, during Aimery's reign it would seem, like Reynald Barlais[22], and Aimery de Rivet, who was made seneschal of Cyprus, should probably also be numbered among them[23].

---

[17] '... et le conte Henri, par l'atrait et la volonté de Ysabiau sa feme, fist don et vente a sa fille del conté de Jaffe, que il li fist doaire et en heritage.' Continuation, c. 167, 177. This clause seems to have taken effect in c.1208 when Henry's daughter Alice married Aimery's son Hugh I of Cyprus, see the marriage contract, Edmond Martène, Ursmer Durand (eds.), Thesaurus Novus Anecdotorum (Paris 1717), I, 806 f. See n. 72 below.

[18] See the alleged comments of the Military Orders at the time of his death, Continuation, c. 189, 199.

[19] Jean Longnon, Les compagnons de Villehardouin (Geneva 1978) 11 ff.

[20] L'Estoire d'Eracles empereur et la conqueste de la Terre d'Outremer, XXVII, V, RHC Occ, II, 223.

[21] In Guy's entourage: Röhricht, nos. 683–4, 690, 693, 698, 701–2 (Gawain of Cheneché); 690, 698, 701 (Rainier of Gibelet); 698, 701–2 (Hugh Martin and Walter lo Bel); in Aimery's entourage: 723, 737 (Hugh Martin); 723 (Walter lo Bel and Rainier of Gibelet), I, 182–8, 193, 196. Gawain of Cheneché who took a prominent part in Cypriote affairs during Henry I's minority would appear to be the son of Guy's supporter with the same name, Philip of Novara, Mémoires, c. xxvii, ed. Charles Kohler (Paris 1913) 7–43.

[22] Probably to be identified with Raynaldus Betlay, who witnessed a diploma of Aimery in 1195, Röhricht, no. 723, I, 193. He was appointed castellan of Jaffa as soon as Aimery became

King Aimery made no attempt to unite his two realms, nor did he at first make any significant changes among his wife's advisers. Milo Breban, the most powerful of Henry of Troyes' western followers, returned to Champagne and later went to Frankish Greece[24], and Aimery clearly relied on the support of Baldwin of Bethsan, the constable of Cyprus, who often accompanied him when he visited the mainland[25]. Nevertheless, Aimery had rights of patronage in Jerusalem which enabled him over the years to build up a group of supporters there. This was facilitated by the recovery of some territory during his reign. Thus Beirut was regained in 1197 with the help of the vanguard of Henry VI's crusade and Aimery was able to keep it as a royal fief because it had belonged to the crown before 1187[26]. Then in 1203 a splinter group of the Fourth Crusade reached Outremer, and partly with their help Aimery was able to regain control over the disputed lands of Sidon[27]. Balian lord of Sidon was a minor, and Aimery arranged the marriage of his widowed mother, Helvis of Ibelin, to Guy of Montfort, one of the new crusaders, who thus became *bailli* of Sidon until his stepson came of age[28]. Jaffa was still part of the crown lands and therefore under Aimery's control, and so he was building up a secure power base in the mainland kingdom. In c.1202 his daughter Burgundia had married Walter of Montbéliard, a knight from Burgund, who had joined the Fourth Crusade, but, following a rather erratic route, had ended up in Cyprus[29]. Aimery wished to appoint him constable of Jerusalem, presumably so that he could command the army of the kingdom in Aimery's absence. That office was held by John of Ibelin and Aimery offered him the fief of Beirut in exchange for it[30]. Aimery made no attempt to diminish the powers of the men patronised by Henry of Troyes, but when in 1204 news of the capture of Constantinople reached the Holy Land some knights from the Crusader States went there. Among them was Thierry of Tenremonde, who no doubt expected to benefit from the patronage of the Champenois like Geoffrey of Villehardouin

King of Jerusalem, Eracles, XXVII, ii, RHC Occ, II, 219. He was probably related to the lords of Montreuil-Bellay, *Peter W. Edbury*, The Kingdom of Cyprus and the Crusades 1191–1374 (Cambridge 1991) 18, n. 25.
[23] Seneschal by 22 November 1197, *Röhricht*, no. 737, I, 196. *Edbury*, 18, n. 25 suggests that the Rivet family may have been Poitevins.
[24] *Longnon*, 48–57.
[25] *Röhricht*, no. 723 (1195, in Cyprus), 740B, 743, 746, 774, 776 (1198, 1200, in Acre) I, 193, 198f., 206f., II, 49.
[26] Eracles, XXVII, viii, RHC Occ, II, 226. *Bernard Hamilton*, Miles of Plancy and the fief of Beirut, in: *Benjamin Z. Kedar* (ed.), The Horns of Hattin (Jerusalem 1992) 136–46.
[27] *Ibn al-Athir*, Sum of World History, RHC Or, II, 96; *al-Maqrizi*, trans. *R. J. C. Broadhurst*, A History of the Ayyubid Sultans of Egypt (Boston, Mass. 1980) 146.
[28] Eracles, XXVIII, xii, RHC Occ, II, 263. *Lamonte*, The Lords of Sidon in the Twelfth and Thirteenth Centuries, in: Byzantion 17 (1944–5) 193–200.
[29] *Longnon*, 20; Eracles, XXVI, 21, RHC Occ, II, 208.
[30] *Philip of Novara*, c. xxvii, 16; Eracles, XXXI, v, RHC Occ, II, 316. *Lamonte*, John of Ibelin, the Old Lord of Beirut, 1177–1236, in: Byzantion 12 (1937) 424 f.

who had played such a large part in the Fourth Crusade, and other men from Champagne who had supported Henry of Troyes may have done the same[31].

By the end of his reign Aimery was therefore in a strong position in the Latin Kingdom. He died early in 1205, it would appear from food poisoning. It had been agreed that Cyprus should be inherited by Hugh, the eldest surviving son of his first marriage, who was still a minor. Isabella survived Aimery by only a few months. She left five daughters and her heir was the eldest of them, Maria, the child of Conrad of Montferrat, who was about fourteen[32]. By the laws of the kingdom John of Ibelin was the rightful regent as Maria's closest kin on her mother's side[33]. When Baldwin V of Montferrat had become king at the age of eight in 1185 his grandfather, William IV, had come to live in the Holy Land partly at least in order to safeguard the family interests[34]; but that did not happen in 1206 because the family had greater concerns elsewhere. Its head, Maria's uncle, Boniface of Montferrat, had led the Fourth Crusade and become king of Thessalonica. But he was killed in 1207 and his kingdom was disputed between the supporters of his eldest son, William V, and those of his infant son Demetrius, whose mother, the dowager Byzantine empress Mary, claimed the regency[35]. This resulted in a long civil war and one consequence of this was that the Montferrats took no interest in the kingdom of Jerusalem, not even in the choice of a husband for their kinswoman, Queen Maria.

King Hugh of Cyprus was also a minor and his regent was his brother-in-law, Walter of Montbéliard[36], who cooperated closely with his fellow regent, John of Ibelin. The agreement which had been made between Aimery of Cyprus and Henry of Troyes was partly implemented by John and Walter in c.1208 when Henry's elder daughter, Alice, married king Hugh, to whom she brought the county of Jaffa as her dowry[37]. At about the same time close family ties were formed between the two regents when John's younger brother, Philip of Ibelin, married Walter's sister Alice, the widow of count Bertold of Neuenburg who had

[31] Baldwin of Flanders 'manda en la terre d'Otre mer et fist crier par tout que, qui vodroit avoir terre ne garison, que il venist a lui'. Eracles, XXIX, ii, RHC Occ, II, 278. Thierry of Tenremonde was killed in 1206 fighting the Bulgarians, Geoffrey of Villehardouin, La Conquête de Constantinople, § 316, 405–6, 408–9, ed. Edmond Faral (Paris 1939) II, 124, 216 ff., 220 ff.
[32] Eracles, XXX, xi, RHC Occ, II, 305. Isabel was pregnant with Maria at the time of Conrad's death in 1192, Continuation, c. 138, 143. Her other surviving daughters were Alice and Philippa, the children of Henry of Troyes, and Melisende and Sibyl, the daughters of Aimery of Lusignan.
[33] 'Et deit remaindre le baillage de la terre en la main dou plus prochein parent ou parente que les anfans aient de par leur mere et de par la reauté meut ...' Le Livre au Roi, c. v, RHC Lois, I, 610.
[34] Continuation, c. 10, 24 f.
[35] Longnon, L'Empire latin de Constantinople et la principauté de Morée (Paris 1949) 106–11.
[36] Eracles, XXX, xii, RHC Occ, II, 305.
[37] Ibid. XXX, xv, RHC Occ, II, 308 f.

come to live in the Latin Kingdom during Aimery's reign[38]. Another index of co-operation between the two regents was the appointment as constable of Cyprus of Walter of Caesarea, John of Ibelin's brother-in-law, who would not inherit his important mainland fief until his mother died[39]. One other man who became prominent during John of Ibelin's regency was Garnier l'Aleman, the name which the French-speaking population of Outremer gave to Werner von Egisheim, who first appeared at the court of Acre in the company of count Bertold[40]. He married Pavia, a member of the Tripolitan family of the lords of Gibelet[41], and became important during John of Ibelin's regency as part of the Montbéliard circle of Philip of Ibelin's wife. By 1210 Garnier and Philip of Ibelin jointly took responsibility for the defence of Acre while the rest of the nobility were attending the coronation of the queen at Tyre[42]. John of Ibelin used his powers while regent to arrange his own marriage to Melisende, Lady of Arsuf, in c.1209, after the death of her first husband, Henry of Troyes' supporter, Thierry d'Orgue[43].

In 1208 the High Court of Jerusalem, following precedents from Baldwin IV's reign, sent an embassy to Philip Augustus asking him to choose a husband for the queen. He nominated John of Brienne, a choice which one version of the *Eracles* attributes to an unworthy desire to rid France of him, and which is generally agreed to have been greeted with some dismay in Acre. For John was a younger son, and he was merely *bailli* for the county of Brienne on behalf of his young nephew, Walter III, who was living in the kingdom of Sicily[44]. On the other hand John was a first cousin of Walter of Montbéliard, regent of Cyprus[45], and this consideration may have influenced Philip II in his choice. In 1210 John of Brienne married the queen thus ending the Ibelin regency.

---

[38] Lignages, c. xiii, RHC Lois, II, 452. Count Bertold and his son Bertold were present in Acre in October 1200, *Röhricht, no. 776*, I, 207; and Count Bertold witnessed charters in May 1206 and February and July 1207, ibid. nos. 812, 818, 819, 821, I, 217, 220. Although he is normally identified with Count Bertold of Katzenellenbogen (e.g. by *Wipertus H. Rudt de Collenberg, Les Ibelin aux XIIIe et XIVe siècles. Généalogie compilée principalement selon les registres du Vatican,* in: Epeteris IX [1979] 203), the latter spent most of his time in Frankish Greece, *Longnon,* Compagnons, 244 f. It seems more probable that Alice of Montbéliard's first husband was Count Berthold of Neuenburg, who on 22 June 1200 left for the Holy Land with his son 'trans mare perpetuo mansurus', *Röhricht,* Die Deutschen im Heiligen Lande (Innsbruck 1894) 87.
[39] First recorded as constable in September 1210, *Röhricht,* Regesta, no. 844, I, 225. Lignages, c. xii, RHC Lois, II, 451.
[40] *Röhricht,* Die Deutschen, 94. *Röhricht,* Regesta, no. 812 (May 1206) I, 217; cf. Ibid., no. 933, I, 247, where as a witness to a charter of Count Otto of Henneberg his name is given in its German form, Wernerus de Egisheim.
[41] *Ducange,* 504; Lignages, xxx, RHC Lois, II, 465.
[42] Eracles, XXXI, i, RHC Occ, II, 312.
[43] Lignages, xi, RHC Lois, II, 451. *Rudt de Collenberg,* 128, places this marriage in c.1209.
[44] 'Cil de la terre ... sorent que li cuenz [Johan] n'estoit pas richez hom ne la conté de Briene ne teneit il que en baillage, car ele estoit de Gauteron son neveu, qui estoit en Puille ...' Eracles, XXX, xiv, RHC Occ, II, 308.
[45] The Eracles wrongly claims that John's mother, Agnes of Montbéliard, was Walter's sister, XXI, v, RHC Occ, II, 316. She was in fact his aunt, *Rudt de Collenberg,* 131, n. 45.

The *Eracles* says that John was accompanied by 300 knights, but these cannot all have been members of his entourage, for he was not a rich man[46]. Nevertheless, two of them, James and Erard, members of the Durnai family of Champagne, stayed in the kingdom, and John appointed James marshal of Jerusalem in the place of Adémar of Lairon[47]. Almost immediately on his arrival John was joined by Walter of Montbéliard, who had quarrelled with king Hugh when he came of age and fled from Cyprus. He was welcomed by John because he was a kinsman and also very rich, and was recognized as constable of the kingdom, a post which had formerly been given to him by king Aimery[48]. John's cousin, Erard of Brienne, also joined him from the West, but proved a liability. He made a clandestine, though undoubtedly valid, marriage with Philippa, the younger daughter of Henry of Champagne, and the full sister of Queen Alice of Cyprus, and returned to France where he laid claim to the county of Champagne in his wife's right. The

* countess Blanche defended Thibaut III's title on the grounds that Henry of Troyes' daughters were illegitimate because the annulment of Isabella I's marriage to her first husband, Humphrey of Toron, had not been valid[49]. John of Brienne had disapproved of Erard's marriage and it caused him problems: first, as *bailli* of

* the lordship of Brienne, he depended on the goodwill of Thibaut III's mother, the countess Blanche, to preserve his nephew's rights there; and secondly, once the validity of the annulment of Isabella's first marriage was called in question the legitimacy of all her children, including that of Queen Maria, would be put in doubt[50].

By the time this scandal broke, John's position had already been weakened by the death of Maria in 1212[51]. She left one daughter, Isabella II, and by the laws of the kingdom John, though undoubtedly rightful regent, was no longer king. At this point, he quarrelled with some senior members of the nobility, for reasons which are unknown to us. They included John and Philip of Ibelin, who did not appear at court again after the queen's death, and Balian, lord of Sidon[52]. The Ibelins went to live in Cyprus, and rather pointedly served under king Hugh on the

[46] Eracles, XXX, xiv, RHC Occ, II, 308.

[47] For Adémar as marshal during John of Ibelin's regency, *Röhricht, Regesta*, no. 812, I, 217. James of Durnai was marshal by 1 July 1211, ibid. no. 853, I, 228, and held the office at least until August 1217, ibid. nos. 898–9, I, 241; Erard of Durnai first appears in John of Brienne's entourage on 1 March 1212, ibid. no. 857, I, 229.

[48] Eracles, XXXI, v, RHC Occ, II, 316.

[49] Erard was a member of the Ramerupt branch of the Brienne family, *Evergates*, 196–9; Eracles, XXXI, viii, p. 320. The documents are printed in an appendix to Innocent III's Registers, *Jacques-Paul Migne, Patrologia Latina*, 216, 968–91.

[50] A legatine inquiry in 1200 had already cast doubt on the validity of the annulment of Isabella's marriage to Humphrey of Toron, ibid. 216, 980f.

[51] '... la reine Marie ... ne vesqui que II anz puis que li rois Johans l'ot esposée ...' Eracles, XXXI, viii, RHC Occ, II, 320.

[52] Philip of Ibelin was present at John and Marie's court in 1211, *Röhricht, Regesta*, no. 853, I, 228, but after the queen's death all three men were conspicuous by their absence. Innocent III was concerned about the disturbances in the Latin East and accused Hugh of Cyprus of supporting the rebels, Regesta, XV, ccviii, ccx, ccxi, PL, 216, 736–9.

Fifth Crusade[53], but it is not known whether Balian of Sidon accompanied them into exile. His control of his fief was certainly unchallenged, since his stepfather and former *bailli*, Guy of Montfort, had returned to France in 1211 in order to assist his brother Simon in laying waste Languedoc[54], but Balian is not mentioned in any source between 1210 and the autumn of 1218[55].

The disaffected nobles retained their fiefs, and so although John tried to build up his own power he had very little room for manoeuvre chiefly because he had no land with which to reward supporters, nor had he any scope to arrange diplomatic marriages, because Philippa of Troyes had been his only ward of marriageable age. The daughters of Isabella I and Aimery of Lusignan were in the guardianship of their brother, Hugh I of Cyprus. However, John did make a diplomatic marriage himself: his second wife was the daughter of Leo II of Cilicia[56]. He had no adult male kin to whom he could delegate power until his cousin Eudes of Montbéliard, the nephew of Walter, was old enough to be appointed constable in 1220[57]. Shortly before this he had sought a reconciliation with Balian of Sidon who in 1219 married the king's niece Marguerite. She was the daughter of John's sister Ida and Ernoul lord of Reynel, and came from the West in the fleet which brought the legate Pelagius to Egypt[58].

In 1223 John went to Italy to discuss the affairs of his kingdom with Pope Honorius III and the emperor Frederick, leaving Eudes of Montbéliard as his *bailli*[59]. At that meeting it was agreed that Isabella II of Jerusalem should marry the emperor whose first wife had recently died. The marriage took place in 1225 and Frederick immediately assumed the powers of king of Jerusalem. Initially he confirmed Eudes of Montbéliard as his *bailli*[60] and it was only when he was ready

[53] Eracles, XXXI, x, RHC Occ, II, 322.
[54] He reached Languedoc by Christmas 1211, *Michel Roquebert*, L'Epopée cathare (Paris 1970–89) I, 456.
[55] Balian ranked first after John of Ibelin among the nobles present at John of Brienne's coronation in 1210, Eracles, XXXI, i, RHC Occ, II, 311; but is next mentioned at the siege of Damietta in September 1218, ibid., XXXII, iii, II, 332. See *LaMonte*, Byzantion 17 (1944–5) 200.
[56] John's marriage, *Röhricht*, Regesta, no. 873, I, 236; Hugh arranged Melisende's marriage to Bohemond IV of Antioch in 1218, Eracles, XXXI, xiii, RHC Occ, II, 325. Sibyl, the elder daughter of Aimery of Lusignan and Isabella I of Jerusalem, had been married in c.1210 to Leo II of Cilicia, ibid. XXX, xi, II, 305. *Rudt de Collenberg*, 'Les Lusignans de Chypre', in: Epeteris X (1979–80) 99f.
[57] One manuscript of the Lignages reports that Eudes was Walter of Montbéliard's nephew, c. xvii, RHC Lois, II, 455, n. 3. He seems to have been held captive for a time by Hugh I of Cyprus. In 1213 Innocent III urged the king to release 'O. [= Odonem?] consanguineum regis [Johannis]', Regesta, XV, ccviii, PL, 216, 736f. Cf. *Edbury*, 46, n. 29. He first appeared at John's court in 1217, but is first named constable in a diploma of May 1220 when he headed the witness list, *Röhricht*, Regesta, nos. 892, 934, I, 240, 248. *LaMonte*, Feudal Monarchy in the Latin Kingdom of Jerusalem, 1100–1291 (Cambridge, Mass. 1932) 253.
[58] Eracles, XXXII, iii, RHC Occ, II, 332. Risnel (Reynel) is a lordship in the bailliage of Chaumont.
[59] Ibid. XXXII, xix, 355.
[60] Ibid. XXXII, xx, 359.

to lead a crusade to the Holy Land and take possession of his wife's kingdom that he replaced him by Thomas of Acerra, count of Aquino[61]. But when Frederick reached Outremer in 1228 his position had changed because Isabella II had died a few months earlier shortly after giving birth to a son, Conrad, and the emperor, in the eyes of his subjects in the Latin Kingdom, ceased to be king and became regent for Conrad[62].

Although his enemies tried to belittle his achievements, Frederick gained considerable territorial concessions from the Sultan of Egypt including Jerusalem, Bethlehem, Nazareth and Toron[63]. His imperial commitments meant that he could not stay in the East, but he nevertheless wanted to exercise real power there. This involved appointing men whom he could trust to positions of authority, and at first he seems to have contemplated using the Montferrats in that capacity. His son Conrad, the King of Jerusalem, was a great-grandson of Conrad of Montferrat, and the Montferrats were imperial vassals. Frederick brought with him on crusade Demetrius of Montferrat, titular king of Thessalonica, who had lost his kingdom in 1224, and I think it probable that the emperor intended to provide him with a suitable fief in the Latin kingdom and appoint him *bailli*, but that proved impossible[64]. Frederick did, however, arrange the marriage of Demetrius's niece, Alice of Montferrat, to his own vassal, the child-king Henry I of Cyprus[65].

Despite his recovery of lost territory, Frederick met with only limited success in his attempt to exercise royal patronage. He had hoped to award the fief of Toron to the Teutonic Order, but in a complicated legal battle the High Court upheld the claims of Alice of Armenia. Interestingly, although she was a widow, Frederick did not attempt to enforce his right of choosing a husband for her, perhaps because she was advanced in age[66]. The only way in which he could acquire more fiefs was by confiscation, but when he attempted to strip John of Ibelin of his fief of Beirut he failed, and this led to civil war[67].

---

[61] Ibid. XXXII, xxiv, 364.

[62] *Philip of Novara*, c. xl, 188.

[63] No full text of the treaty is known and Christian and Muslim sources disagree about the precise terms. See *Joshua Prawer*, trans. G. *Nahon*, Histoire du royaume franque de Jérusalem (Paris 1970) II, 198, n. 37; *Thomas C. Van Cleve*, The Emperor Frederick II of Hohenstaufen (Oxford 1972) 219f. It would appear that the Franks were not able to enforce their claim to Toron until 1240. *Peter Jackson*, The Crusades of 1239–41 and their aftermath, in: Bulletin of the School of Oriental and African Studies, University of London L (I) (1987) 42.

[64] *Philip of Novara*, c. xxiv, 77. *Longnon*, L'Empire, 162ff., wrongly dates Demetrius' death to 1227 on the authority of Benvenuto di S. Giorgio, Historia Montisferrati, published in 1516, ed. L. *M. Muratori*, Rerum Italicarum Scriptores (Milan 1733) VII, 382. This late tradition cannot be preferred to the contemporary evidence of Philip of Novara.

[65] *Philip of Novara*, c. xlv, 92. Alice was the daughter of William V of Montferrat.

[66] *John of Ibelin*, Le Livre des Assises de la Haute Cour, cc. 69, 203, RHC Lois, I, 112f., 325f. Alice was the daughter of Isabella of Toron and Rupen III of Cilicia who married in 1180, and must have been almost fifty by 1229. Cf. *Steven Tibble*, Monarchy and Lordships in the Latin Kingdom of Jerusalem 1099–1291 (Oxford 1989) 90ff.

[67] *Philip of Novara*, passim. *Jonathan S. C. Riley-Smith*, The Feudal Nobility and the Kingdom of Jerusalem, 1174–1277 (London 1973) 163–84.

Frederick therefore exercised power through Sicilian *baillis* whom he could trust, and the Teutonic Order, which had its headquarters at Montfort and was an instrument of imperial authority in the Crusader Kingdom, and to which he gave immense economic and political power in his European lands[68]. His power in the Latin Kingdom was not negligible: his *bailli* Richard Filangieri, marshal of the kingdom of Sicily, controlled the royal city of Tyre[69], and Frederick was also obeyed in Jerusalem, where his lieutenant was Walter Pennenpié. Indeed, when in 1241 Richard of Cornwall succeeded in recovering Ascalon, he handed it over to Walter[70]. But Frederick lost control of Acre[71], and had never had control of the county of Jaffa, which was held by his vassal, Henry I of Cyprus. In c.1235 Henry appointed John of Brienne's nephew, Walter IV, count of Jaffa, when he married Henry's sister Mary[72].

Frederick II's rule came to a practical end in 1242 when his opponents expelled the imperial garrison from Tyre[73]. Although he appointed Thomas of Acerra as his new *bailli*, Thomas was forced to live at the court of Tripoli because the barons of the kingdom would not admit him[74]. In the view of the Jerusalem lawyers king Conrad came of age in 1243 and Frederick's regency ended, but because Conrad remained in Europe a regent was still needed, and the High Court chose Queen Alice of Cyprus, the oldest of Conrad's maternal great-aunts[75]. She had recently married a Frenchman who had come on the crusade of Theobald of Navarre, Ralph, brother of the count of Soissons, who wished to act as *bailli* on his wife's behalf[76]. So the kingdom once again had as ruler the foreign consort of a native princess. But when Ralph asked for the seisin of the royal city of Tyre together with all the royal castles he met with a refusal[77]. The *Eracles* reports that:

[68] *I. Sterns*, The Teutonic Knights in the Crusader States, in: *Kenneth M. Setton* (gen. ed), The History of the Crusades, V (Wisconsin 1985) 315–78; *H. Prutz*, Die Besitzungen des Deutschen Ordens im Heiligen Lande (Leipzig 1877).
[69] For the career of Richard Filangieri see *G. del Giudice*, Riccardo Filangieri sotto il regno di Federico II, di Corrado e di Manfredi (Naples 1893). He was sent to Syria in 1231 as soon as Frederick had stabilised his position in Sicily, *Philip of Novara*, c. lxxvii, 52.
[70] He was in post by 1241, it is not known when he was appointed, Eracles, XXXIII, li, RHC Occ, II, 421.
[71] For a careful assessment of the constitutional position of the commune of Acre, *Riley-Smith*, Feudal Nobility, 173–84.
[72] Eracles, XXXIII, xxxviii, 403. *Jean Richard*, trans. *J. Shirley*, The Latin Kingdom of Jerusalem (Amsterdam 1978) II, 249 suggests that this was the occasion of Walter's becoming count of Jaffa, which seems the most plausible explanation. This has received general assent. See the very full discussion of the whole issue by *Mayer*, John of Jaffa, his opponents and his fiefs, in: Proceedings of the American Philosophical Society 128 (1984) 134–63.
[73] *Jackson*, 20–36; *David Jacoby*, The Kingdom of Jerusalem and the collapse of Hohenstaufen power in the Levant, in: Dumbarton Oaks Papers 40 (1986) 83–101.
[74] *Röhricht*, Regesta, 1118A, 1123A, II, 70. *Riley-Smith*, 210.
[75] Eracles, XXXIII, 1, RHC Occ, II, 420.
[76] Rothelin Continuation of William of Tyre, c. xx; Eracles, XXXIII, 1, RHC Occ, II, 527, 420.
[77] 'Ne ne soufrimes mie que ledit Raou de Saison les eust en son poier, por aucuns perils que peussent avenir, si come il avint dou fait de la Moré as enfanz dou Champeneis, de sire Jofrei

'[Ralph's] wife's relations had more power and authority than he had, and it seemed to him that he was nothing but a shadow'[78]. Not being content with this role, he left the Holy Land, and his wife, and returned to the West[79]. When Alice died in 1246 the regency passed to her son, king Henry of Cyprus[80], but Frederick, despite his deposition from all offices by pope Innocent IV at the Council of Lyons, continued to be treated as king of Jerusalem by many people until he died in December 1250[81]. This left the non-resident Conrad as king, the non-resident Henry of Cyprus as *bailli* and the prospect of anarchy in the Latin Kingdom. That was only averted by the decision of St. Louis to stay there for four years and to give the Latin East a stability it had not known since before the accession of John of Brienne.

The kingdom of Acre had come into being during the strife between Guy of Lusignan and Conrad of Montferrat, and those divisions were never subsequently healed because during the next fifty years there was a succession of king consorts each of whom wanted to place some of his own followers in positions of authority, thereby reducing the opportunities for patronage available to his successor. By the time of Frederick II's accession civil war was almost inevitable in the case of a consort who was not prepared to be a ceremonial figurehead. The emperor throughout the years when he was regent for Conrad fought to maintain his authority but was only partially successful, whereas his successor as regent, Ralph of Soissons, lacking adequate resources, had to admit defeat and return to the West.

Addenda
p. 20, for 'Thibaut III' read 'Thibaut IV' in both cases.

de Villehardoin, en cui mains elle demoura.' Documents relatifs à la successibilité, c. ii, RHC Lois, II, 401.
[78] Eracles, XXXIII, 1, RHC Occ, II, 420.
[79] Ibid, XXXIII, liii, 423.
[80] *Riley-Smith*, 212, 313.
[81] Thus Peter of Brittany, negotiating with the Sultan of Egypt in 1250 about the ransom of St. Louis' Crusade, when asked to surrender fortresses in Palestine replied: 'que il n'i avoit pooir; car on les tenoit de l'empereor d'Alemaingne, qui lor vivoit.' *John of Joinville*, Histoire de Saint Louis, ed. *N. de Wailly* (Paris 1868) 118.

III

Miles of Plancy and the Fief of Beirut

When Amalric of Jerusalem died on 11 July 1174 his heir was a thirteen-year-old boy, Baldwin IV. The fact that he was known to be suffering from leprosy created problems for the future, but made no difference to the immediate need to appoint a regent until he came of age. The government of the kingdom in the new reign was at first conducted by the seneschal, Miles of Plancy, but it is not clear from the sources that he was appointed regent. The *Brevis historia*, a Genoese source dating from about the year 1200, states that King Amalric designated Miles as regent for his son[1] and William of Tyre describes him as acting as regent (*procurante regni negocia*),[2] yet it is clear from William's subsequent narrative that Miles did not hold the official title of regent. It may be inferred from this that although Amalric may have expressed a wish during his last illness that Miles should become regent the High Court failed to ratify his appointment. This decision, I would argue, was made because the High Court wished first to offer the regency to King Henry II of England to whom by the law of Jerusalem it belonged as the closest kinsman of Baldwin IV on his father's side.[3] This policy did not appear unrealistic since it was known that Alexander III had imposed a pilgrimage to Jerusalem on the king of England as a penance for his part in the murder of St. Thomas Becket.[4] If no regent was appointed the government of the kingdom of Jerusalem devolved on the seneschal during a minority. John of Ibelin explained this some eighty years later:

> If the king is absent from the kingdom and his representative (*home qui teigne son leuc*) is also absent, the seneschal by virtue of his office should hold the king's place, save in matters relating to the army...[5]

Miles of Plancy was a member of the royal family, being a third cousin of King

1 *Regni Iherosolymitani brevis historia*, ed. L.T. Belgrano, in *Annali Genovesi di Caffaro e de' suoi continuatori*, vol. 1 (Genoa, 1890), p. 135.
2 WT21,3, p. 963.
3 Henry II was a nephew of King Amalric of Jerusalem and was first cousin of the Leper King. He had no claim to the throne, but the best claim to the regency: *Le Livre au Roi* 5, RHC Lois 1:609-610.
4 *Materials for the History of Thomas Becket, Archbishop of Canterbury*, ed. J.C. Robertson and J.B. Sheppard, RS 67 (London, 1875-85), 7:514.
5 Jean d'Ibelin, *Livre* 256, RHC Lois 1:408.

Amalric.[6] This was the kind of relationship of which the twelfth-century nobility needed to be aware, because of canon law rulings about the prohibited degrees of marriage. Miles had come to Jerusalem from Champagne during Amalric's reign and soon won the king's favor, being appointed seneschal in 1169.[7] Shortly before Amalric's death, and undoubtedly at the king's wish, he married Stephanie of Milly, heiress of the great fief of Oultrejourdain.[8] This was one of the most important lordships in the kingdom: like Sidon it owed the crown service of forty knights.[9]

If William of Tyre's description of him is at all accurate, it is easy to see why Miles was not well liked:

> He was proud and conceited. He loved the sound of his own voice and had far too good an opinion of himself.[10]

In a cryptic passage, William related how, in order to counter criticisms of his rule, Miles ostensibly placed himself under the orders of Rohard, the castellan of Jerusalem. "In fact," William tells us, "the reverse was true. For one man held the title which sounded good but conferred no power, while the other ...dealt with the business of the kingdom as seemed good to himself."[11] Although William does not say what title was given to Rohard, this passage does show that Miles was not the regent, for if he had been then there would have been no higher title which could have been conferred on Rohard except that of king, which was clearly not the case. Jonathan Riley-Smith has suggested that Miles arranged for Rohard to be nominal regent while reserving all real power to himself,[12] but it is difficult to believe that the High Court would have agreed to this in view of its evident reluctance to accept the far stronger claim of Raymond of Tripoli to the regency a few months later. It seems possible that Rohard, a man who had stood high in the esteem of King Amalric,[13] was appointed personal guardian of the young king. During the minority of Baldwin V in 1185 the positions of regent and guardian were kept distinct and there would thus have been nothing contrary to the custom of the kingdom in such an arrangement had it been made in 1174.[14] In such a case Rohard would indeed have had what William of Tyre calls "a title which sounded good but conferred

---

6 Richard, *The Latin Kingdom of Jerusalem* (Amsterdam, 1979), vol. A, p. 152, n. 28, suggests that Miles was descended from the Monthlérys, the family of Baldwin II's mother. Cf. A. Roserot, *Dictionnaire historique de la Champagne méridionale (Aube) des origines à 1790*, publié par J. Roserot de Melin, 4 vols. (Langres, 1945), 2:1129-1136.
7 Delaville, *Cartulaire*, No. 409.
8 WT21,4, p. 964. Miles is first mentioned as lord of Montréal on 18 April 1174: Delaville, *Cartulaire*, No. 463.
9 Jean d'Ibelin, *Livre* 271, RHC Lois 1:422.
10 WT21,4, p. 964.
11 WT21,4, pp. 964-965.
12 J.S.C. Riley-Smith, *The Feudal Nobility and the Kingdom of Jerusalem, 1174-1277* (London, 1973), p. 101.
13 E.g., he formed a member of the king's suite when Amalric visited Constantinople in 1171, WT20,22, p. 940.
14 *Cont. WT*, p. 21.

no power," while Miles, who had power but no special title, would have given the appearance of being guided by Rohard, who controlled access to the king's presence.

The chief complaint made against Miles was that he excluded other barons from the work of government and tried to rule autocratically.[15] This was the kind of temperamental luxury which the kingdom could not afford in its executive head and its consequences were soon apparent. Amalric and his advisers had planned to mount a land attack on Egypt in the summer of 1174 which was timed to coincide with a Sicilian naval attack and with a revolt inside Egypt by pro-Fāṭimid elements against the Sunnite government of Saladin.[16] When Amalric died there was not time for the court of Jerusalem to contact Palermo and seek a postponement, so on 28 July, less than a fortnight after Baldwin IV's coronation, the Sicilian fleet anchored off Alexandria. Within a day of their arrival the Sicilians had established a land-base and driven the Egyptian garrison back inside the walls while to compound Saladin's troubles a pro-Fāṭimid revolt broke out in Upper Egypt.

His spies had informed him of Amalric's plans and he was expecting the Frankish army to invade and therefore stationed his own main army to the east of the Nile delta, but the threat from Jerusalem did not materialize, and so when the garrison of Alexandria sent him an urgent appeal for help, he was able to march his main army to their relief. At his approach the Sicilians abandoned the siege, the revolt in Upper Egypt was rapidly put down and by September peace had been restored throughout Saladin's dominions.[17] Bahā al-Dīn, the Sultan's biographer, called this victory "one of the greatest mercies ever showed by God to the Muslims," and since he did not enter the Sultan's service until many years later, he was probably representing Saladin's own view about the events of 1174.[18]

The Franks had undoubtedly lost an excellent opportunity for attempting to unseat Saladin from power in Egypt. Moreover, such favorable circumstances would prove hard to replicate since the Sicilian attack came only a few months after the death of Nūr al-Dīn which had produced political instability throughout much of western Islam. Miles of Plancy cannot be held directly responsible for the Frankish lack of initiative on this occasion, since his office conferred no military powers, but there seems little doubt that the episode reflected adversely on his government. In the absence of a king or regent military powers were vested solely in the constable.[19] In Baldwin IV's minority this was Humphrey II of Toron, who had held the office for more than twenty years[20]

15   WT21,4, p. 965.
16   Ibn al-Athīr in *RHC HOr.*, 1:599-602.
17   M.C. Lyons and D.E.P. Jackson, *Saladin. The Politics of the Holy War* (Cambridge, 1982), pp. 76-81.
18   Bahā' al-Dīn, *The Life of Saladin*, c. 12, trans. C.W. Wilson in PPTS 13 (London, 1897), p. 67.
19   Jean d'Ibelin, *Livre*, 257, RHC Lois 1:411.
20   Baldwin III appointed him in 1152, WT17,14, p. 779.

and whose bravery and loyalty to the crown were undoubted, for he was later to be killed in an ambush while defending the Leper King.[21] But the feudal host of Jerusalem would not have undertaken an attack on Egypt without the support of the Military Orders over whom Humphrey had no authority. Jobert, the Master of the Hospital, may have been reluctant to commit his Order to a course of action which had overstrained its resources six years before, led to the abdication of the former Master, Gilbert d'Assailly, and left a legacy of debt which Jobert was still striving to clear.[22] The Master of the Temple, Odo of St. Amand, was noted for his independence of mind and his cooperation with the constable could not be taken for granted.

Had Miles been discharging his role as executive head of state satisfactorily he would have summoned a *curia generalis*, attended among others by the constable and the two Masters, to ratify the plans for the Egyptian campaign now that the king was dead. Miles lacked the gifts of persuasion which were needed to secure the adhesion of the commanders to a common plan. In particular he almost certainly found it very difficult to work harmoniously with the Master of the Temple, who is said by William of Tyre to have been a man of imperious temper with little taste for conciliating opponents,[23] faults of character which were very similar to Miles' own. It seems likely in view of what subsequently occurred that Humphrey of Toron deliberately refrained from using his own influence with the Masters of the Military Orders to make the campaign take place, fearing lest should he do so and the attack on Egypt prove successful, Miles' government would gain the credit and the seneschal would be established firmly in power, whereas a failure to attack could be used as a lever to challenge his authority. Certainly a similar policy was followed with great success by the baronage in 1183 in order to break the power of the unpopular regent, Guy of Lusignan.[24]

It is a fact that Miles' power was challenged very soon after the Egyptian fiasco by Count Raymond III of Tripoli, who appeared before the High Court and laid formal claim to the regency with the support of the constable, and of Reynald lord of Sidon, Baldwin of Ibelin, lord of Ramla, and his brother, Balian.[25] When it is remembered that Walter of St. Omer, the Prince of Galilee, had recently died,[26] this meant that all the greatest feudatories in the kingdom had publicly declared their lack of confidence in the seneschal's conduct of affairs of state. Raymond based his claim chiefly on the closeness of his relationship to the young king, for he had been King Amalric's first cousin, but he was not the only member of the royal family with a right to be considered, although William of Tyre tries to make it appear that that was the case. In

---

21   WT21,26 (27), p. 999.
22   J.S.C. Riley-Smith, *The Knights of St. John in Jerusalem and Cyprus, c. 1050-1310* (London, 1967), pp. 60-63, 71-73.
23   WT21,28 (29), p. 1002.
24   WT22,28 (27), p. 1054.
25   WT21,3, pp. 963-964.
26   He died before King Amalric: Delaville, *Cartulaire*, No. 459.

III

140

addition to the descendants of King Fulk who were living in the West, whom I have already mentioned, Prince Bohemund III of Antioch had arguably a better claim to the regency than Count Raymond.[27] It was therefore quite reasonable for Miles to reply that as only a few members of the High Court were present consideration of the count's claim should be deferred until a plenary session could be convoked.[28] Nevertheless, this delay appeared sinister to some of Miles's critics. It was known that he had sent Balian of Jaffa, the brother of Rohard the castellan, to the West with letters and gifts from the king.[29] Almost certainly this mission was intended merely to inform Western rulers about King Amalric's death and Baldwin IV's succession. It is known that messengers from Jerusalem reached Flanders in the autumn or winter of 1174-75, because Count Philip, another of the Leper King's Western cousins, took the cross at Easter 1175.[30] Yet so great was the antipathy in Jerusalem to Miles' autocratic methods of government that rumors began to circulate there that Miles had sent this embassy to the West in order to seek the help of his friends and kinsmen in France to enable him to seize the throne. Such gossip was unfounded, for Miles had no claim to the throne, but it indicates the degree of hostility with which he was viewed.

William of Tyre relates how "certain men" were suborned to make an attempt on Miles' life and how, though warned about this, the seneschal refused to take any precautions. Yet the danger was real enough and one evening in October 1174 he was murdered while walking through the streets of Acre.[31] William does not name the killers and could not have done so even if he had known who they were, for they were never brought to justice, and if he had named them he would have been bringing a charge of murder for which he could have offered no satisfactory legal proof. However, the *Brevis historia*, the Genoese source which was written in about 1200 when all the principals were dead, does name Miles' murderers as the lords of Beirut.[32] This statement merits serious consideration for the following reasons.

In 1174 Beirut formed part of the crown lands and was therefore under Miles of Plancy's control during the king's minority.[33] The lords of Beirut to whom the Genoese writer refers must have been members of the Brisebarre family, who held the fief in the early years of King Amalric's reign. The strange circumstances in which they lost Beirut are recounted in the late-thirteenth-

27 Baldwin IV, Bohemund III, and Raymond III were all descended from Baldwin II in the female line. Baldwin IV was the grandson of Baldwin II's eldest daughter, Queen Melisende; Bohemund III was the grandson of Baldwin II's second daughter, Alice of Antioch; Raymond III was the son of Baldwin II's third daughter, Hodierna of Tripoli. [Cf. the diverging considerations of H.E. Mayer, "The Beginnings of King Amalric of Jerusalem," above. Ed.]
28 WT21,3, p. 964.
29 WT21,4, p. 965.
30 *Sigeberti continuatio Aquicinctina*, MGH SS 6:415.
31 WT21,4, p. 965.
32 *Brevis historia*, p. 135.
33 Jean d'Ibelin, *Livre* 256, RHC Lois 1:408.

century *Lignages d'Outremer*. This relates how Walter Brisebarre and two of his brothers were captured by the Saracens and how their mother, being unable to raise the full price of their ransom, offered herself as a hostage in their place until the outstanding sum had been paid. The crown forbade anyone to lend the brothers money and so they were forced to accept the royal terms: they must exchange the fief of Beirut for the crown-fief of Blanchegarde and the sovereign would then pay the outstanding ransom so that their mother might be set free. They had no alternative but to accept, but their mother only lived for a month after regaining her freedom. The *Lignages* date this episode to the reign of Queen Isabella I (1192-1205) but that is impossible.[34] At the beginning of her reign Beirut was in Muslim hands and when it was recovered from the Ayyūbids in 1197 the queen gave it to her half-brother, John of Ibelin, who held it until his death in 1236 and was, for that reason, known as "the Old Lord of Beirut."[35] As Mary Nickerson pointed out, contemporary documents show conclusively that the exchange of Beirut for Blanchegarde took place in King Amalric's reign, before 1168.[36] The compilers of the *Lignages* appear to have confused two incidents: the exchange of Beirut for Blanchegarde by the Brisebarres in the reign of King Amalric and the granting of Beirut to the Ibelins in the reign of King Aimery, Isabella I's consort. In mitigation it should be said that they are not unique in confusing the names of these two kings.

Walter III Brisebarre had succeeded his father as lord of Beirut in 1157.[37] He had two younger brothers called Guy and Bernard,[38] and the exchange of the fief cannot have occurred until after 1164 for their mother, the Lady Mary Brisebarre, was still alive then,[39] but it had happened before 1167 when King Amalric granted Beirut to Andronicus Comnenus.[40] Even after the ransom money has been taken into account, the exchange was not advantageous to the Brisebarres, for Beirut was one of the great fiefs of the kingdom, owing service of twenty-one knights to the crown, whereas Blanchegarde was a comparatively minor fief owing only nine knights.[41] Yet at first the Brisebarres did not suffer any loss in wealth or prestige.

Walter III Brisebarre had married Helena, the elder daughter of Philip of Milly, lord of Montréal, or Oultrejourdain.[42] This was an even greater fief than Beirut, owing service of forty knights to the crown: indeed, in Amalric's reign

34   *Les Lignages d'Outremer* 20, RHC Lois 2:458.
35   Philippe de Novare, *Mémoires*, c.27, ed. C. Kohler (Paris, 1913), p. 16; J.L. Lamonte, "John d'Ibelin, the Old Lord of Beirut, 1177-1236," *Byzantion* 12 (1937), 424-425.
36   M.E. Nickerson, "The Seigneury of Beirut in the Twelfth Century and the Brisebarre Family of Beirut-Blanchegarde," *Byzantion* 19 (1949), 166-167.
37   Delaville, *Cartulaire*, No. 258.
38   The *Lignages*, c. 20, record a fourth brother, Hugh, mentioned in no other source: RHC Lois 2:458.
39   A. de Marsy, "Fragment d'un cartulaire de l'Ordre de Saint-Lazare en Terre Sainte," *AOL* 2 (1884), No. 23, p. 141.
40   WT20,2, p. 914.
41   Jean d'Ibelin, *Livre* 271, RHC Lois 1:425-426.
42   de Marsy, "Fragment," No. 24, p. 142.

there were no other fiefs in the kingdom which were more important except for those of Sidon and Galilee.[43] At the end of 1165 Philip of Milly, who was a widower, entered the Order of the Temple, of which he later became Master.[44] His only son, Rainier, is not mentioned in any source after 1161[45] and had presumably died without heirs; Philip's only surviving children were his two daughters, Helena, who had married Walter Brisebarre, and Stephanie, the wife of Humphrey III of Toron, the son of the constable of the kingdom.[46] The law of Jerusalem at this time enacted that in the case of female heirs the eldest daughter should have the same rights as an eldest son and should inherit the entire fief.[47] This practice was only changed in 1171 when, with reference to the lands of Henry the Buffalo, Count Stephen of Sancerre persuaded the High Court to alter the law, so that in future when cases of female inheritance arose, all daughters should divide a fief equally between them, the eldest should receive the homage of her sisters and should herself do homage for the whole fief to the king.[48] In 1166, however, the old law was still in force and the fief of Montréal therefore passed in its entirety to Helena of Milly and her husband Walter Brisebarre. This may explain why Amalric forced Walter and his brothers to accept the exchange of Blanchegarde, for this would prevent one man from holding two great fiefs simultaneously.

Walter's position became less secure when his wife died. This happened some time before 18 November 1168 when, as lord of Montréal, he made a gift of forty bezants a year to the Order of St. Lazarus for the repose of her soul. This money is stated to be part of "the exchange of Beirut," presumably part of the money received in compensation in addition to the ransom money. Walter made this gift with the consent of his brother Guy and of his own daughter, Beatrice.[49] There is no evidence that Walter and Helena had any other children. Although he remained the lord of Montréal, Walter was now, by the law of the kingdom, really the *bailli* for his daughter until such time as she married, but if she were to die while a minor the fief would then pass to her mother's closest kin.

Beatrice is mentioned in no later source and, because of the way in which the fief was subsequently transmitted, it must be assumed that she died while still a

---

43   Jean d'Ibelin, *Livre* 271, RHC Lois 1:422.
44   In January 1166 King Amalric confirmed to the Templars the fief of Ahamant which Philip of Milly had given their Order when he was professed: J. Delaville Le Roulx, ed., "Chartes de Terre Sainte," *ROL* 11 (1905-1908), No. 2, pp. 183-185.
45   E. Strehlke, *Tabulae Ordinis Teutonici* (Berlin, 1869), No. 3, p. 4.
46   In 1155 Amalric count of Ascalon confirmed a gift made to the Order of St. Lazarus by Philip of Milly "et Rainerio filio suo, Helena etiam et Stephania filiabus suis": de Marsy, "Fragment," No. 14, pp. 133-134. For Stephanie's marriage see WT21,4, p. 964.
47   Philippe de Novare, *Livre* 71, RHC Lois 1:542.
48   Philippe de Novare (*Livre* 71-72, RHC Lois 1:542-543) records the judgment but does not name Stephen of Sancerre. He is credited with this reform in *Documents relatifs à la successibilité*, 6, RHC Lois 2:408. See H.E. Mayer, "Die Seigneurie der Joscelin," in J. Fleckenstein and M. Hellmann, eds., *Die geistlichen Ritterorden Europas*, Vorträge und Forschungen 26 (Sigmaringen, 1980), p. 183, note 29.
49   de Marsy, "Fragment," No. 24, p. 142.

III

child. Beatrice had certainly died before 24 February 1174 when King Amalric confirmed a gift by Walter Brisebarre to St. Lazarus of income granted to him from the port dues of Acre. In this charter Walter is styled simply "Walter of Beirut, lord of Blanchegarde."[50] The fief of Montréal must by then have passed to Philip of Milly's younger daughter, Stephanie. Her husband, Humphrey III of Toron, died at some unknown time between August 1168 and April 1174[51] leaving two children, a son, also called Humphrey, and a daughter, Isabella.[52] Humphrey III never used the title of Lord of Montréal so far as is known, and this suggests that Stephanie did not inherit the fief during his lifetime. Presumably at King Amalric's bidding she married Miles of Plancy sometime between 24 February and 18 April 1174.[53]

Bernard Brisebarre is not mentioned in any source after 1165[54] and had presumably died by 1174, but both Walter and Guy were alive then and were much reduced in power and wealth since they now had to share the revenues of the minor fief of Blanchegarde. Miles of Plancy could obviously not be held responsible for the decline in the Brisebarre fortunes, but the brothers had some cause to feel resentment towards him after he became effective ruler on the accession of Baldwin IV. Miles was the chief beneficiary through his marriage from the death of Walter Brisebarre's only daughter, the heiress of Montréal. He could have used his powers to help the Brisebarres to recover their lost fortunes, for example by restoring the fief of Beirut to them, for it had reverted to the crown when Andronicus Comnenus had abducted the dowager queen Theodora and sought political asylum at the court of Nūr al-Dīn in 1168.[55] Alternatively Miles could have used his power to arrange a marriage for Walter Brisebarre, who was still a widower, to a suitable heiress, and such a marriage was possible because Eschiva, princess of Galilee, the greatest heiress in the kingdom, had herself been widowed shortly before the king's death.[56] The Brisebarre brothers had some reason to feel aggrieved about Miles of Plancy's conduct towards them

50 Ibid., No. 27, pp. 145-146.
51 He is last mentioned in a charter of 9 August 1168: H.F. Delaborde, ed., *Chartes de la Terre Sainte provenant de l'abbaye de Notre-Dame de Josaphat*, Bibliothèque des Écoles françaises d'Athènes et de Rome 19 (Paris, 1880), No. 36, p. 84. Stephanie had married again by April 1174.
52 WT21,4, p. 964.
53 de Marsy, "Fragment," No. 27, pp. 145-146 of 24 February 1174 is witnessed by Miles of Plancy who does not use the title; Delaville, *Cartulaire*, No. 463 of 18 April 1174 is witnessed by Miles as lord of Montréal.
54 Ch. Kohler, "Chartes de l'abbaye de Notre-Dame de la vallée de Josaphat en Terre Sainte (1108-1291). Analyses et extraits," *ROL* 7 (1899), No. 36, p. 145. Mary Nickerson's identification of him with Bernard of Blanchegarde who owned a house in Jerusalem in 1186 (Delaville, *Cartulaire*, No. 803), is based on insufficient evidence; see Nickerson (note 36 above), p. 169.
55 WT20,2, p. 914. B. Hamilton, "Women in the Crusader States: the Queens of Jerusalem," in D. Baker, ed., *Medieval Women* (Oxford, 1978), pp. 161-162.
56 Her gift to the Hospital of St. John for the repose of her husband's soul was made in 1174 while King Amalric was still alive: Delaville *Cartulaire*, No. 459. This implies that Walter of St. Omer had recently died, since otherwise the king would have arranged a new marriage for the heiress of so important a fief as soon as possible.

and they may have murdered him, as the *Brevis historia* states they did, perhaps having been incited to do so by Miles's more powerful enemies, as William of Tyre implies. If this were so, it would explain William of Tyre's comment that some people held that Miles was murdered "because of the loyalty which he faithfully showed towards the lord king."[57]

Those who praised Miles for his loyalty to the Leper King were certainly right to do so. He had been a faithful steward and had not succumbed to the besetting temptation of guardians for infant kings, that of dissipating the royal demesne, even though to do so would have seemed an easy way of allaying the hostility of his opponents as well as a sure way of building up a clique of loyal supporters. Yet loyalty to the king was not enough in a state like Jerusalem where the survival of the kingdom depended on the ability of a small number of powerful men to work together harmoniously. Miles of Plancy was an autocrat by temperament and was therefore unsuited to have charge of the government in a state built on a tradition of devolved power.

His death left the kingdom without a leader and the fief of Oultrejourdain without a lord, and this occurred at a critical time in Jerusalem's history when Saladin was marching his Egyptian army through the lands beyond Jordan in a bid to seize power in Damascus. The safety of the Crusader Kingdom depended on the existence of a divided Islam whose leaders could be played off against each other, and that situation had been produced by the death of Nūr al-Dīn in May 1174, leaving only a minor heir, which led to the dismemberment of his empire between rival kinsmen and generals, of whom Saladin was one. The Franks could severely have hampered Saladin in his attempts to reunite the dominions of Nūr al-Dīn because they virtually controlled the lines of communication between Egypt and Syria through their military presence in the Sinai and Transjordan. However, they failed to take effective action in 1174 because of their internal disputes and on 28 October Saladin reached Damascus in safety with his army and assumed control there.[58]

It was the knowledge that this had happened which led the High Court to accept Raymond of Tripoli's claim to the regency for Baldwin IV after Miles of Plancy's death. They did so with some misgivings[59] which were perhaps occasioned by the fact that 60,000 bezants of the count's ransom still remained unpaid and that the regents for Nūr al-Dīn's son were holding Frankish hostages in the citadel of Ḥimṣ as surety for this sum.[60] It is never a desirable situation to have a head of state who is open to pressure by a foreign power. If the Brisebarre brothers did murder Miles of Plancy, then Raymond owed his appointment in

---

57 "...dicentibus aliis quia pro sua fidelitate, quam domino regi devotus exhibebat, hoc ei acciderat:" WT21,4, p. 965.

58 Lyons and Jackson, *Saladin* (note 17 above), pp. 81-83, cite a letter from Saladin to his nephew Farrūkh-Shāh relating how during the journey from Cairo to Damascus "we camped [in the land of the Franks] like those who have authority."

59 William of Tyre reports that Raymond was only accepted as regent after a debate which lasted for two whole days: WT21,5, p. 966.

60 WT21,8, p. 972.

part to them, yet he did nothing to improve their fortunes after he became regent. This would have been in character, for even William of Tyre who approved of Raymond admitted that "he was generous to strangers but not to his own men."[61]

No attempt was made to bring Miles' murderers to justice. If Walter and Guy Brisebarre had been suspected of the crime they could have been charged with murder in the High Court and the case would then have been determined in trial by battle between them and their accusers, or their respective champions. Yet as John of Ibelin explained in his treatise on the laws, a plea of murder was very difficult to sustain because if the correct technical procedures were not followed the case would go by default and severe penalties could then be exacted from the plaintiffs.[62]

When Baldwin IV came of age and began his personal rule the Brisebarres still did not receive the fief of Beirut back: that remained part of the royal demesne.[63] Despite this, Walter and Guy enjoyed an honorable position at court, and continued to be called "of Beirut" even though they no longer held the fief, presumably because nobody else had a right to the title. In 1178 Walter "de Beryto" witnessed a royal diploma in favor of the Hospital and took precedence over all those present except for the seneschal, Joscelin of Courtenay, Reynald of Sidon, the king's stepfather, and Baldwin and Balian of Ibelin.[64] In the following year Walter and his brother Guy witnessed another royal diploma in favor of Joscelin of Courtenay, and on that occasion were ranked immediately after Reynald of Châtillon, Reynald of Sidon, and Balian of Ibelin.[65] This is the last time in which Walter is mentioned in any source, while Guy is last recorded in 1182,[66] so presumably neither of them lived until the end of the reign.

According to the *Lignages* Walter Brisebarre married a second time and had a son and four daughters. There is no reason to doubt this, for when the *Lignages* were drawn up there were families in Cyprus who traced their descent from him. His second wife was well born, but not herself a great heiress, for she was Agnes, the niece of Eschiva the princess of Galilee.[67] Raymond of Tripoli almost certainly can be credited with arranging that marriage, for as soon as he became regent, being himself a bachelor, he married the widowed Eschiva and gained control of her fief of Galilee.[68]

It was perhaps as well that the Brisebarre brothers did not live to see Raymond of Tripoli become regent for the child king Baldwin V in 1185, for he was then assigned the fief of Beirut from the royal demesne to defray the

---

61 WT21,5, p. 967.
62 Jean d'Ibelin, *Livre* 82-90, RHC Lois 1:130-147.
63 In 1182 it still had no lord and the bishop and the castellan took charge of its defense when it was besieged by Saladin: WT22,19 (18), p. 1035.
64 Delaville, *Cartulaire*, No. 550.
65 Strehlke, *Tabulae* (note 45 above), No. 11, pp. 11-12.
66 Delaville, *Cartulaire*, No. 621.
67 *Les Lignages d'Outremer* 20,21, RHC Lois 2:458-459.
68 WT21,5, p. 967.

expenses of government.[69] If, as I have argued, the Brisebarres did indeed murder Miles of Plancy, they would have had equal cause to feel resentment towards the count of Tripoli who owed his advancement in part to their action but who had done nothing to restore their fortunes when it had been within his power to do so, and had acquired the greatest heiress in the kingdom and later their former fief of Beirut for himself.

69   *Cont. WT*, p. 21.

IV

The Titular Nobility of the Latin East: the Case of Agnes of Courtenay

THE FRONTIERS of the northern states in Frankish Syria were subject to considerable fluctuation throughout the twelfth century. Any appreciable loss of territory to the Muslims produced a class of titular Frankish noblemen for whom some provision had to be made by the Christian rulers. Yet whereas a few men of this kind could easily be assimilated, the problem became acute after the fall of Edessa.

When eastern Edessa was overrun by Zangī in 1144 the Frankish survivors accompanied Count Joscelin II to Tell Bāshir in western Edessa, which he made his new capital, but when Joscelin was taken prisoner by Nūr al-Dīn in 1150 and then blinded, his wife, Beatrice, sold the remaining lands of Edessa to the Byzantine emperor, Manuel I, in return for a life-pension for herself and her children. King Baldwin III of Jerusalem ratified the treaty and placed the imperial representatives in corporal possession of those territories and the Frankish population withdrew to Antioch.[1] In this way a large number of Frankish noblemen lost their lands and they had no hope of regaining them since they had been granted to Byzantium.

There were no prospects for these men in the principality of Antioch. Nūr al-Dīn had in recent years made considerable conquests there and consequently the principality had a landless nobility of its own to provide for. The situation in the kingdom of Jerusalem was more promising: in 1153 Baldwin III conquered Ascalon and its hinterland and subsequently created the double county of Jaffa-Ascalon which was held as an appanage by his brother, Amalric. The prospect of land which the siege and conquest of Ascalon afforded proved attractive to some of the Edessan nobility, who entered Count Amalric's service.[2] Such men were not seen as a serious threat by the baronage of Jerusalem: they had been granted no important fiefs and they had no powerful patron at court who would seek to further their interests.

For there is no evidence that the Countess Beatrice and her children had come to live in the south at this time.[3] Before she married Joscelin II Beatrice had been the wife of William, lord of Saone, one of the most important fiefs in the principality of Antioch,[4] and in accordance with Antiochene law she would have enjoyed dower-rights there.[5] It may be assumed that in 1150 she retired to her dower-lands where, with the supplement of her Byzantine pension, she and her children could live in some comfort. Two of her children had accompanied her into exile, her son, Joscelin, and her daughter, Agnes. Though still young in 1150, Agnes was already a widow. Her husband, Reynald lord of Marash, had been killed at the battle of Inab in 1149.[6]

Agnes was unpopular with her contemporaries and has been widely criticized by modern historians. Attention has focussed chiefly on her defects of character, particularly on her sexual indiscretions, but Professor Richard has suggested that the antipathy which Agnes provoked in her lifetime might really have been a consequence of her Edessan connections.[7] I believe that this is correct, and it is that theme which I want to explore in this paper.

Agnes was a Courtenay and therefore a member of one of the greatest families in the Frankish East. Her grandfather, Joscelin I of Edessa, had been first cousin to King Baldwin II, and Agnes was thus closely related to the royal house of Jerusalem and to the ruling families of Tripoli and Antioch. In addition she was related to the Capetian royal house, since the heiress of the European branch of the Courtenays had recently married Peter, brother of King Louis VII of France.[8] But good birth was her only advantage. Her dower-lands at Marash were conquered by Mas'ūd of Iconium shortly after her husband's death,[9] her father's lands had all been lost, and she had no claim to her mother's dower-lands at Saone. Apart from her share of the Byzantine pension she was penniless and perhaps that is why she remained unmarried for eight years after the death of her first husband.

In 1157 she came to Jaffa and married Count Amalric.[10] She and her husband were fourth cousins and the marriage was therefore within the prohibited degrees which in the twelfth century extended to the sixth degree of consanguinity. William of Tyre relates that the patriarch Fulcher objected to the marriage on those grounds but was ignored,[11] but a different account is preserved in the late thirteenth-century *Lignages d'Outremer*. This states that Agnes was already betrothed to Hugh of Ibelin and that the patriarch objected to her marriage with Amalric for that reason.[12] No general doubt, however, was expressed at the time about the validity of the marriage, and Agnes bore two children to Amalric, a daughter, Sibyl, and a son, Baldwin, to whom King Baldwin III stood godfather.[13]

Agnes did not herself constitute any threat to the established order in the kingdom. Edessan noblemen were already in her husband's service and although Agnes might have been able to use her personal influence to promote their interests, that influence was limited to the county of Jaffa and Ascalon. However, soon after her marriage, and probably as a consequence of it, her brother Joscelin came to Jerusalem. Like Agnes he had no source of revenue except for his Byzantine pension, but he was a kinsman of the king and had therefore some claim on his generosity, and Baldwin III assigned him an income from the harbour-dues of Acre and also gave him land near the city.[14] Some scholars have suggested that he was made marshal of the kingdom, although I can find no evidence for this.[15] His growing power, it would seem, alarmed the baronage. He was unmarried, the king might confer the hand of a great heiress upon him[16] and he might use his power in the interests of the Edessan exiles at the expense of the barons of the kingdom. Certainly the Edessans would have looked to him for leadership, particularly after 1159 when his father died in prison at Aleppo and he became titular count of Edessa. It was perhaps out of deference to this feeling that Baldwin III removed Joscelin from the kingdom. Early in 1162 the king was called to Antioch where Prince Reynald had been taken prisoner by Nūr al-Dīn, while his heir, Bohemond III, was still a minor.[17] As part of his reorganisation of the defences of the principality the king appointed Joscelin of Courtenay *bailli* of the important frontier-fief of Harim.[18] Thus while giving the titular count of Edessa lands commensurate with his dignity, the king appeased the opposition of the Jerusalem baronage to the growing power of the Courtenays.

A year later Baldwin III died childless. Although there was some baronial opposition to the succession of his brother Amalric, the High Court finally agreed to this provided he put away his wife. The new partriarch, Amalric of Nesle, argued that the marriage between Amalric and Agnes was invalid because they were related within the prohibited degrees. Amalric agreed to this condition, the matter was referred to Pope Alexander III, and the marriage was subsequently annulled by the cardinal of SS. Giovanni e Paolo who, nevertheless, declared that the children of the marriage were legitimate.[19]

Although consanguinity formed the canonical grounds for the annulment, it clearly was not the sole reason for baronial opposition to the marriage. It is sometimes said that the High Court disapproved of Agnes's moral character and the account of the discussions given in the chronicle known as Ernoul is thought to confirm this view. The chronicler reports that the High Court objected that Agnes was not 'the kind of woman who should be queen of so high a city as Jerusalem'.²⁰ It seems doubtful, however, whether the passage in Ernoul will bear this construction. The stories which were afterwards circulated about Agnes's lapses from virtue relate to a much later period in her life²¹ and if her reputation had been notoriously defamed at this stage it is difficult to explain how she was able to make an advantageous marriage after the annulment. Moreover, a version of Ernoul's account of the debate, inserted in the twenty-third book of the Old French continuation of William of Tyre, reports that the High Court's censure was directed at Amalric, not at Agnes: 'he was not worthy to have the crown of the kingdom of Jerusalem'.²² The implication is that by reason of his uncanonical marriage the king was in a state of mortal sin, and if Ernoul's account is preferred it can only be understood to mean that Agnes was being reproached for the same offence. Professor Richard's suggestion that the real reason for baronial opposition to Agnes was that she was a Courtenay seems far more plausible.²³ Her brother Joscelin had recently been sent into honourable exile at Antioch, and the Jerusalem baronage did not want a queen who would be in an even more powerful position to act as patron to the nobility of Edessa than her brother had been.

At the king's request Agnes was freed by special papal dispensation from any moral censure attaching to her by reason of her invalid marriage.²⁴ She retained the title of countess, which she had held as Amalric's wife, and used it for the rest of her life,²⁵ but her children were, of course, removed from her custody. A year later, in 1164, her brother Joscelin was captured by Nūr al-Dīn and imprisoned at Aleppo.²⁶ The threat of Courtenay dominance in the kingdom of Jerusalem seemed to have been effectively ended.

Members of the Edessan nobility who had entered Amalric's service while he was count of Jaffa continued to serve him after he became king and some of them took an active part in his Egyptian campaigns. Joscelin of Samosata was placed in charge of the Frankish infantry during the 1167 campaign, while Arnulf of Turbessel (Tell Bāshir) acted as one of the chief negotiators between the king and Shirkūh.²⁷ Had the king's Egyptian policy succeeded these men would doubtless have been rewarded with lands there, but after it had failed, although Amalric numbered some of them among his close advisers,²⁸ they were not promoted to any high position in the state. Amalric, it would seem, had heeded the strength of baronial opposition to the Edessan exiles which had been expressed at the time of his accession.

Agnes of Courtenay remained in the kingdom but did not have any political power as long as Amalric was alive. Soon after her annulment she married Hugh of Ibelin, lord of Ramla.²⁹ Hugh died in c. 1169, apparently while on a pilgrimage to Compostella.³⁰ The marriage was childless, and Ramla passed to Hugh's brother, Baldwin, but in accordance with the laws of the kingdom Agnes enjoyed the usufruct of half the revenues of Ramla for life.³¹ If the Emperor Manuel was still paying her the pension which he had covenanted twenty years before, and there is no reason to suppose that he was not doing so since he was on excellent terms with the Franks of Jerusalem at this time,³² Agnes would have been a quite rich woman.

Before 1171 she married Reynald, son of Gerard lord of Sidon, one of the four great baronies of the kingdom. A mystery surrounds this marriage. William of Tyre relates that it was annulled by a church court on grounds of consanguinity on the basis of evidence supplied by Gerard of Sidon. This must have happened before Gerard's death, which occurred at the latest in 1171,³³ yet when he is writing of events in the winter of 1175-6 William refers to 'the countess Agnes, wife of Reynald of Sidon'.³⁴ I have argued elsewhere that this was not a slip of the pen, for there is conclusive evidence that Agnes was married to Reynald from that time until the end of her life.³⁵ From this one must infer that the couple had appealed to Rome to obtain a dispensation from the annulment of the local court and that their appeal had been successful, perhaps because the evidence supplied by Gerard had not been conclusive.³⁶

Gerard's reasons for seeking to have this marriage annulled may only be conjectured. Since it cannot have been contracted without his knowledge the impediment of consanguinity can only have been a pretext: he was the only person claiming knowledge of this and it obviously had not bothered him at first. I would like to suggest a possible explanation. Reynald of Sidon was a younger son. The *Lignages* relate that 'Gerard... lord of Sidon had two sons...Eustace and Reynald. Eustace was not at all intelligent, but very good-looking, and he did not marry; Reynald was extremely ugly but very wise and they made him lord'.[37] Eustace was still alive after Reynald became lord,[38] so at some point the High Court must have ruled that Reynald, though younger, was the heir to the lordship, perhaps because Eustace, as the *Lignages* hints, was feeble-minded. If Reynald married Agnes before this ruling was made, she would have seemed a suitable wife for a younger son because she had a large income. She would, however, have seemed less desirable as the wife of the heir of Sidon because she was in her middle thirties and, perhaps, considered beyond the age of child-bearing. Certainly her marriage to Hugh of Ibelin had been childless. Annulments were commonly sought for that reason at this time.

Agnes's position changed when King Amalric died in 1174. He had re-married, but his second wife, Maria Comnena, had borne him only a daughter and the heir to the throne was Agnes's son, Baldwin IV. Baldwin was only thirteen years old and was suffering from leprosy: he therefore could never marry, and his mother could occupy a position of great influence at his court. Yet Agnes had no *locus standi* in her son's household: she was not the dowager queen and she had had no personal contact with her son since he was three years old. It was arguably mutual interest which drew Agnes and Reynald together again and led them to seek to have the annulment of their marriage reversed. Reynald was one of the premier barons of the kingdom and was in a position to secure for Agnes her natural place at court as the king's mother, while, as Agnes's husband, he would share the power which such a position would give her.

Immediately after Amalric's death authority was exercised by the seneschal, Miles of Plancy, but when he was assassinated, as the result, it would seem, of a private vendetta,[39] a group of noblemen led by Agnes's former husband, Reynald of Sidon, and her brothers-in-law, Baldwin and Balian of Ibelin, successfully pressed the claims of Count Raymond of Tripoli to the regency.[40] Because of the antipathy which later existed between Raymond of Tripoli and Agnes it has not been sufficiently appreciated that she returned to court during the time of his first regency. Presumably this was one of the conditions made by Reynald of Sidon and the Ibelins when they gave their support to Raymond, since they hoped to increase their own power with Agnes's help. As has already been seen, at about the same time the pope quashed the annulment of Agnes's marriage to Reynald. Agnes's influence is first discernible in the appointment of Archdeacon Heraclius to the archbishopric of Caesarea in the autumn of 1175,[41] for it was commonly believed that he had once been her lover and he was certainly her protégé.[42] More significantly, a few months later she was able to raise the considerable sum of 50,000 bezants to ransom her brother Joscelin from prison in Aleppo[43] and, when he reached Jerusalem, to secure his appointment as seneschal of the kingdom.[44]

The seneschal was the king's *alter ego*, and when Baldwin IV came of age in 1176 and Raymond of Tripoli's regency ended, Joscelin of Courtenay became the most powerful man in the kingdom. He married Agnes of Milly, daughter and co-heir of Henry the Buffalo,[45] and subsequently acquired other lands by royal gift which made him one of the greatest lords in the kingdom.[46] Agnes of Courtenay herself was granted the lordship of Toron at some time between 1180 and 1185,[47] perhaps in compensation for the loss of her Byzantine pension which must have ceased when the anti-Latin emperor, Andronicus I, came to power in 1182.

By the end of Baldwin IV's reign older members of the High Court may have reflected that it had been a wise instinct which had led them to prevent Agnes of Courtenay from becoming queen-consort twenty years before. It is true that as the king's mother she did not show particular favour to Edessan exiles: death had lessened their numbers by Baldwin IV's reign, and many of the survivors had already been assimilated.[48] Nevertheless, Agnes did favour people in a similar position. It was a titular nobleman, Reynald of Châtillon, former prince of Antioch, who received from the king the hand of the greatest heiress in the kingdom, Stephanie of Milly, lady of Montréal and Hebron, during the time of Agnes's ascendency. Such use of patronage cannot have endeared Agnes to the native nobility.

During the leper king's reign Courtenay influence was paramount, and this was Agnes's creation. At the beginning of the reign she had no position save that of dowager lady of Ramla: by the time of her death in 1186[49] she was first lady in the kingdom, wife of the lord of Sidon, dowager lady of Ramla and lady of Toron in her own right, while her brother was seneschal and held a great lordship which had been specially made for him. William of Tyre was, perhaps, voicing the feelings of the Jerusalem baronage as well as his own when he denounced Agnes as 'the king's mother, a woman hateful to God and relentless in her acquisitiveness'.[50] The titular count of Edessa and his sister had, it seemed to their enemies, become effective rulers of Jerusalem.

Such a view was partial, since it disregarded the personal power of Baldwin the Leper which was, I believe, considerable. Moreover, it does not necessarily follow that the ways in which Agnes and Joscelin used their power were inimical to the true interests of the kingdom, since the sources which imply that this was so reflect the concerns of the Jerusalem baronage who had tried, and failed, to exclude the Courtenays from any share in the government. But the hostility which Agnes aroused among her contemporaries cannot be accounted for solely in terms of moral defects in her character: she was hated because she was powerful and because she used that power to advance the interests of her family which had lost its own lands a generation before.

NOTES

1 William of Tyre, 'Historia rerum in partibus transmarinis gestarum', *RHC Oc*, i, 784-6. Manuel perhaps hoped in this way to contain the threat posed to imperial control of Cilicia by the Roupenid prince Thoros II.

2 By July 1155 Joscelin of Samosata and his brother Baldwin were in Amalric's service; *RRH*, no. 308.

3 Michael the Syrian, *Chronique de Michel le Syrien, Patriarche jacobite d'Antioche (1166-1199)*, ed, with French trans. J.-B. Chabot (Paris, 1899-1924), iii, 297, states that Baldwin III placed the wife and children of Joscelin II in safety in Jerusalem, but this may imply no more than that they left Tell Bāshir under royal escort. 'Les Lignages d'Outremer', *RHC Lois*, ii, 442, state that Agnes entered the kingdom of Jerusalem in 1157, implying that she had previously lived in one of the northern states.

4 William of Tyre, p. 610. C. Cahen, 'Note sur les seigneurs de Saone et de Zerdana', *Syria*, xii (1931), 154-9; P. Deschamps, 'Le château de Saone et ses premiers seigneurs', *Syria*, xvi (1935), 73-88.

5 *Les Assises d'Antioche*, ed. with French trans. L.M. Alishan (Venice, 1876), 18-20.

6 Beatrice's first husband was killed in 1131/2; Deschamps, 'Le château de Saone', p. 78, n.; C. Cahen, *La Syrie du nord à l'époque des Croisades et la principauté franque d'Antioche* (Paris, 1940), 351, n. 12. She cannot have married Joscelin II before 1132. They had three children, Joscelin III, Agnes and Isabel who married Thoros II of Cilicia; W.H. Rüdt-Collenberg, *The Roupenides, Hethumides and Lusignans: the Structure of the Armeno-Cilician Dynasties* (Paris, 1963), 50. Agnes was probably, but not certainly, the canonical age of twelve when she married Reynald of Marash, who was killed in 1149; William of Tyre, p. 773. Her birth may therefore be placed in the years 1133-7. The date of the countess Beatrice's death is not known. I would tentatively suggest 1157 when both Agnes and Joscelin III came to live in the Kingdom of Jerusalem.

7 J. Richard, *Le royaume latin de Jérusalem* (Paris, 1953), 77.

8 Miles of Courtenay, eldest brother of Joscelin I of Edessa, had remained in Europe. In 1150 his granddaughter Elizabeth, heiress to the lordship of Courtenay, married Louis VII's brother, Peter, who took his wife's title.

9 R. Grousset, *Histoire des Croisades et du royaume franc de Jérusalem* (Paris, 1934-6), ii, 288-9.

10 Robert of Torigni, 'Chronica', ed. R. Howlett, *Chronicles of the Reigns of Stephen, Henry II and Richard I* (RS 82; London, 1889), iv, 194.

11 William of Tyre, p. 889. William was absent from the kingdom at the time of Amalric's marriage to Agnes and of its annulment, R.B.C. Huygens, 'Guillaume de Tyr étudiant. Un chapître (XIX, 12), de son 'Histoire' retrouvé', *Latomus*, xxi (1962), 811-29.

12 'Lignages', p. 442.

13 William of Tyre, pp. 871, 888.

14 *La Chronique d'Ernoul et de Bernard le Trésorier*, ed. L. de Mas Latrie (Paris, 1871), 15. R.L. Nicholson, *Joscelyn III and the Fall of the Crusader States, 1134-1199* (Leiden, 1973), 28, affirms that 'Baldwin III made Joscelin III his direct vassal possibly as early as the late Summer of 1150', but the evidence he adduces is not convincing.

15 Nicholson, *Joscelyn*, p. 28, n. 2; J.L. La Monte, *Feudal Monarchy in the Latin Kingdom of Jerusalem, 1100-1291* (Cambridge, Mass., 1932), 121, 254, both cite as their authority C.du Fresne Du Cange, *Les Familles d'Outremer*, ed. E.G. Rey (Paris, 1869), 625, who gives as his sole source the unreliable sixteenth-century antiquary, Estienne de Lusignan.

16 E.g. Philip of Milly, lord of Oultrejourdain from 1161, only had daughters to succeed him.

17 William of Tyre, pp. 868-9, 872-6.

18 Harim, recaptured in 1158 by Baldwin III and Thierry of Flanders, was handed over to Prince Reynald of Antioch; William of Tyre, p. 853. Reynald would have restored it to its former lord, Tancred Fraisnel; Cahen, *La Syrie*, p. 398, n. 6. Tancred, who is not mentioned after 1160, left a daughter, Orgueilleuse, who was a minor, and needed a *bailli* to administer the fief. V. Langlois, *Chronique de Michel le Grand...traduit...sur la version arménienne du prêtre Ischok* (Venice, 1868), 318, states that Joscelin III had been placed in charge of Harim two years before his capture by Nūr al-Dīn in 1164, that is, while the king was at Antioch in 1162. Robert of Torigni's statement (pp. 199-200) that Thierry of Flanders's vassal, Reynald of St Valéry, was placed in charge of Harim in 1158 would seem to be mistaken. Reynald remained in the Holy Land until 1160, but then left Jerusalem and did not style himself lord of Harim. *RRH*, nos. 338, 339, 360. In his notes to the French translation of *Anonymi Auctoris Chronicon ad Annum Christi 1234 pertinens*, trans. A. Abouna, intro., notes and index J.M. Fiey, *Corpus Scriptorum Christianorum Orientalium, Scriptores Syri*, ser III. 154 (Louvain, 1974), 121, Fiey identifies the castellan of Harim in 1164 with Reynald of St Valéry, but there are insufficient grounds for this. Dr Sebastian Brock, who has kindly checked the Syriac text for me, says that the name of the castellan is given as 'RNGD, which has wrongly been translated as Arugad (= 'RWGD) in the French version. Dr. Brock suggests that 'RNGD 'probably does represent a form like Arnald, Reynald, since the G is almost certainly a corruption of an L'. It would therefore appear that Joscelin III had appointed a castellan named Reynald at Harim in 1164.

19 William of Tyre, p. 883, notes the baronial opposition and later gives an account of the annulment, pp. 888-9. The Old French Continuation relates that Amalric appealed to Rome for a dispensation to legitimize the children of the

marriage; M.R. Morgan, ed., *La Continuation de Guillaume de Tyr (1184-1197)* (Paris, 1982), 19-20. William of Tyre (p. 889) confirms that this dispensation was granted by the legate, the cardinal of SS. Giovanni e Paolo, who may still have been present in the kingdom, to which he had first come in 1161 (*ibid.*, pp. 870-1), and have been charged by the Pope to deal with the case.

[20]   *Ernoul*, p. 17.

[21]   Agnes was said to have been the mistress of Aimery of Lusignan and of the patriarch Heraclius, *Ernoul*, pp. 59, 82, neither of whom had come to the East in 1163.

[22]   'Le patriarche li respondi...que il n'estoit mie tels ne si dignes que il deust avoir la corone dou reaume de Jerusalem. Car tant come il sereit el pechié mortel ou il s'estoit mis, ne corone de Jerusalem ne autre honor ne devoit il mie avoir.' Morgan, *Continuation*, p. 19.

[23]   Richard, *Le royaume latin*, p. 77.

[24]   Morgan, *Continuation*, p. 20.

[25]   *RRH*, nos. 410a, 433, 472, 654.

[26]   William of Tyre's testimony, (p. 897) is to be preferred to that of *Anonymi...Chronicon...1234*, p. 119, which places Joscelin III's capture in 1161, shortly before that of Reynald of Châtillon.

[27]   William of Tyre, pp. 927-8, 936.

[28]   E.g. Joscelin of Samosata witnessed one of the king's last acts, *RRH*, no. 514.

[29]   William of Tyre, p. 890; 'Lignages', p. 422; *Ernoul*, p. 17.

[30]   In his last recorded act he stated his intention of making the pilgrimage to St James. *RRH*, no. 472. H.E. Mayer, 'Carving up Crusaders. The Early Ibelins and Ramlas', in *Outremer*, ed. B.Z. Kedar, H.E. Mayer, R.C. Smail (Jerusalem, 1982), 117.

[31]   J.A. Brundage, 'Marriage Law in the Latin Kingdom of Jerusalem', in *Outremer*, p. 265.

[32]   R-J. Lilie, *Byzanz und die Kreuzfahrstaaten* (Munich, 1981), 179-202.

[33]   William of Tyre, p. 890. The marriage occurred before Feb. 1171, when Gerard was dead and Reynald had succeeded to the lordship. *RRH*, no. 487.

[34]   William of Tyre, p. 1023.

[35]   B. Hamilton, 'Women in the Crusader States: the Queens of Jerusalem', in D. Baker, ed., *Medieval Women* (Oxford, 1978), 163-4. Reynald of Sidon did not marry again until after Agnes's death, 'Lignages', p. 456.

[36]   Canon law required detailed evidence of common ancestry in cases of annulment, but Gerard of Sidon merely affirmed on oath that the couple were blood kin. William of Tyre, p. 890.

[37]   'Lignages', p. 456.

[38]   In 1175. William of Tyre, p. 1018.

[39]   *Ibid.*, p.1009. The Brisebarre family are named as the assassins in 'Brevis Regni Hierosolymitani Historia', *MGHS*, xxxviii, 51.

[40]   William of Tyre, p. 1008.

[41]   *Ibid.*, p. 1021. The appointment was after Aug. 1175 when Heraclius was still archdeacon of Jerusalem. *RRH*, no. 528. B.Z. Kedar, 'The Patriarch Eraclius', in *Outremer*, p. 186.

[42]   *Ernoul*, p. 82.

[43]   Michael the Syrian, *Chronique*, iii, 365-6; William of Tyre, p. 1023.

[44]   *RRH*, no. 537, dated 1176, the ninth indiction (i.e. before 1 Sept.).

[45]   Nicholson, *Joscelyn*, pp. 74-5, convincingly argues that the marriage took place soon after Joscelin III's return to Jerusalem.

[46]   H.E. Mayer, 'Die Seigneurie de Joscelin und der Deutsche Orden', in J. Fleckenstein, M. Hellmann, *Die geistlichen Ritterorden Europas*, (Vorträge und Forschungen 26, 1980), 171-216. The lordship of Joscelin ranked immediately after the four great baronies and owed twenty-four knights to the crown. John of Ibelin, 'Livre', *RHC Lois*, i, 422.

[47]   When Humphrey IV of Toron was betrothed to the king's sister, Isabel, in 1180 he surrendered Toron, Chastelneuf and Banias to the crown; William of Tyre, p. 1069. Agnes had acquired Toron by Sept. 1184; Ibn Jubayr, *The Travels of Ibn Jubayr*, trans. R.J.C. Broadhurst (London, 1952), 316.

[48]   The only example of the promotion of an Edessan during Baldwin IV's reign known to me is that of Joscelin of Samosata, appointed castellan of Ascalon. *RRH*, nos. 589, 613, 627.

[49]   The exact date is unknown, but her death occurred before 21 Oct. 1186 when Guy of Lusignan acknowledged that Count Joscelin had satisfactorily discharged the provisions of Agnes's will. *RRH*, no. 654.

[50]   William of Tyre, p. 1078.

V

Manuel I Commenus and Baldwin IV of Jerusalem

Although much has been written about Manuel I Comnenus' relations with the Crusader States before the death of King Amalric of Jerusalem in 1174, comparatively little attention has been given to this aspect of imperial policy during the remaining six years of Manuel's reign[1]. Even Ralph-Johannes Lilie in his excellent study of the whole field of Franco-Byzantine relations in the twelfth century does not consider that Byzantine influence was very important in the Latin East at that time[2]. This is certainly the impression which is given by Byzantine writers, but a rather different picture emerges from the Frankish sources, suggesting that Byzantium remained an important force in the political life of the Crusader Kingdom until 1182 when an anti-Latin government came to power in Constantinople.

There is general agreement among scholars that by abandoning the policy of confrontation with the Franks favoured by John II and by adopting what Lilie has termed 'die Politik der Umarmung' towards them Manuel increased his power in the Latin East. In 1158 his niece Theodora married

1. More recent work includes: S. RUNCIMAN, *A History of the Crusades*, 3 vols (Cambridge, 1951-4), II, pp. 345-426; J.M. HUSSEY, 'Byzantium and the Crusades, 1081-1204', in K.M. SETTON, gen. ed., *A History of the Crusades*, II, ed. R.L. WOLFF and H.W. HAZARD, *The Later Crusades, 1189-1311,* (Philadelphia, 1962), pp. 134-44; S. RUNCIMAN, 'The visit of King Amalric I to Constantinople in 1171', in B.Z. KEDAR, H-E. MAYER, R.C. SMAIL, ed., *Outremer* (Jerusalem, 1982), pp. 153-8; M. ANGOLD, *The Byzantine Empire, 1025-1204* (London, 1984), pp. 184-94. Among older studies J.L. LAMONTE, 'To what extent was the Byzantine Empire the suzerain of the Crusading States?', *B*, 7 (1932), 253-64 remains important.

2. R-J. LILIE, *Byzanz und die Kreuzfahrerstaaten* (Munich, 1981), pp. 200-11, 328-9.

Baldwin III of Jerusalem and in 1167 the emperor's great-niece Maria married Baldwin's brother and successor, Amalric; from 1159 the princes of Antioch acknowledged the emperor as their overlord, while in 1171 Manuel had the satisfaction of receiving a personal visit from Amalric of Jerusalem who besought his help and probably did homage to him for his kingdom. Manuel's political success was paralleled in the ecclesiastical sphere: in 1165 he restored to Antioch the Orthodox Patriarch, Athanasius III, who remained there until 1170 when he was killed by an earthquake, while in the southern kingdom Manuel was able to act as protector of the Holy Places, a role traditionally held by his predecessors before the First Crusade. He exercized his patronage by commissioning mosaics for the shrine of the Holy Sepulchre and for the basilica of the Holy Nativity at Bethlehem, where his icon was placed in the sanctuary even though the church was administered by the Latins[3].

The death of King Amalric of Jerusalem on 11 July 1174 at the age of thirty-eight made the future of the Byzantine protectorate of the Latin Kingdom uncertain. His only son, Baldwin, was thirteen years old and was known to be suffering from leprosy[4]. Nevertheless, the High Court of Jerusalem reached a decision which had no parallel in the medieval Christian world and elected a leper as king. They did so, it would seem, precisely because Baldwin IV was a minor, in the hope that by the time he came of age a suitable husband would have been found for the heir-apparent, his elder sister, Sibyl, and that he would then abdicate in favour of his sister and brother-in-law[5].

During the first months of the new reign no regent was appointed, and the work of government was carried out by the seneschal, Miles of Plancy, who was constitutionally empowered to deputize for the king[6]. This expedient broke down in October 1174 when Miles was assassinated and the High Court then appointed as regent Raymond III Count of Tripoli, King Amalric's first cousin[7]. The political situation in the Latin East at that time was

3. B. HAMILTON, *The Latin Church in the Crusader States. The Secular Church* (London, 1980), pp. 164-7, 174-8, 183-4.

4. *Willelmi Tyrensis Archiepiscopi Chronicon*, XXI, 1-2, ed. R.B.C. HUYGENS (Identification des sources historiques et détermination des dates par H.-E. MAYER, G. RÖSCH), 2 vols, *Corpus Christianorum. Continuatio Mediaevalis*, 63, 63A (Turnhout, 1986) (henceforth WT), II, pp. 961-2.

5. This theme will be examined more fully in my forthcoming book on the reign of King Baldwin IV.

6. WT, XXI, 3, II, pp. 963-4. My reasons for supposing that Miles was not regent will appear in 'Miles of Plancy and the fief of Beirut', in the Acts of the Second Conference of the Society for the Study of the Crusades and the Latin East held in Jerusalem in 1987.

7. WT, XXI, 4-5, II, pp. 964-6.

V

Manuel I Comnenus and Baldwin IV

critical: Nur ed-Din of Damascus, who had united the lands of western Islam, from northern Iraq to Egypt, under his rule, had died shortly before King Amalric, leaving a minor as heir[8]. This led to faction between Nur ed-Din's kinsmen and generals, one of whom, Saladin, the commander in Egypt, gained control of Damascus in October 1174[9]. Common prudence suggested that the Franks in Syria should seek to restrict the growth of his power in order to prevent the empire of Nur ed-Din from being reconstituted, for encirclement by a unified Muslim state was clearly a threat to their survival. Yet in order to attack Egypt, the seat of Saladin's power, the Franks needed a navy, since they had none of their own. For such a purpose the alliance with Byzantium which Amalric had negotiated in 1171 would have proved very useful, but Raymond of Tripoli did not invoke it.

The regent sought instead to place the Kingdom of Jerusalem under the protection of the Western Emperor, Frederick I Barbarossa. This policy was not without attractions: since 1158 the emperor had been seeking to make himself master of Italy, and by 1175 he seemed to be on the verge of success, for his chief enemy, the Lombard League, had opened peace negotiations with him[10]. Saladin watched Frederick's progress with interest after he became ruler of Egypt in 1169, for if the emperor won the war he would have great influence in Lombardy, whose maritime republics handled Egypt's trade with the West, and might also become overlord of Sicily, Egypt's nearest Western Christian neighbour. Embassies therefore passed between Cairo and Frederick's court[11].

Raymond of Tripoli clearly supposed that if Frederick became master of Italy and agreed to act as protector of the Crusader States, Saladin would not dare to attack them. Accordingly he began negotiations with William V, Marquis of Montferrat, who was at that time one of the emperor's most faithful supporters and was assisting him in his campaigns in Lombardy[12], and it was agreed that his eldest son, William Longsword, should come to Jerusalem and marry Sibyl, the leper-king's sister and heir[13]. This match could certainly not be considered in any way disparaging to the royal house of Jerusalem, since the groom was one of the most eli-

---

8. N. ELISSÉEF, *Nūr ad-Din, un grand prince musulman de Syrie au temps des Croisades (511-569 H/ 1118-1174)*, 3 vols (Damascus, 1967).
9. M.C. LYONS and D.E.P. JACKSON, *Saladin. The Politics of the Holy War* (Cambridge, 1982), pp. 80-4.
10. P. MUNZ, *Frederick Barbarossa* (London, 1969), pp. 302-6.
11. *Annales Colonienses Maximi*, ed. G.H. PERTZ, *MGH, SS.* XVII (1861), p. 786.
12. *Chronica regia Colonienses*, ed. G. WAITZ, *SGUS* (Hanover, 1880), p. 126.
13. WT, XXI, 12, II, pp. 977-8.

V

gible bachelors in Christendom, being first cousin both to the Emperor Frederick and to King Louis VII of France[14].

Nevertheless, Raymond of Tripoli's policy had certain disadvantages: notably it was incompatible with the maintenance by Baldwin IV's government of an alliance with Byzantium, for Barbarossa was at war not only with the Lombard League, but also with Pope Alexander III, William II of Sicily and the Emperor Manuel, all of whom had reason to fear an Hohenstaufen victory in Italy[15]. Raymond's abrupt change of policy, which led him to look for protection to the Western rather than to the Eastern Empire, was almost certainly dictated as much by personal rancour as by political expediency. The reasons for this hostility are to be found in the events of 1160 when Manuel Comnenus, who had recently become a widower, sought the hand in marriage of Raymond of Tripoli's only sister, Melisende. She believed that a formal betrothal had taken place and in July 1161 witnessed a diploma of King Baldwin III as 'future empress of Constantinople'[16], but Manuel subsequently received an unfavourable report about her from his ambassadors, repudiated Melisende and later that year married instead her cousin Maria, the sister of Bohemond III of Antioch. Melisende's marriage prospects had been irreparably damaged and it would appear that she died soon afterwards[17]. Raymond III was outraged, not merely by the affront which had been offered to his sister, but also by Manuel's contempt for the honour of the counts of Tripoli, for he claimed descent from the Capetian royal family and considered himself the equal of any king[18]. He therefore equipped a fleet which ravaged the coasts of the Byzantine Empire with great savagery[19]. When he became regent thirteen years later Raymond had no wish to perpetuate an alliance between Jerusalem and Byzantium, particularly one which entailed the recognition by the Frankish government of Manuel's overlordship. Thus when in 1175, the

14. William Longsword's father, William V of Montferrat, was half-brother of Louis VII's mother, Adelaide of Savoy; William Longsword's mother, Giulita, was half-sister of Barbarossa's father, Frederick Duke of Swabia.

15. The best account of Manuel's involvement in the Italian wars is P. LAMMA, *Comneni e Staufer: ricerche sui rapporti fra Bizanzio e l'Occidente nel secolo XII*, 2 vols. (Rome, 1955-7).

16. E. STREHLKE, ed., *Tabulae Ordinis Theutonici*, no. 3 (Berlin, 1869), p. 3.

17. WT, XVIII, 30-1, II, pp. 854-7. Melisende is mentioned in no later source and presumably died young soon after this disgrace. She did not marry: *Les Lignages d'Outremer*, vii, ed. Comte BEUGNOT, *RHC, Lois*, II, p. 448.

18. Raymond's grandmother, Cecilia, wife of Count Pons of Tripoli, was the daughter of Philip I of France and Bertrada of Montfort, who was also the mother (by her marriage to Fulk IV of Anjou) of King Fulk of Jerusalem. Cecilia was thus the half-sister of both Louis VII of France and of King Fulk. WT, XXI, 5, II, p. 966.

19. *Ibid.*, XVIII, 33, II, pp. 858-9.

Manuel I Comnenus and Baldwin IV

first year of Raymond's regency, Manuel, who was planning an attack on the Seljuks of Iconium, appealed to the Catholic powers for help, he received no assurance.of support from his former allies and vassals in the Crusader Kingdom[20].
In the event the regent's policies did not work out at all well. Barbarossa failed to become the master of Italy: on the contrary, when negotiations with the Lombard League broke down and he tried to use force against its member-cities, the emperor was decisively defeated by them at Legnano in May 1176 and had no alternative but to agree to seek a comprehensive peace with all his opponents in Italy[21]. It thus did not appear that he would be in any position to afford protection to the Franks of Outremer and they had begun to need it; for Saladin had greatly strengthened his power in North Syria during Raymond of Tripoli's regency, at the expense of Nur ed-Din's kinsmen, the Zengid princes, over whose confederate army he had won a convincing victory at Tell al-Sultan on 22 April 1176[22]. Although on that occasion Saladin failed to capture Aleppo, there was a high probability that he would soon do so, in which case the Franks would be once more surrounded by a single hostile power.
It would appear that this was the reason why the High Court of Jerusalem did not extend Raymond's tenure of office as regent when in the early summer of 1176 the leper-king came of age at fifteen[23]. Baldwin IV's assumption of power was no doubt intended to be a temporary measure until William of Montferrat came to Jerusalem in the autumn, married Sibyl and was able to take over the work of government, but the end of the regency made it possible to implement a new foreign policy. The fifteen-year old king, inexperienced as he was in public business, cannot be given credit for initiating this: it must have been the work of his chief advisers. Prominent among them were two men who were newcomers to the court of Jerusalem, although neither of them was new to the Latin East: Joscelin of Courtenay and Reynald of Châtillon.
Both men had spent years as prisoners-of-war at Aleppo, Reynald since 1161 and Joscelin since 1164, and they owed their release to Saladin's victory at Tell al-Sultan. For the *atabeg* of Aleppo sought an alliance with

20. DÖLGER, *Regesten* II, 1520. Alexander III responded favourably, JAFFÉ, II, no. 12684. Cf. ANGOLD, *Byzantine Empire*, p. 189.
21. MUNZ, *Frederick Barbarossa*, pp. 310-14.
22. LYONS and JACKSON, *Saladin*, pp. 85-105.
23. The age of majority in the kingdom was fifteen, John of Ibelin, *Livre*, c. 169, ed. Comte BEUGNOT, *RHC, Lois*, I, p. 260. Baldwin IV's birthday is not known but was in the early summer. William of Tyre describes him as 'vix annorum tredecim' in July 1174: WT, XXI, 2, II, p. 962.

357

Bohemond III of Antioch against the sultan, but Bohemond would only agree to this on condition that these two men were set free[24]. Joscelin's ransom was fixed at 50,000 dinars, and that of Reynald at 120,000[25], an index of how important their captors considered them to be. That importance derived entirely from family relationships, since both prisoners were landless men.

Joscelin III was titular Count of Edessa, but he had never ruled any of his patrimony lands. Eastern Edessa had been conquered by the Muslims in 1144 and in 1150, after Joscelin's father had been taken prisoner by Nur ed-Din, his mother, Countess Beatrice, had sold the remaining fortresses of Western Edessa to the Emperor Manuel in return for a life-pension for herself and her children[26]. Joscelin's sister Agnes had married Amalric of Jerusalem in 1157 during Baldwin III's reign, while he was still Count of Jaffa, and had borne him two children, Baldwin and Sibyl. The marriage was annulled in 1163, although the children were declared legitimate by Pope Alexander III, and Agnes had then married Hugh of Ibelin and, after his death in c.1169, Reynald, lord of Sidon. Although she was the mother of the leper-king, she could not act as regent during his minority because she was not the dowager queen. That position was held by Amalric's second wife, the Byzantine princess Maria Comnena, but she was assigned no political role in the new reign and retired with her infant daughter Isabel to her dower-fief of Nablus[27]. Agnes of Courtenay was therefore able to occupy the position of first lady at the court of her son, which allowed her to exercize considerable unofficial powers of patronage[28].

Joscelin of Courtenay was the leper-king's uncle, his closest male relative, and although he had no claim to the throne, this gave Joscelin potentially a great deal of power during the reign of a chronically sick king. Agnes used her influence at court to raise her brother's huge ransom[29] and secured his appointment as seneschal, the king's deputy in all non-military matters, an office left vacant for almost two years since the death of Miles of Plancy[30].

24. ABU SHAMAH, The Book of the Two Gardens (Le Livre des Deux Jardins), RHC, Or., IV (1898), p. 183.
25. MICHAEL THE SYRIAN, Chronicle, XX, 3, ed. with French trans., J.B. CHABOT, 4 vols (Paris, 1899-1924), III, pp. 365-6.
26. WT, XVII, 16, II, pp. 781-2.
27. Ibid., XXI, 17, II, p. 986.
28. B. HAMILTON, 'The Titular Nobility of the Latin East: the Case of Agnes of Courtenay', in R.W. EDBURY, ed., Crusade and Settlement (Cardiff, 1985), pp. 197-201.
29. WT, XXI, 10, II, p. 976.
30. Joscelin was appointed seneschal before 1 September 1176, that is immediately after his release. R. RÖHRICHT, ed., Regesta Regni Hierosolymitani (1097-1291), 2 vols, (Innsbruck, 1893-1904), I, p. 143, no. 537, dated by the ninth indiction which ended on 31 August 1176.

Manuel I Comnenus and Baldwin IV

Reynald of Châtillon who came to Jerusalem with Joscelin was a much more controversial figure. In 1153 he had married Constance, Princess of Antioch, widow of Raymond of Poitiers, and had ruled the principality for eight years. He caused scandal in the Latin East by torturing the patriarch of the city, Aimery of Limoges, when the latter refused to place part of the treasures of the church at his disposal; and soon afterwards he sacked the Byzantine province of Cyprus in the course of a quarrel with the Emperor Manuel who, he claimed, had failed to recompense him for campaigning against Cilician rebels. When Manuel came to Syria in 1159, ·a campaign prompted in part by Reynald's activities, the prince was forced to do an humiliating public penance and to recognize the emperor as his overlord. In 1161 Reynald was captured by one of Nur ed-Din's lieutenants while raiding deep into Muslim territory and was imprisoned at Aleppo. While he was there his situation changed, for his wife died and his step-son, Bohemond III, became prince of Antioch. Thus when Reynald was freed in 1176 he no longer had a principality[31].

Nevertheless, in a strange way his status had improved while he was in prison, for in 1161 his step-daughter, Maria of Antioch, had married Manuel Comnenus[32], while in 1174, through Maria's influence, his own daughter Agnes had married King Bela III of Hungary[33]. Reynald left prison a landless man, but the father-in-law of the King of Hungary and the step-father of the Byzantine Empress, and it was doubtless for that reason that his captors demanded such an astronomical ransom. There was no place for Prince Reynald at Antioch, but he was welcomed at the court of Jerusalem. Like Count Joscelin, Reynald had no claim to the throne and yet was a royal kinsman, for his wife, Constance of Antioch, had been King Amalric's first cousin. Reynald had experience in the work of government and was known to be a good field commander and a man of undoubted courage. His services would be needed in a kingdom where the ruler was young and sick and where the designated heir to the throne was an Italian prince, unfamiliar with methods either of government or of warfare in the Latin East.

Unlike Raymond of Tripoli the new royal advisers favoured a pro-Byzantine policy. Agnes and Joscelin of Courtenay derived part of their income from the life-pension paid by the Emperor Manuel for the reversion

---

31. B. HAMILTON, 'The Elephant of Christ: Reynald of Châtillon', in D. BAKER, ed., *Studies in Church History*, 15 (1978), pp. 97-9.

32. WT, XVIII, 31, II, p. 857; JOHN CINNAMUS, *Historia*, V, 4, ed. A. MEINEKE (*CSHB*, Bonn, 1836) pp. 210-11.

33. CHONIATES (D), I. p. 170; ALBERIC OF TROIS-FONTAINES, *Chronica*, ed. P. SCHEFFER-BOICHORST, *MGH, SS*, XXIII, p. 850.

of Edessa and had every reason to wish to stay on good terms with the Byzantine court. Prince Reynald, despite his clashes with Manuel twenty years before, no longer had any reason to be hostile to the Byzantines: indeed, self-interest required that he should establish good relations with the empire where his step-daughter occupied a position of authority.

Baldwin IV and his advisers wished to renew the treaty which his father had made with Manuel I. Negotiations cannot have taken place until after Raymond of Tripoli's regency had ended in the early summer of 1176 and must have been completed by the following spring[34]. The Frankish plenipotentiary must have been a man whose status was commensurate with so important a mission and the only member of the court of Jerusalem who is known to have been in Constantinople at the relevant time is Reynald of Châtillon. This is known from the covering letter which Hugh Eteriano, Manuel's western adviser on religious affairs, sent to Aimery of Limoges, Latin Patriarch of Antioch, with a copy of his treatise on the dual procession of the Holy Spirit. In this he says that he is sending the manuscript by the hand of Prince Reynald, which shows that the prince was in Constantinople when the letter was written[35]. Now if Reynald's career after he became prince of Antioch in 1153 until his death in 1187 is examined, it will be found that the only point at which he could have visited the imperial capital was during the autumn and winter of 1176-7, for throughout the rest of that time he is known to have been either in the Latin East or in Muslim custody[36]. Reynald would have had a personal reason for going to Constantinople in 1176: the need to raise his ransom. He had no lands of his own which could be sold, the principality of Antioch was too impoverished to raise so large a sum[37], while it is unlikely that the crown of Jerusalem could have paid Reynald's ransom as well as that of Joscelin of Courtenay within a single year. Manuel, on the other hand, had the resources to make a payment of that size and for reasons of international prestige, about which he was very sensitive, he was unlikely to refuse to ransom his wife's step-father. Moreover, by the time Reynald reached the imperial court Manuel would have been in the prince's debt, for on 17 September 1176 Reynald's only son, Baldwin of Antioch, had been killed by the Turks at Myriocepha-

---

34. A copy of the treaty was brought to Jerusalem in September 1177 and it must have been drawn up before the fleet was assembled, presumably during the previous winter: WT, XXI, 15, II, p. 982.

35. E. MARTÈNE, and U. DURAND, eds., *Thesaurus Novus Anecdotorum*, 5 vols (Paris, 1717), I, p. 479.

36. Space does not suffice to prove this here, but the sources corroborate this view.

37. Bohemond III had to ask Manuel for the money to pay his own ransom in 1165: WT, XIX, 11, II, p. 878.

Manuel I Comnenus and Baldwin IV

lum, leading the right wing of the imperial army[38]. Manuel did not habitually bear resentment for long against his enemies[39], and Reynald's long imprisonment coupled with his bereavement would have served to overcome any residual animosity which the emperor might have felt towards him. Reynald's ransom was certainly paid before the summer of 1177: he could not subsequently have behaved with the intransigence towards Islam which he showed had hostages remained in Muslim hands on his account, nor, despite their deep hostility towards him, do any Muslim writers reproach him with failing to pay his ransom. It seems highly probable that Manuel paid this debt, and it seems certain that during his stay in Constantinople Reynald negotiated a new treaty of alliance with Manuel on behalf of Baldwin IV's government.

The defeat of Myriocephalum had been a blow to Manuel's prestige rather than to his military power, for, as Michael Angold has convincingly argued, the imperial army was left virtually intact at the end of the battle, and Kilij Arslan, the Seljuk sultan, did not make any territorial gains[40]. Nevertheless, the defeat weighed heavily on Manuel who likened it to that of Manzikert a century earlier and this opinion has, perhaps, weighed unduly heavily with modern historians[41]. In fact Byzantium remained very powerful, and had a strong navy which Manuel had rebuilt[42] as well as a considerable army, and it was the only state which was in a position to give adequate help to the Franks of Outremer in their attempt to check the growing power of Saladin. Manuel no doubt welcomed the opportunity which the Jerusalem embassy afforded him of launching an expedition against Egypt which he hoped would, if successful, offset the fiasco of Myriocephalum. It is known from William of Tyre that at this time Manuel issued a chrysobull setting out the terms of the treaty between himself and Baldwin IV of Jerusalem[43], and, while it cannot be conclusively proved that Prince Reynald conducted the negotiations, the surviving evidence strongly suggests that he did so.

When Reynald returned to Jerusalem in the spring of 1177 Baldwin IV consented to his marrying the greatest heiress in the kingdom, Stephanie of Milly, which gave him control over the great fiefs of Oultrejourdain and

38. CHONIATES (D), I, p. 181; Cf. RHC, Grecs, II, p. 406.

39. E.g. his treatment of his cousin Andronicus, C. DIEHL, 'Les romanesques aventures d'Andronic Comnène', Figures byzantines (5 edn, Paris, 1918), pp. 86-106.

40. ANGOLD, Byzantine Empire, pp. 192-4.

41. CHONIATES (D), I, p. 191.

42. H. AHRWEILER, Byzance et la Mer (Paris, 1966), pp. 233-79.

43. 'propositus fuit ei [comiti Flandrensium] pactorum inter nos et dominum imperatorem in scriptis fideliter tenor, eius aurea bulla munitus'. WT, XXI, 15, II, p. 982.

Hebron[44]. While Reynald had been in Constantinople William of Montferrat had reached Jerusalem and married Sibyl, but had declined to become king when Baldwin IV offered to abdicate, probably because some members of the High Court were strongly opposed to his doing so[45]. He soon fell ill, and in June 1177 he died, leaving his wife pregnant. The king also became gravely ill at about the same time[46]. He was suffering from lepromatous leprosy, the most severe and debilitating form of the disease, and one of its characteristics is that the patient is liable to contract secondary infections and to run very high fevers[47]. This is what happened to Baldwin IV in the summer of 1177 and it became necessary for him to appoint a regent. He appointed Prince Reynald[48] and this proved to be a wise choice, for the prince was his cousin and an experienced field commander well able to defend the kingdom. The choice was almost certainly influenced by the fact that Reynald had just negotiated an alliance with the Emperor Manuel and would therefore be willing to co-operate in an attack on Egypt with the commanders of the Byzantine forces which were due to reach the kingdom later that summer. Nevertheless, his appointment must have appeared disparaging to Raymond of Tripoli who had been regent throughout the king's minority and whose exclusion indicated that his anti-Byzantine policies were no longer acceptable to the other members of the High Court.

In August 1177, at a time when the king was still extremely ill, Count Philip of Flanders came on crusade to the Holy Land with a substantial force of armed men. He was King Amalric's nephew[49] and his arrival caused great pleasure since it was thought that his troops would strengthen the Christian forces in their projected invasion of Egypt. Prince Reynald was prepared to stand aside and allow Philip to be offered the regency together with command of the Frankish army during the Egyptian campaign, but the count refused this honour saying that he did not intend to

---

44. RÖHRICHT, *Regesta*, II, p. 33, no. 553a, calendars a diploma of November 1177 (no longer extant) in which Baldwin IV confirms a grant made to Count Rodrigo by Reynald Lord of Montréal and Hebron with the consent of his wife Stephanie and of William of Montferrat, Count of Ascalon and Jaffa. Since William died in June 1177, the grant, and consequently Reynald's marriage, must have taken place before then.

45. WT, XXI, 12, II, pp. 977-8. Baldwin's offer of the crown in Sicard of Cremona, *Cronica*, ed. O. HOLDER-EGGER, *MGH SS*, XXXI, p. 173.

46. WT, XXI, 12, II, p. 978.

47. S.N. BRODY, *The Disease of the Soul* (Ithaca, 1974), pp. 21-33, discusses the description of leprosy in medieval writers.

48. WT, XXI, 13, II, pp. 979-80.

49. Philip of Flanders' mother, Sibyl, was the daughter of King Fulk of Jerusalem by his first marriage, and therefore half-sister to Amalric, the son of Fulk's second marriage to Queen Melisende.

stay in the east for very long[50]. He then became involved in a quarrel with the High Court about the marriages of the king's sisters, Sibyl and Isabel, which the count wished to arrange, and that argument was still in progress when the Byzantine fleet reached Acre[51].

This was a large armament, consisting of seventy war-galleys as well as a number of transport ships. The force was commanded by the emperor's cousin, Andronicus Angelus, who was accompanied by three other imperial envoys, John the Megatriarch, George of Sinai, and Alexander, Count of Cosenza, a South Italian nobleman in Manuel's service. Our chief source for the progress of negotiations between the imperial ambassadors and the Frankish court is the account given by William of Tyre, who must have been very well informed about them because he was chancellor of the kingdom. This, however, led him to be extremely reticent when writing about the incident, so that the real reasons for the breakdown of the Franco-Byzantine alliance remain obscure[52].

William is very guarded in his description of the terms of the treaty, saying only that the agreement made between Amalric and Manuel had been renewed by Baldwin IV 'non dissimilis conditionibus'[53]. What those conditions were may only be inferred, since the text of the treaty has not been preserved. H-E. Mayer has pointed out that under the terms of the treaty which William himself negotiated with Manuel in 1168 for a joint attack on Egypt some share of the spoils and of the territories conquered was reserved to the emperor[54], and it seems certain that Manuel would not have reduced his demands in 1177 but might well have included a general claim to the overlordship of Egypt in case of success. Such claims might well have been unacceptable to Philip of Flanders. The treaty of 1177 was a renewal of that of 1171 and therefore almost certainly dealt with Byzantine claims to overlordship in the Crusader States as well as in Egypt and this may have caused other kinds of resentment in the Frankish East.

At about this time Manuel arranged for Bohemond III of Antioch, who had recently become a widower, to marry his own great-niece Theodora, who is thought to have been the daughter of the Protovestiarius John

---

50. WT, XXI, 13, II, pp. 979-80.

51. *Ibid.,* XXI, 14, II, pp. 980-1; *La Chronique d'Ernoul et de Bernard le Trésorier*, ed. L. DE MAS LATRIE (Paris, 1871), pp. 32-3.

52. WT, XXI, 15-17, II, pp. 981-5.

53. *Ibid.,* XXI, 15, II, p. 982.

54. H-E. MAYER, 'Le service militaire des vassaux de Jérusalem à l'étranger et le financement des campagnes en Syrie du Nord et en Égypte au XIIe siècle', *Mélanges sur l'Histoire du royaume latin de Jérusalem, Mémoires de l'Académie des Inscriptions et Belles-Letres*, n.s. V (Paris, 1984), pp. 152-6.

and thus the sister of the dowager-queen Maria of Jerusalem[55]. That this marriage was not to Bohemond's liking is clear from the speed with which he` repudiated Theodora as soon as news reached him of Manuel's death[56]. In arranging the marriage the emperor was almost certainly. acting in his capacity as suzerain, for Bohemond had done homage to him for his principality in 1165[57]. The Pope was fearful that Manuel would seek to implement his authority more fully by instituting a new Orthodox Patriarch in Antioch, and early in 1178 wrote to the clergy and people of the principality urging them to resist any attempt to make the church of Antioch subject to that of Constantinople 'by reason of the affinity contracted between Prince Bohemond and the Emperor Manuel'[58]. In the eyes of contemporaries Theodora was quite clearly a political nominee who was expected to promote imperial interests in a vassal state.

It may reasonably be assumed that Manuel also wished to assert his overlordship in the kingdom of Jerusalem, a position which Amalric had almost certainly acknowledged in the treaty of 1171 which Baldwin IV had renewed. Manuel's problem in the leper-king's reign was to find a representative who would symbolize Byzantine authority and act as imperial 'resident' in the Crusader Kingdom. In Amalric's reign that role had been taken by Queen Maria, but she had retired from court on her step-son's accession, and no parallel alliance could be formed in the new reign because the king, by virtue of his illness, was unable to marry. That Manuel found an alternative solution is suggested by the analysis of the *Life* of St. Leontius recently made by Richard Rose. Leontius, the abbot of Patmos, was appointed Orthodox Patriarch of Jerusalem in c. 1175 by the Emperor Manuel, and his *Life* was written in c. 1200, shortly after his death. It tells of a journey which the patriarch made soon after his election, first to his monastery of Patmos, where he spent the winter, then to Cyprus in the following spring, where he inspected properties belonging to the patriarchal see. In the summer he went to Acre, where he stayed for a while, and in the autumn he made a pilgrimage to Nazareth, before entering Jerusalem in the winter. He stayed there for some months and during that time the Latin Patriarch is said to have hired thugs who made an unsuccessful attempt to assassinate him. Leontius also received an invitation from the ruler of Damascus to

55. C. CAHEN, *La Syrie du nord à l'époque des Croisades et la principauté franc d'Antioche* (Paris, 1940), pp. 419-20; C.M. BRAND, *Byzantium Confronts the West, 1180-1204* (Cambridge Mass., 1968), p. 22.

56. WT, XXII, 6, II, p. 1013.

57. This may be inferred from the restoration of the Orthodox Patriarch at Antioch: HAMILTON, *Latin Church*, pp. 175-6; Lilie, *Byzanz*, pp. 183, 443-4, n. 7.

58. S. LÖWENFELD, *Epistolae Pontificum Romanorum ineditae*, (Leipzig, 1885), p. 164.

come to live in his city and take charge of the church of St. Mary there, but the patriarch was recalled to Constantinople by the emperor and had to decline the emir of Damascus' offer, merely asking him for a *firman* so that he might travel home in a Frankish ship without fear of attack by Muslim warships. Before he left Jerusalem the Frankish attitude towards him mellowed and he was allowed to celebrate the Orthodox liturgy at the Holy Sepulchre, but this had to be done privately, with only a group of Orthodox monks present.

The biographer gives no date for this visit, apart from saying that it took place between Leontius' election in c. 1175 and Manuel's death in September 1180, but Rose is surely right in arguing that the patriarch must have come to Palestine in 1177-8 because the account of his activities there is consonant with the political circumstances of the Latin Kingdom at that time and at none other within the given time-span[59]. The visit was highly unusual: no other Orthodox Patriarch appointed by Constantinople came to Jerusalem during the entire period of Latin rule[60] and Leontius' presence there must be understood in a political context even though his biographer describes it in terms of a pilgrimage. The renewal of the Byzantine alliance by Baldwin IV made such a visit possible: Leontius, I would suggest, came to Acre from Cyprus in the summer of 1177 at the emperor's request to await the arrival of the imperial ambassadors and to travel in their suite to Jerusalem. The failure of the Byzantine embassy made it impractical for Leontius to go to Jerusalem and he therefore withdrew to Nazareth, a centre of religious pilgrimage, but not a centre of government, to await developments.

The presence of Leontius in the kingdom during the discussions about a joint Franco-Byzantine attack on Egypt may have been another factor which contributed to the breakdown of those negotiations, for it is another indication that Manuel I was not prepared to offer military help to the Franks without making certain conditions. It would appear that he wished to assert his overlordship in the Crusader States by restoring an Orthodox Patriarch in Jerusalem and perhaps, as Alexander III supposed, in Antioch also. It has already been remarked that the enforcement of strict Byzantine overlordship at Antioch was not agreeable to Bohemond III, and any recognition of Byzantine suzerainty certainly ran counter to the wishes of Raymond III of Tripoli. Count Raymond remained influential in the Kingdom of Jerusalem even though he was no longer regent, for he had married

59. R.B. ROSE, 'The *Vita* of Saint Leontios and its account of his visit to Palestine during the Crusader period', *Proche-Orient Chrétien*, 35 (1985), 238-57.

60. HAMILTON, *Latin Church*, pp. 179-80.

the Princess of Galilee and thus controlled the greatest fief in the kingdom[61]. William of Tyre reports that Bohemond and Raymond were commonly held responsible for Philip of Flanders' refusal to take part in the attack on Egypt[62]. Unless they had the support of the Western knights who had come with the Count of Flanders and of the contingents from Antioch and Tripoli, as well as the 100 knights whom Raymond III commanded as prince of Galilee, the Franks of Jerusalem could give no adequate support to their Byzantine allies for the projected attack on Egypt. Being unable, after prolonged negotiations, to secure assurances from the Franks that they would be given enough support, the Byzantine ambassadors left Acre in late September 1177 and returned to Constantinople with their war-fleet while the shipping lanes were still open[63].

The failure of this projected joint-attack on Egypt constituted more than a minor diplomatic embarrassment. It could be construed as a calculated affront to the Franks' most powerful ally, the Byzantine Empire. Manuel might reasonably have felt deep resentment: his treasury must have been involved in considerable cost in equipping, provisioning and manning a war-fleet of this size, but any hope which he may have had of recouping this outlay through the spoils of war had been blighted by the Franks' unwillingness to honour their treaty obligations. Moreover, Manuel's wish to restore the prestige of his empire, damaged by the defeat of Myriocephalum, by achieving a signal victory in Egypt had been frustrated. William of Tyre was very conscious of the folly of which the anti-Byzantine party among the Franks had been guilty in antagonizing this great Christian power: 'we did not consider it safe', he wrote, 'to abandon the lord emperor's present offer of help, being fearful of his anger, which could prove very harmful to us'[64].

As soon as the imperial fleet had left, Bohemond of Antioch and Raymond of Tripoli persuaded Philip of Flanders and the Master of the Hospital to join them in a campaign in North Syria which lasted all the winter and achieved nothing. Their departure, which left Jerusalem dangerously short of manpower, was a signal to Saladin to mount an invasion from Egypt with the army he had marshalled to withstand the seemingly imminent Byzantine-Frankish attack. Although he suffered a crushing defeat at Montgisard through the good generalship of Prince Reynald[65], the Franks

61. The marriage took place in 1174 while he was regent, WT, XXI, 5, II, p. 967.

62. *Ibid.*, XXI, 17, II, p. 985.

63. William of Tyre places the planning of the autumn campaign 'circa kalendas Octobris', after the Byzantine fleet had left: XXI, 17, II, p. 985.

64. *Ibid.*, XXI, 16, II, p. 983.

65. Although William of Tyre writes as though the king was in command, Arab historians state that Prince Reynald directed the Frankish army: HAMILTON, 'Elephant', p. 100.

did not have the resources to follow up their victory. Saladin's power was not in the long term weakened and he was able to take the initiative against them once more some eighteen months later.

As has been seen, opposition to the Byzantine alliance had come chiefly from the northern princes: the majority of great lords in the Kingdom of Jerusalem were favourable to it. The young king himself seems in this, as in other ways, to have wished to maintain his father's policy; his uncle, Joscelin the seneschal, and his mother, Agnes of Courtenay, each received a life-pension from Manuel and had reason, therefore, to be well-disposed towards Byzantium, and it is likely that Agnes influenced her husband, Reynald of Sidon, to take a similar view; while Prince Reynald, lord of Montréal and Hebron, was closely related to the imperial family of Constantinople. In the autumn of 1177 the pro-Byzantine party gained a new adherent, for the king agreed to the marriage between Balian of Ibelin and his step-mother, Queen Maria Comnena[66]. As a result of this marriage the Ibelins became one of the greatest families in the kingdom, for Balian became the administrator of his wife's fief of Nablus, while his brother Baldwin already held the lordships of Ramla and Mirabel.

Consequently the pro-Byzantine party continued to dominate the High Court of Jerusalem even after the breakdown of the Byzantine alliance. The Orthodox Patriarch Leontius had stayed at Nazareth after the departure of the imperial fleet and the High Court must have given permission for him to visit Jerusalem, for, as he claimed to be lawful Patriarch and was the emperor's representative, a private visit was not possible. The Franks presumably were anxious to consult with Leontius about how best they might restore good relations with the Byzantine court. His *Life* probably reflects quite accurately the hostility felt by the Latin Patriarch, Amalric of Nesle, towards his Orthodox rival, although it seems unnecessarily melodramatic to suppose that Amalric had recourse to incompetent assassins: that story seems to have been introduced by the biographer merely to show that the saint enjoyed divine protection. The invitation which Leontius is said to have received from the ruler of Damascus to come and live in his city, though unsubstantiated, is quite plausible. Damascus at this time was ruled by Saladin who was anxious to maintain good relations with Eastern Christians living under Frankish rule[67], and his patronage of the Orthodox Patriarch might serve the dual purpose of pleasing the Melkite population of Palestine while widening the rift between the Franks and Byzantium by

---

66. WT, XXI, 17, II, p. 986.
67. C. CAHEN, 'Indigènes et Croisés', *Syria*, 15 (1934), 351-60; cf. ROSE, *'Vita'*, p. 249, n. 14.

suggesting that the Sultan was prepared to recognize the Orthodox hierarchy, whereas the Franks were not. It was, perhaps, in order to counteract this impression that the Latin Patriarch was persuaded by the King and the High Court to allow Leontius to celebrate the liturgy in the church of the Holy Sepulchre, even though this was only sanctioned in the presence of a restricted congregation. The group of monks of whom his biographer speaks were presumably the Orthodox canons of the Sepulchre, responsible for the daily performance there of the liturgy in the Byzantine rite, whose presence is certainly attested from King Amalric's reign[68]. The danger that Leontius might accept Saladin's invitation was averted when Manuel recalled him to Constantinople in the spring of 1178. This must have been done as part of the response by the emperor to the failure of the 1177 negotiations, and the length of time between the two events is to be explained by the closure of the sea-lanes during the winter months, but by ordering the patriarch to return Manuel was in effect breaking off diplomatic relations with the court of Jerusalem.

Although Baldwin IV and his advisers might have wished to restore the Byzantine alliance, there seemed no way to do so at this juncture. The Franks instead put their hope in the Third Lateran Council which had been called to meet in Rome in March 1179 and which their representatives attended. This proved a sad disappointment, since the Council failed to launch a new crusade or to take any effective measures to help the beleaguered Franks of Jerusalem. Bishop Joscius of Acre who was present had been charged by the High Court of Jerusalem to seek to arrange a marriage between the widowed princess Sibyl, heir to the throne, and Hugh III, duke of Burgundy, nephew of the Queen of France[69]. Joscius went to France after the Council had ended and Hugh III agreed to the conditions set out in the draft marriage settlement and gave a solemn undertaking to come to Jerusalem in the near future and marry Sibyl[70]. This news was reassuring to the court of Jerusalem, for it meant that a successor of suitable rank, age and experience had been found for the leper-king, and one whose close ties with the Capetian royal family promised their continuing interest in the survival of the Crusader States.

Louis VII had, indeed, taken the cross in 1177, but he was too old and

---

68. There were five Orthodox canons of the Holy Sepulchre in Amalric's reign: RÖHRICHT, *Regesta*, I, p. 132, no. 502; HAMILTON, *Latin Church*, p. 171.

69. WT, XXI, 25, II, pp. 996-7.

70. J. RICHARD, *Les ducs de Bourgogne et la formation du Duché* (Paris, 1954), p. 158, n.4, has drawn attention to evidence of Joscius' presence in Burgundy in the summer of 1179 in CH. PERRAT, *L'autel d'Avenas. La légende de Ganelon et les expeditions de Louis VII en Bourgogne (1166-72)* (Lyons, 1932), p. 100.

ill to fulfil his vow[71], but he sought to redeem it by helping to finance a party of crusaders led by his brother-in-law, Henry Count of Troyes, his brother, Peter of Courtenay, and his nephew, Philip, bishop-elect of Beauvais. They travelled through Italy in the summer of 1179 and there met with William of Tyre who accompanied them to the port of Brindisi where they took ship to the Holy Land while he embarked for the Byzantine Empire[72]. William does not tell us anything about the circumstances of this meeting, but it was almost certainly not fortuitous. William was chancellor of the kingdom and cannot have stayed in Italy for an indefinite time after the Council ended without the permission of the King. The Council had ended on 19 March, yet William did not leave Italy until some time in July[73]. The apparent reason for his delay was that he was awaiting news of the outcome of the Bishop of Acre's mission to the court of Burgundy, and it was not until he learned of this from Henry of Troyes, who was the duke of Burgundy's uncle, that he set out for Constantinople. Since he stayed there throughout the coming winter, he must have been undertaking an official embassy on behalf of King Baldwin IV.

The delegates from the Crusader States who attended the Third Lateran Council would have had the opportunity to collect news about the Emperor Manuel's relations with the West from the other delegates from all over Western Europe who were present. From them they would have learned how Manuel was seeking new western allies. In 1177 the war between Barbarossa and the pope, the Lombard League and the King of Sicily which had lasted for almost twenty years had been brought to an end by the Peace of Venice, yet Manuel, who had contributed generously to support the Western Emperor's opponents, was not even invited to send representatives to the peace conference. Moreover, in the course of the war, Manuel had antagonized two of the major Italian powers: Venice by his wholesale arrest of Venetian citizens and confiscation of their property in 1171, and Sicily by his refusal to honour his treaty obligations and marry his daughter Maria to the young king William II in 1172. Neither power was in a position to take reprisals so long as the war against Barbarossa lasted, but both were free to do so after 1177. Moreover, after the Peace of Venice Frederick I became increasingly powerful in Italy as well as in Ger-

---

71. Sigebert of Gembloux' continuator, *Chronographia*, ed. D.L.C. BETHMAN, *MGH SS*, VI, p. 416. Cf. W.L. WARREN, *Henry II* (London, 1973), pp. 145-6.

72. WT, XXI, 29, II, p. 1003.

73. The French crusaders must have parted from William of Tyre at Brindisi in July, for they reached Jerusalem shortly before Saladin's attack on Le Chastellet on 24 August: LYONS and JACKSON, *Saladin*, p. 141.

many, and Manuel felt threatened by this growth in Hohenstaufen strength. He therefore began to look for new allies in the West.

In the winter of 1178-9 Byzantine envoys came to Paris and negotiated a marriage between Louis VII's daughter, Agnes, and Manuel's heir, Alexius II[74]. At the same time Manuel looked for possible allies in Italy among Frederick I's discontented vassals. He found one in William V of Montferrat, who had been one of Frederick's most loyal supporters during the Lombard Wars, but who was dissatisfied because his interests were not well protected by the terms of the Peace of Venice[75]. Manuel sought his alliance by offering the hand of his only daughter, Maria, to one of the marquis's sons, and William accepted on behalf of his youngest son, Rainier, who went to live in Constantinople in the late summer of 1179[76]. Both families with whom Manuel was seeking to establish these close ties had links with the Kingdom of Jerusalem. Rainier of Montferrat was the brother of Princess Sibyl's first husband, William Longsword, and uncle of the son of that marriage, the future King Baldwin V[77]. Agnes of France was the cousin of Hugh III of Burgundy, who was betrothed to Sibyl of Jerusalem and who, when he reached the East, was certainly expected to become regent for the leper-king and who would succeed him when he abdicated or died. Because of these new Byzantine alliances, one may assume, it seemed a propitious time to the court of Jerusalem to try to renew diplomatic relations with the Emperor Manuel, and William of Tyre was instructed to undertake this mission once he was assured that the marriage contract between Hugh of Burgundy and Sibyl of Jerusalem had been ratified.

Despite the shameful failure of the Franks of Jerusalem to honour their treaty commitments two years earlier, Manuel was not disposed to reject diplomatic overtures which matched so well with his own new system of alliances and William of Tyre was well received by him. The chancellor stayed in Constantinople throughout the winter and was present at the marriages of both the emperor's children, that of Maria to Rainier of Montferrat in February 1180 and that of Alexius II to Agnes of France on March 2. William says nothing about his mission except that it was business 'very

74. ROBERT OF TORIGNI, Chronicle, in Chronicles of the Reigns of Stephen, Henry II and Richard I, ed. R. HOWLETT, Rolls Series, 82 (IV), (London, 1889), p. 279.

75. BRAND, Byzantium, pp. 18-19.

76. William of Tyre places Rainier's arrival in Constantinople about a fortnight before his own: WT, XXII, 4, II, p. 1010.

77. William considered the fact of this relationship important: [Manuel] 'filiam vero nuptui collocavit apud adolescentem nomine Reinerium, Willelmi senioris marchionis de Monte Ferrato filium, domini item Willelmi fratrem, cui nos regis nostri sororem contuleramus': XXII, 4, II, p. 1010.

useful to ourselves and to our church', but clearly his negotiations had more than ecclesiastical significance[78]. His embassy was successful, for he returned to Syria soon after Easter 1180 accompanied by a fleet of four imperial galleys and by envoys to the rulers of the Frankish East: diplomatic relations had been restored between the Crusader Kingdom and Constantinople. The envoys first called at Antioch and saw both Prince Bohemond and the Latin Patriarch, Aimery of Limoges, before travelling on to Beirut where they met King Baldwin[79]. It is possible that William, or some of the emperor's other Western contacts, had succeeded in convincing him that he should stop trying to restore Orthodox Patriarchs in the sees of Antioch and Jerusalem because that policy alienated support for him both in the Frankish East and the Latin West. The evidence for this is inferential: the envoys were charged with a special message from Manuel to the Latin Patriarch of Antioch, who had previously been hostile to Byzantium, but who subsequently became a staunch supporter of Byzantine interests in the city represented by Theodora, Bohemond III's Byzantine wife[80]. Manuel certainly made no further attempt to restore an Orthodox Patriarch in Jerusalem and perhaps that is what William of Tyre meant by describing the results of his mission as 'very useful to... our church'.

The imperial envoys would have learned from Baldwin IV of the attempted *coup d'état* led by Bohemond III and Raymond of Tripoli who at Easter 1180 had sought to depose the king and marry princess Sibyl to a husband of their choice; and how, in order to frustrate their treachery, the king had married Sibyl to a candidate of his own choice, Guy of Lusignan, because he had not dared to await the arrival of her betrothed husband, the duke of Burgundy. The envoys would also have been told of the truce which the King had recently concluded with Saladin[81]. Neither of these events would have prejudiced negotiations about the projected alliance between the two powers: although the links between the ruling houses of Constantinople and Jerusalem were, as a result of the Lusignan marriage, less close than they would have been had Sibyl married Hugh of Burgundy, the Lusignans were not hostile to Byzantine interests.

Baldwin IV sent back to Constantinople as his representative to finalize the terms of the new treaty his uncle, Joscelin of Courtenay. The significance of this choice has not hitherto been remarked, but Joscelin was the

---

78. 'moram nobis et ecclesie nostre perutilem fecissemus': *Ibid.,* XXII, 4, II, p. 1009.

79. *Ibid.,* XXII, 4, II, pp. 1009-11.

80. The Patriarch excommunicated the prince when he repudiated Theodora: *Ibid.,* XXII, 6, II, pp. 1013-14.

81. *Ibid.,* XXII, i, II, pp. 1007-8.

seneschal, the king's *alter ego,* empowered to deputize for him in all civil functions, and, as Baldwin IV was too ill to travel, Joscelin's visit to the Byzantine court resembled that of King Amalric in 1171. This is an index of the importance which the Franks attached to the Byzantine alliance. Joscelin was accompanied by Baldwin of Ibelin, who had been taken prisoner by Saladin in 1179 and released at Easter 1180 in return for a huge ransom, estimated by some Muslim writers at 150,000 dinars and the exchange of 1,000 Muslim prisoners-of-war[82]. Although one source, the Chronicle of Ernoul, relates that Baldwin's ransom was fixed so high because he aspired to marry Princess Sibyl who encouraged his suit, so that Saladin, learning of this, expected him to become King of Jerusalem, this story deserves to be treated with more scepticism than it has usually received[83]. It must be remembered that until her sudden marriage to Guy of Lusignan Sibyl had been betrothed to the duke of Burgundy and in no position to encourage other suitors. Further discussion of this issue would be out of place here: what is relevant to this argument is that Baldwin, being unable to raise the ransom himself, appealed to Manuel for help[84]. It is true that he was related to the emperor by marriage, but the degree of kinship was fairly distant, since Baldwin was only the brother-in-law of Manuel's great-niece; nevertheless, the emperor paid the huge ransom. This indicates that he too was anxious to renew the alliance with the Franks of Jerusalem and build up a group of supporters among the powerful men in the kingdom[85].

C.M. Brand has suggested that an important element in Manuel's readiness to form closer links with the Franks of Jerusalem at this time was a desire to guarantee his son's succession should Manuel die while he was still a minor. He cites the evidence of Eustathius of Thessalonica who relates that refugees from the oppression of Andronicus I later sought refuge in the Frankish East claiming that Bohemond III, Aimery of Limoges and Baldwin IV 'owed genuine brotherly love and succor...next after Manuel to his wronged son Alexius'[86]. There seems no reason to doubt that such a clause was inserted in the treaties and that the Franks felt bound to honour it; nevertheless, at the time those treaties were drafted a reference to the rights of Alexius II may have had only formal significance because he was already associated in power with his father as co-emperor.

Manuel died on 24 September 1180 while the embassy from Jerusalem

---

82. ABU SHAMAH, *The Book of the Two Gardens,* p. 199; IBN AL-ATHIR, 'Sum of World History', *RHC, Or.,* I, p. 636.
83. *La Chronique d'Ernoul,* pp. 56-60.
84. WT, XXII, 5, II, p. 1013.
85. *La Chronique d'Ernoul,* pp. 58-9.
86. BRAND, *Byzantium,* pp. 26-7.

V

Manuel I Comnenus and Baldwin IV

was still in Constantinople. His heir was his eleven-year old son, the co-emperor Alexius II, who was married to Agnes of France, but the regency was exercized by Manuel's widow, Maria of Antioch, the sister of Bohemond III, who was assisted by Manuel's nephew, the *protosebastus* Alexius, uncle of Maria the queen-dowager of Jerusalem[87]. The pro-Latin character of Manuel's court was thus in no way diminished after his death, and Joscelin of Courtenay stayed in the capital throughout the winter to complete his negotiations with the new government.

The news of Manuel's death provoked a reaction in Antioch where Bohemond III repudiated his Byzantine wife, Theodora, and married Sibyl, the daughter of a Frankish nobleman. For this he was excommunicated by the Latin Patriarch, Aimery of Limoges, and although William of Tyre represents this as an attempt by the church authorities to defend the sacrament of marriage, it would appear that the patriarch was also concerned to uphold the Byzantine protectorate which Bohemond's marriage to Theodora symbolized and which he had undertaken to respect in his negotiations with the Byzantine envoys a few months previously. Bohemond's divorce occurred at a particularly sensitive time when the existing treaties needed to be ratified by the new government in Constantinople. Aimery of Limoges was anxious to maintain the Byzantine protectorate because the power of Saladin continued to grow in North Syria: in 1180 he had brought his army once again to the confines of Antioch and attacked the Armenian principality of Cilicia[88]. In this situation it would be inadvisable for the Franks of Antioch to antagonize their only powerful Christian ally. The quarrel between prince and patriarch escalated into a dispute about church property in which members of the baronage took different sides. A civil war broke out in Antioch which was only ended by the intervention of a delegation of Frankish leaders from Jerusalem, who mediated a compromise whereby the prince should keep his new wife while remaining excommunicate, while the church should receive back all its former property[89]. It would appear that Bohemond also agreed to honour his treaty commitments to Byzantium[90].

Joscelin of Courtenay had returned to the Holy Land by the late summer of 1181 having, it may be inferred, brought the negotiations to a successful conclusion[91]. But in that same summer the Byzantine regent,

87. See the genealogy in Brand, *op.cit.,* p. 276.
88. Lyons and Jackson, *Saladin,* p. 151.
89. WT, XXII, 6-7, II, pp. 1013-16.
90. According to Eustathius of Thessalonica, Bohemond III and the Patriarch Aimery were willing to receive with sympathy refugees from the regime of Andronicus I, considering themselves still bound by treaty obligations to supporters of Alexius II. De capta Thessalonica narratio, ed. I. Bekker (*CSHB,* Bonn, 1842), p. 416; Brand, *Byzantium,* pp. 26-7.
91. He was in Acre again by 13 November 1181, Strehlke, *Tabulae,* p. 13, no. 13.

373

V

Maria of Antioch, sent an embassy to Cairo to negotiate a truce with Saladin, perhaps wishing to use him as a counterpoise to the Seljuks of Iconium. Saladin welcomed these proposals and a peace was concluded between the two powers in that autumn[92]. This caused no difficulties to the Franks who already had a truce with Saladin at that time. Indeed, peace between Byzantium and Cairo was not incompatible with a Byzantine protectorate of the Crusader States, for Saladin would then be unable to attack the Franks after his truce with them expired without incurring the hostility of Byzantium.

By the time the truce did expire in the spring of 1182 the government of Byzantium had changed. The regency of Maria of Antioch was overthrown in April 1182 by a revolt led by Andronicus Comnenus, an elderly cousin of the Emperor Manuel. He was well known in the Frankish East. Appointed governor of Tarsus in 1166 he had caused grave scandal by seducing the empress's sister, Philippa of Antioch, and had fled to Jerusalem. There he was welcomed by King Amalric, who enfeoffed him with Beirut, but a few months later Andronicus caused even greater scandal by eloping with Baldwin III's young widow, the dowager-queen Theodora Comnena, and seeking political asylum in Damascus at the court of Nur ed-Din. After living in Muslim territory for many years he was reconciled to Manuel shortly before the emperor's death and allowed to live in Pontus[93].

Andronicus' contacts with the Franks had not made him feel well disposed towards them. Indeed, in 1182 he came to power on a wave of anti-Latin feeling, for the Westerners who had occupied a privileged position in Constantinople in Manuel's reign had caused great resentment there. When Andronicus marched on the capital there was a spontaneous uprising by the mob, who attacked the western quarters and massacred those whom they found there, regardless of age, sex or status. Even the hospital of St. John was sacked and its sick inmates murdered. Some of the more agile Latins sought refuge aboard western ships anchored in the Golden Horn, while some even found shelter on Byzantine ships which had western crews. In the summer of 1182 some of those ships made their way to the Crusader Kingdom and it was thus from eyewitnesses that William of Tyre learned of the massacre of which his *History* gives the most detailed account[94].

In this dramatic way the Franks of Jerusalem learned that they could

---

92. 'In Safar [16 June - 14 July 1181] the envoy of the Emperor of Constantinople arrived in Cairo and peace with its sovereign was concluded': AL-MAQRIZI, *A History of the Ayyubid Sultans of Egypt,* trans. R.J.C. BROADHURST (Boston, 1980), p. 64.
93. B. HAMILTON, 'Women in the Crusader States: the Queens of Jerusalem (1100-90)', in D. BAKER, ed., *Medieval Women* (Oxford, 1978), pp. 161-2.
94. WT, XXII, 11-14, II, pp. 1020-5.

V

Manuel I Comnenus and Baldwin IV

expect no further help from Byzantium. Andronicus within a short time eliminated the western elements in the imperial government. He at first claimed to be acting as regent for Alexius II, and ordered the execution of Manuel's daughter, Maria and of her husband, Rainier of Montferrat, then that of Manuel's widow, Maria of Antioch. In 1183 Andronicus took the title of co-emperor, and soon afterwards had Alexius II murdered and thus became sole emperor. The only westerner of consequence to survive this purge was Alexius II's widow, the eleven-year old Agnes of France, whom Andronicus married, thus eliminating any potential focus of opposition among Manuel's former supporters[95].

Thus by 1183 there were no longer any Latins or philo-Latins left in positions of influence in the Byzantine government and the court of Jerusalem could no longer look to Constantinople for protection as it had been able to do since 1158 when Baldwin III first made an alliance with Manuel. There seems no doubt that the Byzantine protectorate of the Crusader Kingdom had acted as a deterrent to Saladin's aggression during Baldwin IV's reign. The only serious attacks on Frankish territory which the Sultan made were between November 1177 and September 1179 while the treaty was in abeyance, but they were resumed again after Andronicus seized power and instituted an anti-Latin regime in Constantinople in 1182. Saladin's attacks continued without intermission for the rest of Baldwin IV's reign, and although the Franks suffered no loss of territory as long as the king lived, they received no help from the West and could not check the growth of Saladin's power. After Baldwin IV's death in 1185 the Sultan completed his conquest of the former Zengid dominions and was able to bring his superior military resources to bear on the Franks with disastrous consequences for them. The loss of the Kingdom in 1187 is commonly ascribed to the prevalence of divisions among the Franks, but it is arguable that an equally important factor was the end of the Byzantine protectorate of the Crusader Kingdom which had come about with the fall of Maria of Antioch's government in 1182.

Addenda
p. 372, it seems more likely that Baldwin's ransom was paid after Manuel's death by the Frankish regent, Mary of Antioch.

95. O. JUREWICZ, *Andronikos I Komnenos* (Amsterdam, 1970), pp. 84-125.

375

VI

Eleanor of Castile and the Crusading Movement

Eleanor of Castile was centrally involved in the crusading movement both by birth and by marriage. She was the daughter of Ferdinand III of Castile, better known as San Fernando, who brought the whole of Andalusia under Christian sovereignty,[1] and also the niece of John of Brienne, king of Jerusalem.[2] From the start the wars against the Muslims in Spain and in the Holy Land had been seen as part of a single enterprise, and archbishop Diego Gelmirez of Compostella addressed a Church council in 1125 about his hope of reaching Jerusalem by way of North Africa.[3] San Fernando was planning to implement this policy by carrying the war into Morocco when he died on 30 May 1252.

His son Alfonso X initially shared this vision. In March 1254 he concluded a treaty with Henry III of England by which he renounced Castilian claims to Gascony, and this was sealed by the marriage at Burgos in October between the Lord Edward, Henry's elder son, and Fernando's half-sister Eleanor. One of the conditions of the alliance was that Henry would obtain the Pope's permission to substitute a joint expedition to Morocco with Alfonso for his projected crusade to the Holy Land.[4]

---

1. At the time of Fernando's death, client Moorish kings remained in Murcia, Granada, and Niebla, paying tribute to Castile.
2. John of Brienne married Berengaria, sister of S. Fernando, in 1223; see *L'Estoire de Eracles Empereur, XXXII*, Ch. XX, *Recueil des Historiens des Croisades* (hereafter *RHC*), *Historiens Occidentaux*, Vol. II, p. 356.
3. See the letter of Urban II in P. Kehr (ed.), *Papsturkunden in Spanien*, Vol. I, *Katalonien* (Berlin, 1926), pp. 287-8; Archbishop Diego's speech is cited by J. Riley-Smith in *The Crusades: A Short History* (London, 1987), p. 92.
4. J.O. Baylen, 'John Maunsell and the Castilian Treaty of 1254: A Study of the Clerical Diplomat', *Traditio*, 17 (1961), 482-91; T. Rymer (ed.), *Foedera, Conventiones, Litterae et Acta Publica* (London, 1704), Vol. I, pp. 504-6.

So Eleanor did not leave the world of crusading behind when she married, for the English royal family was also deeply concerned about the holy war. Henry III was the nephew of Richard I, the hero of the Third Crusade, while Henry's brother, Richard of Cornwall, in 1240-41 had led a crusade to the East which had gained large territorial concessions from the Ayyubids without striking a blow.[5] Henry III himself was also a potential crusader. He had first taken the cross at his coronation in 1216, but had been absolved from his vow by Honorius III because he was only nine at the time. But when he took the cross again in 1250, while St Louis was in Egypt, he was old enough to know his own mind,[6] although some of his subjects speculated that his crusading zeal was only a ruse to enable him to tax the clergy.[7] Alfonso X's proposal about a joint attack on Morocco remained a dead letter because of Henry's Sicilian ambitions. When Conrad IV died in 1254 Pope Innocent IV offered the Sicilian crown to Henry III's younger son Edmund, aged nine. But because the Hohenstaufen were firmly entrenched in Sicily it was obvious that Edmund's candidacy would only succeed if backed by force, and Alexander IV (1255-61) refused Henry's request to be allowed to crusade in Morocco instead of Syria and tried to persuade him to commute his crusading vow into a war against Sicily.[8]

Henry, who had no wish to offend Alfonso X and jeopardize the Gascony settlement, continued, albeit rather half-heartedly, to press the Pope to allow him to go to Morocco, and although Alexander IV would not agree to this, he allowed Henry to use the crusader taxes to promote his son's Sicilian interests.[9] Thus Henry spent all the crusading funds in a fruitless attempt to secure the Sicilian crown, so that when Alfonso X finally launched his crusade against Morocco in 1260, Henry had neither the necessary dispensation nor the money to take part in it.

5. P. Jackson, 'The Crusades of 1239-41 and their Aftermath', *Bulletin of the School of Oriental and African Studies*, 50 (1987), 33-60.
6. A. Forey, 'The Crusading Vows of the English King Henry III', *Durham University Journal*, 65 (1973), 229-30.
7. Matthew Paris, *Chronica Majora*, ed. H.R. Luard, Rolls Series (London, 1880), Vol. V, p. 102.
8. Rymer, *Foedera*, Vol. I, pp. 545-6, 548.
9. *Annales de Burton*, in *Annales Monasti*, ed. H.R. Luard, Rolls Series (London, 1864), Vol. I, p. 351; cf. Forey, 'Crusading Vows', 233-45, on the financing of the Sicilian expedition.

Alfonso's troops captured Salé on the Atlantic coast and held it for three weeks, a victory which, though ephemeral, was psychologically important as C.J. Bishko has pointed out, because for the first time Spanish Christians had carried the war into Africa.[10]

Alfonso made no further attack on Morocco, so the opportunity of a joint English-Castilian crusade against the Moors did not arise again. But Henry III had still not fulfilled his vow and could not do so during the baronial wars of the early 1260s. However, when Clement IV began to preach a new crusade and St Louis once again took the cross in 1267, the situation in England had become more peaceful. On Midsummer Day 1268 both the Lord Edward and his brother Edmund received the cross from the papal legate Cardinal Ottobuoni.[11] Henry III initially said that he would accompany them, but he was an elderly man and the Pope gave him permission to allow one of his sons to crusade on his behalf. Although, as Alan Forey has shown, Henry was initially reluctant to use this dispensation, he finally agreed to do so, because it was thought inadvisable that the king and both his sons should be absent from the kingdom at the same time.[12] So Edward fulfilled his father's vow as well as his own.

Eleanor of Castile also took the cross.[13] This was by no means an automatic consequence of her husband's doing so, but rather the reverse. The position of women in the crusading movement was an anomalous one. When Pope Urban called the First Crusade he did not forbid women to take part, because the crusade was conceived as an armed pilgrimage with special spiritual benefits which could not be denied to any Christian. Nevertheless, he did specify that a woman must be accompanied by a man who would protect her: her husband, brother, father, or legal guardian.[14] Subsequently the Church tried to dissuade women from going on crusade, and the religious reasons for their doing so were effectively abolished when Innocent III decreed that women and other non-combatants might receive the full spiritual benefits of crusading by commuting their vows in return for a

---

10. C.J. Bishko, 'The Spanish and Portuguese Reconquest, 1095-1492', in K.M. Setton (gen. ed.), *History of the Crusades*, Vol. III (Madison, 1975), p. 434; A. Ballesteros, 'La Toma de Salé en tiempos de Alfonso el Sabio', *Al-Andalus*, 8 (1943), 89-196.

11. *Annales de Oseneia*, in *Annales Monastici*, Vol. IV (London, 1869), pp. 217-18.

12. Forey, 'Crusading Vows', 246.

13. Details of her retinue on the crusade in S. Lloyd, *English Society and the Crusade, 1216-1307* (Oxford, 1988), p. 124 and App. 4.

14. J.A. Brundage, *Medieval Canon Law and the Crusader* (Madison, 1969), p. 32.

contribution to crusading funds which would be used to support active crusaders. But women were never forbidden to take the cross.[15]

Eleanor's reasons for going on crusade are not known. There were precedents in her husband's family: the Spanish princess, Berengaria of Navarre, had gone on the Third Crusade as the betrothed bride of Richard I whom she married in Cyprus,[16] while Eleanor of Aquitaine, from whom both Edward and Eleanor were descended, had taken part in the Second Crusade while married to Louis VII of France.[17] It seems probable that Eleanor of Castile was more influenced by the example of Queen Marguerite of France than by that of these earlier queens of England. Her mother-in-law, Eleanor of Provence, was one of four sisters all of whom made distinguished marriages: Marguerite to St Louis; Sanchia to Richard of Cornwall; and Beatrice to Louis's brother, Charles of Anjou. All the sisters were present at the Christmas court in Paris in 1254, held to celebrate the return of St Louis from the Holy Land after his first crusade, and there would have learned from Marguerite, who had accompanied him, about the decisive role she had taken during the Egyptian campaign.[18] She had been left in charge of Damietta in 1250 while the main army marched on Cairo, and when news reached the city of the king's defeat Marguerite prevailed on the Italian merchant community to stay at their posts and not flee back to the West. Although she had given birth to a son only three days before, the queen rose from her confinement and addressed the Italian consuls, pointing out that if Damietta were lost the king would have no bargaining counter with which to secure the safety of his army, and chiefly as a result of her decisive intervention the king and the entire French army was ransomed.[19] Eleanor of Castile must have heard this story from her mother-in-law, Eleanor of Provence, and perhaps also from her husband's aunt, Sanchia Countess of Cornwall.[20] Queen

15. J.A. Brundage, 'The Crusader's Wife: A Canonistic Quandary', *Studia Gratiana*, 12 (1967), 427-41.
16. Itinerarium Regis Ricardi, Bk. II, Ch. XXXV, ed. W. Stubbs, Rolls Series (London, 1864), pp. 195-6.
17. Odo of Deuil, *De Profectione Ludovici VII in Orientem*, ed. V.G. Berry (New York, 1948).
18. F.M. Powicke, *King Henry III and the Lord Edward* (Oxford, 1947), Vol. I, pp. 240-41.
19. John of Joinville, *Histoire de Saint Louis*, Ch. LXXVIII, ed. N. de Wailly (Paris, 1868), pp. 141-2.
20. Sanchia of Cornwall died in 1262; Eleanor of Provence outlived her daughter-in-law and died in 1291.

Marguerite had proved that a woman might play an active part on crusade even though she could not fight, and this may have influenced Eleanor in her decision.

Even for a princess, taking the cross involved courage and sacrifice. Courage was needed, for although women were non-combatants, they were exposed to the risks of malnutrition which all too often beset crusader armies, to diseases endemic in Africa and the Levant to which they had no immunity, and to the hazards of shipwreck and of capture by the infidel. Crusading involved sacrifice because the participants had no way of telling how long the war would last. A crusader accepted a self-imposed exile of uncertain duration. In Eleanor's case this meant being separated from her children. She had three in 1268: Eleanor aged four, John aged two, and Henry, who was one year old. In an era when infant mortality was high a long absence must have been a cause of anxiety to any mother. Eleanor paid a high price for her crusading venture, since John died before her return to England and Henry two months after she came back.[21]

The Lord Edward might not have been able to prevent his wife from taking the crusade vow, but he could have persuaded her to commute it for a generous donation to crusading funds had he not wished her to go with him. The fact that he did not do so is perhaps evidence that he and Eleanor were happily married, but there may have been an additional reason. It was axiomatic that crusades were pleasing to God, yet it was self-evident that most of them failed. The unvarying explanation of this paradox, as Elizabeth Siberry has shown, was that failure was the result of human sin: God withdrew his support from crusaders who lived unchristian lives.[22] Crusader leaders were therefore anxious to avoid committing sins which would jeopardize the success of the expeditions which they commanded. Sexual sins were clearly a hazard, especially in the case of married men. For fornication, which was not thought very serious by moral theologians, was only an option for bachelors; the sexual misdemeanours of married men were adulterous, and those were serious sins because they involved the breaking of marriage vows.[23] A

21. John died on 3 Aug. 1271; Henry on 14 Oct. 1274; Edward and Eleanor reached England on 2 Aug. 1274; see E.B. Fryde *et al.* (eds.), *Handbook of British Chronology*, 3rd edn. (London, 1986), p. 38.
22. E. Siberry, *Criticism of Crusading, 1095-1274* (Oxford, 1985).
23. John of Joinville, a married man, was very conscious of this while on crusade: 'Mes lis estoit fais en mon paveillon en tel maniere, que nus ne pooit entrer ens, que il ne me veist gesir en mon lit; et ce fesoie-je pour oster toutes mescreances de femmes', Ch. XCVIII, p. 179.

happily married prince was less likely to commit adultery if he took his wife with him, and that may have been why Edward wanted Eleanor to accompany him.

The response to the call for a crusade was disappointing in England, and Edward, recognizing that he could not lead a separate army, agreed to serve under St Louis.[24] Louis's brother, Charles of Anjou, had become King of Sicily in 1266 after attempts to enthrone Edmund of England there had proved ineffective. Charles agreed to take part in the crusade, but persuaded Louis to direct it in the first instance against the emir of Tunis. Jean Richard has argued convincingly that St Louis was not being manipulated by Charles of Anjou to use the crusade in the political interests of Sicily, but that Louis himself considered that the Christian cause would be greatly strengthened by gaining control of some north African ports, though he envisaged this as only a first stage in an expedition to succour the Crusader States.[25]

Edward and Eleanor had agreed to liaison with Louis at Aigues-Mortes, but were delayed in leaving England and Louis therefore sailed ahead of them.[26] Landing on 18 July near the site of ancient Carthage, he was preparing to besiege Tunis when he fell victim to an epidemic which killed many of his men, and died on 25 August. The crusade then had to be abandoned so that Philip III could return to France, and Charles of Anjou negotiated peace with the emir of Tunis. The English army reached the camp on 10 November, just before the crusade embarked for Sicily.[27] It is, I think, legitimate to speculate that Eleanor, who owned a large collection of vernacular romances and patronized writers, may have appreciated this brief visit to the home of Queen Dido more than most of the army.[28] The other leaders decided to defer the main crusade for three years, but Edward was adamant that he would continue to the Holy Land alone. He wintered in Sicily at the court of Charles of Anjou because sailing in the winter months was too

24. Lloyd, *English Society*, pp. 114-19.
25. J. Richard, *Saint Louis, Roi d'une France féodale, soutien de la Terre sainte* (Paris, 1983), pp. 558-66.
26. For the organization and composition of Edward's crusading force, see Lloyd, *English Society*, pp. 113-53. The evidence for Edward's itinerary to Aigues-Mortes is unclear. I have followed M. Prestwich, *Edward I* (London, 1988), p. 73.
27. Richard, *Saint Louis*, pp. 566-73.
28. The Wardrobe Account for Eleanor for 1290 contains the item, 'pro j coffro empto . . . pro Romanciis Regine'; see J.C. Parsons (ed.), *The Court and Household of Eleanor of Castile in 1290* (Toronto, 1977), p. 90; see also p. 13, n. 39.

dangerous, and it was not until May 1271 that he and Eleanor finally reached Acre, having made a brief call at Cyprus on the way.[29]

The crusader settlements were desperately in need of help. The remnants of the Latin Kingdom were torn by faction and threatened by the Mamluks of Egypt, whose power had become formidable since the First Crusade of St Louis, for they had succeeded in harnessing the economic resources of their large empire, which stretched from Libya to north Syria, to support a huge professional standing army. Nevertheless, they feared the possibility of an alliance between a new crusade and the Mongols of Persia, and this led the sultan Baybars to attempt to destroy the remaining Frankish outposts in Syria, so that future crusades would have no bases from which to operate. In the winter of 1270-71 he had captured the great fortresses of Crac des Chevaliers and Chastel Blanc in the county of Tripoli; and in June 1271, that is after the Lord Edward had landed, the sultan captured the castle of Montfort, headquarters of the Teutonic Knights, which was not far from Acre.[30]

This shows that he did not consider Edward a very serious threat, for he probably had fewer than 1,000 men under his command, together with small independent contingents of Bretons and Flemings.[31] Arguably Edward had a sensible threefold plan of action: he sought to activate the alliance with the Mongol Ilkhan Abagha and sent an embassy to his court; he wanted to co-ordinate the armed forces in the Crusader States because together with his own troops they would make a quite substantial army, and summoned a conference of representatives from the three states, Jerusalem, Cyprus, and Tripoli, to plan a campaign; and he wished to impose a trade embargo on Egypt. Acre was one of the greatest ports in the Levant and its trade was almost entirely in the hands of Italian merchants who did not scruple, despite papal prohibitions, to sell war materials, notably iron and timber, to the Egyptian sultan. None of Edward's plans proved effective. The Venetians, who were the dominant mercantile power in Acre, flatly

29. *Les Gestes des Chyprois*, RHC, *Documents Arméniens*, Vol. II, p. 777; Marino Sanuto, *Liber Secretorum Fidelium Crucis*, Bk. III, Pt. XII, Ch. XI (Hanover, 1611), p. 224.
30. R. Irwin, *The Middle East in the Middle Ages: The Early Mamluk Sultanate, 1250-1382* (London, 1986), pp. 36-61; P. Thoreau, trans. P.M. Holt, *The Lion of Egypt: Sultan Baybars I and the Near East in the Thirteenth Century* (London, 1987), pp. 187-208.
31. There are no precise figures for Edward's army: Lloyd, *English Society*, pp. 113-53, 262-81; Prestwich, *Edward I*, p. 71.

refused to acknowledge his jurisdiction and continued to trade with the infidel, while the barons of Cyprus claimed that they were under no obligation to fight on the mainland, thus making it impossible for Edward to raise an adequate force.[32]

Although the Ilkhan was engaged in a war on his northern frontier and was unable to divert his main army to Syria, he instructed his commander in eastern Turkey to dispatch such troops as he could spare, and a force of 10,000 Mongol irregulars swept down as far south as Apamea. But Edward did not have enough troops to effect a liaison with them, and in mid-November the Mongols returned home because they were not numerous enough to take on the main Egyptian army.[33] Their presence had led the sultan to concentrate his own forces at Damascus, which left Edward a free hand in Palestine; however, because he had so few men he was not able to take advantage of this situation.

Among those who had accompanied Edward was Tebaldo Visconti, archdeacon of Liège, who in the autumn of 1271 was informed that he had been elected Pope, thus ending a three-year long papal vacancy. Before leaving for Rome he preached an impassioned sermon in the Cathedral of the Holy Cross at Acre on the text; 'If I forget thee, O Jerusalem, let my right hand forget its cunning'.[34] Baybars was aware that the new Pope was intent on raising a crusade, and events in north Syria had shown that the prospect of co-ordinated Mongol-Christian action was not an illusion. This made him prepared to negotiate a truce with the government of Jerusalem in April 1272 which was to last ten years, ten months, and ten days. Charles of Anjou, rather than the Lord Edward, seems to have been responsible for brokering this treaty, which brought Edward's crusade to an end.[35] Although its terms allowed Christians free access to the Holy Places, the papacy had forbidden Catholics to visit Jerusalem while it was in Muslim hands on

32. The main accounts of the campaign of the Lord Edward are those of R. Röhricht, 'Etudes sur les derniers temps du royaume de Jérusalem. A. La croisade du prince Edouard d'Angleterre (1270-1274)', *Archives de l'Orient latin* (hereafter *AOL*), Vol. I (1881), pp. 617-32; Powicke, *Henry III*, Vol. II, pp. 596-617; C.J. Tyerman, *England and the Crusades, 1095-1588* (Chicago, 1988), pp. 124-32.
33. Thoreau, *Lion*, pp. 208-10.
34. *Gregorii X vita anonymo scripta*, ed. R.L. Muratori, *Rerum Italicarum Scriptores* (hereafter *RIS*), new edn. G. Carducci and V. Fiorine (Città di Castello, 1900), Vol. III (I), p. 599.
35. Thoreau, *Lion*, pp. 209-10; Prestwich, *Edward I*, pp. 77-8.

pain of excommunication; but Edward and Eleanor may have visited Nazareth. This, the site of the childhood of Christ, would have been an appropriate place of pilgrimage for them, because in the spring of 1272 Eleanor had given birth to a daughter, who was named Jeanne after Eleanor's mother, and who became known in England as Joan of Acre.[36] The Catholic cathedral of Nazareth, built by the crusaders, had been ruined by Baybars when he captured the city in 1263, but the rock chapels in the crypt, which contained the most holy shrines, remained in liturgical use.[37]

Before he left Acre an attempt was made on Edward's life by a member of the Order of Assassins, a Nizarite Isma'īlī group which had been subdued by Baybars, who had taken some of its highly trained assassins into his service. Although the Lord Edward was wounded, he succeeded in wresting the knife from his opponent and stabbing him to death.[38] With justifiable pride he took the murder weapon back to England and displayed it in the royal treasury.[39] This attack shows that, despite the ineffectiveness of his military intervention, the sultan thought Edward potentially dangerous. He would one day be ruler of the Angevin dominions; he was a friend of the new Pope; he had established contact with the Mongol Ilkhan; but above all he had proved that he was dedicated to the crusading cause by staying in the East for so long.

36. Fryde et al.(eds.), Handbook, p. 38.
37. Annales de Terre Sainte, AOL, Vol. II, p. 451; J. Folda, The Nazareth Capitals and the Crusader Shrine of the Annunciation (Pennsylvania, 1986), pp. 12-13. Powicke suggested that Edward may have visited Nazareth, see Henry III, Vol. II, p. 603.
38. Although Prestwich doubts whether the murderer was a Nizarite Isma'īlī, see Edward I, pp. 78-9, F. Daftary, in a recent work sympathetic to this religious community, reports the widely held belief that the Assassins carried out this attempt on Baybars' orders: The Isma'īlīs: Their History and Doctrines (Cambridge, 1992), p. 434. The Syrian branch of the Order had recently been subdued by Baybars; see Thoreau, Lion, pp. 201-3.
39. It was still there in the reign of Edward III. 'Un cotel dont le Roi Edward estoit navre en la T're Seinte en Acres sanz pris', is Item 68 in the Treasury Inventory of Robert de Wodehouse in 1338, The Antient (sic) Kalendars and Inventories of the Treasury of his Majesty's Exchequer, ed. Sir Francis Palgrave, Vol. III (London, 1836), p. 174. This is repeated two years later in the Inventory of Robert Sadington in 1340, ibid., p. 198. Dr. Sarah Barter Bailey, Librarian of the Royal Armouries in the Tower of London, tells me in a private letter that she can find no later evidence for this item, and 'that no knife that might correspond to that description has been identified in the collection surviving in the Royal Armouries'.

Apart perhaps from a pilgrimage to Nazareth, Eleanor stayed in Acre throughout her time in the Holy Land. It was an important centre of book production and manuscript illumination, and while she was there she commissioned an English scholar, master Richard, to translate Vegetius' treatise, *De re militari*, into Old French; the text was then illuminated for her by Acre miniaturists and she gave this edition as a present to her husband. This was the earliest known Old French translation of Vegetius. The presentation copy no longer survives, but Marlay Add. MS 1 in the Fitzwilliam Museum at Cambridge is a later copy of it, and contains an earlier miniature of a sea battle which may have been produced in Acre and possibly formed part of the Lord Edward's book.[40]

Eleanor and Edward left for the West on 22 September, and spent the winter at the court of Charles of Anjou. While there they learnt that Henry III had died and that they were now rulers of England, but they could not cross the Alps until the spring.[41] Eleanor spent part of her time negotiating with Charles of Anjou about the release of her brother, Prince Henry of Castile, who some years earlier had quarrelled with Alfonso X and come to Italy, where he had a distinguished career as a freelance adventurer until he took the losing side in the war of the Sicilian succession and ended up as Charles's prisoner. Although Eleanor failed to secure his release, Charles allowed three of the queen's procurators to visit her brother and supervise the conditions in which he was being held. This was a political issue, not simply a matter of family affection. The imprisonment of a prince reflected adversely on his kin by marriage as well as by blood, and Edward continued to press the Sicilian Crown for his brother-in-law's release even after Eleanor's death.[42]

In 1273 Edward and Eleanor had an audience with Tebaldo Visconti, now Pope Gregory X, at Viterbo,[43] and Edward then went on to Paris to do homage for Gascony to the new king, Philip III.[44] Eleanor

40. J. Folda, *Crusader Manuscript Illumination at Saint-Jean d'Acre, 1275-1291* (Princeton, 1976), pp. 16-17, 129-30, 199, No. 18 (description of the manuscript with bibliography).

41. *Willelmi Rishanger Chronica et Annales*, ed. H.T. Riley, Rolls Series (London, 1865), p. 78.

42. On the career of the Infant Henry, see S. Runciman, *The Sicilian Vespers* (Cambridge, 1958), pp. 99-116; for Eleanor's intervention, see Powicke, *Henry III*, Vol. II, p. 608, n. 2.

43. *Annales Urbevetani, Monumenta Germaniae Historica Scriptores*, Vol. XIX, p. 270; Prestwich, *Edward I*, p. 83.

44. *Rishanger*, ed. Riley, p. 80; Prestwich, *Edward I*, p. 85.

VI

did not accompany him but went to the court of her brother, Alfonso X, in Seville. Inevitably that visit had a political dimension: Alfonso entrusted her with state business, which she was to discuss verbally with Edward.[45] This is an indication of the extent to which her husband and her brother considered her politically competent. The queen was once again pregnant and when she reached Gascony gave birth on 27 November to a son who was called Alfonso after her brother.[46] It was not until 1274 that she and Edward returned to England.

Edward I retained his interest in the Holy Land and paid for a tower to be built in Acre to strengthen the city's defences, which was entrusted to the small English confraternity of St Edward.[47] After the truce with Egypt expired in 1282 and the situation of the Crusader States grew more desperate, Edward was pressed to return there, but his commitments in Western Europe made that impossible. Among those who sent embassies to him were the Mongol Ilkhans of Persia, Abagha, and after 1282 his son Arghun, both of whom were anxious to promote a new crusade to hold the power of the Mamluks in check.[48] In 1286 Arghun sent an embassy led by a Nestorian monk, Rabban Sauma, who had been born in Peking and later became a close adviser of the Nestorian Patriarch of Baghdad. So far as is known he was the first Chinese visitor to Western Europe: certainly he was the first to leave an account of it. He went to Italy, then visited Philip IV in Paris, and learning that the king of England was in Gasony went on to Bordeaux. There he delivered the Ilkhan's letters and gifts to Edward and at the king's request celebrated the Nestorian liturgy at which Edward is said to have received Holy Communion and to have declared that he had once more taken the cross.[49] Rabban Sauma does not mention the queen in his account, but there is no reason to doubt that she was present with

45. Rymer, *Foedera*, II, p. 11; Powicke, *Henry III*. Vol. II, p. 614, n. 1.
46. Born 24 Nov. 1273, see Fryde *et al.* (eds.), *Handbook*, p. 38.
47. *Calendar of Patent Rolls 1272-81 . . . in the Public Record Office, Edward I, AD 1272-78* (London, 1901), p. 296; J. Riley-Smith, 'A Note on Confraternities in the Latin Kingdom of Jerusalem', *Bulletin of the Institute of Historical Research* (hereafter *BIHR*), 44 (1971), 303.
48. L. Lockhart, 'The Relations between Edward I and Edward II of England and the Mongol Il-Khans of Persia', *Iran*, 6 (1968), 23-31.
49. M. Rossabi, *Voyager from Xanadu: Rabban Sauma and the First Journey from China to the West* (New York, 1992), pp. 153-6; Rabban Sauma's account is translated by E.A. Wallis Budge in *The Monks of Kublai Khan* (London, 1928), pp. 185-7.

the rest of the court, and Tyerman has conjectured that she also may have taken the cross again at this time.[50]

For Eleanor retained her interest in the East although she never returned there. Right up to the end of her life she bought luxury goods from the merchants of Acre: in January 1290, for example, she bought, three basins of Damascene work, thirteen ounces of silk, and two dozen camlets made in Tripoli from Roger of Acre.[51] She did not live to see the loss of Acre and of all the remaining Frankish strongholds in the Latin Kingdom which took place a few months after her death.[52]

The Lord Edward was the last important Western leader to crusade in the Holy Land, and although he achieved very little, he was celebrated in later romances as a model of the chivalric, crusading prince. Some of this idealization rubbed off on Eleanor as well, and the story was told of how she had saved her husband's life by sucking the poison from his wound when he was struck down at Acre by the assassin's dagger. There is no warrant for this in any contemporary source; the story was first told by Ptolemy of Lucca 100 years later.[53]

That tale was a story-teller's view of how a good crusader's wife should behave. The reality is, I think, more interesting. Eleanor went on crusade from a sense of personal conviction and at some cost to herself. Unlike Queen Marguerite of France she did not have the chance to play any dramatic role in the crusade, but that was the result of a lack of opportunity rather than a lack of initiative, for the crusade of the Lord Edward was extremely uneventful. During much of her time abroad she was pregnant, and while in Acre she interested herself in the intellectual life of the city and shared that interest with her husband by commissioning a translation of Vegetius for him. On the homeward journey she also shared with him the work of forging closer links with Castile, by seeking to defend Castilian interests in the Kingdom of Sicily and by acting as an ambassador on her husband's behalf to the court of Alfonso X. Her marriage had been arranged to draw England and Castile more closely together, but Eleanor did not construe her role in this as a passive one. The picture of the marriage which emerges from Eleanor's crusading activity is one of a relationship of parity, and it goes far to explain, I think, why the king mourned his wife so deeply when she died.

50. Eleanor's presence with Edward in Gascony from 1286-89 is widely attested:
    J.P. Trabut-Cussac, 'Itinéraire d'Edouard Ier en France du 13 mai 1286 au 1?
    août 1289', *BIHR*, 25 (1952), 160-203; Tyerman, *England*, pp. 237-8.
51. Parsons, *Court*, p. 85.
52. Eleanor died on 28 Nov. 1290; see Prestwich, *Edward I*, p. 363.
53. Ptolemy of Lucca, in Muratori (ed.), *RIS*, Vol. XI, p. 1168.

VII

Ralph of Domfront,
Patriarch of Antioch (1135-40)

During the twelfth century the Latin East offered good career prospects to young men of noble birth from Western Europe. A steady stream of them made their way to the Crusader States: some were knights, others were priests, but they mostly came from the same social class and frequently shared a common interest in the exercise of power. One of the most arresting examples of a clerk from the West who sought to make his authority felt in Frankish Syria was Ralph of Domfront, second Latin patriarch of Antioch.

The extent of his ambition has hitherto excited little comment.[1] The reason for this is to be found perhaps in the nature of the principal source for Ralph's pontificate, the *History* of William of Tyre.[2] Books XIV and XV of William's *History*, which deal with the reign of King Fulk (1131-43), are the least satisfactory parts of his work: he had no good chronicle sources about that period on which to draw, as he had for the earlier years of the twelfth century, nor could he write from his own experience, as he did in the later parts of his work, since he had only been a child at that time. He gives very few dates for the events which he describes in those years, presumably because he was uncertain about them, and he treats the ecclesiastical history of Antioch in that period largely in isolation from its political context. He interprets the pontificate of Ralph of Domfront chiefly in terms of a personality clash between the patriarch and the prince of Antioch, and although he does suggest that there were political dimensions to this quarrel, he does not clearly define them. However, if Ralph's career is examined in the context of international politics it becomes more comprehensible, and it also becomes possible to form a more precise judgment of his talents.

The church of Antioch over which Ralph presided claimed to have been founded, like that of Rome, by St. Peter. The patriarchate came under Frankish

---

[1] The chief accounts of Ralph's career are: S. Runciman, *A History of the Crusades* (Cambridge, 1951-4, 3 vols), ii. 198-222; R. Grousset, *Histoire des Croisades et du royaume franc de Jérusalem* (Paris, 1934-6, 3 vols), ii. 33-50; C. Cahen, *La Syrie du nord à l'époque des Croisades et la principauté franque d'Antioche* (Paris, 1940), pp. 501-4; H.E. Mayer, *The Crusades*, English trans. (Oxford, 1972), pp. 90-2; G. Fedalto, *La Chiesa Latina in Oriente* (revised ed., Verona, 1981), i. 167-8.
[2] William of Tyre, *Historia rerum in partibus transmarinis gestarum, Recueil des Historiens des Croisades, Historiens Occidentaux* (Paris, 1844-95, 5 vols) (Henceforth *RHC Oc*), i.

2

political control in 1098 when the First Crusade captured the city and although the pope's legate, Adhémar, initially restored the Orthodox patriarch to power this experiment was short-lived. In 1100 Prince Bohemond I drove out the Orthodox patriarch, John IV, and appointed in his place a Latin patriarch, Bernard of Valence. Theoretically the patriarch of Antioch ruled over the whole church of Asia except for Palestine, which was under the jurisdiction of the patriarch of Jerusalem, but in practice the Latin patriarchs of Antioch only ruled those areas which were under Frankish political control. In the first half of the twelfth century their jurisdiction extended to the principality of Antioch, the province of Cilicia and the county of Edessa, while they also exercised *de facto* religious authority in the county of Tripoli.[3] The Byzantine emperors did not accept the latinisation of the patriarchate and maintained a line of titular Orthodox patriarchs who lived in exile in Constantinople. In adopting this policy the Byzantine government was partly responding to a practical need, since Orthodox bishops continued to function in some parts of the patriarchate of Antioch which remained under Muslim rule and were not allowed by the Islamic authorities to acknowledge the Latin patriarchs, but the policy also reflected Byzantine hostility towards the existence of independent Frankish states in northern Syria which had once formed part of their empire.[4]

Although the Latin patriarch of Antioch was responsible for the spiritual oversight of the counts of Tripoli and Edessa, he had a special need to live harmoniously with the prince of Antioch whose capital city was also his patriarchal see. The political situation there was unusually delicate when Ralph of Domfront became patriarch in 1135. Five years before the young prince Bohemond II had been killed. His only child was his daughter, Constance, who was aged two. Her right to succeed was unchallenged, but a dispute arose over the appointment of a regent. Bohemond's widow, Alice, was the second daughter of Baldwin II of Jerusalem and considered that she had the best claim to be regent, but she did not enjoy the support of a substantial section of the baronage and when she assumed power her opponents appealed to her father, who deprived her of office. When her father died in 1131 Alice attempted to seize power once more. This time her opponents asked the new king of Jerusalem to intervene. This was Fulk of Anjou, who had married Alice's elder sister, Melisende. Fulk excluded Alice from power and appointed the constable, Reynald le Mazoir, lord of Margat, as his *bailli*, to

---

[3] J.G. Rowe, 'The Papacy and the ecclesiastical province of Tyre', *Bulletin of the John Rylands Library*, xliii (1960-1), 160-89.
[4] B. Hamilton, *The Latin Church in the Crusader States. The Secular Church* (London, 1980), pp. 172-9.

rule in the name of the princess Constance.[5]

Because the king could not remain permanently in the north during Constance's minority the High Court of Antioch consulted him about the choice of a husband for the young princess. He suggested Raymond of Poitiers, younger brother of William X of Aquitaine, who was living at the court of Henry I of England. A messenger was sent to put the proposal to him, but this plan had to be carried out with great secrecy since the envoy had to travel through the lands of Roger II of Sicily who considered that he had a better right than King Fulk to arrange the princess of Antioch's marriage.[6]

Roger II of Sicily was Constance's closest kinsman on her father's side. Constance was the great-granddaughter and only living descendant of the south Italian Norman prince, Robert Guiscard, while Roger II was the only surviving son of Guiscard's younger brother, Roger I, count of Sicily. Roger II had been unable to intervene in Antioch when Bohemond II died in 1130 because he had only recently succeeded in uniting all the Norman dominions of southern Italy under his sole rule and needed to keep all his forces in the West to consolidate his authority. Nevertheless, he had ambitions to extend his power in the eastern Mediterranean at the expense of the Byzantine empire and control of Antioch would have provided him with a useful base for operations in the Levant. It seems unlikely that William of Tyre is right in his conjecture that Roger II planned to disinherit the princess Constance and assume direct rule in Antioch:[7] his purpose would have been equally well served by appointing a Norman regent there and, in due time, arranging a marriage between the princess and one of his own sons. Roger had supporters in Antioch, particularly among the higher clergy, some of whom may have been appointed by Bohemond II, himself a south Italian.[8] To evade Roger's vigilance the Antiochenes therefore chose a brother of the Hospital, Gerald Jeberrus, as their envoy to the English court, since they supposed, rightly it would seem, that he would arouse no suspicion.[9]

Another ruler who was interested in Antioch was the Byzantine emperor, John II Comnenus. The Byzantines had not forgotten either that the city had been part of their empire before the Turkish invasions or that Bohemond I had been

[5] Cahen, La Syrie, 349-56; William of Tyre, Historia, XIV, v, RHC Oc, i. 614.
[6] Ibid., XIV, ix, RHC Oc, i. 618-19; William does not give a date for this but Mayer, Crusades, p. 90, suggests that negotiations were opened in 1133.
[7] William of Tyre, Historia, XIV, ix, RHC Oc, i. 619.
[8] E.g. Canon Arnulf of Antioch was a Calabrian nobleman who later became archbishop of Cosenza, ibid., XV, xii, RHC Oc, i. 677.
[9] Ibid., XIV, ix, RHC Oc, i. 618-19.

forced in 1108 to agree to the humiliating Peace of Devol, under the terms of which he did liege homage to the emperor Alexius I for Antioch and bound his heirs to do the same.[10] Although this undertaking had never been implemented, John II, who had succeeded Alexius I in 1118, was looking for a favourable opportunity to intervene in the affairs of northern Syria, because Antioch was of great strategic importance in his plans for regaining control of Anatolia.

The principality was gravely weakened by the power struggles which occurred there in the years following Bohemond II's death. In 1132 the Armenian prince, Leo I, took from Antioch the coastal plain of Cilicia, thereby considerably reducing the military and economic resources of the principality.[11] He showed no special antipathy towards the Latin church and Frankish bishops continued to live in the Cilician cities under Armenian rule.[12] A more serious threat to Antioch was posed by Zengi, *atabeg* of Mosul and Aleppo, who in the spring of 1135 captured a number of important fortresses on the eastern frontier of the principality. This attack brought King Fulk to Antioch once more to organise the defences.[13]

The patriarch, Bernard of Valence, died in the late summer of 1135 soon after the king had returned to Jerusalem.[14] The election of his successor canonically belonged to the canons of Antioch cathedral. The normal procedure would have been for them to elect a candidate whom the prince had intimated that he wanted them to chose, confirmation would then have been sought from the pope, and the new patriarch would have been granted a *pallium*, signifying that he was in communion with the Holy See. At the patriarchal election of 1135 this procedure was not followed. In the absence of a prince, the bishops of Antioch met in synod to choose a new patriarch, but while they were deliberating the people of the city elevated Ralph of Domfront by popular acclaim. Because he was already archbishop of Mamistra in Cilicia he did not need to be consecrated, but simply took his seat on St. Peter's throne.[15] Although William of Tyre represents his election as a spontaneous action by the people of Antioch,

---

[10] Anna Comnena, *Alexiad*, XIII, xii, ed. with French trans. B. Leib (Paris, 1937-45, 3 vols), iii. 134.

[11] S. Der Nersessian, 'The kingdom of Cilician Armenia', in K.M. Setton, gen. ed., *History of the Crusades* (Philadelphia, Madison, Wisconsin, 1958-77, 4 vols), ii, *The Later Crusades, 1189-1311*, ed. R.L. Wolff, H.W. Hazard (Philadelphia, 1962), p. 636.

[12] Hamilton, *Latin Church*, p. 33.

[13] Cahen, *La Syrie*, p. 355.

[14] *Regesta Regni Hierosolymitani (MXCVII-MCCXCI)*, ed. R. Röhricht, (Oeniponti, 1893-1904, 2 vols) (henceforth *RRH*), i. 157. This document of 2 August 1135 was witnessed by Bernard of Valence and is his last recorded act.

[15] William of Tyre, *Historia*, XIV, x, *RHC Oc*, i. 619-20.

analogous to that which had raised Gregory VII to the papacy sixty years before, there is reason to suppose that it was premeditated. In the first place it is noticeable that Ralph was not present at the synod with his fellow bishops, but was available to be acclaimed, and secondly it cannot be supposed that he owed his appointment to the common people of Antioch alone. He must have had the support of the nobility, headed by King Fulk's *bailli*, Reynald Le Mazoir, and in that case he was brought to power by the party which favoured the marriage of Constance and Raymond of Poitiers.

Ralph came from Domfront, the great fortress-city on the southern borders of the duchy of Normandy, and this may help to explain his popularity with the Antiochene nobility, since, although most of them came from south Italy, they were mainly Norman in race and speech. Virtually nothing is known about Ralph's earlier career: he first appears as archbishop of Mamistra in two documents issued towards the end of the reign of Bernard of Valence[16] but since the records of the church of Mamistra are very scanty for the early twelfth century it is not known for how long he had held that office, or who had appointed him.[17] William of Tyre describes him as 'a military man, very magnificent and generous, a great favourite with the common people and with those of knightly birth',[18] which implies that he had been trained as a knight and had subsequently taken holy orders.

William of Tyre met Ralph when he was a child. He gives no details of the circumstances of this encounter, but it clearly made a great impression on him as is plain from the description which he gave of Ralph years afterwards when he came to write that section of his *History*:

> The lord Ralph was a tall, handsome man. He squinted a little, but not excessively. He was not very well-educated, but was a fluent speaker and a cheerful companion and had good manners. Because he was very generous he gained the favour both of the knights and of the burgesses. He was not good at keeping agreements and promises which he had made, and would say first one thing and then another.

---

[16] *RRH*, i. 157, ii. 161a.
[17] Hamilton, *Latin Church*, pp. 24-5.
[18] William of Tyre, *Historia*, XIV, x, *RHC Oc*, i. 619-20.

6

His was a complex character, cunning, cautious and discerning. ... He was called arrogant and conceited and this was true.[19]

In the view of Western churchmen Ralph showed evidence of his arrogance from the moment of his enthronement. The Latin patriarchs of Jerusalem and Antioch regarded themselves as successors of the Orthodox patriarchs who had held office before the First Crusade. There was one important difference: the Orthodox patriarchs, while recognising the pope as senior-ranking bishop in the Christian world, had not supposed that the Roman see had jurisdiction over the eastern patriarchates. In their view each patriarch was autonomous within his own sphere of influence. The early Latin patriarchs, trained in the West, naturally regarded the Holy See as the fount of all ecclesiastical jurisdiction and were encouraged in this view by the Reformed Papacy, which was anxious that its supremacy should be accepted by all the churches of East and West. Although during the twelfth century the popes did not directly intervene in the election of Latin patriarchs, they claimed the right to scrutinise such elections and to invest new patriarchs with the *pallium*.

Alone of all the Latin patriarchs of Jerusalem and Antioch Ralph of Domfront disregarded papal claims to supremacy. At his enthronement he simply took his predecessor's *pallium* from the high altar and wore it.[20] He is alleged to have had no great respect for the Roman see and to have said of the churches of Rome and Antioch that 'each was the see of Peter and Antioch was the firstborn and therefore distinguished in its prerogatives'.[21] This high-handed attitude provoked no reaction from Rome. Since 1130 there had been two rival popes, Innocent II and Anacletus II. Innocent II has come to be regarded as lawful pope and his rival as antipope, but at this time the situation must have seemed less obvious, since the current election procedure allowed only for a unanimous choice by the Sacred College, so that it was arguable that either, or neither, of the popes was lawful vicar of St. Peter. Innocent II was acknowledged throughout the Christian West except in the Norman kingdom of Sicily where Roger II supported Anacletus II. During the pontificate of Bernard of Valence Innocent II had been acknowledged in the patriarchate of Antioch,[22] but Ralph's gesture of

---

[19] *Ibid.*, XV, xvii, *RHC Oc*, i. 686. William is generally thought to have been born in c. 1130; R.B.C. Huygens, 'Guillaume de Tyr étudiant. Un chapltre (XIX, 12) de son "Histoire" retrouvé', *Latomus*, xxi (1962), 819.

[20] William of Tyre, *Historia*, XIV, x, *RHC Oc*, i. 620.

[21] *Ibid.*, XV, xiii, *RHC Oc*, i. 679.

[22] *Regesta Pontificum Romanorum a condita Ecclesia ad annum ... 1198*, ed. P. Jaffé, W. Wattenbach, S. Loewenfeld, P. Kaltenbrunner, P. Ewald, (Leipzig, 1881-8, 2 vols), ii, no. 7531.

independence placed the pope in a difficult position, for if he sought to intervene Ralph might well give his allegiance to Anacletus II, thereby increasing the influence of the rival pope. Innocent II therefore took no action.

Ralph showed evidence of political versatility when a radical change occurred in the government of Antioch soon after his election. He had come to power as the nominee of the baronial party led by Reynald Le Mazoir, King Fulk's *bailli*, a group which was bitterly hostile to the dowager-princess Alice. Alice's elder sister, Melisende, was the wife of Fulk of Jerusalem and, as daughter of Baldwin II, co-ruler with Fulk. The couple had been estranged as a result of the rebellion in 1134 of Hugh of Le Puiset, which was designed to give Melisende a greater share in the work of government. A reconciliation was effected between them after Fulk's return from Antioch in the late summer of 1135, as a result of which Melisende was admitted to an equal place with her husband in the exercise of sovereignty. One of the queen's first acts was to persuade her husband to relinquish the regency of Antioch to her sister, the dowager-princess Alice.[23] Alice resumed direct rule in the winter of 1135-6 and this could have proved difficult for Ralph, but he handled the situation with tact, gave unqualified support to Alice and, as a result, came to enjoy considerable power.[24]

Yet there was one area in which the interests of Ralph and those of Alice were diametrically opposed. When Alice returned to power she learned of the negotiations for the marriage of her daughter to Raymond of Poitiers. She did not approve of the proposal, partly perhaps for personal reasons, since the marriage would mark the end of her regency, but perhaps also because, as Sir Steven Runciman has suggested, she may have considered it politically inexpedient.[25] Raymond would bring no military aid beyond his own gifts of leadership to a principality which stood in need of such help, whereas an alliance with the Byzantine empire would afford military and diplomatic protection to Antioch. Alice therefore sent an embassy to John II Comnenus, acknowledging his overlordship and suggesting that her daughter, Constance, should marry his son, Manuel.[26] Since Constance was only seven the marriage would not take place for

[23] H.E. Mayer, 'Studies in the history of Queen Melisende of Jerusalem', *Dumbarton Oaks Papers*, xxvi (1972), 100-13; B. Hamilton, 'Women in the Crusader States: the Queens of Jerusalem', in *Medieval Women*, ed. D. Baker (Oxford, 1978), pp. 149-51.

[24] William of Tyre, *Historia*, XIV, xx, *RHC Oc*, i, 636.

[25] Runciman, *Crusades*, ii. 198-9.

[26] John Cinnamus, *Epitome rerum ab Ioanne et Alexio Comnenis gestarum*, I, vii, ed. A. Meineke, *Corpus Scriptorum Historiae Byzantinae* (Bonn, 1836), p. 22. No date is given for these negotiations, but Cinnamus describes them immediately before his account of John II's Syrian campaign of 1137.

VII

8

some years, during which time Alice would continue to act as regent, while Antioch would enjoy protection both from possible Sicilian intervention and from the aggression of the *atabeg* Zengi who, it was hoped, would hesitate to embroil himself in a war with Byzantium by attacking a client state of that empire.

Such a policy was not without merit, but the patriarch Ralph could not be expected to endorse it. The Byzantines had always refused to accept the latinisation of the church of Antioch, and continued to support a line of titular Orthodox patriarchs who lived in Constantinople. Moreover at the Peace of Devol in 1108 Behemond I had agreed that

> the patriarch of Antioch shall not any more be one of our race, but a man whom Your Majesties shall promote and choose from the clergy of the great church of Constantinople.[27]

If John were acknowledged as overlord of Antioch he would be likely to insist on the restoration of the Orthodox patriarch-in-exile and Ralph would then be deprived of his dignity. However, Ralph made no protest about this until an opportunity presented itself to him to take some practical steps to reverse Alice's policy. He realised, perhaps, that he could afford to wait because most of the baronage of Antioch shared his distaste for Byzantine overlordship.

While Alice was planning a Byzantine alliance Raymond of Poitiers was travelling to Syria.[28] His journey was not without incident, for Roger II of Sicily had learned of his intentions and had ordered that he should be arrested as he travelled through South Italy.[29] By a series of ingenious subterfuges Raymond evaded the king's agents and reached Antioch in Summer 1136.[30] Although he was welcomed by Alice's opponents, who had prevailed on King Fulk to invite him to the east, this did not guarantee his success. For Alice's position was strong: she controlled the government and the citadel of Antioch and, short of persuading the garrison to mutiny, her opponents could not dislodge her from power.

In this situation the patriarch's reactions were crucial. If he refused to perform the marriage between Raymond and Constance Raymond would be excluded from power. Ralph appears to have reasoned that if he supported Alice

[27] Anna Comnena, *Alexiad*, XIII, xii, ed. Leib, iii. 134.
[28] He left England after the death of Henry I on 1 December 1135; Orderic Vitalis, *The Ecclesiastical History*, XIII, xxxiv, ed. and trans. M. Chibnall (Oxford, 1969-80, 6 vols), vi, 505.
[29] William of Tyre, *Historia*, XIV, 20, *RHC Oc*, i. 635.
[30] He did not reach Antioch until after 19 April 1136, because a document of 19 April 1140 is dated 'anno principatus quarto', *RRH*, i. 195.

in this crisis he would still have no guarantee that her Byzantine overlord, John Comnenus, would not remove him from power. Conversely, if Raymond married Constance the Byzantine threat would be averted and the patriarch's religious position assured, but he would lose his influence in temporal politics because Antioch would once more have an adult prince. In the event, Ralph decided to support Raymond, but to impose terms which would preserve his own temporal authority.

Ralph insisted as a condition of his help that Raymond should do liege-homage to him for the principality. The prince had no alternative but to agree and a written contract was drawn up between them. Ralph succeeded in allaying Alice's fears by persuading her that Raymond of Poitiers had come to marry her, not her daughter, and she therefore made no attempt to prevent Raymond from entering the city. Once he was inside the patriarch immediately solemnized the marriage between him and the eight-year old princess Constance. Since even her own supporters would hesitate to fight against the husband of the lawful princess, Alice conceded defeat and withdrew to her dower lands.[31]

There was a precedent for Ralph's making Raymond do homage to him, because in 1099 Bohemond I had done homage for the principality to the pope's legate, Daimbert of Pisa, possibly as a way of evading the consequences of the oath which he had earlier sworn to the emperor Alexius.[32] There is no evidence that Bohemond II had ever held his lands as a fief of the Church, and there is a considerable difference between holding a state as a fief of the Holy See (as the Norman rulers of South Italy had done since 1059), and holding it as a fief from the patriarch who lived in the same city as the prince. The new situation at Antioch was bound to cause tension. William of Tyre explains how, after Raymond's accession

> the lord patriarch in his customary way behaved more arrogantly, believing himself superior to the lord prince, and he was, indeed, deceived; for the prince thought it most shameful that he had exacted an oath of fealty from him and ... began to behave hostilely towards him and, dispensing with the oath he had taken, allied with his enemies.[33]

[31] William of Tyre, *Historia*, XIV, xx, *RHC Oc*, i. 636-7.
[32] Fulcher of Chartres, *Gesta Francorum Iherusalem peregrinantium*, III, xxxiv, 16, ed. H. Hagenmeyer (Heidelberg, 1913), pp. 741-2.
[33] William of Tyre, *Historia*, XIV, xx, *RHC Oc*, i. 637.

VII

An open conflict was averted by the intervention in Syria of the emperor John II whom both Raymond of Poitiers and Ralph of Domfront feared. John's presence in south-east Asia Minor was made necessary because of attacks which the Armenian prince of Cilicia was making on Byzantine possessions in that area,[34] but his resolve to subdue Antioch at the same time seems to have been hardened by a desire to avenge the affront to Byzantium caused by the marriage of Constance to Raymond of Poitiers, made without reference to himself as overlord and in contravention of the engagement entered upon with his own son. John could only move his armies from Europe if he was assured that Roger II of Sicily would not take advantage of his absence to attack Greece. He therefore formed an alliance with the western emperor Lothair against Sicily, and this was joined by Pope Innocent II who wanted Lothair to overthrow Roger II and the rival pope, Anacletus II, whom Roger supported. Lothair brought his army to Italy in the winter of 1136-7,[35] and that same winter John mustered his forces at Attalia and attacked Cilicia in the following spring.[36] He subdued the province and by late August 1137 had reached Antioch.[37]

Although Raymond of Poitiers had no wish to acknowledge John as his overlord he was left with no alternative. His own forces were insufficient to resist the imperial army, while King Fulk, who had just been defeated by Zengi counselled Raymond to do homage to John because he could expect no military aid from the kingdom of Jerusalem.[38] The terms of the Peace of Devol were therefore in part fulfilled: Raymond of Poitiers did liege-homage to the emperor for his lands, and John also stipulated that if, during the following campaign season, he should succeed in conquering Aleppo, Shaizar, Hama and Homs Raymond should receive them in exchange for the principality of Antioch which should revert to Byzantine rule.[39]

There was a place in the projected imperial settlement for Raymond of Poitiers, even if it was not the one he would ideally have preferred, but it seemed doubtful whether there would be any place at all for Ralph of Domfront. His

---

[34] John Cinnamus, *Epitome*, I, vii, ed. Meineke, p. 22.
[35] F. Chalandon, *Histoire de la domination normande en Italie et en Sicile* (Paris, 1907, 2 vols), ii. 54-7; P. Lamma, *Comneni e Staufer. Ricerche sui rapporti fra Bisanzio e l'Occidente nel secolo XII* (Rome, 1955-7, 2 vols), i. 25-6.
[36] Cahen, *La Syrie*, p. 359.
[37] F. Chalandon, *Les Comnènes: Jean II Comnène (1118-43) et Manuel I Comnène (1143-80)* (Paris, 1912, 2 vols), ii. 129, n. 1.
[38] Orderic Vitalis, *Ecclesiastical History*, XIII, 34, ed. M. Chibnall, vi. 506-8.
[39] William of Tyre, *Historia*, XIV, xxx, *RHC Oc*, i. 651-3; F. Dölger, *Regesten der Kaiserurkunden des oströmischen Reiches* (Munich, Berlin, 1924-65, 5 vols), no. 1314, ii. 61.

claim to be temporal overlord of Antioch had been demolished by imperial intervention, and it was inconceivable that John would leave a Latin patriarch in Antioch if the city did revert to direct Byzantine rule. John did not approve of the presence of Latin bishops in Orthodox sees and had shown this when he annexed Cilicia by expelling the Latin hierarchy whom the previous Armenian ruler had left undisturbed.[40] At this point Ralph, as head of the Latin Church in north Syria, appealed to Innocent II whose authority he had not hitherto recognised.[41] This was an embarrassment to Raymond, who was seeking to avoid a confrontation with superior Byzantine forces, and he imprisoned Ralph, presumably in order to prevent him from stirring up anti-Byzantine feeling among the people and barons of Antioch. This was reported by a Muslim writer, Ibn al-Qalanisi, living in Damascus:

> A report was received that the lord of Antioch had arrested the Frankish patriarch there and had plundered his house. The reason for this was said to be that the king of the Greeks ... had stipulated as one of the conditions of peace that he should set up in Antioch a patriarch of the Greeks, as had been the custom of old ... .[42]

At the time when Ralph made his appeal, in the autumn of 1137, Innocent II was allied with John Comnenus and the emperor Lothair against Sicily and it seemed unlikely that he would be willing to imperil this alliance by quarrelling with the Byzantine emperor. In December 1137 Lothair died and, as the western empire was elective, the alliance was automatically dissolved because it could not be binding on Lothair's successor. Innocent was therefore free to respond to Ralph of Domfront's appeal. He had no wish to see the Latin church lose control of one of the five ancient patriarchates, and he must, in any case, have been annoyed by the tactless speech attacking the papacy which John II's envoy to Lothair had made at the western imperial court during the time of *détente*. In March 1138 he wrote an encyclical to all Latin Christians serving in the armies of John Comnenus threatening them with damnation if they took part in any attack which the emperor might make on Antioch 'or any other place which faithful Christians possess'.[43]

---

[40] Odo of Dueil, *De Profectione Ludovici VII in Orientem*, IV, ed. and trans. V.G. Berry (New York, 1948), p. 68.

[41] The text of his letter has not survived. That he wrote to the pope may be inferred from Innocent II's encyclical, discussed below, which shows a knowledge of events at Antioch.

[42] Ibn al-Qalanisi, partially trans. H.A.R. Gibb, *The Damascus Chronicle of the Crusades* (London, 1932), pp. 245-6. This event is dated A.H. 532, i.e. A.D. 19 September 1137 - 8 September 1138.

[43] *Cartulaire de l'Église du Saint-Sépulcre de Jérusalem*, ed. E. de Rozière, *Collection des*

Neither his fears nor those of Ralph of Domfront proved to be justified. John Comnenus did campaign in Muslim Syria in the spring of 1138 but, for a variety of reasons not germane to the present argument, he made no substantial and lasting territorial gains.[44] At the end of May he returned to Antioch. By that time Ralph of Domfront had been released from prison, almost certainly because a copy of the pope's encyclical had reached Syria. This would have given Raymond a reason for not accepting an Orthodox patriarch in Antioch until he had referred the matter to the pope, while John II would have been reluctant to antagonise Innocent II whose co-operation he would need if he were to form a new western alliance against Roger II of Sicily. It was Ralph of Domfront, therefore who presided at the solemn liturgy in Antioch cathedral which marked the end of the emperor's Syrian campaign.[45] When John expressed a wish to place a Byzantine garrison in the citadel of Antioch there was a riot in the city, fomented by Count Joscelin II of Edessa, and the emperor, fearing for his safety, withdrew.[46] This was tantamount to a declaration of war against Byzantium by the Franks, but John II had no wish to press the issue at that time since a number of commitment demanded his presence in other parts of the empire.[47] One of his chief concern was to protect the western approaches to Byzantium against a possible Sicilian attack now that the German alliance had been dissolved.

Once the imperial army had withdrawn from Syria the quarrel between Raymond and the patriarch was resumed. Raymond realised that he could not take the law into his own hands and depose Ralph without reference to Rome because while the emperor was campaigning in Syria in 1138 the papal schism had come to an end. Anacletus II had died on 25 January and although his clergy had elected a successor, the antipope Victor IV, he had little support and made his submission to Innocent II on 29 May.[48] Innocent thus became undisputed head of the Latin Church, and Raymond of Poitiers realised that his rights must be respected because he needed papal help to recruit Western support against the threat of attack by Zengi of Aleppo now that he had quarrelled with John

documents inédits sur l'histoire de France, sér. I, v (Paris, 1849), 86-7. The speech of John II's ambassador to the court of Lothair in Peter the Deacon, *Chronica monasterii Casinensis*, III, 115-16, *Monumenta Germaniae Historica, Scriptores* (henceforth *MGH SS*), vii. 833.

[44] Chalandon, *Les Comnènes*, ii. 134-46; Cahen, *La Syrie*, pp. 360-2.

[45] William of Tyre, *Historia*, XV, iii, *RHC Oc*, i. 659.

[46] *Ibid.*, XV, iii-v, *RHC Oc*, i. 658-65.

[47] For example, while John was in Syria the Seljuk sultan of Iconium had attacked Adana in Cilicia, Michael the Syrian, *Chronicle*, XVI, viii, ed. with French trans. J.B. Chabot, (Paris, 1899-1924, 4 vols), iii. 245.

[48] Jaffé, *Regesta*, ii. 919.

VII

Comnenus. It was necessary to find canonical grounds for criticising Ralph of Domfront and these were at hand. At the beginning of his reign Ralph had become involved in a dispute with the canons of Antioch about the apportionment of revenues. His chief opponents were Archdeacon Lambert, 'a learned man of upright life with little or no experience in worldly affairs', and Canon Arnulf, a Calabrian nobleman, whom William of Tyre calls 'learned and worldly-wise'. Disputes of this kind were not uncommon in twelfth-century Syria, but Ralph's reactions might be considered excessive: he deprived Lambert and Arnulf of their benefices and imprisoned them on the charge that they were conspiring against his life. William of Tyre's simple narrative of this quarrel may leave some important factors out of consideration. Canon Arnulf, as later events were to show, was on excellent terms with Roger II of Sicily and may have been conspiring to overthrow the government of King Fulk's *bailli* in Antioch, Reynald Le Mazoir, as well as the patriarch whom he had appointed.[49] It is certainly difficult to believe that Ralph could have arrested members of the higher clergy without the connivance of the civil authorities, and this supports the view that this quarrel had a political dimension. Arnulf and Lambert were released when Raymond of Poitiers became prince, but he could take no action against the patriarch while John Comnenus was in Syria since that might have proved divisive and have weakened his own authority, but immediately after the emperor's departure Raymond persuaded Arnulf and Lambert to appeal to the pope against the patriarch and he compelled Ralph to go to Rome to answer the charges. No doubt he hoped that Ralph would be deposed and a more malleable patriarch appointed.

The prince's straightforward plan was complicated by the intrigues of Arnulf. He was a South Italian nobleman and on his way to Rome he contacted Roger II and persuaded him that Ralph of Domfront had been responsible for bringing Raymond of Poitiers to power in Antioch, thereby effectively wrecking Roger's ambitions to gain control of the regency during the minority of the princess Constance. Consequently when Ralph landed at Brindisi he was arrested on the king's orders, his property was confiscated, his suite dismissed and he was placed in the custody of Arnulf's family while waiting a summons to the court.

When the king and the patriarch finally met Roger II was favourably impressed, for Ralph of Domfront had great presence and was a persuasive talker. He seems to have convinced the king that relations between himself and Raymond of Poitiers were very bad and that he would be prepared to give his support to Roger if he were to intervene at Antioch. The king restored Ralph to liberty, gave

49 William of Tyre, *Historia*,XIV, 10, *RHC Oc*, i. 620. Cf. note 8 above.

VII

back to him his property and his retinue and sent him to Rome on the understanding that he should call and discuss matters further on his return journey.[50]

When Ralph reached the papal court his welcome was at first far from cordial. No pope would have approved of the low esteem in which Ralph was reputed to hold the Holy See. Nevertheless, the patriarch was able to swing curial opinion in his favour: his eloquence no doubt helped him, but so also did the firm opposition which he had shown to Byzantine attempts to restore an Orthodox patriarch in Antioch. Innocent II may well have considered that he could not afford to lose so staunch a supporter of *Latinitas* in the Frankish East. The pope therefore recognised Ralph as lawful patriarch and invested him with a *pallium*. The consistory ruled that, as there was insufficient evidence to decide the charges brought against him, a legate should be sent to the East to receive full testimony and make a judgment. On his homeward journey Ralph once again met Roger II and held long discussions with him and returned to Syria in the Autumn of 1138 escorted by a fleet of Sicilian galleys.[51]

Prince Raymond's plan had gone badly awry. It is true that the case against Ralph was still *sub judice*, but it seemed unlikely that a legate would depose the patriarch now that the pope himself had confirmed him in office. Moreover, Ralph had found a powerful new ally in the king of Sicily. The alliance of Ralph of Domfront and Roger II constituted a serious threat to Raymond, for the patriarch might, if he chose, secure the annulment of Raymond's marriage on the grounds that Constance had been below the canonical age of twelve when it was solemnized.[52] If that were to happen, Raymond would no longer have a claim to the principality; the king of Sicily, as Constance's closest kinsman, would be able to arrange a new marriage for her; Antioch would become a Sicilian protectorate in which Ralph would enjoy a favoured position because he had made Sicilian dominance possible; while Byzantine intervention, which Ralph had reason to fear, would be excluded.

Prince Raymond found himself in a difficult position. He could not arrest Ralph when he landed without antagonizing the pope, which he could not afford to do since he needed Western aid. He therefore tried to neutralise Ralph's influence by forbidding him to enter the city of Antioch, and the patriarch stayed in one of

[50] William of Tyre, *Historia*, XV, xii, *RHC Oc*, i. 676-8.
[51] *Ibid.*, XV, xiii, *RHC Oc*, i. 678-9.
[52] Isabella I of Jerusalem had her marriage to Humphrey IV of Toron annulled on the grounds that she had only been eight when it was contracted, Hamilton, 'Queens', pp. 172-3.

the monasteries on the Black Mountain outside the city. Joscelin II of Edessa, who, although willing to make common cause with Raymond against the Byzantine emperor, had no love for the prince of Antioch who had forced him to become his vassal,[53] saw in Ralph of Domfront a potential ally and therefore invited him to stay in Edessa. Ralph accepted the invitation and remained there during the winter of 1138-9. In the spring of 1139 Raymond expressed a desire for reconciliation. He knew that the pope's legate was about to reach Syria and wished it to be seen that his own conduct towards the patriarch had been correct. Ralph acted circumspectly. He returned to Antioch, but was accompanied by the three Latin archbishops of the county of Edessa, who were not political subjects of Raymond and who would therefore be able to inform the legate if the prince attempted to coerce the patriarch in any way.[54]

The legate was an elderly man, Peter, archbishop of Lyons. He reached Palestine with the spring sailing, accompanied by Ralph's opponents, Arnulf and Lambert, and he went first to Jerusalem to visit the Holy Sepulchre and perhaps to keep Easter there. Lambert and Arnulf were anxious that he should reach Antioch as soon as possible and hastened his departure, but when he arrived at Acre he fell gravely ill, and he died there on 25 May.[55] When Arnulf and Lambert returned to Antioch and reported this, it seemed to Ralph's opponents that the legate's death had removed any hope of bringing the case against him to a conclusion satisfactory to themselves.[56] This is in itself surprising. The charges against Ralph had not yet been examined and the normal procedure would have been for the pope to appoint a new legate to conduct the inquiry. Events in Italy had made it unlikely that he would be prepared to do so. In June 1139, soon after the death of Peter of Lyons, Innocent II had led the papal army in an invasion of Sicily in an attempt to settle certain outstanding territorial disputes, but Roger II defeated his forces and took the pope prisoner at the battle of Mignano on 22 July.[57] Innocent II had no alternative but to make peace with the king of Sicily and to invest him with his lands, which he did five days later.[58] In these circumstances it seemed improbable that the pope would proceed with the case against Ralph of Domfront who was a friend of Roger II's and who had, in any case, regularised his own position in regard to the Holy See.

[53] Cahen, La Syrie, p. 368.
[54] William of Tyre, Historia, XV, xiv, RHC Oc, i. 680-1.
[55] Ibid., XV, xv, RHC Oc, i. 681-2. Peter of Lyon's date of death has been established by P. Pelliott, 'Mélanges sur l'époque des Croisades', Mémoires de l'Institut national de France, Académie des Inscriptions et Belles-Lettres, xliv (I) (1960), 4 n. 1.
[56] William of Tyre, Historia, XV, xv, RHC Oc, i. 682.
[57] Chalandon, Domination normande, ii. 83-90.
[58] Jaffé, Regesta, no. 8043.

Arnulf and Lambert therefore decided to make peace with the patriarch, offering to withdraw the charges against him if he would restore their benefices to them. Ralph agreed to re-instate Lambert as archdeacon, but he refused to be reconciled to Arnulf. He had cause for rancour, since it was Arnulf who had persuaded Roger II to arrest Ralph in the previous year and Arnulf's family who had held him captive. Nevertheless, Ralph's intransigence was an error, since Prince Raymond had no difficulty in persuading Arnulf to continue his vendetta and that autumn the canon set off to Rome again to prevail upon the pope to re-open the case against Ralph. Innocent II was willing to do this, although he was not very enthusiastic about it. Relations between him and Roger II had deteriorated since the Peace of Mignano had been signed: the king of Sicily refused to give the pope military help to quell disturbances in Rome; the king's sons had annexed territory which the pope claimed formed part of the States of the Church; and the pope disputed the extent of the legatine powers which Roger II claimed to hold in the Sicilian church.[59] All these factors may have influenced Innocent II in his decision to disregard the wishes of the king of Sicily and to appoint a new legate, Alberic, cardinal bishop of Ostia, to investigate the charges against Ralph.[60]

While awaiting the new legate's arrival Raymond allowed Ralph to stay in Antioch, but there is some evidence to suggest that he tried to restrict him in the exercise of his office. In 1139 Raymond had gone on pilgrimage to Jerusalem where he had been approached by the patriarch William and Peter, prior of the Holy Sepulchre, about property which had belonged to the Sepulchre at Antioch before the First Crusade, but which had since passed into other hands. The prince invited them to come to Antioch and state their case and in February 1140 Prior Peter and the provost of the Sepulchre arrived in the city. Some of the property which they claimed had passed into the hands of the Latin monastery of St. Paul's at Antioch and, when the prince heard the case in the High Court, Abbot Robert of St. Paul's lodged a formal complaint:

> The discussion of this matter is not within the competence of a secular court but belongs only to that of the lord patriarch of Antioch and his church.

The abbot's protest, although undoubtedly sound in canon law, was ignored by the prince, and the High Court gave judgment in favour of the Holy Sepulchre.[61] The

---

[59] Chalandon, *Domination normande*, ii. 96.
[60] William of Tyre, *Historia*, XV, xv, *RHC Oc*, i. 682.
[61] De Rozière, *Cartulaire*, pp. 172-8.

prince was clearly concerned to restrict Ralph even in the exercise of his ecclesiastical jurisdiction.

Cardinal Alberic, whose departure from the West was much lamented by his friend Peter the Venerable, abbot of Cluny,[62] left Rome after 6 May 1140 and reached Sidon early in June.[63] He immediately went to join the confederate Frankish armies which, under King Fulk's leadership, were laying siege to Banias. Among the Frankish leaders present was Raymond of Poitiers. When the city fell in mid-June the Christian leaders, including Raymond, went to Jerusalem to give thanks for their victory and the legate accompanied them. The prince was thus able to discuss Ralph of Domfront with the cardinal.[64] Raymond then returned to Antioch, while the legate summoned the bishops from the patriarchates of Jerusalem and Antioch to attend a synod in Antioch on November 30.[65]

By the time the synod met Raymond knew that the legate's decision would be favourable to him. Innocent II might have hesitated to depose Ralph of Domfront while there was a possibility that Roger II would intervene in Antioch, since such a move would have antagonised the king of Sicily to no purpose. But by the autumn of 1140 it was clear to the entire Christian world that Roger II would not embark on an expedition to the eastern Mediterranean. In the early months of 1140 John Comnenus had sent an embassy to the new Western emperor, Conrad III, seeking to renew the alliance against Sicily between the two empires which had been formed in Lothair's reign, and suggested that this should be cemented by a marriage alliance between his son Manuel and a German princess.[66] Conrad accepted the proposals in principle and proposed his own sister-in-law, Bertha of Salzbach, as a wife for Manuel.[67] Although Conrad III never did attack Sicily, the fear that he might do so not only inhibited Roger II from attacking Byzantium, which had been the emperor John's chief purpose in making the German alliance, it also deterred him from intervening in the affairs of Antioch. By the Autumn of

---

[62] Peter the Venerable, *Epistolarum Libri Sex*, II, xlviii, ed. J.P. Migne, *Patrologiae cursus completus. Series Latina* (Henceforth *PL*), clxxxix. 271.
[63] His visit to Syria has been variously dated between 1139 and 1141, but it is certain that he left Rome after 6 May 1140 and reached the Holy Land early in June, R. Manselli, 'Alberico cardinale vescovo d'Ostia e la sua attività di legato pontificio', *Archivio della Società romana di storia patria*, lxxviii (1955), 39, n. 2.
[64] William of Tyre, *Historia*, XV, xi, *RHC Oc*, i. 674-6; Ibn al-Qalanisi states that Banias fell at the end of Shawal, A.H. 534, that is in mid-June A.D. 1140, *Damascus Chronicle*, p. 261.
[65] William of Tyre, *Historia*, XV, xv, *RHC Oc*, i. 682.
[66] Dölger, *Regesten*, no. 1320.
[67] Chalandon, *Les Comnènes*, ii. 170; Lamma, *Comneni*, i. 34-5.

1140 both Prince Raymond and Innocent II knew that Roger II would not try to come to the aid of Ralph of Domfront.

The synod which met in Antioch cathedral from 30 November to 2 December 1140 was attended by a group of clergy from the patriarchate of Jerusalem, led by the patriarch William I, who was accompanied by the archbishops of Tyre, Caesarea and Nazareth[68] and the bishops of Bethlehem, Sidon and Beirut. From the principality of Antioch came the archbishops of Tarsus and Apamea and the bishops of Latakia and Jabala, while the county of Edessa was represented by the archbishops of Hierapolis and Cyrrhus. No clergy were present from the county of Tripoli.[69] The two archbishops from Edessa favoured Ralph, as did the archbishop of Apamea, but the other Antiochene prelates sided with Raymond, while the sympathies of the Jerusalem delegation also lay with the prince: he was a benefactor of the religious houses of Jerusalem[70] and he had sided with the canons of the Holy Sepulchre in their dispute with the Antiochene abbey of St Paul's.

The case against the patriarch was brought by his two former enemies, Arnulf and Lambert. Despite Ralph's reconciliation with the latter in the previous year, Lambert made no attempt to fulfil his promise and withdraw his allegations. Ralph of Domfront was charged with being uncanonically elected, and with being guilty of fornication and of simony since his election. He refused to appear before the synod, perhaps because he was afraid that he might be coerced into admitting the truth of the charges. This would make an appeal to the pope against a sentence very difficult, whereas, if he refused to plead, he might lodge such an appeal against any decision which the synod reached. On the second day, when the patriarch still refused to attend, archbishop Serlo of Apamea is alleged to have questioned the competence of the synod to judge the case. This assertion scarcely

---

[68] Robert, archbishop of Nazareth, is not named among those present by William of Tyre, *Historia*, XV, xvi, *RHC Oc*, i. 683, but clearly was of their number. See the grants made to the Holy Sepulchre by Raymond II of Tripoli in December 1140 and January 1141, witnessed by Robert, together with other clergy from Jerusalem, 'returning from Antioch', de Rozière, *Cartulaire*, pp. 184-7.

[69] Fulcher, archbishop of Tyre, had claimed jurisdiction over the bishops of the county of Tripoli and this had been accorded to him by Innocent II on 17 January 1139, Jaffé, *Regesta*, ii, no. 7940. If put into effect this would have made the church of Tripoli subject to the patriarch of Jerusalem. Raymond II of Tripoli may have objected to this and therefore forbidden bishops from his county to attend the legatine synod at which this ruling might be enforced.

[70] E.g. the Holy Sepulchre, de Rozière, *Cartulaire*, pp. 169-72; the Hospital of St John, *RRH*, i. 188a.

seems credible, and it is more likely that he questioned the competence of the synod to proceed with the case in the absence of the defendant, perhaps because Ralph had not been summoned in due form. William of Tyre, who is the only source for the proceedings, is almost certainly merely recording what he found in the *acta* of the synod. The legate dealt severely with this dissenting prelate: Serlo was deposed from his see and unfrocked from the orders of bishop and priest.

The patriarch meanwhile remained in his palace. He had the full support of the people of Antioch. William of Tyre relates that:

> If they had not feared the power of the prince they would have been prepared to expel the legate with contumely from the city together with all those who had assembled to depose the patriarch.

Raymond of Poitiers had the upper hand because he controlled the garrison of the city and, when Ralph refused to appear before the synod on the third day, the legate went to his palace with an armed escort and read the sentence of deposition to him. The patriarch was then handed over to Raymond who had him put in irons and imprisoned him in the monastery of St Symeon on the Black Mountain.[71] There seems to have been a long delay before the new patriarch, Aimery of Limoges, was enthroned, perhaps because Ralph's deposition needed papal confirmation.[72]

William of Tyre relates that after Ralph had been held captive for a long time he escaped and made his way to Rome, where he appealed to the pope against the judgment of the legatine synod and was re-instated as patriarch. While he was preparing to return to his see he was poisoned by an unknown assassin.[73] William of Tyre does not date these events, but Cahen has suggested that Ralph's appeal occurred in c. 1144,[74] because when Otto of Freising visited the papal court in the following year he met there the bishop of Jabala who had come to complain about

---

[71] William of Tyre, *Historia*, XV, xvi, xvii, *RHC Oc*, i. 683-6.

[72] *Ibid.*, XV, 18, *RHC Oc*, i. 688, implies that Aimery's election followed immediately after Ralph's deposition. The first secure date in Aimery's reign is April 1143 when he witnessed Prince Raymond's charter for Venice, *Urkunden zur älteren Handels- und Staatsgeschichte der Republik Venedig mit besonderer Beziehung auf Byzanz und die Levante*, ed. G.L.F. Tafel and G.M. Thomas, *Fontes Rerum Austriacarum*, section III, 12-14 (Vienna, 1856-7 3 vols), i. 102-3, no. xlvi, which is wrongly dated 1140 by the editors. The text states that it was issued in the seventh year of Raymond of Poitiers's reign, i.e. in 1143. Pelliott, *op. cit.* (n. 55 above), pp. 9-10, argues that Aimery's election was delayed until c. 1142, citing William of Tyre, *Historia*, XIX, i, *RHC Oc*, i. 883, where Amalric of Jerusalem's coronation in February 1163 is said to have occurred in the twentieth year of the reign of Aimery, patriarch of Antioch.

[73] William of Tyre, *Historia*, XV, xvii, *RHC Oc*, i. 686.

[74] Cahen, *La Syrie*, p. 504.

the patriarch of Antioch. Otto does not name the patriarch against whom this complaint was lodged, but speaks of Hugh of Jabala as the man 'mainly through whose efforts Antioch began to be fully subject to the Roman see'.[75] Hugh had been one of Ralph of Domfront's chief critics at the legatine synod of 1140[76] and since Ralph was the only patriarch of Antioch during the twelfth century who questioned the papal supremacy it seems likely that Hugh had been sent to Rome to protest against Ralph's re-instatement. If this interpretation is correct, it would appear that Ralph's appeal had been heard by Pope Lucius II (12 March 1144 - 15 February 1145). Lucius tried quite hard to reach some accommodation with Roger II of Sicily, who may have persuaded the pope to give Ralph a friendly hearing.[77] Moreover, Cardinal Alberic of Ostia, who had presided over Ralph's deposition, was absent from Rome on a legation to France from the late spring of 1144 until after the end of Lucius's pontificate.[78] Little serious attention need be given to William of Tyre's remarks about the manner of Ralph's death, since it was common throughout the Middle Ages to attribute sudden deaths to poison, often on completely inadequate evidence. It is not known when Ralph died. He may have been alive while Otto of Freising was in Rome, but his death certainly occurred before 1149 by which time Aimery of Limoges was recognised as lawful patriarch.[79]

Ralph of Domfront was not unusual among Latin prelates in the twelfth century in having a will to power. St Thomas Becket displayed many of the same traits of character and is only one among many examples which could be cited. What distinguished Ralph from other, like-minded bishops was that he did not claim that he was fighting for the liberty of the Church. He does not seem to have been interested in theocratic power, as many bishops, formed in the tradition of the Reformed Papacy, undoubtedly were: he was simply interested in exercising supreme temporal authority in Antioch in his own right, and he exploited the political situation to his own advantage.

[75] Otto of Freising, Chronica, sive historia de duabus civitatibus, VII, xxxiii, ed. A. Hofmeister, MGH SS rerum Germanicarum in usum scholarum separatim editae (Hanover, Leipzig, 1912), pp. 363-4.
[76] William of Tyre, Historia, XV, xvi, RHC Oc, i. 683.
[77] Chalandon, Domination normande, ii. 113-14. Lucius II made a truce with Roger II hoping to enlist his help against the newly formed Rome commune, Lucius II, Epistolae, lxiv, PL, clxxix. 905.
[78] Manselli (op. cit., n. 63 above), p. 50.
[79] No source mentions Aimery as patriarch between 1143 and 1149, William of Tyre, Historia, XVII, x, RHC Oc, i. 775.

Inevitably this brought him into conflict with Raymond of Poitiers. The two men were very much alike, except that the prince was perhaps more conventionally devout.[80] Ralph was popular with the knightly class because he had many of the social gifts which they esteemed: liberality, affability and a distinguished presence. He proved to be both able and gifted, and entered on equal terms, with no resources save his own intelligence, into a conflict which involved the various rulers of Antioch and their opponents, as well as the Holy See, the Byzantine emperor and the king of Sicily.

Ralph resembles more closely some of the great prince-bishops of the post-Carolingian age, men who used their skills to build up virtually independent states for themselves, than he does any of his contemporaries. The Latin Church in Syria still offered scope for men of this kind during the twelfth century, whereas it was more difficult for them to find a place in the Western Church unless they were prepared to identify themselves with the theocratic ideals of the Reformed Papacy.

It is not surprising that, while a child, William of Tyre, who was intending to take holy orders when he grew up, was impressed by the able and flamboyant personality of Ralph of Domfront. When years later he came to write his *History*, he gave Ralph this epitaph:

He was like Marius: he experienced in his own life the extremes of good and ill fortune.[81]

The comparison is just, but it is significant that William should have turned to the history of Republican Rome rather than to that of the Christian Church when he wished to find a parallel to this patriarch of Antioch whom he so much admired.

---

[80] William of Tyre, while making no comment about Ralph's piety, says of Raymond that he was 'observant in his religious duties and punctilious in his attendance at church services, particularly on great feast days', *Historia*, XIV, xxi, *RHC Oc*, i. 637.
[81] *Ibid.*, XV, xvii, *RHC Oc*, i. 686.

VIII

Aimery of Limoges, Patriarch of Antioch: Ecumenist, Scholar and Patron of Hermits

I FIRST MET Father Jean at the Spoleto Conference on the *alto medioevo* in 1956. I was a student at the British School at Rome and had just begun work on my Ph. D. thesis. Jean immediately took a friendly interest in my research, which involved the impact of Cluny and Camaldoli on tenth-century Rome, introduced me to some of the eminent scholars who were present, and helped me to gain access to the archive of Saint John Lateran. We remained firm friends ever afterwards and over the years I have received a stream of learned and supportive postcards from him from all over the world, as well as the gift of a huge number of offprints. Since I came to live in Nottingham I have seen Jean regularly when he visited the nearby Mount Saint Bernard Cistercian Abbey, and it has been a pleasure over the years to have him stay with me and meet the rest of my family.

Father Jean has been an important influence on my work: partly through his advice; partly through the opportunities which he has given me of meeting with other scholars sharing similar concerns (for example, by inviting me to speak at the Congress on Saint Peter Damian at Ravenna in 1972); but chiefly because his scholarship and his monastic profession were so firmly integrated that his life gave me an insight into the learned monastic tradition of the Middle Ages which I could not have obtained from research alone. One of the greatest satisfactions of my academic career was to know that he approved of my book on *Religion in the Medieval West*.

I have chosen this subject as my way of saying thanks, because Aimery of Limoges combined many of the characteristics of Father Jean in his life: he was a distinguished scholar, he was untiring in his zeal for the unity of Christendom, and he combined a very active life with a high regard for the eremitical ideal.

Aimery of Limoges, third Latin Patriarch of Antioch, has un- doubtedly been the victim of character assassination. William of Tyre, writing about the deposition of Ralph of Domfront, the second Latin Patriarch, in 1140, says of the choice of his successor:

> the clergy of Antioch and specially those who had plotted to depose the Lord Ralph, at the bidding and suggestion of the prince and chiefly, it is said, through bribery, elected a certain subdeacon of the church called Aimery. He came from Limoges, and was an uneducated man and not at all honourable in his conduct. The aforesaid Lord Ralph had appointed him dean . . . intending thereby to place him under an obligation and to ensure his loyalty to himself, but this was a vain hope for from that time forward he is said to have joined with Ralph's enemies, and unmindful of the good faith he owed to his benefactor he had plotted his downfall.[1]

The reason for William's antipathy is not known: he was only a child at the time of Aimery's succession, and the two men seldom met in adult life. Most probably it reflected the dispute over ecclesi- astical jurisdiction in the County of Tripoli. In Orthodox times the sees of Tripoli, Tortosa, and Jubail, together with those of Beirut, Sidon, and Acre, had formed part of the ecclesiastical province of Tyre. When Tyre was captured by the Franks in 1124 and a latin archbishop enthroned there, his claim to jurisdiction over the three northern dioceses was contested by the patriarch of Antioch. This led to prolonged litigation in the papal courts. This revolved round the question whether the Orthodox provincial boundaries should continue to be observed, or whether, as Paschal II had ruled in 1111, ecclesiastical boundaries should follow newly established political boundaries in the Latin East. In 1139 Pope Innocent II upheld the claim of the archbishop of Tyre to jurisdiction over the three northern seas, but interestingly this ruling was never enforced, not even by Alberic of Ostia, the cardinal who presided at the legatine synod of 1140 convoked specifically to regulate the affairs of the Church of Antioch, and at which Aimery's predecessor, Ralph of Domfront, was deposed. The tripolitan sees therefore remained under the jurisdiction of Antioch, and this was a major source of grievance to William of Tyre, who as archbishop was deprived of half of his province.[2] His antipathy to Aimery may well have arisen because of this dispute.

William's unflattering portrait has undoubtedly influenced modern scholars who have written about Aimery, but attention has recently been drawn to a range of evidence which makes it possible to achieve a more balanced view of his personality and achievements. Rudolph Hiestand has drawn attention to *La Fazienda de ultra mare*, a pilgrim's guide to the Holy Land, written for Archbishop Raymond of Toledo (1124/5–1152) by Aimery, archdeacon of Antioch.[3] Hiestand argues convincingly that his author must be Aimery of Limoges, and from the correspondence which is annexed to the work it is clear that he knew Raymond of Toledo well. Given their respective life spans, Aimery was clearly much younger than Raymond and it is therefore reasonable to infer that he had been Raymond's pupil before he went to live in the Latin East. This would give an approximate date of birth of 1110 for Aimery. Raymond of Toledo was one of the leaders of the intellectual revival in Western Europe in the early twelfth century, and was the patron of a school of translators of classical and arabic works into Latin. *La Fazienda* makes it plain that Aimery had studied in Toledo and had received an excellent academic training, for it is written in Castilian, and is based in part on a study of the hebrew text of the Old Testament as well as on the Vulgate text. On internal evidence the treatise was written before 1144, and almost certainly dates from before Aimery's appointment as dean of Antioch in 1140.[4]

Aimery was probably attracted to the latin East because of his intellectual interests, and he also had connections there. His uncle, Peter Armoin, was part of the entourage of Prince Raymond of Poitiers, who had appointed him castellan of Antioch.[5] Raymond was concerned to give office to men from his native Aquitaine in order to counter the power of the Normans who had ruled in Antioch since the First Crusade, and Peter Armoin's well qualified nephew, who was destined for a career in the church, soon attained preferment. Aimery cannot have come to the Levant until after 1136, when Raymond came to power, and his rise was meteoric. Raymond was involved in a bitter power struggle with the Patriarch Ralph of Domfront, a very ambitious man who attempted to make the prince a vassal of the church.[6] When Aimery arrived in Antioch the office of archdeacon was vacant, because the previous holder, Lambert, had been deposed by Ralph at the beginning of his reign.[7] The patriarch must have been responsible for Aimery's appointment: his abilities were undoubted and Ralph may well have thought that Prince Raymond would see this appointment as a conciliatory gesture. But in 1139 Ralph decided for tactical reasons to reinstate archdeacon Lambert, and that was the occasion, I infer, for Aimery's promotion to dean.[8]

Late in 1140 Ralph of Domfront was deposed by a legatine synod and was imprisoned in a monastery on the Black Mountain.[9] Aimery of Limoges was elected as new patriarch: he was an obvious choice, since he was a man of mature life, who already held senior office in the church, who was well educated and had been respected and promoted by the previous patriarch, but who also enjoyed the full confidence of Prince Raymond. William of Tyre implies that Aimery was not elected until after the legate had left for Rome in 1141 and the first secure reference to him as patriarch is found in a document of 1143.[10] Although this implies that the pope had confirmed Aimery's appointment by that date, his position was again put in doubt when Ralph of Domfront escaped from prison and fled to Rome where he appealed in person against his deposition. William of Tyre relates that the pope reinstated Ralph and that he was preparing to return to Antioch, when he was poisoned.[11] He does not date these events, but in 1145 the bishop of Jabala was sent by Prince Raymond to lodge a complaint about the patriarch to the new pope, Eugenius III, and Cahen rightly interprets this as a request to reverse his predecessor's decision to reinstate Ralph.[12] So far as is known that judgment was not revised, but with Ralph's death Aimery's position became secure. It is generally assumed that Ralph died before 1149, though there is one piece of evidence which might suggest a later date. When in 1149 Cardinal Guido of Florence, Eugenius III's legate, convoked a synod in Jerusalem, Aimery forbade any of his suffragans to attend, because of the political crisis in North Syria following the battle of Inab. The bishop-elect of Tripoli, who obeyed this injunction, had his appointment quashed by the legate and had later to go to Rome to be reinstated by the pope. It is possible, as Cahen suggests, that Aimery feared that if his patriarchate was represented at the synod his own position would be called in question because Ralph of Domfront was still alive, but it is more likely that Aimery was unable to be present himself because of the situation in north Syria and did not want the question of the province of Tyre reopened in his absence.[13] After this time Aimery's patriarchal status was never called in question. Eugenius III recognised it: when he wanted a copy of the homilies of Saint John Chrysostom on Saint Matthew's Gospel, he asked Aimery to procure a latin translation for him. Aimery sent him a copy of the greek text instead, which was then translated by Burgundio of Pisa, who presented it to the pope in 1151.[14]

As well as being a gifted scholar Aimery had considerable gifts of leadership which were frequently called upon during his long reign. This first happened when, on 29 June 1149, Prince Raymond was killed, together with many of his knights, at the battle of Inab by the army of Nur ad-Din of Aleppo. Raymond's heir, Bohemond III, was a minor and government devolved on Raymond's widow, the twenty-one year old Constance, hereditary princess of Antioch. In that emergency she received the full support of the Patriarch Aimery: even William of Tyre relates that he 'proved himself to be a true guardian of the stricken province', raising an army of mercenaries at his own expense.[15] Inevitably this led to Aimery's enemies to accuse him of wishing to rule Antioch himself. Baldwin III of Jerusalem was anxious that his cousin Constance should remarry, and in 1152 convoked a *curia generalis* at Tripoli which she attended with the barons of Antioch, and at which Aimery of Limoges and his suffragans were also present, together with several members of the royal family. Not even the admonitions of her aunts, Queen Melisende of Jerusalem and Hodierna, Countess of Tripoli, could persuade Constance to take a husband, and William of Tyre reports that the patriarch was thought to be responsible for her intransigence:

because he was a clever and subtle man he was said to have encouraged her in this mistaken course of action, so that he might in the meantime more freely rule the whole land, which he was very desirous of doing.[16]

William was not writing from personal knowledge; he was a student in Western Europe at this time,[17] and he may simply have been repeating a malicious rumour because he disliked Aimery. Nevertheless, his observation gains a certain force from what happened next. In 1153 Constance of Antioch did remarry: her husband was Reynald of Chatillon and Aimery is said to have been critical of the new prince. Moreover, the Church of Antioch was rich whereas recent territorial losses had impoverished the prince whose defence expenditure nevertheless remained extremely high. The reason for this disparity in income is not known, because the archive of Antioch has never been found and there is very little evidence about the property of the patriarch or of the rest of the church in the twelfth century. Nevertheless, all contemporary writers are unanimous in asserting that Aimery of Limoges was rich. It would appear from William of Tyre's account that Reynald sequestered some church property and when Aimery protested, imprisoned him in the citadel of Antioch. He humiliated the patriarch by causing him to sit bareheaded on the roof of the keep throughout a summer's day, for good measure pouring honey over his head, which made him a prey to mosquitoes and midges. William of Tyre gives his only sympathetic account of Aimery on this occasion—perhaps because he disliked Reynald of Chatillon even more—describing the patriarch as 'a very old priest, the successor of Peter, prince of the Apostles, a sick man, almost continually ailing'.[18] This seems for the most part to be invention. Aimery at this time was probably aged about forty-four, and appears to have had robust health: he was certainly to live an active life for another forty years.

Nevertheless, the news of this very public quarrel disturbed the court of Jerusalem and Baldwin III sent the bishop of Acre and Ralph the Chancellor of the Kingdom to restore peace. Reynald agreed to release Aimery and to return all church property. The patriarch nevertheless refused to go on living in Antioch and went into exile in Jerusalem in 1153.[19] He was still there in 1158 when Theodora Comnena, niece of the Emperor Manual and bride of

King Baldwin III, reached the Holy Land. At that time the pope had
not ratified the appointment of Amalric of Nesle, the new patriarch-
elect of Jerusalem; and because this marriage was of the greatest
diplomatic importance and the rites needed to be performed with
the fullest solemnity, Aimery of Limoges was commissioned to
anoint Theodora as queen and to solemnize her marriage to the
king.[20] This was the only occasion on which a Latin Patriarch of
Antioch exercised full liturgical functions in the Catholic cathedral
of Jerusalem.

The Emperor Manuel campaigned in Cilicia and Syria in the
winter of 1158–9, and Aimery accompanied Baldwin III who went
to meet him when the emperor visited Antioch at Easter 1159.[21]
Prince Reynald did not seek to reopen his quarrel with the patriarch, who was therefore able to stay on in the city after Baldwin left.
He and Reynald were not required to work together for long. In
November 1161 Reynald was captured by the governor of Aleppo
and spent the next fifteen years in prison.[22] This led to a contest
between Princess Constance who wished to act as regent, and the
barons who wished to make Bohemond III prince, although he was
still underage, which was only resolved in *c.* 1163, when Aimery
and the High Court invoked the military aid of prince Thoros of
Cilicia and placed Bohemond III in power.[23] About a year later,
on 10 August 1164, the confederate christian armies of north Syria
were defeated at the battle of Artah by Nur ad-Din and Bohemond
was taken prisoner. As in 1149 Aimery of Limoges took charge
of the government during this emergency and sent an appeal for
help to Louis VII of France.[24] But Nur ad-Din made no attempt to
attack Antioch, fearing Byzantine reprisals if he did so, for not only
had Manuel established his protectorate there in 1159, he had also,
in 1161, married Bohemond's sister, Mary. Nur ad-Din therefore
released Bohemond on bail and he went to Constantinople to ask
his imperial brother-in-law to pay his ransom and Manuel agreed to
this on condition that a greek patriarch was restored to Antioch.[25]

Aimery of Limoges, like his latin predecessors, claimed to be
the lawful successor of Saint Peter in the see of Antioch and to
have canonical jurisdiction over all the Orthodox as well as the
Latins in his patriarchate. The Byzantine rulers contested this claim;
when Manuel's father, John II, had restored byzantine rule in Cilicia
in 1138, he had expelled the latin bishops and replaced them by

Greeks,[26] and all the Comnenian Emperors had appointed titular Orthodox patriarchs of Antioch who lived in Constantinople.[27] In 1165 Bohemond III returned to Antioch with the current titular patriarch, Athanasius III, and Aimery was required to cede his cathedral to his greek rival. He did so with an ill grace, anathematizing all the Latins in Antioch who accepted Athanasius as their canonical superior, and went to live in his castle of al-Qusair.[28] Athanasius' installation provoked no reaction either from the court of Jerusalem or from the pope. The Franks in the East realised the importance of the byzantine protectorate and did not wish to offend the emperor: William of Tyre does not even mention the restoration of Anastasius III in his official history of the crusader kingdom. Pope Alexander III was likewise unwilling to antagonize Manuel, who was an important ally in his struggle against the western emperor, Frederick Barbarossa.[29]

Aimery was restored to power by what he certainly regarded as an act of God. In 1170 there was a severe earthquake in north Syria and Athanasius was mortally wounded when the sanctuary of Antioch cathedral collapsed during the liturgy. Aimery was therefore left in undisputed possession of his see,[30] for although Manuel appointed a new titular Orthodox patriarch, Cyril II, he did not attempt to instal him in power at Antioch. But as overlord of the principality, he did in c. 1177 arrange a marriage between Bohemond III, who had recently become a widower, and his own great-niece Theodora.[31] Alexander III seems to have feared that this might lead to the restoration of a greek Patriarch, and in 1178 wrote urging the clergy and people of Antioch to resist any attempt to make their church subject to that of Constantinople.[32] This is an indication of how much the political situation had changed since 1165. Having in 1177 brought his long war against the Emperor Frederick to an end at the Peace of Venice, Alexander was in a position to take a firm stand about the rights of the latin patriarch of Antioch, while Manuel did not wish to antagonize the pope, since he was seeking western allies.[33] This was the context of William of Tyre's embassy to Constantinople in the winter of 1178–9, on behalf of Baldwin IV of Jerusalem. Since he went by way of the Third Lateran Council he would also have had the opportunity to speak to the pope about the needs of the latin East. On his way back to Jerusalem in the spring of 1180, William reports that his mission called at Antioch, where 'we carried out with the prince and the lord patriarch the business enjoined upon us by his imperial highness'. This business was, of course, confidential, and the only indication which William gives of its nature is when he speaks of the time spent at Manuel's court as 'very useful to us and to our church'. This may indicate that Manuel had been persuaded by William—who had been advised by the pope and the court of Jerusalem—not to seek to restore an Orthodox patriarch in Antioch. Certainly William's guarded account seems to indicate that Manuel treated Aimery as legitimate incumbent in 1180.[34]

When Manuel died in the autumn of that year, Bohemond promptly repudiated his byzantine wife Theodora, and married Sibyl, a frankish noblewoman who was said to be of doubtful moral character. Aimery of Limoges refused to recognise the legitimacy of this marriage and excommunicated the prince. The quarrel between them then escalated, for Bohemond began seizing church property, while the patriarch withdrew with his supporters to al-Qusair, placing Antioch under an interdict. Civil war broke out: the Patriarch's supporters were led by Reynald Masoier, lord of al-Marqab, and Bohemond laid siege to the patriarch's castle. Baldwin IV of Jerusalem was rightly disturbed by news of this, since it jeopardized the security of north Syria, and he sent an impressive delegation to Antioch to mediate peace, led by the new Patriarch of Jerusalem, Heraclius, the Masters of the Temple and the Hospital, Count Raymond of Tripoli and Bohemond's stepfather, Reynald of Chatillon. After lengthy negotiations the envoys succeeded in producing a compromise solution: Bohemond would restore confiscated church property, but would remain excommunicated until he regularized his marriage (though as Cahen pointed out, the church soon came to accept Sibyl as lawful princess of Antioch).[35]

This quarrel bears a striking similarity to that between Aimery and Reynald of Chatillon thirty years earlier. No marriage irregularities had been at issue then, and it seems probable that the chief problem in 1180–81, as in 1153, was that of church property, and that Bohemond's divorce was simply a catalyst in this dispute. Whereas prince Reynald had won his struggle with Aimery and had been able to exclude him from Antioch for several years, Bohemond III was forced to make peace with him. By 1180 Aimery had become an elder statesman in the Latin East: he had held office for

forty years and had an international reputation, and his exclusion
would have caused protests throughout the Catholic world. Indeed,
it was Bohemond, not the patriarch, who was weakened by this
quarrel, since a substantial group of noblemen left his service and
entered that of Thoros the Roupenid, Lord of Cilicia.[36]

Throughout Aimery's long term of office the lands of the church
of Antioch had been contracting. At its greatest extent the latin
patriarchate was made up of six archbishoprics and ten bishoprics
in addition to the patriarchal see. Rafaniyah had been lost to the
Muslims in 1137, and the archbishops of Mamistra and Tarsus had
been driven from their sees by John Comnenus in c. 1138, before
Aimery came to power. In the first eleven years of his reign the
county of Edessa with its three archbishoprics of Edessa, Hierapolis,
and Quris were lost to the Muslims, as were the sees of Artah,
Marash, and Kesoun and the archdiocese of Apǿmea in the principality of Antioch. These events effectively reduced the suffragan
sees of Antioch to six: Latakia, Jabala, Valania, in the principality;
and Tortosa, Tripoli, and Jubail in the County of Tripoli; and
this explains why Aimery was determined to retain control over
those three northern sees of the province of Tyre.[37] Even there his
authority was not unchallenged, for in 1152 the Knights Templar
acquired the fief of Tortosa, where their powers of exemption
greatly reduced the authority of the latin bishop.[38] Because of the
steady decline of his ecclesiastical jurisdiction, Aimery might have
been notable chiefly for his strenuous intervention in the secular
affairs of the principality. But in fact he was an important religious
leader because of his dealings with the oriental Christians in his
patriarchate.

Although Aimery's friendly relations with the separated Eastern
Churches was rooted in part in a common antipathy to the byzantine
Church, it was no doubt also stimulated by the efforts which the
Emperor Manuel made to restore unity between the Church of
Constantinople and the non-Chalcedonian Christians of the East.
From 1170–2 Theorianus, the Emperor's envoy, presided at a series
of negotiations with representatives of the Jacobite and Armenian
Churches, trying to unite them with the Orthodox Church, but
the discussions proved inconclusive.[39]

Aimery began to develop close relations with the Jacobites when
their new patriarch, Michael the Syrian, was elected in 1166. He

fixed his see at Mardin in northern Iraq[40] but soon established friendly relations with his frankish neighbours. In 1168 he went on pilgrimage to Jerusalem and returned home by way of Antioch. At that time the Orthodox Patriarch Athanasius III was in power, but Michael ignored him and paid his respects to Aimery at his castle of al-Qusair.[41] Michael claimed to be lawful patriarch of Antioch, and his preference for meeting his latin rather than his greek rival is explained by a comment in his history:

> The Franks never made any difficulty about matters of doctrine, or tried to formulate it in one way only for Christians of differing race and language, but they accepted as a Christian anybody who venerated the cross without further examination.[42]

No doubt this had been true of all the frankish prelates who had ruled in north Syria since the First Crusade, but Michael was writing out of his own experience of Aimery of Limoges. The Greeks were much more concerned with theological exactitude—which the Jacobites resented.

In personal terms Michael had much in common with his fellow patriarch, for he too was a scholar and the author of a very important history. He stayed in Antioch until Easter 1169, and according to the anonymous syriac *Chronicle of 1234* was allowed by the frankish authorities to be solemnly enthroned in the cathedral and presumably to preside at the Jacobite liturgy there.[43] This may indeed have happened, even though Michael himself says nothing about it, because the greek patriarch was not popular with the frankish rulers who may have felt no scruples about offending him. Certainly Michael's long stay at Antioch led him to form an enduring friendship with Aimery and the Franks.

Michael the Syrian came to Antioch again in 1178 and Aimery of Limoges invited him to attend the Third Lateran Council which was going to meet at Easter 1179. Michael declined, but when he learned that the Cathar heresy was on the council's agenda he wrote a treatise against it for the consideration of the pope.[44] Aimery's invitation was revolutionary: Michael had not made any profession of Catholic faith or even expressed a wish to be in communion with the Roman See. Moreover he claimed to be the lawful incumbent of the see of Antioch. But Aimery seems to have supposed that Michael's presence at the Council might be the first step in restoring unity between the Catholic and Jacobite churches. Michael remained a loyal friend to the Franks until his death in 1199, appointing as his vicar in Antioch his own brother Athanasius who had fled there from Jerusalem in 1187 after its capture by Saladin.[45] The Jacobite Church in Michael's reign never entered into communion with the Latins, and political circumstances would certainly have made that very difficult because most Jacobites lived under Muslim rule, but nevertheless the warmth of the relations between the two communities was appreciable, and that was a consequence of Aimery's efforts.

When Aimery became patriarch, the Armenians of Cilicia were under byzantine rule and had little direct contact with the church of Antioch because the Emperor John had driven the latin hierarchy from the province and replaced them with Greeks.[46] The Catholicus of Armenia, Gregory III (1113–66), while maintaining friendly contacts with the papacy, lived in muslim territory and had no close dealings with the Franks of Antioch.[47] Relations between the two churches improved after Cilicia regained her independence in c. 1172, and Rupen III (1175–87) who wanted a frankish alliance, allowed latin archbishops to be restored at Tarsus in 1178 and at Mamistra by 1186.[48] The chief link between the Armenians and Aimery would seem to have been Saint Nerses of Lampron, armenian archbishop of Tarsus, a churchman of truly ecumenical spirit, who made no difficulty about admitting a rival latin archbishop in his own see. As he later explained to Leo the first-crowned, when he had visited the Crusader States he had observed the Latin Church in action and had found many things about it which were admirable. He had received a particularly warm welcome at Antioch:

> The latin churches of the East as well as those of the West showed their approval of my sound views before the arrival of the Roman Emperor [Frederick I in 1190]. At a synod of bishops, finding that I was well instructed in their disciplines and that I was extending the benefits of this to my own country through the practice of good works, they glorified the heavenly Father. I also recall how the churches of the Latins and the Greeks at Antioch, solemnly greeted me as Paul, unworthy though I am, and said that I was the

worthy successor in that Apostle's see [of Tarsus]. Those
churches opened their doors to me and their clergy listened
attentively to my preaching.[49]

These discussions culminated in 1184 in the dispatch of an embassy
to Pope Lucius III by the Catholicus Gregory IV with a profession
of faith. Lucius obviously regarded this as an act of submission to the
Holy See and sent a *pallium* to the Catholicus, together with a text
of the *Rituale Romanum*. The Armenians may not have understood
this exchange in the same way as the Catholic authorities, but there
seems no doubt that they wished to establish full communion with
the Roman Church. Aimery's name is not directly mentioned in
the negotiations, but he must have been involved in them, since
by recognising the Armenians the pope was licensing an alternative
Catholic hierarchy within the jurisdiction of the latin patriarch of
Antioch. Saint Nerses translated the Roman Ritual into Armenian,
because it would form the basis for bringing the practices of his
church into conformity with those of the Roman see.[50] Lucius III
obviously thought that full religious unity had been restored with
the Armenian Church, and in 1184 he ordered armenian clergy
in the diocese of Valania, who had no bishop of their own, to
obey the latin bishop.[51] Pope Clement III likewise assumed that
the union was in force and wrote about this to the Catholicus
Gregory IV in 1189.[52] Relations between the Armenian Church
and the Latins remained cordial in the years immediately following
the Third Crusade, and this culminated in the formal act of union
in 1198.[53] Aimery of Limoges did not live to see this, but there is no
doubt that by his tactful handling of the situation he had contributed
in a very central way towards it.

His greatest success in promoting unity with the oriental churches
was with the Maronites. William of Tyre relates how in *c.* 1181
they renounced their error, by which he presumably means Monotheletism, and

> returned to the unity of the Catholic Church, receiving the
> orthodox faith and being willing to embrace and devoutly
> observe all the traditions of the Roman Church.[54]

The Maronites lived in the County of Tripoli, and therefore within
the latin patriarchate of Antioch. William of Tyre gives a more

triumphalist account of the union than the facts warrant, for in 1181 only some of the maronite hierarchy came into communion with Rome, while there was strong opposition to this on the part of many others. Nevertheless, the union was slowly implemented: in 1215 the maronite patriarch attended the Fourth Lateran Council, and the union, although it has had a chequered history, has survived until the present day.[55] The settlement which Aimery of Limoges devised for the Maronites was to become the blueprint for uniate churches of the eastern rite. The Maronites preserved their own liturgy, canon law and forms of religious observance insofar as these were compatible with Catholic norms. They retained their own hierarchy, which was subject to the maronite patriarch who was answerable to the pope alone, and the local Catholic hierarchy had no jurisdiction over the Maronite Church.[56]

Thus by the time of his death Aimery had succeeded in taking the first steps towards union with all three of the main groups of non-byzantine Christians living in his patriarchate, although full union had not yet been achieved with any of them. It was a remarkable achievement, because it involved the recognition of independent ecclesiastical jurisdictions within his own patriarchate, and, as future events were to show, this was the way forward in ecumenical relations between Rome and the eastern Churches.

Aimery believed that the orthodox Christians, both Syrians and Greeks, were in full communion with the Western Church already. There were a substantial number of them in the city of Antioch and among the monasteries on the Black Mountain and he had no doubt that they owned him canonical obedience.[57] So far as I am aware he did not recognise the existence of the titular Orthodox patriarchs who succeeded Athanasius III, Cyril II (c. 1173–9) and Theodore IV Balsamon (pre 1189 – post 1195), a learned canonist who had a profound contempt for the Latin Church which he regarded as schismatic.[58] But Aimery's attitude to the greek members of his flock was in no way negative. He corresponded with Hugo Eteriano, the pisan scholar who was one of the Emperor Manuel's principal advisers on western affairs.[59] In 1176 he wrote to thank Hugo for sending him a copy of his treatise on the procession of the Holy Spirit, a matter about which he wished to be fully informed because it was the chief point of theological contention between the Orthodox and Latin churches. Aimery's letter implies that he had by this time learned Greek, for he speaks of 'reading with admiration the books written both in Latin and Greek which you have sent'.[60] He also asks Hugo to procure more books for him: a copy of Saint John Chrysostom's commentary on the pauline Epistles; a history of the Byzantine Empire 'from the time at which their emperors split away from the Roman Empire until the present day'; and finally a copy of the acts of the Council of Nicaea 'which we have heard is held by the Lord Emperor'.[61] Aimery was obviously wishing to be better informed about the history of the byzantine church and people and about the way in which they understood the faith. His purpose may have been polemical, but it may equally well have been eirenical: a desire to understand the Orthodox and to promote true unity among the Greeks and Latins in his obedience whom he believed were members of the one Church. This would certainly have been in keeping with the rest of his dealings with eastern Christians.

Aimery was also concerned with the spiritual needs of Latin Christians under his care. One such group were the hermits who lived on the Black Mountain of Antioch. This is known from the writings of Gerard of Nazareth who had himself been a hermit there and who later during Aimery's reign became Bishop of Latakia (1139–61). He relates how Aimery enacted that every solitary who lived on the Black Mountain must have a spiritual director. This was no doubt a necessary reform, for, as Gerard's writings make plain, large numbers of Latins, as well as of oriental Christians, lived as hermits on the Black Mountain in the twelfth century, and although some of them lived in community, like those of Jubin, others had no training at all in the religious life.[62] Aimery's legislation was evidently found beneficial and was continued after his death: in 1235 Pope Gregory IX sent an instruction to the Minister of the hermits of the Black Mountain.[63]

According to a treatise by the Dominican Stephen of Salagnac (†1291), Aimery of Limoges was also responsible for drawing up the first rule for the hermits of Carmel.[64] It is known that both greek and latin hermits were living on Carmel in the twelfth century and it is therefore possible that Aimery was asked to advise them, or that they adopted the same kind of rule which he had drawn up for the hermits of the Black Mountain.[65] Nevertheless, there is no contemporary evidence for this, and it is *prima facie* unlikely that a patriarch of Antioch would have been able to exercise that degree of religious influence in the patriarchate of Jerusalem, even though he did live there for some years in Baldwin III's reign.[66]

Saint Nerses of Lampron was favourably impressed by the charity of the latin clergy of Antioch towards the poor during Aimery's reign, and the patriarch clearly set his fellow priests a good example, for Michael the Syrian records with admiration his generosity to the poor during the drought which afflicted Syria in 1178.[67] He was also concerned with maintaining the defences of his patriarchate. Not only did he improve the fortifications of his own castle of al-Qusair—which might be regarded as simple self-interest[68]—he also seems to have used his early links with Castile to persuade the Master of the Order of Santiago to undertake the defence of the antiochene frontier in 1180.[69] It is also very much to Aimery's credit that in 1186 he encouraged his friend, Reynald Mazoier, to sell his great lordship of al-Marqab to the Knights of St. John because he could no longer satisfactorily undertake its defence. The lordship encompassed most of the bishopric of Valania, which consequently came under the influence of the Order and was lost to the secular church,[70] and Aimery must have been aware that the sale would be potentially damaging to his own ecclesiastical interests.

When the news of the disastrous frankish defeat at Hattin reached Antioch, Aimery sent a mission to England, led by the bishop of Jabala, to invoke the assistance of Henry II, perhaps building on earlier links between the principality and the angevin crown.[71] When Saladin campaigned in north Syria in 1188, he failed to capture Antioch city and certain other fortresses, including the patriarch's castle of al-Qusair.[72] Although a late source, the *Anonymi Rhenani Historia*, relates that Aimery of Limoges bought off an attack, this does not find support in contemporary sources.[73] al-Qusair was a well fortified castle: Bohemond III had not been able to capture it, and it was later to resist the Mamluks for some years after they captured Antioch in 1268.[74] Saladin did not return to the north, and the lands of Antioch remaining in frankish hands were confirmed to them by him in the Treaty of Jaffa in 1192, a pact subsequently ratified by Prince Bohemond who visited the sultan at Beirut in October 1192.[75]

Saladin's conquests had diminished the ecclesiastical powers of the patriarchate and these were not restored in Aimery's lifetime. The dioceses of Latakia, Jabala, and Jubail all passed into muslim hands.[76] Thus by the time Aimery died he had only five suffragans: the archbishops of Tarsus and Mamistra, whose powers were nominal; the bishop of Tortosa, who was overshadowed by the Knights Templar; the bishop of Valania who was virtually a chaplain of the Knights of Saint John; and the bishop of Tripoli, who alone had any real power.

According to the contemporary chronicle of Michael the Syrian, Aimery died in 1193 in his castle of al-Qusair and was buried in Antioch cathedral. Michael adds 'they appointed in his place an aged priest called Ranulf'.[77] Cahen, who points out that the death of an unnamed patriarch of Antioch is also recorded in the *Bustan* for 1193, accepts this dating, but this is not without problems:[78] no other source mentions Ranulph, and the Old French Continuation of William of Tyre ascribes to Aimery a leading role in the events of 1193–4. In October 1193, Bohemond III and some of his chief supporters were seized and imprisoned by Leo II of Cilicia who then attempted to gain control of Antioch with the help of frankish dissident noblemen who had been in his service since 1181. This led to a riot in the city, and the Patriarch Aimery presided over an assembly in the cathedral at which a commune was set up and Bohemond's eldest son Raymond recognised as regent. Aimery, Raymond, and his brother Bohemond [IV] then appealed to Henry of Troyes, ruler of Jerusalem, to mediate with Leo. He did so in 1194 and Bohemond III was released, but the commune of Antioch remained in existence and was the earliest such body to be formed in the Frankish East.[79] This kind of initiative is so much in keeping with the rest of Aimery of Limoges' career that I am reluctant to attribute it to an otherwise unknown Patriarch Ranulph on the sole evidence of a passage in Michael the Syrian. Since Cahen wrote, Ruth Morgan has edited the earliest redaction of the Old French continuation of William of Tyre, and this names Aimery as the patriarch in 1194.[80] *The Chronicle of the Holy Land* which forms part of the *Gestes des Chiprois* contains this entry:

> In the year 1196 died Saladin . . . And in this same year died Aimery, Patriarch of Antioch, and Peter of Angouleme, who was bishop of Tripoli, succeeded him.[81]

Saladin, of course, died in 1193, as Michael the Syrian says Aimery did: and Peter of Angouleme did become patriarch of Antioch, although there is no evidence apart from this entry of his holding office until 1197.[82] No final resolution of this problem is possible unless fresh evidence comes to light; but one suggestion would be that Michael the Syrian gives correct information under the wrong date: that Aimery died in 1196, and that Ranulph did briefly succeed him as patriarch-elect but that his appointment never received papal confirmation.

Aimery of Limoges may justly be counted one of the greatest churchmen to hold office in the Crusader States. He ruled the Church of Antioch for almost sixty years and was distinguished by his learning, his desire to promote unity between Catholics and oriental Christians, and his concern for the spiritual wellbeing of solitaries. But he coupled those qualities with considerable force of character and political, diplomatic and even military skills, which earned him a place among the great secular leaders of the Latin East.

NOTES

1. *Willelmi Tyrensis Archiepiscopi Chronicon*, XV.18; ed. R. B. C. Huygens (identification des sources historiques et détermination des dates par H-E. Mayer, G. Rösch), *Corpus Christianorum Continuatio Medievalis*, 63, 63A (Turnhout, 1986) [henceforth WT], pp. 699–700.

2. *Ibid.*, XVI.14; pp. 650–1; J. G. Rowe, 'The Papacy and the Ecclesiastical Province of Tyre', *Bulletin of the John Rylands Library*, 43 (1960–1) 160–89.

3. M. Lazar, ed., *La fazienda de ultra mar*, Acta Salamanticensia. Filosofia y Letras, 18 (2) (Salamanca, 1965).

4. R. Hiestand, 'Un centre intellectuel en Syrie du Nord? Notes sur la personnalité d'Aimery d'Antioche, Albert de Tarse et *Rorgo Fretellus*', *Le Moyen Age*, 100 (1994) 8–16. Hiestand points out that *La Fazienda* must have been written before 1145 because the author does not know about the finding of the head of Saint John the Baptist at Sebastea in that year. For Raymond of Toledo, see J. Kritzeck, *Peter the Venerable and Islam* (Princeton, 1964) 53–55.

5. WT XV.16; p. 697.

6. B. Hamilton, 'Ralph of Domfront, Patriarch of Antioch (1135–40), *Nottingham Medieval Studies*, 28 (1984) pp. 1–21.

7. WT XIV.10; p. 642.

8. *Ibid.*, XV.15; p. 695. Aimery had become dean by April 1140; G. Bresc-Bautier, ed., *Le cartulaire du chapitre du Saint-Sépulcre de Jérusalem*, Documents relatifs à l'histoire des croisades publiés par l'Académie des Inscriptions et Belles-Lettres, 15 (Paris, 1984), nos. 76, 77, pp. 178, 182.

9. R. Hiestand, 'Ein neuer Bericht über das Konzil von Antiochia 1140', *Annuarium Historiae Conciliorum*, 20 (1988) 314–50.

10. WT XV.18; pp. 699–700. P. Pelliot, 'Mélanges sur l'époque des croisades', *Mémoires de l'Institut national de France, Académie des Inscriptions et Belles-Lettres*,

44/1 (1960) 9–10, argued that Aimery was not confirmed in office until 1142. He cites William of Tyre's assertion that Amalric of Jerusalem was crowned 'on 18 February 1163 in the twentieth year of the Lord Aimery, third Latin patriarch of the holy church of Antioch' (WT, XIX.1; p. 864). This is congruent with a privilege for Venice issued by Prince Roger of Antioch: *factum anno principatus VII, Aimerico patriarcha*. The seventh year of Raymond's reign began in 1143, although * the editors wrongly date this charter to 1140 (G. L. F. Tafel and G. M. Thomas, eds., *Urkunden zur älteren Handels- und Staatsgeschichte der Republik Venedig mit besonderer Beziehung auf Byzanz und die Levante, Fontes rerum austriacarum*, section III, 12–14, 3 vols [Vienna, 1856–7], I, no. xlvi, pp. 102–3).

    11. WT XV.17; p. 699.

    12. Otto of Freising, *Chronica, sive historia de duabus civitatibus*, VII. xxxiii; ed. A. Hofmeister, *Monumenta Germaniae Historica Scriptores* [henceforth *MGH SS*] *rerum Germanicarum in usum scholarum separatim editae* (Hanover, Leipzig, 1912) pp. 363–4; cf. C. Cahen, *La Syrie du nord à l'époque des croisades et la principauté franque d'Antioche* (Paris, 1940) p. 504.

    13. Continuator of Sigebert of Gembloux, *Historia Pontificalis*, xxxvi; *MGH SS*, 20: pp. 540–1; Cahen, *Syrie*, p. 505; B. Hamilton, *The Latin Church in the Crusader States. The Secular Church* (London, 1980) 41–2.

    14. E. Martène & U. Durand, eds., *Veterum Scriptorum et Monumentorum amplissima collectio*, 9 Vols (Paris, 1724–33) 1: 817–18.

    15. WT XVII.10; pp. 772–4.

    16. *Ibid.*, XVII.18; p. 786.

    17. *Ibid.*, XIX.12; 879–82; R. B. C. Huygens, 'Guillaume de Tyr étudiant. Un chapitre (XIX, 12) de son "Histoire" retrouvé', *Latomus* 21 (1962) 811–29; P. W. Edbury & J. G. Rowe, *William of Tyre. Historian of the Latin East* (Cambridge, 1988) p. 15.

    18. WT XVIII.1; p. 809: . . . *sacerdotem longevum, Petri apostolorum principis successorem, virum egrotativum, pene perpetuo infirmantem*. The account is substantially confirmed by Michael the Syrian, *Chronicle*, ed. with French trans. by J. B. Chabot, 4 vols (Paris, 1899–1924) [henceforth MS], XXI.viii; III, pp. 411–412.

    19. WT XVIII.1; p. 809. His presence in Jerusalem is attested in a document of 1155, ed. Bresc-Bautier (n. 8 above), no 37, p. 106.

    20. WT XVIII.xxii; p. 843; B. Hamilton, 'Women in the Crusader States: the Queens of Jerusalem 1100–90', in D. Baker, ed., *Medieval Women* (Oxford, 1978) 157–8.

    21. WT XVIII.25; p. 847; John Cinnamus, *Epitome rerum ab Ioanne et Alexio Comnenis gestarum*, ed. A. Meineke, *Corpus Scriptorum Historiae Byzantinae* (Bonn, 1836) p. 187; P. Magdalino, *The Empire of Manuel Komnenos 1143–1180* (Cambridge, 1993) pp. 66–72.

    22. The date is sometimes given as 1160, but see B. Hamilton, 'The Elephant of Christ: Reynald of Châtillon', *Studies in Church History* [henceforth *SCH*] 15 (1978) p. 98, n. 13.

    23. MS XVIII.x; vol. 3: p. 324.

    24. Cahen, *La Syrie*, pp. 408–9; R. Röhricht, *Regesta Regni Hierosolymitani (MXCVII–MCCXCI)*, 2 vols (Oeniponti, 1893–1904) I, no. 405.

    25. R-J. Lilie, *Byzantium and the Crusader States, 1096–1204*, revised edn. 1988, English trans. J. C. Morris & J. E. Ridings (Oxford, 1993) pp. 184–93; MS XVIII.xi; vol. 3: 326.

VIII

288

26. Odo of Deuil, *De Profectione Ludovici VII in Orientem*, ed. & trans. V. G. Berry (New York, 1948) p. 68.

27. Hamilton, *Latin Church*, pp. 173–5.

28. MS XVIII.xi; vol. 3: 326; King Fulk had captured al-Qusair with the help of the Patriarch Bernard of Valence in 1134, *ibid.*, XVI, v. vol. III, p. 234, and it may have been granted to the patriarchs from that time. P. Deschamps, *Les chateaux des croisés en Terre Sainte*. III. *La défense du comté de Tripoli et de la principauté d'Antioche* (Paris, 1973) pp. 351–7.

29. Lilie, *Byzantium and the Crusader States*, pp. 189–93; P. Lamma, *Comneni e Staufer. Ricerche sui rapporti fra Bisanzio e l'Occidente nel secolo XII*, 2 vols (Rome, 1955–7).

30. MS XIX.vi; vol. 3: 339.

31. Cahen, *La Syrie*, pp. 419–20; C. M. Brand, *Byzantium Confronts the West, 1180–1204* (Cambridge, Mass., 1968) p. 22.

32. S. Löwenfeld, *Epistolae Pontificum Romanorum ineditae* (Leipzig, 1885) p. 164.

33. Magdalino, *Manuel*, pp. 98–104.

34. WT XXII.4; pp. 1009–1011.

35. *Ibid.*, XXII.6–7; pp. 1013–1017; Cahen, *La Syrie*, p. 423, n. 6.

36. Listed in WT XXII.7; p. 1016.

37. Hamilton, *Latin Church*, pp. 38–41.

38. J. Riley-Smith, 'The Templars and the castle of Tortosa in Syria: an unknown document concerning the acquisition of the fortress', *English Historical Review*, 84 (1969) pp. 278–88.

39. P. Tekeyan, *Controverses christologiques en Arméno-Cilicie dans la seconde moitié du xiie siècle (1165–98)*, *Orientalia Christiana Analecta* 124 (Rome, 1939) 14–42.

40. MS XIX.ii; vol. 3: 329–331.

41. *Ibid.*, XIX.iii; 3: 332.

42. *Ibid.*, VI.i; 3: 222.

43. *Anonymi Chronicon ad annum Christi 1234 pertinens*, trans. A. Abouna, introduction etc., J. M. Fiey, *Corpus Scriptorum Christianorum Orientalium*, Scriptores Syri, 154 (Louvain, 1974), *Historia Ecclesiastica*, p. 230.

44. MS XX.vii; vol. 3: 377–8.

45. *Ibid.*, XXI.vii; viii; vol. 3: 409, 411–412.

46. See n. 26 above.

47. B. Hamilton, 'The Armenian Church and the Papacy at the time of the Crusades', *Eastern Churches Review* X (1978) pp. 65–8.

48. MS XX.vii; vol. 3: 377 (Tarsus); J. Delaville Le Roulx, *Cartulaire général de l'Ordre des Hospitaliers de St Jean de Jérusalem (1100–1310)*, 4 vols (Paris 1894–1906) [henceforth CGOH], no. 783 (Mamistra).

49. Saint Nerses of Lampron, 'Lettre adressée au roi Léon II', *Recueil des Historiens des Croisades* [henceforth RHC], *Documents Arméniens*, ed. E. Dulaurier (Paris, 1869), i: pp. 592–3.

50. *Pontificia Commissio ad redigendum codicem iuris canonici orientalis*, *Fontes*, series III, [henceforth CICO] vol. I, *Acta Romanorum pontificum a s. Clemente I . . . ad Coelestinum III . . .* (Vatican City, 1943), no. 395, pp. 811–13.

51. CICO, vol. III, *Acta Honorii III et Gregorii IX (1216–41)*, ed A. L. Tautu (Vatican City, 1950), no. 132, pp. 178–80.

52. This is a reissue of Lucius III's bull, P. Jaffé, W. Wattenbach, S. Löwenfeld, *Regesta Pontificum Romanorum ab condita ecclesia ad annum post Christi natum 1198*, 2 vols (Leipzig, 1885–8), no. 16463.

53. Hamilton, 'Armenian Church', *Eastern Churches Review* 10 (1978) pp. 70–1.

54. WT XXII.9; p. 1018.

55. K. S. Salibi, 'The Maronite Church in the Middle Ages and its Union with Rome', *Oriens Christianus*, 42 (1958) 92–104.

56. For the later history of the Union, see P. Dib, 'Maronites', *Dictionnaire de Théologie Catholique*, ed. A. Vacant and others, 30 vols (Paris, 1903–50) 10/1: cols, 1–142.

57. S. Runciman, 'The Greeks in Antioch at the time of the Crusades', *Proceedings of the International Congress of Byzantine Studies, Thessalonica, 1953*, vol II (Athens, 1956) pp. 583–91.

58. Hamilton, *Latin Church*, p. 178

59. A. Dondaine, 'Hugues Éthérien et Léon Toscan', *Archives d'histoire doctrinale et littéraire du moyen age* 19 (1952) 67–134; 'Hugues Éthérien et le concile de Constantinople de 1166', *Historisches Jahrbuch* 77 (1958) pp. 473–83.

60. *Propterea libros de processione Spiritus Sancti, quos tam Graece quam Latine scriptos misistis, cum magna suscipimus cordis alacritate, et mox ut in perlegendis illis studii nostri curam potuimus adhibere, vestrum ingenium et facundiam et modum loquendi, plurimum sumus admirati.* ed. E. Martène & U. Durand, *Thesaurus Novus Anecdotorum*, 5 vols (Paris, 1717) 1: 480.

61. This correspondence can be precisely dated to 1176 because Hugo says that he is sending the books by the hand of Prince Reynald. Martène-Durand, 1: 479–81. Reynald's only visit to Constantinople occurred in that year; B. Hamilton, 'Manuel I Comnenus and Baldwin IV of Jerusalem', in J. Chrysostomides, ed., *Kathegetria. Essays presented to Joan Hussey for her 80th birthday* (Camberley, 1988) 360–1.

62. B. Z. Kedar, 'Gerard of Nazareth, a neglected twelfth-century writer in the Latin East', *Dumbarton Oaks Papers*, 37 (1983) pp. 55–77. The passage about Aimery (p. 74) reads: *sedulus vitae monasticae promotor fuit . . . Legem tulit, ne quis in Monte Nigro sine maiore inspectore viveret solitarius.*

63. L. Auvray, ed., *Les Registres de Grégoire IX*, 3 vols (Paris, 1896–1955), no. 2660.

64. *De quattuor in quibus Deus ordinem Praedicatorum insignivit*, a work completed after Stephen's death by Bernard Gui in 1304. Melchior de Ste Marie, 'Carmel. Origine', *Dictionnaire d'histoire et de géographie ecclesiastiques*, vol. 11: col 1073.

65. John Phocas, 'A general description . . . of the Holy Places of Palestine', in J. Wilkinson, *Jerusalem Pilgrimage 1099–1185*, Hakluyt Society, ser. II, no. 167 (London, 1988) pp. 335–6.

66. A. Jotischky, *The Perfection of Solitude: Hermits and Monks in the Crusader States* (Pennsylvania State University Press, 1995) pp.100–138.

67. MS XX, vi; vol. 3: 374.

68. See n. 28 above.

69. *Bullarium Equestris Ordinis S. Iacobi de Spatha*, eds., A. F. Aguado de Cordova, A. A. Aleman et Rosales, I. L. Agurleta (Madrid, 1719) pp. 22–3.

70. CGOH, no. 783; cf. CGOH, no. 799 about the ecclesiastical consequences of this sale.

71. *The Chronicle of the Regions of Henry II and Richard I* [published as *The Chronicle of Benedict of Peterborough*], ed. W. Stubbs, Rolls Series, 49 (I, II) (London, 1867), 2: p. 38; the Pipe Roll for 1178–9, for example, records the presence in England of Robert, an envoy from Manuel Comnenus, and Prince Bohemond of Antioch;

A. A. Vasiliev, 'Manuel Comnenus and Henry Plantagenet', *Byzantinische Zeitschrift* 29 (1929–30) 233–44.

72. M. C. Lyons & D. E. P. Jackson, *Saladin. The Politics of the Holy War* (Cambridge, 1982) 286–91.

73. *Anonymi Rhenani Historia*, c. xlv, *RHC, Historiens Occidentaux*, 5 vols (Paris, 1844–95), 5: p. 521.

74. Deschamps, *Les chateaux des croisés*, 3: pp. 351–7.

75. Cahen, *La Syrie*, pp. 432–3; Lyons & Jackson, *Saladin*, pp. 360, 362.

76. Hamilton, *Latin Church*, p. 48.

77. MS XXI.viii; vol. 3: 412.

78. Cahen, *La Syrie*, pp. 507–9.

79. M. R. Morgan, ed. *La continuation de Guillaume de Tyr (1184–1197), Documents relatifs à l'histoire des croisades publiés par l'Académie des Inscriptions et Belles-Lettres*, 14 (Paris, 1982) pp. 168–70, 177; J. Prawer, 'The "community of Antioch" ', *Crusader Institutions* (Oxford, 1980) pp. 68–76, has no doubt that the patriarch involved in this was Aimery of Limoges.

80. Ruth Morgan argued that the compiler of manuscript d, which she edited, had access to the lost chronicle of Ernoul, or to a manuscript closely related to it, which gives this continuation a special value for the period to 1197; *La continuation*, p. 8. See also M. R. Morgan, *The Chronicle of Ernoul and the Continuations of William of Tyre* (Oxford, 1973).

81. 'Chronique de Terre Sainte', in G. Raynaud, ed., *Les Gestes des Chiprois, Société de l'Orient latin, sér. historique*, vol. 5 (Geneva, 1887) p. 15.

82. Hamilton, *Latin Church*, p. 214–15.

Addenda
p. 287, n. 10, for 'Prince Roger of Antioch' read 'Prince Raymond of Antioch'.

IX

THE LATIN CHURCH IN THE CRUSADER STATES

Before 1095 the permanent Latin presence in the Patriarchates of Jerusalem and Antioch was limited to the Benedictine community of St Mary of the Latins in Jerusalem, founded in *c.* 1070, the nearby convent of St Mary Magdalen, and the adjacent hospital of St John, which were intended to give spiritual direction and pastoral care to pilgrims from the West. They accepted that they were part of a single communion with the Orthodox and therefore did not question, or pose any challenge to the canonical authority of the Orthodox Patriarch of Jerusalem[1]. They had no need to formulate any independent policy in their relations with the non-Chalcedonian Churches, which, in any case, had few direct dealings with Rome in the eleventh century, except for the Armenian Church which had entered into friendly correspondence with Gregory VII[2]. Urban II had no wish to change this, and certainly the establishment of a Latin Church in the Levant was no part of his intention when he launched the First Crusade. Indeed, it is arguable that the foundation of independent Frankish states in the Eastern Mediterranean was not part of his plan either. One of his chief aims, revealed in his letter to the people of Flanders, was to aid the Christians of the East who were being attacked by the Turks[3]. He considered that the legitimate secular authority in the Eastern Mediterranean was the Byzantine Emperor, Alexius I Comnenus, and that the canonical church authorities were the three Orthodox Patriarchs: Nicholas III Grammaticus of Constantinople, John IV, the Oxite, of Antioch, and Symeon II of Jerusalem[4].

---

[1] *Willelmi Tyrensis Archiepiscopi Chronicon*, IX, 18, XVIII, 5, ed. R.B.C. Huygens, Corpus Christianorum, Continuatio Mediaevalis, LXIII, 2 vols (Turnholt, 1986), I, p. 445, II, pp. 815-817.

[2] *Pontificia Commissio ad redigendum codicem iuris canonici orientalis* [henceforth *CICO*], *Fontes*, Series III, I, Acta Pontificum Romanorum a S. Clemente ... ad Coelestinum III (Vatican City, 1943), no. 379, pp. 789-790.

[3] H. Hagenmeyer, *Epistulae et chartae ad historiam primi belli sacri spectantes* (Innsbruck, 1901, reprinted Hildesheim and New York, 1973), no. II, pp. 136-137.

[4] B. Leib, *Rome, Kiev et Byzance à la fin du XIe siècle* (Paris, 1924, reprinted New York, 1968), pp. 119-126.

Reprinted from B. Hamilton, *The Latin Church in the Crusader States* in: *East and West in the Crusader States* (1996), edited by K. Ciggaar, A. Davids, H. Teule, by permission of Peeters Publishers.

When the leaders of the First Crusade reached Constantinople they made an agreement with the Emperor, which was confirmed by oaths in western form, that they would restore to him all the lands which had formerly been part of his Empire and would hold from him any other lands which they might capture[5]. They certainly observed these obligations in Asia Minor, where cities were either restored to Alexius, as Nicea was, or were held from him by the western commanders whom the crusaders appointed, as happened at Comana which was entrusted to Peter of Aulps[6]. In these circumstances the question of appointing Catholic bishops did not arise and the authority of the Patriarch of Constantinople was not challenged.

When the Crusade entered the Patriarchate of Antioch they could not establish communication with John IV because he was living in Antioch city under Turkish rule. But his colleague, Symeon of Jerusalem, left his see when he heard of the Crusade's arrival in Syria, and took refuge in Byzantine Cyprus. He contacted the Crusade leaders, probably in the early months of 1098[7], and was welcomed by the Pope's legate, Adhémar of Le Puy. An encyclical letter was sent in their joint names to all the Christians of the West asking urgently for reinforcements[8]. Adhémar apparently considered it important to emphasize that the expedition had the support of eastern Christian leaders in whose lands it was now operating. Although Jerusalem was the most junior patriarchate in terms of canon law, it enjoyed greater prestige than any of the other Eastern Churches among western Christians in the eleventh century, and it was the Church which the Crusade was seeking to liberate. A further appeal for support was sent in the spring of 1098, the protocol of which deserves attention:

> "The Patriarch of Jerusalem and the Greek and Latin bishops and all the army of the Lord and of the Church [send greeting] to the Church of the West that it may enjoy the fellowship of the Heavenly Jerusalem and have some share in the reward of their endeavours[9]."

[5] Albert of Aix, *Liber Christianae Expeditionis*, II, xvi, RHC Occ., IV, p. 311; Anna Comnena, *Alexiad*, X, 9, ed. B. Leib, 3 vols (Paris, 1937-45), II, p. 226.

[6] *Gesta Francorum*, IV, xi, ed. and trans. R. Hill (London, 1962), p. 25.

[7] "Migravit enim idem patriarcha ab Iherusalem ..., audito adventu et sede Christianorum circa moenia Antiochiae, profectus ad insulam Cypri propter minas Turcorum et importunitatem Sarracenorum." Albert of Aix, *Liber Christianae*, VI, xxxix (see n. 5), IV, p. 489.

[8] Hagenmeyer, *Epistulae* (see n. 3), no. VI, pp. 141-2, dated this letter October 1097, because of the reference it makes to a third victory over the Turks, H. Hagenmeyer, *Chronologie de la Première Croisade* (Paris, 1902), no. 205, p. 106, but this is not consonant with the information given by Albert of Aix, and the reference is probably to the defeat of Duqaq of Damascus on 31 December 1097.

[9] "Ierosolymitanus patriarcha et episcopi tam Graeci quam Latini universaque militia Domini et ecclesiae, sui laboris praemii portionem", Hagenmeyer, *Epistulae*, no. IX, p. 146.

The Patriarch Symeon, who was then living in Cyprus, was writing in the name of the Orthodox hierarchy (there were, after all, no Greek bishops in the crusader army) and associating the Latin bishops on the Crusade with them as a matter of politeness. He concluded the letter:

> "I, the apostolic patriarch, and the bishops and the whole communion of the Orthodox excommunicate those who have taken [crusader] vows, unless they shall come and fulfil them, and we completely exclude them from the communion of the Church. And do you do the same, and let them be denied Christian burial unless they have stayed behind for sufficient cause[10]."

Bishop Adhémar must have agreed to the wording of this encyclical and probably have arranged for its translation into Latin, and it seems clear that he assumed that the Orthodox hierarchies would be maintained in the lands conquered by the crusaders. After Antioch had been captured in June 1098, the crusader leaders sent envoys to ask Alexius to come and take possession[11], and John IV was enthroned once more in his cathedral as "Prince of the Church of Antioch"[12]. To this point the agreement with Byzantium had been honoured and its ecclesiastical consequences had been implemented. But later that summer it became known to the crusaders that Alexius, far from marching to join them as he had undertaken to do, had turned back at Philomelium when he learned that they were in grave danger from the Turks[13]. The crusader princes considered that this dispensed them from their obligations to the Emperor, and thereafter began to found independent states for which they did no homage to him. It then seemed to them desirable to establish a Latin Church in those states.

Bishop Adhémar's death in August 1098 removed the only crusader leader who might have sought to defend the rights of the Orthodox Churches[14]. The change of policy which then took place became evident when the Crusade conquered Jerusalem in July 1099. The Patriarch Symeon had died in Cyprus during the siege of the city[15], and the

---

[10] *Ibid.*, pp. 148-149.

[11] *Gesta Francorum*, X, xxx (see n. 6), p. 72.

[12] "[Franci] Patriarcham ... urbis ... decenter in cathedra sua relocaverunt, et principem Antiochenae Ecclesiae cum omni subjectione et religione praefecerunt." Albert of Aix, *Liber Christianae*, V, i, (see n. 5), IV, p. 433.

[13] The story widely believed among the Franks is that in *Gesta Francorum*, IX, xxvii, (see n. 6), pp. 63-65.

[14] *Ibid.*, X, xxx, p. 74. The best treatment of Bishop Adhémar's role on the crusade is J.A. Brundage, "Adhémar of Puy: The Bishop and his Critics", *Speculum*, 34 (1959), pp. 201-212.

[15] "Nam [ecclesia Hierosolimitana] viduata erat pastore suo, patriarcha, viro sanctissimo, in insula Cypri, tempore obsidionis Iherusalem, ex hac luce subtracto." Albert of Aix, *Liber Christianae*, Vl, xxxix (see n. 5), IV, p. 489; V. Grumel dates Symeon's death June/July 1099, *Traité d'Études byzantines*, 1, *La Chronologie* (Paris, 1958), p. 452.

4

crusader clergy immediately appointed one of their own number, Arnulf of Chocques, the chaplain of Robert of Normandy, as new Patriarch[16]. They do not seem even to have considered consulting the Orthodox clergy of Jerusalem: they were intending to make Jerusalem the capital of an independent Frankish state, and it seemed natural to them to establish the Latin Church there. At Antioch Prince Bohemond, who had made himself independent, was attacked by the Byzantines in 1100 and expelled John the Oxite, presumably because he doubted his loyalty[17]. The Franks regarded the see as vacant and appointed Bernard of Valence, the chaplain of Bishop Adhémar, as first Latin Patriarch. Pope Urban's death in July 1099 was a blow to harmonious relations between the Churches of East and West. His successor, Paschal II, did not question the propriety of appointing Latins to the patriarchal sees, although he was concerned about the calibre of the men appointed[18]. Paschal did not share his predecessor's oecumenical vision, but seems rather to have welcomed the opportunity of extending papal authority in the eastern patriarchates[19].

The Franks at Antioch made no attempt to co-operate with the Orthodox hierarchy, but expelled all the Orthodox bishops and cathedral clergy and replaced them by Latins[20]. The reason for this would seem to have been political rather than religious: the Franks were few, bishops occupied positions of authority in key cities, and the loyalty of the Orthodox was bound to be suspect because for the first ten years of its existence Frankish Antioch was at war with Byzantium[21].

[16] B. Hamilton, *The Latin Church in the Crusader States: The Secular Church* (London, 1980), pp. 12-14.

[17] William of Tyre tactfully records that John "videns ... quod non satis utiliter preesset Grecus Latinis, urbe cedens Constantinopolim abiit", *Willelmi Tyrensis Chronicon*, VI, 23 (see n. 1), I, p. 340. John considered he had been expelled, V. Benechewitch, *Catalogus Codicum Manuscriptorum Graecorum qui in Monasterio Sanctae Catherinae in Monte Sinai asservantur* (St Petersburg, 1911), p. 279.

[18] Paschal's legate, Cardinal Maurice, who reached Syria shortly after John's deposition, made no attempt to restore Orthodox patriarchs in either Antioch or Jerusalem, although he, and the subsequent legates whom Paschal sent to the Latin Kingdom, were concerned about the suitability of the Latin patriarchs of Jerusalem: Hamilton, *Latin Church*, pp. 52-63.

[19] This is clear from Paschal's letter of 4 May 1100 to the Latin clergy and the Crusaders in the East, introducing Cardinal Maurice: "Cui nimirum in praeceptis dedimus, ut Ecclesiae, quam per vos Dominus liberavit ... ordinationi vigilanter immineat; quae si minus canonicis regulis apta repererit, corrigat; et in eisdem cum vestro auxilio, plantanda plantet, aedificanda aedificet." *CICO* (see n. 2), ser. III, I, no. 384, p. 796. There is no mention of the Orthodox clergy.

[20] Michael the Syrian, *Chronicle*, XV, 9, ed. with French trans., J.B. Chabot, 4 vols (Paris, 1899-1924), III, p. 191.

[21] C. Cahen, *La Syrie du nord à l'époque des Croisades et la principauté franque d'Antioche* (Paris, 1940), pp. 227-256.

The Kingdom of Jerusalem was not at war with Byzantium, and although a Catholic hierarchy was established there some Orthodox bishops may have been allowed to remain as coadjutors to their Latin colleagues[22]. The real focus for the Orthodox in the Kingdom were the great monasteries, led by St Sabas, which were treated with considerable respect by the crown[23]. Paschal II in 1111 decreed that all the lands conquered by the crown should be subject to the ecclesiastical jurisdiction of the Patriarch of Jerusalem, thereby in effect making the Patriarchate co-extensive with the Kingdom[24]. This ruling recognised the importance of cooperation between Church and state in a frontier area, even though it led to the ecclesiastical province of Tyre being divided between the two Latin patriarchs, whereas in Orthodox times it had been subject to the Patriarch of Antioch, a situation which William of Tyre deplored because it halved his metropolitan authority[25].

The Franks claimed to be continuing the traditions of the ancient patriarchates of the East, and merely to be changing their rites. They preserved the Orthodox lists of dioceses and translated them into Latin and even Old French[26]. The Antioch list was copied into the *Liber Censuum* of the Roman Church, where its 153 cathedral churches were likened to the miraculous draught of fishes[27]. Yet this should not disguise from us the fact that neither the Franks in the East nor the Papacy wanted to keep the patriarchates unchanged. Some local changes were made. The Franks were distressed to find that Bethlehem was only an Orthodox parish, and Nazareth a simple bishopric, and they translated the Bishopric of Ascalon to Bethlehem and the metropolitan see of Bethsan to Nazareth to give them ecclesiastical status comparable with their spiritual importance[28].

[22] Hamilton, *Latin Church* (see n. 16), pp. 179-84.

[23] *Vie et Pèlerinage de Daniel, Hégoumène russe*, trans. B. de Khitrowo, *Itinéraires Russes en Orient* (Geneva, 1889), cc. 1, 38-39, 97 (describing the honour shown to the Abbot of St Sabas by Baldwin I at the Easter ceremonies), pp. 5, 33-35, 75-83.

[24] "Secundum mutationes temporum", *Willelmi Tyrensis Chronicon*, XI, 28 (see n. 1), I, p. 538.

[25] J.G. Rowe, "The Papacy and the Ecclesiastical Province of Tyre", *Bulletin of the John Rylands Library*, 43 (1960-61), pp. 160-189.

[26] Latin lists, *Itinera Hierosolymitana*, ed. T. Tobler and A. Molinier, Publications de la Société de l'Orient Latin, Série géographique, 1, II (Geneva, 1879-80), I, pp. 323-343; Old French lists, *Itinéraires à Jérusalem*, ed. H. Michelant and G. Raynaud, Publications de la Société de l'Orient Latin, Série Géographique, III (Paris, 1882), pp. 11-19.

[27] *Le Liber Censuum de l'Eglise romaine*, ed. P. Fabre, L. Duchesne and G. Mollat, 3 vols (Paris, 1910-52), I, p. 239.

[28] Bethlehem was made a bishopric in 1108, H.-E. Mayer, *Bistümer, Klöster und Stifte im Königreich Jerusalem*, Monumenta Germaniae Historica, Schriften, 26 (Stuttgart, 1977), pp. 44-80. Nazareth was made an archbishopric between 1125-28, Hamilton, *Latin Church* (see n. 16), p. 67.

6

They also amalgamated the numerous small Orthodox sees into a few larger dioceses, "lest the dignity of a bishop should be made cheap", as James of Vitry explained[29].

But far more radical were the changes which were made to the status of the Patriarchs of Antioch and Jerusalem. Yael Katzir has discussed the situation in Jerusalem, but the same pattern may be observed at Antioch. The popes claimed that the Latin incumbents were the lawful successors to the Orthodox patriarchs[30], yet treated them as though their authority was on a par with that of metropolitans of western provinces. Their appointments were subject to papal scrutiny and they were expected to travel to Rome to receive the pallium after their enthronement; they were required to enforce western canon law in their churches; and ordinary, not extraordinary appeals lay to Rome from their courts[31]. They lacked the autonomy enjoyed by their Orthodox predecessors. This happened partly because the first Latin patriarchs had themselves grown up in the western tradition and accepted the monarchical model of papal authority as normative. But it was also partly the result of papal fears lest the Latins in the East should seek independence of Rome. Such fears were not unrealistic: the dynamic view of papal power associated with the reform movement of the eleventh century was of very recent growth when the Crusader Kingdom was first established. Moreover, it was not unchallenged: for quite long periods in the first quarter of the twelfth century large parts of Western Europe withdrew from the obedience of the Roman pontiffs and in some cases acknowledged antipopes, and even when unity was restored to the Church it proved fragile, as the schism of 1130 showed[32]. In those circumstances an independent Latin patriarch in one of the eastern sees might have been a serious focus of disaffection for Latin Christians in general. In the early years of the Frankish settlement papal anxiety in this regard focussed on Jerusalem. Paschal II accepted the appointment of Bernard of Valence to the see of Antioch, which ranked fourth in the hierarchy of the universal Church, even though he lacked the range of experience which might have been

---

[29] James of Vitry, *Historia Orientalis* (Douai, 1597), p. 98.

[30] For example, by giving them precedence at General Councils, "De dignitate patriarchum" Canon V of the Fourth Lateran Council, ed. G.D. Mansi, *Sacrorum Conciliorum nova et amplissima collectio*, 31 vols (Florence and Venice, 1759-98), XXII, cols 990-991.

[31] Yael Katzir, "The Patriarch of Jerusalem, primate of the Latin Kingdom", in P.W. Edbury, ed., *Crusade and Settlement* (Cardiff, 1984), pp. 169-175.

[32] Antipopes: Clement III (1080-1100); Sylvester IV (1105-11); Gregory VIII (1118-21); Anacletus II (1130-38); Victor IV (1138-39).

considered essential for the holder of such an office[33]. But Paschal sent a constant stream of legates to Jerusalem to supervise the Latin patriarchs[34].

It was therefore ironic that the only serious challenge to papal authority in the Latin East should have come from Ralph of Domfront, second Latin Patriarch of Antioch. He was an ambitious man who was elected to succeed Bernard of Valence, it is said by popular acclaim, in 1135, during the minority of the Princess Constance and also during the papal schism between Innocent II and Anacletus II[35]. Although the Church of Antioch did not have the same degree of popular prestige in Western Christendom as Jerusalem, it nevertheless had great potential power, in that, like Rome, it claimed St Peter as its founder. Ralph did not seek papal ratification of his election, allegedly claiming that the Churches of Rome and Antioch were both the sees of Peter, but that "Antioch was the firstborn and therefore distinguished in its prerogatives"[36]. Ralph was also able to exploit the political situation in Antioch by arranging the marriage of Princess Alice to Raymond on condition that Raymond   *
did homage to him for the principality[37]. Ralph therefore showed a disposition to be like a twelfth-century pope by claiming, as St Peter's successor, to be the supreme authority in temporal as well as spiritual affairs within his patriarchate. Inevitably his ambition made him enemies, and he was finally deposed by a legatine council and imprisoned in a monastery on the Black Mountain[38]. But he succeeded in escaping to Rome where he successfully appealed to the new Pope, Lucius II, against his sentence and was reinstated, although he died before he could return to the Levant[39]. Otto of Freising comments that it was only after this that "Antioch began to be fully subject to the Roman see"[40].

---

[33] He received a pallium, *Willelmi Tyrensis Chronicon*, XIV, 10 (see n. 1), II, p. 642.

[34] Hamilton, *Latin Church* (see n. 16), pp. 52-64.

[35] B. Hamilton, "Ralph of Domfront, Patriarch of Antioch (1135-40)", *Nottingham Medieval Studies*, 28 (1984), pp. 1-21.

[36] "... sedem cui preerat, Antiochenam videlicet, Romanae subiacere dedignabatur, sed ei eandem in omnibus parificare contendebat, dicens utramque Petri esse cathedram eamque quasi primogenite insignem prerogativa." *Willelmi Tyrensis Chronicon*, XV, 13 (see n. 1), II, pp. 692-693.

[37] "Exigitur ergo a domino Raimundo ut, iuramento corporaliter prestito, domino patriarche fidelitatem exhibeat ...", *ibid.*, XIV, 20, II, p. 658.

[38] Hamilton, "Ralph of Domfront" (see n. 35), pp. 9-19.

[39] *Willelmi Tyrensis Chronicon*, XV, 17 (see n. 1), II, p. 699.

[40] Otto of Freising, *Chronica, sive historia de duabus civitatibus*, VII, XXXIII, ed. A. Hofmeister, Monumenta Germaniae Historica, Scriptores rerum germanicarum in usum scholarum (Hanover and Leipzig, 1912), pp. 363-364.

Addendum
For 'marriage of the Princess Alice to Raymond' read 'the marriage of Princess Constance to Raymond.

The Latin patriarchs claimed canonical authority over the Orthodox as well as the western Catholic faithful in their territories. One consequence of this was that all Orthodox cathedrals which were in use were taken over by Latin clergy. This included the Church of the Holy Sepulchre, which in 1099 consisted of the rotunda of the present church, with a walled courtyard containing chapels, including that of Calvary. This complex had been completed under the patronage of the Emperor Constantine IX in 1048 and incorporated the remains of the Constantinian *Anastasis*[41]. The crusaders entrusted the church to a Catholic community of Austin canons, while allowing the Orthodox certain rights there from the beginning. But other Eastern Christian Churches were not at first allowed to have chapels there[42].

Churches of the Orthodox rite, in which the liturgy was performed either in Greek or in Syriac, remained open for the use of the native population, but their clergy were made subject to the Latin hierarchy[43]. The exception to this general rule was the Church of the Holy Nativity at Bethlehem, where the Orthodox clergy were replaced by Catholic Austin Canons, and the basilica was reserved for the Latin rite[44].

That the Latins did not sequester more Orthodox churches at the time of the conquest was partly a matter of chance. When the First Crusade entered the Holy Land in 1099 they found that most of the great shrine-churches, with the exception of the Holy Sepulchre and the Holy Nativity, were in ruins[45]. They therefore embarked on an ambitious building programme. A new Latin cathedral was consecrated at Nazareth before

[41] V.C. Corbo, *Il Santo Sepolcro a Gerusalemme*, Studium Biblicum Franciscanum, Collectio Maior, 29, 3 vols (Jerusalem, 1981-82), I, pp. 139-181, II, pl. 4, 5.

[42] *Le "Liber" de Raymond d'Aguilers*, ed. J.H. and L.L. Hill, Documents relatifs à l'histoire des Croisades publiés par l'Académie des Inscriptions et Belles-Lettres, 9 (Paris, 1969), p. 154; discussion of the events of Easter 1101 which led to the readmission of the Orthodox, Fulcher of Chartres, *Historia Hierosolymitana (1095-1127)*, ed. H. Hagenmeyer (Heidelberg, 1913), Appendix III, pp. 831-837; when Abbot Daniel spent Easter in Jerusalem some years later the Orthodox and Latin liturgies were both celebrated in the Anastasis on Easter Eve, *Vie et Pèlerinage de Daniel*, c. icvii, ed. de Khitrowo (see n. 23), pp. 75-83.

[43] Hamilton, *Latin Church* (see n. 16), pp. 161-166.

[44] It would appear to have been Latinized as early as Christmas 1100, when Baldwin I was crowned there. Fulcher of Chartres, *Historia* (see n. 42), II, 6, pp. 384-385; D. Pringle, *The Churches of the Crusader Kingdom of Jerusalem: A Corpus* (Cambridge, 1993), I, p. 138.

[45] Saewulf, *Certa Relatio de Situ Jerusalem*, c. 21, 22, ed. with Italian trans. by S. de Sandoli, *Itinera Hierosolymitana Crucesignatorum (saec. XII — XIII)*, Pubblicazioni dello Studium Biblicum Franciscanum, Collectio Maior, 24, 3 vols (Jerusalem, 1978-83), II, p. 22.

1109[46], and by 1112 a new group of churches had been built in and around Jerusalem. These were the Church of Our Lady of Sion, traditional site of the Last Supper, Pentecost, and the Dormition of the Virgin[47]; the Church of the Ascension on the Mount of Olives[48]; and the Church of Our Lady of Josaphat, it was believed, of Mary's burial and assumption into heaven[49]. The Dome of the Rock, supposed site of Christ's presentation, had been converted into the Church of the Temple of the Lord[50]. The chief early Latin shrine-churches in other parts of the Kingdom were built at Mount Tabor, in Galilee, site of Christ's Transfiguration[51], and over the tombs of the patriarchs at Hebron[52]. Many of these sites had formerly been in Orthodox hands but were untenanted at the time of the Frankish conquest. The Franks entrusted them to communities of Austin Canons or Benedictines[53].

But the most Orthodox monasteries which were still in use were not disturbed. Many of them were in places which were of no devotional significance to western pilgrims, like St Sabas and St Euthymius in the Judaean Desert[54], but others were on sacred sites, like the monastery of St John the Baptist in the Jordan valley, which was alleged to stand near the place where Christ had been baptized[55]. The Franks made no attempt to Latinize this shrine, perhaps because initially there were not enough

[46] The Latin diocese of Nazareth is first recorded in 1109, Ch. Kohler, "Chartes de l'abbaye de Notre-Dame de la vallée de Josaphat en Terre Sainte (1108-1291)", *Revue de l'Orient Latin*, 7 (1899), no. 2, pp. 113-114.

[47] The Franks first restored the ruined Byzantine church, but soon after rebuilt it in western style, B. Hamilton, "Rebuilding Zion: The Holy Places of Jerusalem in the Twelfth Century", in *Studies in Church History*, ed. D. Baker, 14 (Oxford, 1977), pp. 107-108.

[48] *Ibid.*, p. 109; John of Würzburg, *Descriptio Terrae Sanctae*, c. 14, ed. de Sandoli, *Itinera* (see n. 45), II, pp. 264-266; Theodoric, *De Locis Sanctis*, c. 27, ed. de Sandoli, *Itinera*, II, p. 356.

[49] John of Würzburg, *Descriptio*, c. 17, pp. 272-6; Theodoric, *De Locis Sanctis*, c. 23, pp. 350-2; Hamilton, "Rebuilding Zion" (see n. 47), p. 108.

[50] *Ibid.*, pp. 109-110; John of Würzburg, *Descriptio*, c. 4, pp. 236-44; Theodoric, *De Locis Sanctis*, cc. 14, 15, pp. 334-340.

[51] Prince Tancred was a benefactor of the shrine, *Willelmi Tyrensis Chronicon*, IX, 13 (see n. 1), I, p. 438; a Benedictine community had been established there by 1103, Hamilton, *Latin Church*, p. 60.

[52] The foundation antedates 1119, *Tractatus de Inventione Sanctorum Patriarcharum Abraham, Ysaac et Jacob*, ed. de Sandoli, *Itinera* (see n. 45), I, pp. 331-337; Pringle, *Churches* (see. n. 44), I, pp. 223-239.

[53] Benedictine communities were given charge of Our Lady of Josaphat and Mount Tabor; the other shrines were entrusted to Austin Canons.

[54] Daniel, cc. 38-39 (see n. 23), pp. 33-35.

[55] *Ibid.*, cc. 27, 29, pp. 26-27.

Latin regular clergy to serve it. But in the Kingdom of Jerusalem Orthodox shrines which were not expropriated within the first few years of the conquest remained in Orthodox hands thereafter[56]. In addition to the Orthodox places of worship, there were many churches and monasteries in the Crusader Kingdom belonging to other Eastern Christian Churches. The clergy who accompanied the First Crusade did not know very much about them, as is clear from the letter which the princes wrote to Urban II in 1098 informing him of Bishop Adhémar's death, in which they invited the Pope himself to come and deal with the religious problems which confronted them: "we have beaten the Turks and the heathen, but we do not know how to defeat the heretics, the Greeks and Armenians and Syrian Jacobites[57]."

At that stage they had not met the Maronites. But Frankish practice proved to be more enlightened than this initial reaction might suggest. This was partly due to the absence of a theologically sophisticated Latin clergy on the First Crusade, which was a consequence of Urban II's not intending to set up a Latin Church in the East. Michael the Syrian commented with surprise:

> "The Franks never raised any difficulty about matters of doctrine, or tried to formulate it in one way only for Christians of differing race and language, but ... accepted as a Christian anybody who venerated the cross, without further examination[58]."

They granted non-Byzantine Christians complete religious freedom under the authority of their own ecclesiastical leaders, a continuation of the Islamic system, but freed all Christians from the payment of the religious poll-tax[59].

Armenians, Jacobites and Maronites were allowed to keep their own churches and monasteries, even in cases where these were the shrines of saints whom all Christians venerated, like the house of St James held by the Armenians of Jerusalem[60]. The sole exception was the Church of the Holy Sepulchre from which all eastern-rite Christians were expelled by the Franks in 1099. Although the non-Byzantine Christians were not

---

[56] This may be seen by comparing the information given by Abbot Daniel, see n. 23 above, with that of John Phocas, *Ekphrasis*, in RHC, Historiens Grecs, 2 vols (Paris, 1875-81), I, pp. 527-558. There is not enough information about the other Crusader States to make any definite statement on this point.

[57] Hagenmeyer, *Epistulae* (see n. 3), no. XVI, p. 164.

[58] Michael the Syrian, *Chronicle*, XVI, i (see n. 20), III, p. 222.

[59] Hamilton, *Latin Church* (see n. 16), pp. 189-190.

[60] John of Würzburg, *Descriptio*, c. 15 (see n. 48), p. 268.

readmitted to the main church, when the new Latin cathedral was built provision was made for the Armenians and Jacobites to use the surviving Byzantine chapels along the western side of the southern courtyard[61]. Some arrangement of that kind may have been adopted from the first, but if so it is not documented.

The first generation of Frankish settlers, both clergy and laity, came to understand eastern Christianity in its diversity of confessions through contact with people rather than through theological explanations. This led to a realisation of the very large areas of belief which they had in common, rather than to an emphasis on the small, but acrimonious areas of doctrinal and disciplinary divergence. Good relations between the Franks and the native Christian population were also helped by intermarriage. This occurred at all social levels, including the royal family. Both Baldwin I and Baldwin II of Jerusalem had Armenian consorts; and through the marriages of Baldwin II's children Armenian blood passed into the ruling houses of Antioch and Tripoli. The royal family gave an example of how eastern Christians should be treated with tolerance and respect, and this was widely followed. It was, no doubt, through royal patronage that the Armenian community of Jerusalem were able to build a great cathedral in western architectural style, but designed for Armenian liturgical use, to incorporate the shrine-church of St James. This was constructed towards the end of the First Kingdom by masons trained in the western tradition[62]. The Armenians were in an unusually privileged position among the eastern Christians, because they had a powerful and independent nobility at the time of the Latin conquest and this led to their being treated on terms of social equality by the Franks. But this was not an unmixed blessing, particularly in the northern states, because the Franks coveted and often seized their lands[63]. Yet this did not erode religious goodwill among churchmen on both sides.

The Maronites of Lebanon, despite a few brushes with the counts of Tripoli[64], were well regarded by the Frankish settlers as a whole because

[61] Hamilton, *Latin Church* (see n. 16), pp. 195, 202; Corbo, *Il Santo Sepolcro* (see n. 41), I, pp. 179-181, II, pl. 4.

[62] It is first recorded in *c.* 1170 by John of Würzburg, *Descriptio,* c. 15 (see n. 48), p. 268; K. Hintlian, *History of the Armenians in the Holy Land* (Jerusalem, 1976), pp. 51-56.

[63] B. Hamilton, "The Armenian Church and the Papacy at the time of the Crusades", *Eastern Churches Review,* 10 (1978), p. 63.

[64] They were held responsible, for example, for the death of Count Pons in 1137. *Willelmi Tyrensis Chronicon,* XIV, 23 (see n. 1), II, p. 661.

they were good fighting men[65]; while the Jacobites were treated with considerable respect by the Franks. Except in the case of a few great monasteries, their social position in Frankish territory was fairly modest, but their leaders ruled over a large diaspora in the Islamic world and their friendship was important to the Frankish governments. But Frankish goodwill towards them was not entirely calculated, many Franks seem to have felt a genuine respect for them[66].

Later in the twelfth century, when learned clergy began to be appointed to high office in the Latin Church, good relations already existed between the Franks and the native Christians, and this enabled theological discussions to take place in a friendly atmosphere. The churchman who contributed most to Christian unity in the Crusader States in the twelfth century was Aimery of Limoges, third Latin Patriarch of Antioch. William of Tyre's description of him as "an uneducated man from Limoux whose general behaviour left much to be desired"[67] is quite unfounded and seems to be the product of personal dislike. Aimery was a learned man, interested in theology, who corresponded with Hugo Eteriano, the western theological adviser of the Emperor Manuel, about the Byzantine doctrine of the Holy Spirit[68]. But he also showed a deep sympathy with and understanding for eastern Christian communions, which was perhaps a product of his fifty-three year long tenure of the see of Antioch. In c. 1180 he succeeded in bringing the Maronite Patriarch and some of his followers into full communion with the Latin Church. They renounced their Monotheletism, made a statement of willingness to accept the traditions of the Roman Church where these differed significantly from their own, but preserved their own hierarchy, liturgy, canon law and autonomy[69]. The Maronites formed the first Uniate Church. The process was less tidy than William of Tyre would have us believe, because there was strong opposition on the part of some Maronites and it took a long time to negotiate the changes which the act of union required[70].

---

[65] "... erant ... veri fortes et in armis strenui, nostris in maioribus negociis, que cum hostibus habebant frequentissima, valde utiles ...", *ibid.*, XXII, 9, II, p. 1018.

[66] Hamilton, *Latin Church* (see n. 16), pp. 190-199.

[67] "... Lemovicensem natione, hominem absque litteris et conversationis non satis honeste", *Willelmi Tyrensis Chronicon*, XV, 18 (see n. 1), Il, p. 700.

[68] *Thesaurus Novus Anecdotorum*, ed. E. Martène and U. Durand, 5 vols (Paris, 1717), I, p. 479; P. Magdalino, *The Empire of Manuel I Komnenos, 1143-1180* (Cambridge, 1993), pp. 90-91.

[69] *Willelmi Tyrensis Chronicon*, XXII, 9 (see n. 1), II, pp. 1018-1019.

[70] K.S. Salibi, "The Maronite Church in the Middle Ages and its Union with Rome", *Or. Chr.*, 42 (1958), pp. 92-104.

But Aimery had sought the corporate reunion of the Maronite Church, not partial reunion or individual conversions, and this was in the end achieved[71]. This became the blueprint for Catholic attitudes towards religious unity in the Crusader States.

Aimery of Limoges may also have been responsible for moves towards closer unity with the papacy on the part of the Armenian Church. These were built on older initiatives which had been inconclusive[72]. But in 1184 the Catholicus Gregory IV sent an embassy to Pope Lucius III with a profession of faith. In return the Pope sent Gregory a pallium, signifying that in the eyes of the Pope he was in communion with the Holy See and was the accredited papal representative in his Church. The Pope also sent him a copy of the *Rituale Romanum* which St Nerses of Lampron is said to have translated into Armenian[73]. These negotiations had no immediate sequel because of the dislocation caused by Saladin's campaigns in 1187-92, but they helped to lay the foundations for the official act of union which was achieved under Celestine III in 1198[74].

Although the Jacobites did not come into communion with Rome in the twelfth century, or make any attempt to do so, Aimery of Limoges was on very cordial terms with their Patriarch, Michael the Syrian. A later Jacobite source claims that Aimery allowed him to pontificate in Antioch cathedral, admittedly when it was briefly under Orthodox control again, so that Michael's enthronement there must have taken place on the orders of Prince Bohemond III[75]. Aimery certainly invited Michael to attend the Third Lateran Council, which indicates that he did not regard the Jacobites as heterodox. It was, nevertheless, a remarkable invitation, because had it been accepted it would have meant that two Patriarchs of Antioch would have been present. Michael declined to go, but wrote a treatise against the Cathars, who were on the agenda of the Council, for consideration by the fathers[76]. Aimery of Limoges therefore came near to achieving the unity of all eastern Christians with the Latin

---

[71] P. Dib, "Maronites", *Dictionnaire de Théologie Catholique*, ed. A. Vacant *et al.*, 30 vols (Paris, 1903-50), X (I), cols 1-142.

[72] *CICO* (see n. 2), ser. III, I, no. 379, pp. 789-790.

[73] *Ibid.*, no. 395, pp. 811-813.

[74] In 1189 Clement III reissued the letters of Lucius III for the Catholicus of Armenia, P. Jaffé *et al.*, *Regesta Pontificum Romanorum*, 2 vols (Leipzig, 1881-88), no. 16463; Hamilton, "Armenian Church" (see n. 63), pp. 69-71.

[75] *Anonymi Auctoris Chronicon ad annum Christi 1234 pertinens*, trans. A. Abouna, CSCO, Scriptores Syri, ser. III, 154 (Louvain, 1974), p. 230.

[76] Michael the Syrian, *Chronicle*, XX, 7 (see n. 20), III, pp. 377-378.

Church. He sought corporate reunion on a basis which would allow each Church to keep its own traditions and its own cultural and hierarchical identity.

The Emperor Manuel had tried in the 1170s to unite eastern Christians with the Oecumenical Patriarch[77], but neither his model of Church unity nor that of Aimery of Limoges was able to accommodate both an Orthodox and a Catholic patriarch in the Churches of Antioch and Jerusalem. Manuel restored the Orthodox Patriarch, Athanasius III, at Antioch in 1165. This was an index of his political power at that time[78], but it was extremely unpopular with the Franks, and when Athanasius was killed by an earthquake in 1170 Manuel was unable to replace him because the Franks of Antioch were opposed to this and had full papal support[79]. Similarly, when Manuel tried to introduce an Orthodox patriarch at Jerusalem in Baldwin IV's reign he was unsuccessful. Leontios II came to the Holy Land almost certainly in 1177, but was only given grudging permission by the Franks to celebrate the liturgy privately in the Church of the Holy Sepulchre, assisted only by the Greek canons and behind locked doors. Soon after this he was required to leave the Kingdom, and he never returned[80].

It has not been sufficiently remarked that the chief religious conse-quence of crusader settlement in the Levant was that the Kingdom of Jerusalem became a Catholic country. Not only was the Orthodox hierarchy replaced by Latins, but also the cathedrals in the thirty-one dioceses which the Franks established were either newly built in western style or were adapted for western liturgical use. In the Church of the Holy Sepulchre, the Franks retained the rotunda of Constantine IX but demolished the apse and built a new cathedral adjoining it[81].

The shrine-churches which the Franks had rebuilt were all designed in western style, and their number continued to grow throughout the First Kingdom. Some were very small, like the chapels of the Agony in the

[77] P. Tekeyan, "Controverses Christologiques en Arménie-Cilicie dans la seconde moitié du xiie siècle (1165-98)", *Orientalia Christiana Analecta*, 124 (Rome, 1939), pp. 14-42; Magdalino, *Empire* (see n. 68), pp. 75-76 and n. 189.
[78] Hamilton, *Latin Church* (see n. 16), pp. 175-176; Magdalino, *Empire*, pp. 72-73.
[79] Michael the Syrian, *Chronicle*, XIX, 6 (see n. 20), III, p. 339. See Alexander III's letter to the clergy and people of Antioch, urging them to resist any attempt to make their Church subject to Constantinople, ed. S. Löwenfeld, *Epistolae Pontificum Romanorum Ineditae* (Leipzig, 1885), p. 164; Magdalino, *Empire*, pp. 75-108, with special reference to pp. 75, 103.
[80] R.B. Rose, "The *Vita* of Saint Leontios and its account of his visit to Palestine dur-ing the crusader period", *Proche Orient Chrétien*, 35 (1985), pp. 238-257.
[81] Corbo, *Il Santo Sepolcro* (see n. 41), I, pp. 183-209, II, pl. 6,7.

Garden and the Sleep of the Apostles, which the monks of Our Lady of Josaphat built in Gethsemane to commemorate the events of the Passion[82]; but others were more considerable, like the convent of Bethany, founded by Queen Melisende in 1138 on the site of the house of Mary, Martha and Lazarus[83]; the abbey of Mountjoy, burial place of the prophet Samuel, staffed by Praemonstratensian Canons, and standing at the point where pilgrims from the north gained their first view of Jerusalem[84]; the priory of Quarantena, a dependency of the Holy Sepulchre, situated in the mountains above the Jordan on the site of the Temptation of Christ[85]; the Hospitaller church at Abu Ghosh, which the crusaders supposed was Emmaus[86]; and the shrine of St John in the Woods, the place, it was thought, of John the Baptist's birth, which was administered by Cistercians[87]. Outside the environs of Jerusalem rural Catholic shrines were less common, although there were many churches and chapels of the Latin rite in the cities, and in administrative centres in the countryside. But as the Kingdom became more peaceful in the course of the twelfth century because of the patrols by the Military Orders, the Franks began to build churches in undefended sites, like that of Jacob's Well at Sychar near Nablus, where Jesus had talked to the woman of Samaria[88]. These churches were built in western architectural style so that the Latin liturgy might be performed in them.

Few changes were made in the Western rite by the Frankish settlers: some eastern saints, notably the early bishops of Jerusalem and Antioch, were incorporated in the church calendars[89]; and in the Easter Liturgy of the Church of the Holy Sepulchre the ceremony of the new fire replaced

---

[82] Theodoric, *De Locis Sanctis*, c. 24 (see n. 48), II, p. 352.

[83] *Willelmi Tyrensis Chronicon*, XV, 26 (see n. 1), II, pp. 709-10; John of Würzburg, *Descriptio*, c. 6, Theodoric, *De Locis Sanctis*, c. 28 (see n. 48), ll, pp. 246, 358; S.J. Saller, *Excavations at Bethany (1949-1953)*, Publications of the Studium Biblicum Franciscanum, 12 (Jerusalem, 1957); Pringle, *Churches* (see n. 44), I, pp. 122-137.

[84] Hamilton, *Latin Church* (see n. 16), p. 94; Theodoric, *De Locis Sanctis*, c. 29 (see n. 48), ll, pp. 358-360; Pringle, "Jabal Quruntul", *Churches* (see n. 44), l, pp. 252-258.

[85] H.-E. Mayer, "Sankt Samuel auf dem Freudenberge und sein Besitz nach einem unbekannten Diplom König Balduins V", *Quellen und Forschungen aus italienischen Archiven und Bibliotheken*, 44 (1964), pp. 35-71.

[86] Hamilton, *Latin Church*, pp. 105-106; L.-H. Vincent and F. M. Abel, *Emmaüs, sa basilique et son histoire* (Paris, 1932); Pringle, *Churches* (see n. 44), I, pp. 7-17.

[87] Theodoric, *De Locis Sanctis*, c. 38 (see n. 48), ll, p. 368; D. Pringle, "Cistercian Houses in the Kingdom of Jerusalem", in *The Second Crusade and the Cistercians*, M. Gervers ed. (New York, 1992), pp. 185-188, 191-192; Pringle, *Churches*, I, pp. 38-47.

[88] Theodoric, *De Locis Sanctis*, c. 42, II, pp. 372-374; Pringle, *Churches*, I, pp. 258-264.

[89] F.M. Wormald, "Liturgical Notes", in *Miniature Painting in the Latin Kingdom of Jerusalem*, ed. H. Buchthal (Oxford, 1957), pp. 107-134.

IX

16

the traditional western practice of kindling fire in the church courtyard to light the Paschal candle[90]. But the liturgy in the main remained western, and in that, as in other ways, the Papacy was concerned that the churches of the Crusader Kingdom should conform to the Roman tradition[91].

During the twelfth century the Holy Land remained the greatest focus of pilgrimage in the entire Christian world. Western pilgrims came there in greater numbers than ever before once the ports were in Christian hands and the journey could be made swiftly in Christian shipping[92], but there may also have been an increase in eastern-rite pilgrims to the Kingdom because it had Christian rulers. The Catholic authorities did not discriminate against any eastern Christian visitors, whether they were Orthodox or non-Chalcedonian. The churches of their own rite were open and they might worship freely in them while no barrier was placed in their way if they wished to make their private devotions in shrines administered by the Latins. For example, the Russian Princess, Euphrosyne of Polotsk, who died in Jerusalem in 1173, was allowed to hang a golden votive lamp in the sanctuary of the Holy Sepulchre itself[93]. The Orthodox were more privileged than other eastern Christians because in the Churches of the Holy Sepulchre and Our Lady of Josaphat the Orthodox liturgy was celebrated regularly at side altars[94]. Furthermore, in the 1170s the Franks of Jerusalem who valued the protection of the Emperor Manuel allowed him to resume what had been the traditional role of his predecessors in the time of the Fatimid Caliphs, that of protector of Orthodox Christians in the Holy Land[95]. Manuel not only endowed and in some cases rebuilt the Orthodox

[90] A.J. MacGregor, *Fire and Light in the Western Church*, Alcuin Club Collection, 71 (Collegeville, 1992), pp. 154-247; Ch. Kohler, "Un Rituel et un Bréviaire du Saint Sépulcre de Jérusalem (xiie-xiiie siècle)", *Revue de l'Orient Latin*, VIII (1900-1901), p. 421.

[91] Paschal II ordered the Benedictines of Latina: "Psalmorum etiam modulatio sic apud vos teneatur, sicut Romana psallat ecclesia", "Papst-Kaiser und Normannenurkunden aus Unteritalien", ed. W. Holtzmann, no. 1, *Quellen und Forschungen aus italienischen Archiven und Bibliotheken*, 35 (1955), p. 51.

[92] "Thirteenth-century data confirm that the majority of ships bound for the Holy Land left the West in the last weeks of March and early April. With an average passage eastwards taking about four to six weeks, ships would not arrive in Acre before mid to late April." J.H. Pryor, *Geography, Technology and War* (Cambridge, 1988), p. 3.

[93] B. de Khitrowo, "Pèlerinage en Palestine de l'abbesse Euphrosine, princesse de Polotsk", *Revue de l'Orient Latin*, III (1895), p. 33.

[94] Hamilton, *Latin Church* (see n. 16), p. 171.

[95] S. Runciman, "The Byzantine 'Protectorate' in the Holy Land in the XIth Century", *Byzantion*, 18 (1948), pp. 207-215; S. Runciman, "The Visit of King Amalric I to Constantinople in 1171", in *Outremer: Studies in the History of the Crusading Kingdom of Jerusalem Presented to Joshua Prawer*, ed. B.Z. Kedar, H.-E. Mayer and R.C. Smail (Jerusalem, 1982), pp. 153-158; B. Hamilton, "Manuel I Comnenus and Baldwin IV of Jerusalem", in *Kathegetria: Essays presented to Joan Hussey for her 80th birthday*, J. Chrysostomides ed. (Camberley, 1988), pp. 353-375.

monasteries of Judaea[96], the Franks also allowed him to commission Byzantine craftsmen to embellish the Holy Places with mosaics executed in accordance with Orthodox iconography. The shrine of the Anastasis, at the centre of the Christian faith in the Crusader Kingdom, was embellished with Byzantine mosaics[97]; while in the Latin cathedral of Bethlehem a series of monumental mosaics of the oecumenical councils was commissioned by Manuel, whose panel portrait was hung in the sanctuary. These mosaics were remarkable because they set out the Orthodox and not the Latin tradition of conciliar teaching[98].

Yet despite these concessions to eastern spirituality the majority of important shrines in the Holy Land during the twelfth century were built in the western tradition and were served by Catholic clergy who performed the Latin liturgy. Eastern-rite pilgrims might perform their private devotions in the Catholic shrine-churches, but if they wished to assist at the liturgy in their own rite then they had to attend their own churches. Only the Catholic liturgy was performed with solemnity in the shrine-churches. This reached its climax in Holy Week, which began early on Palm Sunday, when the Latin patriarch and his entourage, bearing the Holy Cross in its jewelled reliquary, rode out to Bethany while it was still dark, and at dawn descended the Mount of Olives to be greeted by the faithful, led by the Catholic monks and canons of Jerusalem, who were holding branches of palm and olive blessed in the Garden of Gethsemane. The whole crowd then led the patriarch and the cross, symbolizing Christ, through the Golden Gate into the Temple precinct. Holy Week continued in that way. On Maundy Thursday the patriarch led the faithful to the Church of Mount Sion where the Last Supper had been celebrated; on Good Friday, before dawn, he and his canons led the faithful barefoot up the stairs to the Calvary chapel in the Holy Sepulchre to venerate the reliquary of the Holy Cross on the spot where that Cross, they believed, had once stood; and there, at the hour of the Crucifixion, the patriarch celebrated the Good Friday Liturgy. On Holy Saturday the patriarch sat enthroned behind the high altar, facing down the choir of the Holy Sepulchre towards the Anastasis, flanked by

---

[96] For a general survey of Orthodox monasticism in Judaea in Manuel's reign, John Phokas, *Ekphrasis*, c. xvi-xxvi (see n. 56), I, pp. 545-552, Manuel's intervention is commented on *ibid.*, c. xxii, xxvii, pp. 549, 553.

[97] *Ibid.*, c. xiv, p. 541.

[98] *Ibid.*, c. xxvii, pp. 553-554; H. Stern, "Les représentations des Conciles dans l'Église de la Nativité à Bethléem", *Byzantion*, 11 (1936), pp. 101-152; 13 (1938), pp. 415-459; L.-A. Hunt, "Art and Colonialism: The Mosaics of the Church of the Nativity in Bethlehem (1169) and the Problem of 'Crusader Art', *Dumbarton Oaks Papers*, 45 (1991), pp. 69-85; Pringle, *Churches* (see n. 44), I, pp. 141-146.

his canons, while the prophecies were sung. A procession was formed of four eminent pilgrims, often laymen, preceded by acolytes, all of them holding unlighted tapers and walking barefoot, who brought the Holy Cross from its chapel. Proceeding down the choir they circled the shrine of the Anastasis, kneeling each time they passed the entrance to see whether the holy fire had kindled. In some years this process had to be repeated six or seven times before a light appeared. When it did, the cross-bearer entered the Sepulchre and lit his candle from that fire, and took the light to the patriarch, from whose candle it gradually spread throughout the congregation, a symbol of the Light of the World. Then the patriarch continued with the Latin Easter Liturgy[99].

Eastern Christians who came to the Holy land during the time of Frankish rule were not uniformly hostile to the Latins. The more thoughtful among them found admirable features in Catholic spirituality. St Nerses of Lampron, Armenian Archbishop of Tarsus, for example, was particularly impressed by the daily recitation of the Divine Office in the Catholic cathedrals of the Crusader States, by the good order which the Franks observed in their public worship, and by the impressive range of charitable works which the Latin clergy undertook[100]. But it is noteworthy that those who viewed Catholicism sympathetically were not Byzantine Christians, who tended to be critical. John Phocas, who visited the Holy Land shortly before the invasion of Saladin, says little about the Latins until near the end of his short treatise, when he relates how the Catholic Bishop "intruded" at Lydda and had tried to open the tomb of St George:

> "But when he was trying to open it, fire blazed out of the tomb, causing one of those who sought to lay hands on it to be severely burned and instantaneously killing another[101]."

The First Kingdom came to an end in 1187 as a result of the Frankish defeat at Hattin. Although they later regained control of the coast of Palestine and Syria, the Franks did not permanently recover most of the Holy Places, and their presence in them was confined to a few priests who were allowed to say Mass for western pilgrims[102]. Even when the Franks regained temporary control of some of the holy places in 1229 as

---

[99] Kohler, "Un Rituel" (see n. 90), pp. 412-424.
[100] St Nerses of Lampron, Réflections sur les Institutions de l'Eglise, RHC, Historiens Arméniens, 2 vols (Paris, 1869-1906), I, p. 574.
[101] John Phocas, Ekphrasis, c. xxix (see n. 56), I, p. 557.
[102] This was arranged with Saladin by Hubert Walter, Bishop of Salisbury, Itinerarium Regis Ricardi, VI, 34, ed. W. Stubbs, Rerum Brittannicarum Medii Aevi Scriptores, Rolls Series, 99 vols (London, 1858-1911), 38 (I) (1864), p. 438.

IX

LATIN CHURCH IN THE CRUSADER STATES   19

a result of Frederick II's treaty with al-Kamil[103], their custodianship was half-hearted. Nazareth, for example, was in Christian hands from 1229-1265, yet as Archbishop Henry sadly recorded in 1251:

> "the Holy Places of the Kingdom, and specially Nazareth, have been neglected and left without clergy, and have suffered grave and irreparable damage on both a spiritual and a material level through the neglect and indeed the total absence of canons, for so far scarcely anyone ... could be found who was prepared to devote his life there to the service of God[104]."

The holy places of Jerusalem experienced similar problems: most of the Catholic clergy refused to leave Acre to come to live there, and only a few canons took over the Holy Sepulchre, which became a kind of priory of its own daughter-house, the Holy Sepulchre at Acre[105]. The shrine-churches of the Holy Land in the thirteenth century either fell into ruins once more and were not rebuilt, or they returned to the control of eastern-rite Christians who had held them before the First Crusade. The reasons for this decline in Latin zeal for the Holy Places are complex and cannot be treated in this paper. The Latins in their coastal cities continued to maintain a titular hierarchy for the sees they no longer ruled, and a full complement of religious communities for the shrines they no longer administered[106]. But there were few shrines of any importance in the areas which were securely under Frankish control, with the exception of Our Lady of Tortosa[107], and Mount Carmel[108]. The Orthodox who lived in the Frankish states were more resentful of Catholic dominance than they had been in the twelfth century, because their own hierarchy had been restored in the lands under Muslim rule[109]. With the Mameluke conquests of 1291 this ceased to be a problem. The Latin political presence ended, and the Catholic religious presence was institutionalized a generation later by the establishment of the Franciscan *Custodia Terrae Sanctae* to minister to Catholic pilgrims visiting the Holy Places[110].

[103] J.-L. Huillard-Bréholles, *Historia Diplomatica Friderici Secundi*, 12 vols (Paris, 1852-61), III, pp. 86-90.
[104] *Les Registres d'Innocent IV*, ed. E. Berger, 4 vols (Paris 1884-1921), no. 5538.
[105] Gerold of Lausanne, Patriarch 1225-39, did not return to Jerusalem, but appointed the Dean of Jaffa and the Abbot of the Mount of Olives as his vicars there, *Le Cartulaire du Chapitre du Saint-Sépulcre de Jérusalem*, no. 184., ed. G. Bresc-Bautier, Documents relatifs à l'histoire des Croisades publiés par l'Académie des Inscriptions et Belles-Lettres, XV (Paris, 1984), pp. 341-342.
[106] Hamilton, *Latin Church* (see n. 16), pp. 243-281.
[107] Jean de Joinville, *Vie de S. Louis*, c. cxviii, ed. N. de Wailly (Paris, 1868), p. 214.
[108] The best treatment of Carmel in the time of Crusader rule is the unpublished doctoral thesis of A. Jotischky, *Hermits and Eremitical Monasticism in the Holy Land, 1095-1291* (Yale University, 1991).
[109] *Les Lettres de Jacques de Vitry*, no. 2, lines 35-55, ed. R.B.C. Huygens (Leiden, 1960), pp. 84-85; James of Vitry, *Historia Orientalis* (see n. 29), c. 75, pp. 139-144.
[110] L. Lemmens, *Die Franziskaner im Heilige Lande*, I, *Die Franziskaner auf dem Sion (1335-1552)* (Münster, 1925²).

The *status quo ante* of 1090 had in appearance been restored, and it is therefore pertinent to ask whether the Latin Kingdom of Jerusalem during its two centuries of existence had made any significant contribution to the development of the universal Church. In one regard that contribution was clearly negative. Relations with the Orthodox had been damaged by the latinization of the hierarchy in the Crusader States, by the demotion of the Orthodox liturgy to a minor place in the great shrine-churches, and by the subordination of the Latin patriarchs, who claimed to be the successors of the Orthodox, to the authority of the pope. It was arguably this which confirmed the Orthodox in their mistrust of the way in which popes in the twelfth and thirteenth centuries understood the Petrine office. But in the case of the non-Byzantine eastern Christians the crusader settlement had a more positive outcome. For in the Kingdom of Jerusalem Catholic churchmen had come into contact for the first time with large groups of separated Christians and had had to consider how best to establish unity with them. The concept of uniate churches which respected the traditions and autonomy of the eastern communities was a fruitful one, even though it was arguably handled with a lack of sensitivity in the early modern period.

It remains to consider the impact of the crusader occupation of Jerusalem on the Catholic Church of the West. The fact that western pilgrims had far easier access to the Holy Places in the twelfth century than at any other time, and that when they came to the Crusader Kingdom in great numbers they found the familiar Catholic liturgy being performed in all the important shrines, profoundly influenced, I would maintain, the way in which western spirituality developed. This visually powerful public liturgy, which showed forth the central events of the Christian faith in the places where they had first happened, arguably led to the growth of a western piety which was far more Christocentric and affective than it had previously been. In that sense the words of the unknown author of the *Gesta Francorum*, writing about the religious motivation of those who went on the First Crusade, had proved predictive:

> "the Franks hearing [Urban II's appeal] straightway began to sew the cross on the right shoulders of their garments, saying that they would all with one accord follow in the footsteps of Christ, by whom they had been redeemed from the power of hell[111]."

* By the time Acre fell in 1291 that desire to imitate Christ in his early life had become a central strand in the piety of the Western Church.

---

[111] *Gesta Francorum* (see n. 6), I, i, p. 2.

Addendum
For 'imitate Christ in his early life' read 'imitate Christ in his earthly life'.

X

A MEDIEVAL URBAN CHURCH: THE CASE OF THE CRUSADER STATES

ALTHOUGH the great majority of first-generation western settlers in the crusader states must have come from rural areas, most of them lived in towns when they reached the levant. This presented no problem: there was plenty of space in the towns of Outremer, for the Franks either slaughtered their Moslem inhabitants[1] or, more commonly, expelled them.[2] Initially, therefore, the towns of Frankish Syria were inhabited only by Franks and native Christians. The crusaders did not pursue a similar policy in the countryside because they were conscious of the need to keep an adequate labour-force. Native Christian peasants presented no problem in any case, while the Moslem peasants, who were probably the more numerous, were left undisturbed by their new rulers.[3]

Western forms of land tenure were introduced in Syria by the crusaders, but manorialism was not. The new Frankish landlords had very few demesne lands, and normally lived from the dues which their peasants paid them, which were usually a percentage of the crops.[4] Some of the Frankish lords lived in cities, but others lived in castles around which small townships often grew up. The only other forms of primary Frankish settlement outside the towns were a few fortified administrative centres and a few fortified churches and

This paper is a report on work in progress on a book which I am writing on the Latin church in the crusader states. In it I intend to substantiate more fully some of the controversial generalisations I have made here, which cannot be more fully treated in an article of this length.

[1] At Antioch in 1098, Jerusalem in 1099, Caesaraea in 1101.

[2] For example at Arsuf in 1101, Acre in 1104.

[3] In 1184, for example, most of the villages between Toron and Acre were inhabited by Moslem peasants. [*The Travels of*] *Ibn Jubayr*, [trans R. J. C. Broadhurst] (London 1952) pp 316–17.

[4] Some examples of fortified Frankish manor houses dating from the twelfth century have been discovered. Their function is not clear. Possibly they were collecting centres for Frankish landlords. M. Benvenisti, *The Crusaders in the Holy Land* (Jerusalem 1970), pp 233–45. On the rural organisation of Frankish Syria see J. Riley-Smith, *The Feudal Nobility and the Kingdom of Jerusalem, 1174–1277* (London 1973) cap 3, 'The Domain in the Countryside', pp 40–61.

monasteries which served important shrines.[5] Only slowly were Franks persuaded to settle in villages under the patronage of the church or of the crown, and such settlements were rare: less than a dozen of them are known, and their inhabitants were all Franks.[6]

The crusaders were very tolerant of the religion of their native subjects. Moslems were allowed the free practice of their faith, and as the twelfth century wore on were even permitted to open mosques in some of the cities from which they had at first been expelled.[7] Few attempts were made to convert them to Christianity,[8] although there were some Moslems who voluntarily became Christians.[9]

Except in Jerusalem, where exotic sects like the Saint Thomas's Christians and the Ethiopian Copts were found,[10] the native Christian population of the crusader states belonged mainly to four confessions. Armenians and Syrian Jacobites were found in large numbers in Edessa and Antioch, with a few congregations in some of the cities of the south; while the Maronites formed a close-knit community in the mountains of the county of Tripoli. In the view of the western church members of all three of these communions were heretics; but, to the surprise of some of the native Christian prelates, the crusaders made no attempt to force these dissident groups into union with the Roman see, but allowed them to keep their property and granted them complete religious freedom.[11]

---

[5] The *casale* of Saint Gilles to the north of Jerusalem is an example of a rural administrative centre; the mount Thabor monastery in Galilee and the convent of Bethany in Judaea are examples of fortified shrines.

[6] Darum was founded as a royal Frankish village by Amalric I, W[illiam of] T[yre, *Historia rerum in partibus transmarinis gestarum*,] bk 20 cap 19, *RHC Occ* I, p 975; Beth-Gibelin was a Frankish village founded by the Hospitallers in 1168, *CGOH* p 399.

[7] There were mosques at Acre and Tyre in 1184, Ibn Jubayr pp 318, 321.

[8] An exception was the Praemonstratensian house of Saint Habacuc at Ramleh whose first abbot, Amalric, was commissioned by Innocent II to preach to the pagans in the holy land, N. Backmund, *Monasticon Praemonstratense*, (Straubing 1949–   ) I, pp 397–9.

[9] For example, Abu 'l-Durr of the Mahgrib who became a Christian monk in Syria, Ibn Jubayr p 323. He seems to have been motivated by religious conviction, but many Moslem converts were deserters and, even at the time, Christians were sceptical about their sincerity. *Itinerarium Peregrinorum et Gesta Regis Ricardi auctore ut videtur Ricardo, canonico S. Trinitatis Londonensis*, bk 3 cap 16, ed W. Stubbs, *Chronicles and Memorials of the Reign of Richard I*, I, RS 38, I (1864) p 230.

[10] *Description of the Holy Land by John of Würzburg, A.D. 1160–1170*, trans C. W. Wilson, PPTS 14 (1890) p 69.

[11] 'The Franks never raised any difficulties about matters of faith, nor [sought] to reach a single definition [of belief] among the Christians of different races. . . . They accepted as a Christian anybody who venerated the Cross, without [further] . . . examination.' [*Chronique de*] M[ichel le] S[yrien, *patriarche jacobite d'Antioche (1166–99)*,] bk 16 cap 1, [ed with French translation J. B.] Chabot, 4 vols (Paris 1899–1924) 3, p 222.

A medieval urban church

The fourth group of native Christians were the Orthodox, who in the sources are sometimes called Greeks and sometimes Syrians, depending on which liturgical language they used.[12] The majority of the native Christians in the kingdom of Jerusalem were of this faith and there were substantial groups of them also in the cities of the northern states. In the eyes of the crusaders the Orthodox formed part of the one, holy, catholic church to which they themselves belonged. Unlike the separated eastern Christians, the Orthodox were required by the Franks to recognise the authority of the holy see, but if they did so they were allowed to keep their own churches and monasteries and to use their own rites. Indeed, they were allowed considerable latitude in matters of usage and doctrine when those diverged from western norms.[13] However, one consequence of the crusaders' belief in the unity of Catholics and Orthodox was that only one bishop could exercise authority over both communities in each diocese. In places where Orthodox bishops held office the crusaders initially expelled them and replaced them by Latins.[14] But the need to provide for the spiritual oversight of Orthodox clergy led the Franks during the twelfth century to modify their ecclesiastical system and to appoint Orthodox co-adjutor bishops to assist the Latin bishops. This practice had certainly been adopted by Amalric I's reign[15] and it may well have come into being at an earlier date, for when ratifying a similar settlement for the church of Cyprus in 1223, Honorius III affirmed that it was modelled on the traditional practice

[12] When the sources speak of Greeks they clearly mean Orthodox. Syrian is an imprecise term which could mean either Orthodox or Jacobite unless it is qualified – for example, 'Suriens de la loy de Grèce', *Chronique du Templier de Tyr (1242–1309)*, *Les Gestes des Chiprois*, ed G. Raynaud, *Publications de la Société de l'Orient Latin, série historique* 5 (Geneva 1887) pp 151, 239. From the context it is clear that most references to Syrians in the kingdom of Jerusalem relate to Orthodox. This has been convincingly argued by G. Every, 'Syrian Christians in Palestine in the early Middle Ages', *Eastern Churches Quarterly* 6 (Ramsgate 1945–6) pp 363–72.

[13] For example, at a time when feelings ran high between Rome and Constantinople on the subject of the *Filioque* clause, Greek artists commissioned by the Byzantine emperor Manuel I executed a mosaic illustrating the council of Constantinople of 381 in the Latin cathedral of Bethlehem in which belief in the Holy Spirit is formulated in the Orthodox way without the addition of the *Filioque*. H. Stern, 'Les répresentations des Conciles dans l'Église de la Nativité à Bethléem', *B* 11 (1936) pp 101–54; 13 (1938) pp 415–59; text of the mosaic *ibid* 13, p 421, see also p 437.

[14] This was the situation in north Syria, *MS* bk 14 cap 9, Chabot 3, p 191. There is no information known to me about initial crusader treatment of Orthodox bishops in the patriarchate of Jerusalem.

[15] A document of 1173 mentions an Orthodox 'archbishop of all the Syrians and Greeks living in Gaza and Jabin' who was in communion with the Latin church. Gaza and Jabin were in the Latin diocese of Hebron. *CGOH*, p 443.

of the kingdom of Jerusalem.[16] As a result of this modification the Orthodox in the crusader states came to form a virtually self-governing community under the authority of Latin bishops.

Therefore, the Latin church which the crusaders established in their territories ministered solely to western settlers, who formed only a fraction of the total population. At the head of the Latin establishment were the patriarchs of Antioch and Jerusalem and they were assisted by a varying number of bishops of whom, at the period of maximum Frankish territorial expansion, there were thirty.[17] Each bishop had his own household officials, and was assisted by an archdeacon who was responsible for the judicial and administrative business of the see. Each Latin cathedral was administered by a dean and chapter of canons, who were sometimes regulars, but more often seculars, and whose numbers varied from twelve to eighteen. The diocesan structure or Frankish Syria resembled that of western Europe and compared favourably with it: there were, for example, fourteen dioceses in the twelfth-century kingdom of Jerusalem and only seventeen in the far larger Angevin kingdom of England. On a parish level, however, there was no parity between the Syrian and western churches.

In the twelfth century there was normally one Latin parish in each crusader town. In towns which were episcopal sees the cathedral fulfilled this function, but in other towns a church of the Latin rite was built and given parish status.[18] Only in cases where the town grew beyond the walls was a new parish set up to serve the *faubourg*.[19] Most Frankish castles had chapels, and chaplains were appointed by the castellans,[20] but such chapels did not usually enjoy parochial rights.

[16] '. . . quatuor . . . episcopi graeci, qui de consensu nostro . . . semper remanebunt in Cypro, oboedientes erunt Romanae Ecclesiae et archiepiscopo et episcopis Latinis, secundum consuetudinem regni Hierosolymitani.' *Pontificia Commissio ad redigendum codicem iuris canonici Orientalis, Fontes*, 3 series, 3, ed A. L. Tautu, *Acta Honorii III et Gregorii IX* (Vatican City 1950) pp 144–8, no 108.

[17] Patriarchate of Antioch, Latin sees at Antioch, Mamistra, Tarsus, Edessa, Coricium, Hierapolis, Apamea, Marasch, Keiçoun, Artah, Raphaniah, Laodicea, Tortosa, Tripoli, Biblos, Jabala. Patriarchate of Jerusalem, Latin sees at Jerusalem, Tyre, Petra, Nazareth, Caesaraea, Bethlehem, Hebron, Lydda, Sebaste, Tiberias, Banias, Acre, Sidon, Beirut.

[18] For example, Saint Peter's, Jaffa, [*Cartulaire de l'Église du St-Sépulcre de Jérusalem*, ed E.] de Rozière, *Collection des documents inédits sur l'histoire de France*, 1 series, 5 (Paris 1849) pp 15–17, no 14; Saint Paul's, Ascalon, WT bk 17 cap 30, *RHC Occ* 1, p 812.

[19] For example, Saint Nicholas, built to serve the *faubourg* of Jaffa, de Rozière, pp 289–90, no 161.

[20] See Baldwin IV's letter of appointment of William Lovell as chaplain of the royal castle of Jaffa, [H.-F.] Delaborde, [*Chartes de la Terre Sainte provenant de l'Abbaye de Notre-Dame de Josaphat*], BEFAR 19 (1880) pp 85–6, no 38.

A medieval urban church

If a township grew up around the castle a separate church was customarily built to serve the Frankish inhabitants.[21] The few Frankish villages had their own parish churches[22] and there were a few other rural churches of the Latin rite in important administrative centres.[23] But, overall, rural parishes were exceptional in Outremer and town parishes not numerous, so that Latin bishops had comparatively few subordinate clergy.

The Latin clergy drew their income from various sources of which the most important was the tithe payable by all Frankish landowners, but not levied on lands owned by eastern-rite Christians before the fourth Lateran council.[24] Bishops and chapters also took over any endowments which had formerly belonged to Orthodox dioceses,[25] while the churches of Jerusalem, Bethlehem and Nazareth, because of the esteem in which they were held, received landed endowments from the faithful in Outremer and throughout the west.[26] In marked contrast to western Europe, laymen in the crusader states in the twelfth century did not own tithes,[27] although some of them attempted to evade payment of tithe by nominally conveyancing land to eastern Christians who were not liable to pay tithe.[28]

The few Latin clergy of Outremer should therefore have been

[21] For example Nostre-Dame du Bourg in the Hospitaller castle of Krak des Chevaliers, J. Delaville Le Roulx, 'Inventaire des pièces de Terre Sainte de l'Ordre de l'Hôpital', R[evue de l'] O[rient] L[atin] 3 (Paris 1895) p 87, no 267.

[22] For example those built by the canons of the Holy Sepulchre in villages which they founded, de Rozière, pp 233–8, no 128.

[23] For example the church cum iure parrochiali in the royal casale of Saint Gilles, de Rozière, pp 258–60, no 142.

[24] The consequences of this ruling are explained in a letter of Innocent IV to the abbot of Sainte Margarite de Agros, in the archdiocese of Nicosia, L. de Mas Latrie, Histoire de l'Ile de Chypre sous le règne des princes de la maison de Lusignan, 3 vols (Paris 1852–61) 3 pp 643–4.

[25] For example, in 1140 the prior of the Holy Sepulchre successfully laid claim to property at Antioch which had belonged to his cathedral temporibus antiquorum Grecorum, de Rozière pp 178–80, no 90.

[26] For example, Eugenius III's confirmation of the lands of the Holy Sepulchre, de Rozière pp 36–41, no 23; Gregory IX's confirmation of the lands of the church of Bethlehem, [P.] Riant, [Études sur l'Église de Bethléem], 2 vols (Genoa 1889, Paris 1896) 1, pp 140–7, no 11; and documents relating to the property of the church of Nazareth in Italy, Società di Storia Patria per la Puglia, Codice diplomatico Barese, 18 vols (Bari 1897–1950) 8, pp 123–4 no 85, pp 155–6 no 110, p 170 no 125, pp 178–9 no 134, p 210 no 164, pp 244–5 no 190, pp 342–3 no 269, pp 337–8 no 267, pp 343–4 no 270, pp 346–7 no 273, pp 359–60 no 279, pp 360–1 no 280.

[27] [G.] Constable, [Monastic Tithes from their origins to the Twelfth Century] (Cambridge 1964) p 85, n 2.

[28] [Les Régistres de Grégoire IX, ed L.] Auvray, 3 vols, BEFAR, 2 series (Paris 1896–1955) no 4474.

affluent and episcopal authority should have been strong. This was not so, because the Frankish secular clergy had to share their resources and their authority with other groups of western churchmen. First there were the monks. The chief shrines of the holy land, which were the official *raison d'être* of the crusading movement, were entrusted to communities of monks and nuns who built and served churches on those sites. In some ways they were of help to the secular clergy, for they ministered to the large, but seasonal, influx of western pilgrims who came to Syria each year, but in other ways they proved something of a mixed blessing to their secular colleagues. For these communities received endowments throughout the crusader states and founded priories in some of the cities to act as administrative centres for their lands.[29] The mother houses and each of their priories had their own chapels which, while not enjoying parochial status, tended to attract some Franks away from their parish churches. The secular clergy were particularly concerned when their parishioners were buried in monastic churches and left legacies to those communities which would otherwise have been made to their parish churches.[30] Conflicts also arose at times between monks and bishops about the appointment of priests to rural parishes in monastic estates, but since such parishes were few those disputes were rare.[31] More serious were monastic exemptions from payment of tithe. In 1103, for example, pope Paschal II exempted all the lands of the Mount Thabor monastery from tithe,[32] and although total exemptions were uncommon, partial exemptions became relatively frequent.[33]

But the bishops faced a more serious threat when the new orders of

[29] For example, the Benedictine monastery of Our Lady of Josaphat at Jerusalem had daughter-houses at Tiberias, Ch. Köhler, 'Chartes de l'Abbaye de Notre-Dame de la Vallée de Josaphat en Terre Sainte (1108–1291). – Analyses et extraits', *ROL* 7 (1899) pp 113–14, no 2; at Sidon, *ibid* p 124, no 14; at Sichem, *ibid* pp 156–7, no 48; at Antioch, *ibid* pp 172–3, no 64.

[30] Many of these monasteries received privileges similar to that which Paschal II granted to Santa Maria Latina, Jerusalem: 'Cimiterium quoque, quod vel in ipso monasterii claustro vel in ecclesiis ad ipsum pertinentibus habetur, omnino liberum esse decernimus, ut eorum, qui illic sepeliri deliberaverint, petitioni et extremi voluntati, nisi forte excommunicati sint, nullus obsistat.' ed W. Holtzmann, 'Papst-Kaiser-und Normannenurkunden aus Unteritalien', *QFIAB* 35 (1955) pp 50–3, no 1.

[31] For example, archbishop William of Nazareth disputed the right of the monks of Josaphat to control the parish church in the *casale* of Ligio which his predecessor had given them, Delaborde, pp 56–8, no 24.

[32] Jaffé 5948, Constable, pp 95–6.

[33] See, for example, the large number of grants of tithe confirmed to the monastery of Josaphat by Anastasius IV, Delaborde pp 63–7, no 28.

A medieval urban church

fighting monks were founded, the Templars in 1128, and the Hospitallers, who became militarised soon after. Both orders came to have their own chaplains and to receive from the holy see virtual rights of exemption from the ordinary, the Templars in 1139, the Hospitallers in 1154.[34] They established houses in many of the cities of the crusader states and their chapels, which possessed many papal privileges such as the right to say mass even during an interdict, attracted lay congregations. Moreover, the orders soon came to acquire large tracts of territory, by gift or by purchase, particularly in frontier districts, and this often led to disputes with the local bishop about his right to collect tithes in those areas or to exercise jurisdiction in chapels or parish churches which the orders owned. Although William of Tyre's account of the degree of exemption which the orders enjoyed is clearly much exaggerated,[35] it remains true that the powers and revenues of Latin bishops were much diminished as a result of the orders' growth. Take, for example, the case of Tortosa where in 1152 the castle and its dependencies were granted to the Templars. It was agreed that the bishop of Tortosa should control the churches of the city, but that churches elsewhere in the fief belonging to the order should be exempt from episcopal jurisidiction; that the demesne lands of the order should not pay tithe, but that the tithe on all other lands owned by the order should be divided with the bishop.[36] This was fairly typical of the compromises reached between bishops and members of both orders.

The power of the secular church was also threatened by the Italian maritime communes whose shipping gave the crusader states naval protection, kept open their lines of communication with the west and handled the bulk of their commerce. In return for their support these cities received important concessions in the Frankish east, which normally included the gift of quarters in some of the ports in which they might build churches for the use of their nationals. In the more important ports all three communes, the Genoese, Pisans and Venetians, had their own chapels. Although these chapels did not at first have parochial status, most of them later tried to obtain it, and

[34] The Templars in the bull *Omne Datum Optimum* of 1139. The Hospitallers' right to have brother priests and to become a completely exempt order was formally recognised in the bull *Christiane fidei religio* of 1154. [J.] Riley-Smith, [*The [Knights] of St John in Jerusalem and Cyprus, 1050–1310*] (London 1967) pp 235–6.

[35] WT bk 18 cap 6, *RHC Occ* I, pp 826–7.

[36] J. Riley-Smith, 'The Templars and the castle of Tortosa in Syria: an unknown document concerning the acquisition of the fortress', *EHR* 84 (1969) pp 278–88.

also to gain total exemption from the authority of the local bishop.[37] Some of them succeeded in this ambition, so that when Jacques de Vitry went to Acre as bishop in 1216 he found that the Italian churches there did not acknowledge his jurisidiction at all, and their clergy even refused to allow him to preach in them.[38]

The problem of exempt churches was not peculiar to the crusader states but common to the whole of Latin Christendom. What was unique in the case of Frankish Syria was that during the twelfth century the secular clergy, who were few, came to be outnumbered by the monastic clergy, the chaplains of the military orders and the priests of the Italian communes, and that their powers and their financial resources were seriously eroded by the rights of partial or total exemption which those clergy enjoyed.

Nevertheless, before 1187 there were adequate resources to support the entire religious establishment of Frankish Syria, and although episcopal powers were curtailed by the exempt clergy they were not, in most cases, dangerously impaired. This changed after the battle of Hattin, for the Franks were then restricted to a narrow strip of coastal territory, with only intermittent control over parts of Galilee. The Frankish population was not greatly diminished, since refugees from Moslem-occupied territory came to live in the coastal cities. To meet this increase in population bishops created extra parishes in some towns.[39]

The secular church was hardest hit by this change in fortune, although in some ways it was its own worst enemy. In the thirteenth century only four of the fourteen dioceses of the kingdom of Jerusalem remained permanently in Christian hands.[40] Nevertheless, bishops continued to be appointed to twelve of the former sees and the patriarch of Jerusalem, together with seven other bishops whose cathedrals were in enemy hands, came to the new capital, Acre, with their

---

[37] The exemption of the Venetian churches at Acre and Tyre is attested in [*Urkunden zur älteren Handels- und Staatsgeschichte der Republik Venedig mit besonders Beziehung auf Byzanz und die Levante*, ed G. L. F.] Tafel and [G. M.] Thomas, *Fontes rerum Austriacarum*, Sectio 2, 12–14, 3 vols (Vienna 1856–7) 2 pp 445–8, nos 212, 213; that of the Pisan church of Acre in [G.] Müller, [*Documenti sulle relazioni delle città toscane coll 'Oriente cristiano e coi Turchi fino all' anno 1531*], Documenti degli archivi toscani, 3 (Florence 1879) pp 82–3, no 52.

[38] *Lettres [de Jacques de Vitry (1160/70–1240), évêque de Saint-Jean d'Acre*, ed R. B. C. Huygens] (Leiden 1960) pp 85–6, no 2.

[39] For example, two new parishes are named in Acre in 1200, Müller pp 82–3, no 52; and two in Antioch in 1227, Riant I, p 145, no 11.

[40] Acre, Tyre, Caesaraea, Beirut.

A medieval urban church

households and their chapters of canons, and set up pro-cathedrals which were exempt from the authority of the bishop of the city.[41] They were always anxious to increase their often meagre revenues, drawn chiefly from endowments still in Christian hands, and were not above trying to collect tithes from their former parishioners who, like themselves, had sought refuge in Acre.[42] The secular church, therefore, had to support a hierarchy of almost pre-1187 size while its resources were only a fraction of what they had formerly been.

The situation was made worse because they faced increased competition for a share of those resources from the other groups of clergy. The monastic establishment grew in size after 1187, for all the many religious communities of Jerusalem set up houses at Acre after the third crusade[43] and during the thirteenth century new religious orders founded houses there and in some of the other coastal cities. The most important of these new orders, but by no means the only ones, were the Dominicans, the Franciscans and the Carmelites.[44] All these foundations attracted landed endowments together, often, with some part of the tithe which was thus lost to the secular church; and they also took Frankish laymen, and their legacies, away from the parish churches.[45]

The chapels belonging to the Italian maritime cities were virtually unaffected by the conquests of Saladin, since they were situated in ports most of which remained in crusader hands. As the volume of Mediterranean trade increased in the thirteenth century new groups of merchants, like the Provençals and the Anconitans, came to the Syrian ports and they too built chapels for their nationals,[46] so that the

[41] The patriarch of Jerusalem, the archbishop of Nazareth and the bishops of Bethlehem, Lydda, Hebron, Sebaste, Tiberias and Sidon.
[42] Innocent III, *Regesta, PL* 214-16 (1856) *an* I, no 516; *PL* 214, col 476.
[43] Our Lady of Josaphat, Our Lady of Sion, Mount of Olives, Santa Maria Latina, Templum Domini, Saint Anne's, Sainte Marie la Grande, Convent of Bethany, Saint Samuel's, and the hospital of Saint Lazarus.
[44] Carmelite church at Acre, [*Les Registres d'Alexandre IV*, ed C.] Bourel de la Roncière, *BEFAR*, 2 series, 2 vols (Paris 1902-31) no 3250. On the Franciscans, Golubovich 1, *passim*. References to the Dominicans in the crusader states in F. M. Abel, 'Le couvent des frères prêcheurs à Saint-Jean d'Acre', *Révue Biblique* 43 (Paris 1934) pp 265-84. Some of the more important of the minor houses at Acre were Sancta Trinitas Captivorum, Auvray no 4014; the Cistercian nuns of Saint Mary Magdalen's, *CGOH* no 1828; Saint Catherine's, E. Strehlke, *Tabulae Ordinis Theutonici* (Berlin 1869) pp 68-9, no 86; Saint Thomas of Canterbury, Bourel de la Roncière, no 1553.
[45] For example the many bequests listed in the will of Saliba, burgess of Acre, in 1264, *CGOH* no 3105.
[46] Anconitan church, S. Pauli, *Codice diplomatico del sacro militare ordine gerosolimitano oggi di Malta*, 2 vols (Lucca 1733-7) 1, pp 157-61; church of the Provençals, Tafel and Thomas,

authority of the secular clergy was correspondingly weakened. But the most serious threat to the authority of the bishops came from the military orders, which now included the Teutonic knights, founded after the third crusade, as well as the two older orders. During the thirteenth century they came to control between them most of the castles and much of the land of Frankish Syria, and this led to a further decline in episcopal patronage and revenue.[47]

When Jacques de Vitry came to Acre in 1216 he complained to friends in Paris that his new see was like a nine-headed monster.[48] This was, if anything, an understatement, for the ecclesiastical condition of Outremer at that time was one of chaos, tempered only by expensive, and often not very effective, appeals to Rome. This remained true until James Pantaleon, patriarch of Jerusalem, became pope Urban IV. Having personal experience of the situation, he attempted to remedy matters by uniting the see of Acre to the patriarchate of Jerusalem in 1262, so that the head of the Latin church in the holy land should have an adequate power-base,[49] and by giving the patriarch legatine powers over all the remaining crusader territories.[50] In theory at least the patriarch as legate could exercise authority in the pope's name over the exempt clergy as well as over his own suffragans; but a situation which had taken so long to develop would have taken time to put right and time was not on the patriarch's side, for within thirty years of this settlement the Mameluks had overrun all crusader territory.

The fact that the Latin church in Syria existed only for a ruling minority which lived almost exclusively in a few cities certainly brought about a collapse in episcopal authority, for the bishops had to compete in resources and spiritual influence with exempt groups of clergy who out-numbered them and who were vying for control of the same

---

3, p 32. The commune churches sometimes faced setbacks. Thus the Pisan church of Acre was deprived of its parochial status by pope Innocent IV in 1247, *Les Registres d'Innocent IV*, ed E. Berger, BEFAR, 2 series, 4 vols (Paris 1884–1921) no 2801.

[47] Bishops fought tenaciously for their rights, sometimes with success. Thus the compromise reached between the bishop of Acre and the Hospitallers about payment of dues and parochial rights in 1221, (*CGOH* no 1718), was re-negotiated in 1228 in the bishop's favour (*ibid* no 1911). On the other hand the archbishop of Nazareth in 1263 renounced all his episcopal rights over the Mount Thabor monastery and the lands which it owned in his diocese in favour of the Hospital, who had gained possession of it (*ibid* no 3054).

[48] *Lettres*, p 83, no 2.

[49] *Les Registres d'Urbain IV*, ed J. Guiraud, BEFAR, 2 series, 4 vols (Paris 1901–29) no 168.

[50] *Ibid* no 241.

A medieval urban church

limited number of souls and the same restricted amount of real estate. Reading the surviving sources, one can easily form the impression that the crusader clergy spent most of their time wrangling about who should have the largest slice of an ever-diminishing economic cake.

But such a negative assessment of their work would be distorted, for they achieved much that was of value. The orders of the Temple and the Hospital which, in their different ways, had a profound influence on the whole of Catholic Christendom, had their inception in Outremer and in their formative stages received much encouragement from the secular church there.[51] The crusader clergy were also responsible for building an impressive number of shrine churches as a visible expression of their veneration for the holy places,[52] while the extent of their work as patrons of a flourishing school of manuscript illumination is only now receiving full recognition.[53]

But their most remarkable achievement was to promote a spirit of religious tolerance in an age when that was rare. Although the union between Latin and Orthodox broke down in the thirteenth century, that was the result largely of political pressures generated by the fourth crusade rather than of any failure of consideration for the Orthodox on the part of the Latin hierarchy.[54] Moreover, the good relations which the Franks maintained with the other Christian confessions who lived among them produced positive results. For the Maronites, Jacobites and Armenians all entered voluntarily into union with the western church during the crusader period, although only the Maronite union outlasted the collapse of Frankish political power in Syria.[55] This achievement seems all the more remarkable

[51] Riley-Smith, *Knights* pp 32–59; WT bk 12 cap 7, *RHC Occ* I, p 520 gives details of support for the early Templars.
[52] T. S. R. Boase, 'Ecclesiastical Art in the Crusader States in Palestine and Syria. A. Architecture and Sculpture', *A History of the Crusades*, ed K. M. Setton, 4 vols (Philadelphia 1955–) 4, ed H. W. Hazard, *The Art and Architecture of the Crusader States* (Wisconsin 1977) pp 69–116; B. Hamilton, 'Rebuilding Zion: the holy places of Jerusalem in the twelfth century', *SCH* 14 (1977) pp 105–116.
[53] H. Buchtal, *Miniature Painting in the Latin Kingdom of Jerusalem* (Oxford 1957); J. Folda, *Crusader Manuscript Illumination at Saint-Jean d'Acre, 1275–91* (Princeton 1975).
[54] There is some discussion of this in S. Runciman, *The Eastern Schism* (Oxford 1955) pp 112–17, but a fuller treatment of this subject is needed.
[55] The Maronites were reconciled in 1182, WT bk 22 cap 8, *RHC Occ* I, pp 1076–7; the Jacobite union lasted from 1236 (see Gregory IX's bull, *Causam Conditoris Omnium*, Auvray no 3789), until 1263, Bar Hebraeus, *Chronicon*, cap 96, ed J. B. Abbeloos, T. J. Lamy, 2 vols (Louvain 1872–4) I cols 746–50. For the Armenian union, formally inaugurated in 1198, see B. Hamilton, 'The Armenian Church and the Papacy at the time of the Crusades', *Eastern Churches Review* 10 (1978) pp 61–87.

X

when it is considered how intolerant the Latin church in western Europe became of any deviation from Catholic norms in the course of the thirteenth century. It is arguable that the weakness of the Latin episcopate in Syria and the fact that much of their energy was directed into struggles with other groups of western clergy contributed in some measure towards their tolerance of eastern Christian confessions who constituted no kind of threat to the authority or the resources of the Frankish bishops.

Addenda
p. 161, n. 15, for '*CGOH*, p. 443' read '*CGOH*, no. 443'.

Knowing the Enemy: Western Understanding of Islam

at the Time of the Crusades*

In 1076, some twenty years before the First Crusade was launched, Pope Gregory VII
wrote to al-Nāṣir, Sultan of Bougie in what is now Algeria:

For there is nothing which Almighty God, who wishes that all men should be saved and that no man
should perish, more approves in our conduct, than that a man should first love God and then his
fellow men ... Most certainly you and we ought to love each other in this way more than other races
of men, because we believe and confess one God, albeit in different ways, whom each day we praise
and reverence as the creator of all ages and the governor of this world. For, as the Apostle says: "He is
our peace, who hath made both one".[1]

This enlightened view of Islam was not widely shared in Latin Christendom at that time,
nor was it rooted in any very profound knowledge of the Muslim religion. B. Z. Kedar is, I
think, correct in his view that a good deal of information about Islam was available in the
West before the crusades, both in written and oral sources, but because there was a general
lack of interest in the subject, no attempt had been made to coordinate this knowledge.[2]
Typical of the laconic character of pre-crusade comments about Islam are the remarks of
the Cluniac historian Ralph Glaber, writing in c. 1030:

For the Saracens read the Hebrew prophets ... claiming that what they foretold of Jesus Christ, Lord
of all, is now fulfilled in the person of Muhammad, one of their people. To support them in their
error, they have in their possession a genealogy of their own, similar to that found in the Gospel of St.
Matthew, who recounts the descent of Jesus from Abraham through Isaac ... But theirs says that
"Ishmael begat Negajoth", and continues with an erroneous fiction, which, in deviating from the
holy catholic account, strays equally from the truth.[3]

This is an inaccurate account, but it is not written with the intention of wilfully misleading
the reader, whereas some accounts written after the preaching of the First Crusade in 1095

---

* This is the text of a paper given at the 65th Anglo-American Conference of Historians held at the Institute of
Historical Research of the University of London from 3–5 July 1996 on the theme *Religion and Society*.
Note. A word about vocabulary for readers who are not specialists in this field. "Saracens" was used by Western
writers at the time of the Crusades as a generic term to describe all Muslims. "Franks" was a term quite commonly
used by participants in the crusades to the Levant and Egypt, and by Western settlers in the Crusader States, to
describe themselves. It was also used by the Muslims of the Near East as a generic term to describe Westerners.

[1] E. Caspar, ed., *Das Register Gregors VII*, Bk. III, no. 21, *Epistolae Selectae in usum scholarum ex Monumentis
Germaniae Historicis separatim editae* (Berlin, 1955), ii(1), p. 288 (citing Eph. 2, 14).

[2] B. Z. Kedar, *Crusade and Mission. European Approaches towards the Muslims* (Princeton, 1984), pp. 3–41, who
takes issue with R. W. Southern's description of the pre-crusade period as the "age of ignorance" in regard to
western knowledge of Islam, *Western Views of Islam in the Middle Ages* (Harvard, 1962), pp. 1–33.

[3] J. France, ed. and trans., *Rodulfi Glabri Historiarum Libri Quinque*, Bk. I, c. 9 (Oxford, 1989), pp. 20–3.

undoubtedly were. The *Song of Roland*, for example, in the form which we now have it, represents the Muslims as idolaters, worshipping a trinity of gods called Mahomet, Tervagant and Apollin, while the author of the *Historia Peregrinorum* recounted how the First Crusade had found an idol of Mahomet in the Dome of the Rock, when they captured Jerusalem.[4] But such statements, intended in part to inflame hostility to Islam at a time of war, should not be taken seriously as evidence of what the West knew about Islam. As John France has pointed out, these writers or their informants had been on crusade, had sacked mosques, and knew that there were no images in them and that these stories were untrue.[5]

Despite this inauspicious beginning, it was the crusades which in the long term led to a deeper knowledge of Islam in the West. Seen in historical perspective the crusades were part of an ongoing war between Muslim and Christian powers for control of the Mediterranean, which had begun with the rise of the Arab Empire in the seventh century and which has lasted until living memory. One of the ways in which the crusades differed from earlier phases of these wars was that those who took part in them were recruited from all over western Europe and not simply from the frontier regions. The crusade movement lasted for many centuries, but I wish to concentrate on the period from c. 1100 to c. 1300 when substantial Muslim communities were for the first time brought under Western rule in Spain, Sicily and the Latin Kingdom of Jerusalem. In that period there was no diminution in crusading zeal: Muslims, in theory at least, remained the principal enemies of the Christian world, but, nevertheless, a wide range of Western people had the opportunity of prolonged contact with them in the newly conquered territories. One consequence of this was that it became possible for Western Catholics to obtain a more accurate picture of the Islamic faith.

This only happened gradually. When Guibert of Nogent wrote his history of the First Crusade in c. 1110 he sought to explain to his readers how the former Christian lands of the Levant had become Muslim:

It is the common opinion, if I understand it aright, that there was a certain man called Mathomus who drew [those people] away from belief in the Son and the Holy Spirit and taught them that in the Godhead there was the Father, the creator, alone. He taught that Jesus Christ was a sinless man, and let me briefly conclude this account of his teaching by saying that he enjoined circumcision, while completely freeing them from restraining their lusts.

He goes on to give a garbled account of Muḥammad's life, which he admits that he knew only from hearsay, telling how Muḥammad had grown up poor and illiterate and owed his power to his marriage with his master's widow. He was epileptic, but he concealed this from his wife by pretending that he had visions: but in fact he derived his religious

---

[4] E.g. Dedevant sei fait porter sun dragon
    Et l'estandart Tervagan e Mahum
    E un'ymagene Apolin le felun.
La Chanson de Roland, ll. 3266–8, ed. C. Segre, French trans. M. Tyssens (Geneva, 1989), i, p. 256; C. Meredith Jones, 'The traditional Saracen of the songs of Geste', *Speculum*, XVII (1942), pp. 201–25; *Historia peregrinorum euntium Jerosolimam*, ccxxiv, *Recueil des Historiens des Croisades, Historiens Occidentaux* [henceforth *RHC Occ*] (Paris, 1866), iii, p. 222.
[5] J. France, "The First Crusade and Islam", *The Muslim World*, LXVII (1977), pp. 247–57.

teachings from a renegade Christian monk, who was inspired by the devil to use Muḥammad for the subversion of Christendom. Guibert concludes:

[Muslims] do not think that [Mathomus] is god, as some people assert, but a good man and the benefactor through whom they received the divine laws.[6]

Walter of Compiègne, writing his *Anecdotes of Mahomet* a generation later, is no better informed. He tells much the same story of the Prophet's life, and summarises his teaching in this way:

[he ordered] that the sacrament of baptism should be discontinued and the law of circumcision restored; that the sacrifice of the Body and Blood of Christ should be brought to an end, and the offering of rams, heifers, sheep and calves should be substituted; that one man should marry twelve wives and the chaste bonds of marriage should be abandoned. It is said that Mahomet wrote many other things, but I have thought it better to say nothing about those matters of which I have little knowledge.[7]

But during Walter's lifetime a change took place. This was due to the work of Peter the Venerable, Abbot of Cluny, who visited Spain in 1142 and was concerned about the conversion of the considerable Moorish population who had come under Christian rule as a result of the *reconquista*. He engaged two of the most skilled academic translators of Arabic texts, Robert of Ketton and Herman of Carinthia, to produce a corpus of works about Islam. The most important of these was Robert of Ketton's version of the Qur'ān, the first translation of that work into a Western language.[8] Robert also translated a collection of Muslim traditions about the history of the pre-Islamic world and the early years of the caliphate. Herman of Carinthia translated an account of the succession of the prophets from Seth, son of Adam, to Muḥammad, together with a treatise by ʿAbdallāh ibn-Salām about the Prophet's teaching. The collection was supervised by Peter of Toledo, a Spanish Christian who knew Arabic, and who was probably the author of the glosses, the marginal commentary which accompanied Robert of Ketton's Qur'ān, explaining the work to Christian readers. Peter of Toledo was certainly responsible for the translation of a critique of Islam written in Iraq in c. 900 by a native Christian and attributed to al-Kindī. Peter the Venerable also employed a practising Muslim, named Muḥammad, to check these translations, to ensure that they were accurate and complete.[9]

The West also learned about Islam at the same time through other channels. An important source of information was Moshe Sephardi, an Arabic speaking Spanish Jew, who was baptized in 1106 and became known as Peter Alfonsi because Alfonso the Battler of Aragon was his godfather. He wrote an account of his conversion in the form of a

---

[6] Guibert of Nogent, *Gesta Dei per Francos*, I, iii–iv, *RHC Occ*, iv (Paris, 1879), pp. 127–30.

[7] R. B. C. Huygens, ed., 'Otia de Machomete Gedicht von Walter von Compiègne', *Sacris Erudiri*, VIII (1956), pp. 287–328. Huygens dates this poem 1137–55. The quotation is from p. 320 (lines 851–8).

[8] In terms of Islamic orthodoxy, of course, the Uncreated Qur'ān could not be translated, only paraphrased. Kees Versteegh has suggested that a Greek translation might have been made in the ninth century but the evidence for this is conjectural: "Greek translations of the Qur'ān in Christian polemics (9th century A.D.)", *Zeitschrift der deutschen Morgenlandischen Gesellschaft*, CXLI (1991), pp. 52–68.

[9] J. Kritzeck, *Peter the Venerable and Islam* (Princeton, 1964); M-T. d'Alverney, "Deux traductions latines du Coran au Moyen Age", *Archives de l'histoire doctrinale et littéraire du Moyen Age*, XXII–III (1946–8), pp. 69–113. Most of these works were printed by Theodor Buchmann (known as Bibliander), *Machumetis Saracenorum principis eiusque successorum vitae ac doctrina, ipseque Alcoran* (Basle, 1543).

dialogue with a Jew, in which, among other issues, he discusses why he had not become a Muslim instead, and in so doing he provides an accurate and succinct account of Islam.[10] The account of that faith written in the eighth century by the Greek theologian, St John of Damascus, born c. 675, also became available in a Latin translation, made by Burgundio of Pisa in c. 1150. St John had lived at the St Sabas monastery in Jerusalem under the Umayyad Caliphs and was well informed about Islam.[11]

Peter the Venerable's wish to evangelize Muslims, though not unparalleled, was uncommon at the time, but this changed with the foundation of the mendicant Orders in the early thirteenth century. The Dominicans required their missionaries to learn native languages so that they could dispense with interpreters, and some of those who worked in the Crusader States, William of Tripoli, for example, became very knowledgeable about Islam.[12] The scope of such activity was at first restricted by the laws of Islamic states which, while permitting religious disputations, did not allow the Prophet and his teaching to be publicly criticized, and treated the conversion of Muslims to Christianity as a capital offence. In the case of Iran and Iraq this changed after the Mongol conquest in 1258. Mongol law granted parity of status to all faiths, and after diplomatic relations had been established with the Roman curia in 1263 Western missionaries were able to work freely in the lands of the Il-Khanate whose population was overwhelmingly Muslim. Although they made few Muslim converts, those missionaries had a unique opportunity to live and preach openly in an Islamic society.[13]

Of course, despite all these new sources of information about the Muslim faith, older, unenlightened views persisted. As late as 1257 Matthew Paris, the St Albans chronicler, recorded that the Master of the English Military Order of St Thomas of Acre, when visiting the abbey, had told the community how:

in the previous year, the statue of Mahomet, which hung solemnly in the air at Mecca to be reverently worshipped, had been destroyed by lightning because it angered God . . .[14]

Although the West seems at first to have regarded Islam as a monolithic religion, it gradually became aware of the divisions within that faith. William of Tyre (d. 1186), the historian of the crusader Kingdom of Jerusalem, is, so far as I know, the first Western author to attempt to explain them. After giving a brief account of the early history of the caliphate to the time of 'Alī (d. 661) he writes:

And so a schism arose among those people, which has persisted right down to our own times, for some of them say that Muḥammad is the greater and the most important of all the prophets, and these

---

[10] *Petri Alfonsi ex Judaeo Christiani Dialogi contra Judaeos, Titulus* V, ed. J. P. Migne, *Patrologia Latina* [henceforth *PL*], CLVII, cols 597–606.

[11] J. de Ghellinck, "L'entrée de Jean de Damas dans le monde littéraire occidental", *Byzantinische Zeitschrift*, XXI (1912), pp. 448–57. A revised translation was made in the thirteenth century by Robert Grosseteste, R. W. Southern, *Robert Grosseteste. The Growth of an English Mind in Medieval Europe* (Oxford, 2nd edn, 1992), pp. 199–200.

[12] Kedar, *Crusade and Mission*, pp. 136–58; J. Richard, *La papauté et les missions d'Orient au moyen âge (xiii–xve siècles)* (Rome, 1977), pp. 37–47; William of Tripoli, *De statu Saracenorum*, ed. H. Prutz, *Kulturgeschichte der Kreuzzüge* (Berlin, 1883, reprinted Hildesheim, 1964), pp. 575–98.

[13] Richard, *Papauté et missions*, pp. 98–116.

[14] Matthew Paris, *Chronica Majora, Additamenta*, no. 183, ed. H. R. Luard, *Rolls Series* [henceforth *RS*], 57 (I–VII) (London, 1872–83), vi, pp. 348–9.

in their language are called Sunnites, but others say that 'Alī alone is the prophet of the Lord, and these are called Shi'ites.[15]

It is clear that William did not understand the theological position of the Shi'ites, that 'Alī was the lawful successor and the guaranteed interpreter of the revelation of Muḥammad. But thereafter Western writers did distinguish between the two main branches of Islam.

The group of Shi'ites with whom the Franks had closest dealings in the thirteenth century were the Nizarite Ismā'īlīs, commonly called the Order of Assassins. They were one of the most radical Shi'ite groups, with an esoteric understanding of their faith.[16] St Louis, while staying at Acre in 1252, exchanged embassies with the head of the Syrian Nizārīs, whom the Franks called the Old Man of the Mountain. Louis's chief negotiator was a Dominican, Yves Le Breton, who lived in the Holy Land and spoke Arabic. Unfortunately we do not have his own report of the mission, but an account of it is given by Joinville in his *Life of St Louis*, who tells us that:

By the head of the Old Man's bed brother Yves found a book in which were written some of Our Lord's sayings to Saint Peter when he was on earth. Brother Yves said to the Old Man: "Ah, sir, in God's name study this book often, for it is excellent doctrine." The Old Man said that it was his custom to do so. "For I am devoted to my Lord Saint Peter, since at the beginning of the world the soul of Abel, after his murder, passed into the body of Noah; and after Noah's death into that of Abraham; and after Abraham's death it passed, when God came on earth, into the body of Saint Peter." Hearing this, Brother Yves showed him that his faith was mistaken, and taught him of the good truth; but the Old Man refused to believe.[17]

What Yves Le Breton would seem to have been reporting was a discussion of the Ismā'īlī belief in the succession of speaking prophets each succeeded by a silent, spiritual legatee who interpreted the esoteric meaning of the prophet's revelation to the initiated. According to that tradition Simon Peter (Shamūn al-Ṣafā) was the silent interpreter of the teaching of the prophet Jesus. It is clear that Joinville did not understand this doctrine, and, if his report is accurate, it would seem that Yves Le Breton did not understand it either. This shows how very difficult it could be for Western inquirers, even those who were well-educated, who spoke Arabic, and who were prepared to discuss theology with Muslim religious leaders, to understand the information they were given.[18]

Yet although by the end of the thirteenth century some Catholic scholars possessed a very full range of information about the faith and practice of Sunnite Islam and a more limited and imperfect knowledge of some of the Shi'ite schools, this did not add up to an

---

[15] William of Tyre, *Chronicon* [henceforth WT], XIX, 21, ed. R. B. C. Huygens, Corpus Christianorum, Continuatio Medieavalis, LXIII, LXIIIA (Turnholt, 1986), ii, p. 891.

[16] M. G. S. Hodgson, *The Order of Assassins. The Struggle of the Early Nizari Isma'ilis against the Islamic World* (The Hague, 1955); B. Lewis, *The Assassins. A Radical Sect in Islam* (London, 1967); F. Daftary, *The Ismā'ilis. Their History and Doctrines* (Cambridge, 1990).

[17] John of Joinville, *Histoire de Saint Louis*, cc. 462–3, ed. N. de Wailly (Paris, 1868), pp. 164–5; I cite the translation of R. Hague, *The Life of St. Louis* (London, 1955), p. 141.

[18] Daftary, *The Ismā'ilis*, p. 139. Joinville implies that the Nizarites believed in reincarnation, and some members of the Syrian Lodge may have done so in the thirteenth century, *ibid*., p. 401; cf. N. Daniel, *Islam and the West* (Edinburgh, 1960), p. 325, n. 24. The book which the Nizārī Shaykh was reading seems to have been related to the text known as the *Kerygmata Petrou* which is embedded in the Clementine Recognitions and Homilies. It is not possible to determine in what form it was known to the Shaykh. G. Strecker, ed. "The Kerygmata Petrou", in E. Hennecke, *New Testament Apocrypha*, ed. W. Schneemelcher, trans. R. McL. Wilson (London, 1965), ii, pp. 102–27.

understanding of Islam as a religion. Muslims and Christians had much in common: they all believed in One God, and agreed in outline about the early history of mankind from Adam to Abraham. Yet paradoxically the main hindrance to a full Western understanding of Islam, so it seems to me, arose from the warmth with which the Qur'ān speaks of Jesus and Mary, 'Īsā and Maryam. In the Qur'ān Jesus is recognized as a prophet sent by God, who although only human, was nevertheless unusually privileged, being virgin-born by the breath of God, and at the end of his earthly ministry taken up bodily into Heaven by God.[19] Islam also evinced immense respect towards his mother, about whom the Qur'ān contains passages like:

Remember when the angels said, O Maryam, verily Allāh has elected thee and purified thee and elected thee above all the women of all created beings. O Maryam be obedient unto thy Lord and prostrate thyself and bow down with those who bow down.[20]

In medieval Islam devotion to Jesus and Mary was not simply theoretical. When by the Treaty of Jaffa in 1229 the Sultan al-Kāmil restored the Holy Places to Christian rule under Frederick II, it was stipulated that "no Saracen shall be forbidden freely to make the pilgrimage to Bethlehem ..."[21]

But this very reverence for Jesus and Mary led Christian theologians to measure Islam by Christian standards instead of viewing it, as Gregory VII had seemed to do, as a different religion which had certain elements in common with their own. Even St Thomas Aquinas, who had read the metaphysical works of the Muslim philosopher Avicenna, judged Islam by Christian standards and found it wanting:

None of the divine oracles of the prophets who went before him bear witness to him [he writes of Muḥammad]; nay rather he has perverted almost all the books of the Old and New Testaments by a fictitious account, as is apparent to anyone who looks at his teaching. For that reason, as a result of clever thinking, he has not bequeathed the books of the Old and New Testaments to be read by his followers, lest through them he might be convicted of deceit.[22]

This attitude, which ranged the followers of Islam in the ranks of spiritual opposition to the true faith of Christ, should have commanded general assent in an age which supported the crusades. Intellectually it did, but in other ways it failed to carry conviction. One important reason for this, which is often underestimated except by historians of literature, was the way in which during the twelfth century the Western imagination began to be infiltrated by the world of Islam.[23] A crucial role in this process was played by Peter Alfonsi, the convert Jew. In addition to his theological treatise he also wrote the *Disciplina Clericalis*, a collection of stories translated from the Arabic. This work was immensely popular, no doubt chiefly for its entertainment value, and from it Western people learned

[19] G. C. Anawati, "'Īsā", *Encyclopaedia of Islam* [henceforth *EI*] (new edn, 1978), iv, pp. 81–6. G. Parrinder, *Jesus in the Qur'an* (London, 1965).
[20] Sūra III, 37–8, cited in the translation of A. J. Wensinck, "Maryam", *EI* (new edn, 1991), vi, pp. 628–32; J.-M. Abd-el-Jalil, *Marie et l'Islam. Études sur l'histoire des religions*, viii (Paris, 1950); Parrinder, *op. cit.*, pp. 60–82.
[21] Letter of the Patriarch Gerold to Pope Gregory IX, c. III, ed. J. L. A. Huillard-Bréholles, *Historia diplomatica Friderici Secundi* (7 vols in 12, Paris, 1852–61), iii, p. 88.
[22] *Summa ... contra Gentiles*, I, vi (Paris, 1925), p. 7; J. C. Doig, *Aquinas on Metaphysics. A Historico-Doctrinal Study of the Commentary on the Metaphysics* (The Hague, 1972).
[23] An excellent study of this kind by an historian of literature is that of D. Metlitzki, *The Matter of Araby in Medieval England* (New Haven and London, 1977).

about Muslims in a quite different context from the theological or military ones to which they were used. Take, for example, the beginning of Peter's story of the Ten Chests:

I was once told of how a Spaniard journeyed to Mecca, and while on his journey went through Egypt. As he had a desire to go into the desert and cross it, he thought that he would leave his money in Egypt ... The local people pointed out an old man whose trustworthiness and uprightness were famous. So he gave this man more than a thousand talents of his money ...[24]

This is the world of the Arabian Nights, and it was possible for people all over the West to enter it, even those who had never seen a Muslim. The corpus of Arabic stories which entered the West by different routes, of which the work of Peter Alfonsi was one, was a kind of Trojan horse in the imagination of Christendom. An imaginative awareness of the Islamic world made it more difficult to think of Muslims in the black and white terms which the logic of twelfth-century Christian theology required.

Western Christians who lived in frontier societies like Spain, Sicily and the Latin Kingdom of Jerusalem, came to know Muslims as human beings, and to feel affection and respect for some of them. Among those who felt this most keenly were scholars, for the crusade movement coincided with, and was arguably part of that growth in western European civilization which is commonly called "the twelfth-century renaissance". One of the first scholars to profit from the increased contact with Islamic learning which the crusades made possible was an Englishman, Adelard of Bath. Fairly soon after the First Crusade he had visited Norman Sicily and from there had gone on to the Norman principality of Antioch. Although he may also have visited Jerusalem, the chief purpose of his journey was not to make a pilgrimage, but to study under Arab masters, and he spent seven years in this way before returning to England where he wrote the *Quaestiones Naturales* to show what he had learned. This is cast in the form of a dialogue between him and his nephew, educated in the schools of northern France, and Adelard is concerned to show his own regard for the superior learning, and indeed method, of the Arab world. At one point, while talking about zoology, he says to his nephew in exasperation:

It is difficult to discuss animals with you. For I have learned one thing from the Arab masters by inductive reasoning, but you have been led to form a different opinion, having been tethered, so to speak, by the halter of authority. For what other name should we give to authority but that of halter?[25]

Adelard was one of the earliest of a great number of Western scholars who were indebted to Arabic scholarship in the twelfth and thirteenth centuries, when a huge number of logical, philosophical and scientific works were translated into Latin: some of these were classical Greek texts which came to the West through Arabic versions, but many were original works of Arabic scholarship. In this way, at a time when the crusades were at their height, the scholars of western Europe came to have a great respect for Islamic learning.[26]

---

[24] *Petri Alfonsi Disciplina Clericalis*, eds. A. Hilka, W. Soderhjelm, *Acta Societatis Scientiarum Fennicae*, 38, no. 4, (Helsinki, 1911). I cite the translation by P. R. Quarrie of E. Hermes's edition, *The "Disciplina Clericalis" of Petrus Alfonsi* (London, 1977), p. 128.

[25] *Die "Quaestiones Naturales" des Adelardus von Bath*, c. v, ed. M. Müller, *Beiträge zur Geschichte der Philosophie und Theologie des Mittelalters*, xxxi(2) (Munster, 1934), p. 11. C. Burnett, ed., *Adelard of Bath: An English Scientist and Arabist of the Early Twelfth Century* (London, 1987).

[26] E. Gilson, *History of Christian Philosophy in the Middle Ages* (London, 1955), pp. 181–246; G. Leff, *Medieval*

Western understanding of Islam at the time of the crusades

Some of the Franks who lived in the Levant came to feel a respect for some Muslim leaders, including those who were their most dangerous opponents. Consider William of Tyre's obituary notice for Nūr al-Dīn, atabeg of Aleppo, the chief enemy of the Franks for a quarter of a century before his death in 1174:

Nūr al-Dīn, the greatest persecutor of the Christian faith and cause, and yet a righteous prince, subtle and farsighted, and devout in the observance of the faith of his own people, died in the month of May, in the twenty-ninth year of his reign.[27]

But even the military classes, who made up the crusader armies and who fought to defend the Crusader States, came to have a respect for the fighting qualities of their Muslim enemies. This was true from the beginning. The author of the *Gesta Francorum*, a south Italian knight who went on the First Crusade, wrote of the Turks:

They have a saying that they are of common stock with the Franks, and that no men, except the Franks and themselves, are naturally born to be knights. This is true, and nobody can deny it, that if only they had stood firm in the faith of Christ and holy Christendom ... you could not find stronger or braver or more skilful soldiers; and yet by God's grace they were beaten by our men.[28]

People taking part in the crusades, particularly those who lived in the frontier societies which the crusaders conquered, therefore faced a dilemma. Faith and reason combined to demonstrate that the Muslims were in the wrong. The application of logic to the study of everything including theology, which was one of the chief innovations of the twelfth century renaissance, made it more difficult for Catholics to take the pragmatic view of Islam held by Pope Gregory VII that "we believe and confess one God, albeit in different ways". The more accurate the information they gained about Islam, the plainer it became that Muslims were on the wrong side in the ongoing spiritual war which determined the shape of human history. Western Christians believed that the general outline of the future had been revealed by God, in symbolic terms, in the Apocalypse of St John and that the spiritual war would reach its climax with the coming of Antichrist.[29] No Western Christian contested this world view in general terms, but some of them were disquieted by the place assigned to Muslims in it, because their experience of individual Muslims and even, in some cases, their experience of the way in which they practised their faith, was not consonant with the belief that they were minions of antichrist.

The theologically correct solution to this problem was that of conversion. Through baptism a Muslim would become a Christian and share parity with his fellow believers in this world and the next. Certainly most Christian theologians who studied Islam did so with a view to hastening Muslim conversions. Peter the Venerable used his corpus of translations to compose a *Book against the Sect or Heresy of the Saracens*, in which he appealed

---

Thought (Harmondsworth, 1958), pp. 141–67; C. H. Harkins, *The Renaissance of the Twelfth Century* (Cambridge, Mass., 1939); *Studies in the History of Medieval Science* (Cambridge, Mass., 1927).

[27] WT, XX, 31, ii, p. 956. Cf. R. C. Schwinges, *Kreuzzugsideologie und Toleranz. Studien zu Wilhelm von Tyrus*, *Monographien zur Geschichte des Mittelalters*, xvi (Stuttgart, 1977).

[28] The author supposes that the Turks, like other peoples in the Near East, had been Christians before the rise of Islam. *Gesta Francorum et aliorum Hierosolimitanorum*, Bk. III, ed. and trans. R. Hill (London, 1962), p. 21.

[29] R. K. Emmerson and B. McGinn, eds, *The Apocalypse in the Middle Ages* (Ithaca and London, 1992); R. K. Emmerson, *Antichrist in the Middle Ages* (Manchester, 1981).

to Muslims to accept the Christian faith.[30] The same hope inspired the missionaries of the thirteenth century: the Dominican William of Tripoli, who lived in Acre and completed his Treatise *On the State of the Saracens* in 1273, clearly felt a considerable affinity for the Muslims among whom he worked, but this did not lead him to accept their faith as licit. Rather it made him hope that because their beliefs were so close to those of Catholics their conversion would be a simple matter:

The Saracens believe in their hearts and confess with their lips that the words of God written in their Koran concerning the praise and honour of Jesus Christ, of his teaching and of his holy Gospel, of the Blessed Virgin Mary his mother, and of those who model themselves on her by believing in him, are true; although these truths are mixed up with many lies and embroidered with romances, yet it is clear enough that these people are near to the Christian faith and to the way of salvation.[31]

The hope evinced by William and his colleagues in the missionfield was not altogether illusory: quite large numbers of Muslims were converted in lands brought under Christian rule, while some Muslims voluntarily went to live in the Kingdom of Jerusalem during the twelfth century in order to embrace the Christian faith.[32]

The problem remained: that many of the Muslims whom Christians most admired showed no inclination to change their religion. I want to consider in detail how this problem was resolved in one particular case: that of the Sultan Saladin. Saladin succeeded in uniting much of western Islam under his rule, and in 1187 defeated the Frankish army in battle and occupied most of the Kingdom of Jerusalem. The Third Crusade led by Richard of England fought him to a standstill, but was unable to recover Jerusalem from him. He should have been regarded in the West as the chief enemy of Christendom, and in some quarters he was. While Richard I was staying in Messina in 1190 on his way to the Holy Land he asked to see Abbot Joachim, who was writing a commentary on the Book of Revelation and was credited with prophetic powers. For Richard knew a good deal about apocalyptic matters and obviously considered that the loss of Jerusalem was a sign that the Last Days had begun. An eyewitness relates how Joachim and the king discussed the meaning of the twelfth chapter of Revelation: the vision of the woman crowned with twelve stars needed little explanation, since she was clearly an allegory of Holy Church, but St John then writes: "And there appeared another wonder in heaven: and behold a great red dragon, having seven heads and ten horns, and seven crowns upon his heads" [Rev. 12, 3]. Joachim explained that the dragon was the devil, and the seven heads the chief persecutors of the Church, and he continued:

these are their names: Herod, Nero, Constantius, Mahomet, Melsemutus, Saladin and Antichrist; five of these have fallen, and one now stands, that is Saladin, who at this present time persecutes the church of God; and has led her into captivity with the Lord's Sepulchre and the Holy City of Jerusalem, and the land in which the Lord walked [as man] . . .[33]

---

[30] ed. Kritzeck, *Peter the Venerable*, pp. 220–91.
[31] William of Tripoli, *Tractatus*, c. xlvii, ed. Prutz, *Kulturgeschichte*, pp. 595–6.
[32] J. M. Powell, ed., *Muslims under Latin Rule 1100–1300* (Princeton, 1990); *The Travels of Ibn Jubayr*, trans. R. J. C. Broadhurst (London, 1952), p. 323.
[33] This passage appears in the *Gesta Regis Ricardi*, commonly though wrongly ascribed to Benedict of Peterborough, which incorporates material from what appears to be an eye-witness account of the Third Crusade, ed. W. Stubbs, RS (London, 1867), ii, p. 151; A. Gransden, *Historical Writing in England c. 550–1307* (London, 1974), pp. 232–8. The first five heads relate to Herod, who persecuted the infant Christ; Nero, the first emperor to

Joachim later made some modifications to this exegesis, but he did not change his views about the role of Saladin. In two of the oldest manuscripts of the *Liber Figurarum*, which contain illustrations of Joachim's themes, the sixth head of the great red dragon is the only one to wear a crown and is labelled "Saladinus", and captioned: "The sixth persecution [of the Church] has begun, the seventh will follow."[34]

Joachim's hostile reaction to Saladin was not an isolated one. A Latin poem written soon after the defeat of Ḥaṭṭīn gives a lurid biography of Saladin. It relates that he had been of servile birth, had entered the service of Nūr al-Dīn, but had repaid his master's trust by seducing his wife; he had then fled to Egypt where he had treacherously killed the Fatimid Caliph. Next he had arranged for Nūr al-Dīn to be poisoned, returned to Syria, married his widow and dispossessed his infant son. He had then attacked the Christians of Jerusalem. Although this account has some basis in fact, in that Saladin did bring about the end of the Fatimid Caliphate, and dispossess the lawful heirs of Nūr al-Dīn, it is written as an exercise in black propaganda.[35] One of the most swingeing invectives against Saladin is in the *Itinerarium Peregrinorum*, an account of the background to the Third Crusade, written in c. 1191–2 by an Englishman who was probably a Templar chaplain. It describes the Sultan's career in this way:

That pimp, whose kingdom was located in brothels, whose army was found in taverns, whose education consisted in gambling, was suddenly raised up: he became the equal of princes, indeed he was greater than princes ... for he ruled over the Egyptians, he subdued Damascus, he occupied the land of Edessa and northern Iraq, and he carried his rule into the heartlands of nearer India.[36]

It was very understandable that a member of the Order of the Temple should describe the Sultan in these terms, since he had executed all the knights of that Order whom he had taken prisoner at Ḥaṭṭīn. What is astonishing is the inclusion of the following passage by the same author in his account of the Sultan's early years:

when [Saladin] reached an age when more exacting military duties were required of him, he came to Humphrey of Toron, the noble prince in Palestine, to be made an officer, and was girded by him as a knight in a Frankish ceremony.[37]

The Templar chaplain, who had come from the West with the Third Crusade and who was so hostile to Saladin, cannot be credited with inventing this story himself: it must have been current among the Franks of Syria at the time when he was writing. A version of it is indeed found in the chronicle composed in the Holy Land which is usually known as the

---

persecute the Church; Constantius, who patronised the Arian heresy; the Prophet Muḥammad; and Melsemutus the Sultan of Morocco: M. Reeves and B. Hirsch-Reich, *The 'Figurae' of Joachim of Fiore* (Oxford, 1972), pp. 86–8. M. Reeves comments on this passage: "So similar to the Dragon figure in the *Liber Figurarum* is this exposition that possibly Joachim had this actual figure on display". *Joachim of Fiore and the Prophetic Future* (London, 1976), p. 23.

[34] For example, in his *Expositio in Apocalypsim* Joachim identified the fifth head as the Emperor Henry IV, but Saladin continued to be shown as the sixth head in the Oxford and Dresden manuscripts of the *Liber Figurarum*, Reeves and Hirsch-Reich, *The 'Figurae'*, pp. 87, 146–50, and Plates 21, 22.

[35] G. Paris, "Un poème latin contemporain sur Saladin", *Revue de l'Orient Latin* [henceforth *ROL*], i (1893), pp. 433–44.

[36] *Das Itinerarium Peregrinorum*, ed. H. E. Mayer, *Monumenta Germaniae Historica* [henceforth *MGH*] *Schriften*, xviii (Stuttgart, 1962), pp. 252–3; this text was used by Richard, Canon of the Holy Trinity London, in Book I of his *Itinerarium peregrinorum et Gesta Regis Ricardi* (compiled c. 1216–22), ed. W. Stubbs, RS (London, 1864), pp. 10–11; Gransden, *English Historical Writing*, pp. 238–42.

[37] *Itinerarium*, ed. Mayer, p. 251.

Chronicle of Ernoul. The textual history of this source, which the late Ruth Morgan did so much to elucidate, is a complex one, and this is not the place to discuss it. Suffice it to say that although the text which we now have dates from the first half of the thirteenth century, it incorporates material relating to the history of the Latin Kingdom before 1187, which formed part of the lost Chronicle of Ernoul composed in the late 1190s. Professor Richard has suggested that the surviving version should be called the pseudo-Ernoul, and I shall use that name. This source relates how as a young man Saladin had been knighted by the Lord of Kerak who had held him prisoner.[38] This incident is placed immediately before Saladin's Egyptian campaign: Humphrey of Toron was Constable of the Kingdom at that time, and although he was not Lord of Kerak himself, his son was married to a daughter of that Lord. The story in the Pseudo-Ernoul is therefore in substantial agreement with that in the Templar source and they both presumably derive from a common oral tradition circulating in the Latin Kingdom at the time of the Third Crusade.[39]

The story of Saladin's knighting became the subject of a short romance, L'Ordene de Chevalerie, which appears to have been written in northern France at some time before 1250. In this version Saladin is knighted not by Humphrey of Toron, but by Hue de Tabarie, that is Hugh of Tiberias.[40] Various explanations for this change have been advanced, the simplest being that of Gaston Paris that it was the result of a copyist's error, since both men had the same initials.[41] Hue de Tabarie really existed: he was captured in battle by Saladin in 1179 and held to ransom.[42] The Ordene relates how during his captivity Saladin prevailed on him to confer the Order of knighthood upon him, and how Hugh explained the significance of all the parts of the ceremony. There could be no doubt in the mind of readers that Saladin had been truly initiated as a Christian knight, and had understood what was happening to him. This poem was immensely popular, and prose versions were also made of it.

A second romance which related to Saladin, La fille du comte de Ponthieu, was written in

[38] Chronique d'Ernoul et de Bernard le Trésorier, ed. L. de Mas Latrie (Paris, 1871), p. 36. The complex textual history of this source was examined by M. R. Morgan, The Chronicle of Ernoul and the Continuations of William of Tyre (Oxford, 1973). J. Richard, 'L'arrière-plan historique des deux cycles de la croisade', in Croisades et États latins d'Orient (Aldershot, 1992), No. v, p. 12.

[39] It seems possible that the knighting of Saladin was originally ascribed to Humphrey II of Toron, Constable of the Kingdom of Jerusalem from 1152–79, and that it was to him that the Itinerarium referred, J. L. Lamonte, Feudal Monarchy in the Latin Kingdom of Jerusalem (Cambridge, Mass., 1932), p. 253. His son, Humphrey III, married Stephanie de Milly, who inherited the lordship of Kerak, although not until after his death. The fief later passed to their son, Humphrey IV of Toron, who was titular lord at the time that the lost chronicle of Ernoul was compiled in the late 1190s, and the author may therefore mistakenly have supposed that Kerak had been held by members of the Toron family in the 1160s. H-E. Mayer, Die Kreuzfahrerherrschaft Montréal (Sobak). Jordanen im 12 Jahrhundert, Abhandlungen des deutschen Palästinavereins, 14 (Wiesbaden, 1990), pp. 215–28.

[40] There is a critical edition of the verse text by Roy Temple House, L'Ordene de Chevalerie, University of Oklahoma Bulletin, February I (1919), which I have been unable to consult. The text of Paris, Bibliothèque Nationale, MS f. fr. 25462, ff. 149–57, ed. M. Barbazan, L'Ordene de Chevalerie (Paris, 1759), was reprinted with an English translation by William Morris, The Order of Chivalry (Hammersmith, 1893), pp. 107–25. For the prose versions: H. Kjellman, ed., "Les rédactions en prose de l'Ordre de Chevalerie", Studier i modern Språkvetenskap utgivna av Nyfilologiska Sällskapet i Stockholm, VII (1920), pp. 139–77; see M. Keen, Chivalry (New Haven and London, 1984), pp. 6–8; R. F. Cook and L. S. Crist, Le deuxième cycle de la croisade. Deux études sur son développement (Geneva, 1972), pp. 124–31.

[41] G. Paris, "La légende du Saladin", Journal des savants (1891), p. 290, n. 1.

[42] WT, XXI, 28, ii, p. 1002; M. C. Lyons and D. E. P. Jackson, Saladin. The Politics of the Holy War (Cambridge, 1982), p. 140; M. Rheinheimer, Das Kreuzfahrerfürstentum Galiläa (Frankfurt-am-Main, 1989), pp. 62–3.

the same area and at about the same time as the *Ordene* for Marie, the daughter of Count William of Ponthieu, who died in 1251.[43] The author is concerned to show how her family is related to Saladin, though the connection, it must be admitted, is a distant one. Saladin is said to be the great-grandson, through his mother, of the eponymous heroine of the romance, the daughter of the Count of Ponthieu, by her marriage to the Sultan of Almeria (called *Aumarie* in the romance).

These stories soon became associated with the history of the Latin Kingdom and with the loss of Jerusalem. A prose version of the *Ordene de Chevalerie* together with a text of *La fille du comte de Ponthieu* were incorporated in the *Estoires d'Outremer,* a work which is very closely related to the chronicle of the Pseudo-Ernoul, and which Margaret Jubb has recently edited. Although the earliest manuscript in which the integrated version of these three texts appears dates from c. 1300, Jean Richard has argued that its archetype probably dates from about 1250.[44]

It has sometimes been maintained that these stories represent an attempt by Western Christians to put a good face on defeat. Saladin had been able to beat them because he was really one of them, a crypto-Christian knight. I think this argument may well hold good of the treatment of Muslim leaders in the Second Crusade Cycle written in the second half of the fourteenth century, and in later works, for by then the time when any part of the Holy Land had been in Christian hands was beyond living memory.[45] But I do not think that the argument has any validity in the context of the period 1190–1250 when the stories about Saladin which I have been discussing were written. When they first began to circulate Saladin was still alive, and his descendants, the Ayyubid Sultans of Egypt, continued to rule Jerusalem until 1250. Crusading zeal had never been as strong as it was in those years: the Third Crusade was still in progress when the stories began to be told, and six more crusades were launched before 1250 to recover the Holy Places.[46] These circumstances were not conducive to the idealization of an enemy leader who was responsible for the loss of Jerusalem. So why were they written?

First one must consider whether there is any foundation of fact in these stories about Saladin. The report that he had a Christian great-grandmother from the Pas de Calais probably tells us more about the character of Marie de Ponthieu, who commissioned the romance, than about the Sultan's ancestry, but the question of his knighting is less easy to determine. Certainly the Pseudo-Ernoul version is unlikely to be true, since there does not seem to have been a space in Saladin's life during which he could have been a prisoner-of-war at Kerak.[47] All that can be said with certainty is that his being knighted by a Frank was not thought implausible by Christian chroniclers. There are two other accounts of the knighting of Muslims in this period. First, the *Itinerarium Regis Ricardi,* which was not

---

[43] Cl. Brunel, ed., *La fille du comte de Ponthieu . . . versions de XIIIe et du XVe siècle* (Paris, Société des anciens textes français, 1923).

[44] M. A. Jubb, *A Critical Edition of the "Estoires d'Outremer et de la naissance Salehadin",* (London, 1990); Richard, "L'arrière-plan", p. 14.

[45] R. F. Cook, "Crusade propaganda in the epic cycles of the Crusade", in B. N. Sargent-Baur, ed., *Journeys towards God. Pilgrimage and Crusade* (Kalamazoo, 1992), pp. 157–75.

[46] The Crusade of Henry VI (1197); the Fourth Crusade (1203–4), preached to deliver the Holy Land although diverted to Constantinople; the Fifth Crusade (1217–21); Frederick II's Crusade (1227–9); the Crusades of Theobald of Navarre and Richard of Cornwall (1239–41); and the first Crusade of St Louis (1248–54).

[47] Lyons and Jackson, *Saladin,* pp. 1–46.

written until after 1215, but which uses earlier sources, relates that on Palm Sunday 1192 Richard I knighted Saladin's nephew, the son of his younger brother al-ʿĀdil, at his father's request.[48] Secondly, Joinville, in his *Life of St Louis* which was completed only in 1309, reported that Fakhr al-Dīn, commander-in-chief of the Egyptian army at the time of St Louis's first crusade in 1249–50, "was the most esteemed of all the pagans. He bore on his banner the arms of the Emperor, who had made him a knight". That Emperor was Frederick II, and Fakhr al-Dīn had, in 1229, helped to negotiate the peace between him and the Sultan al-Kāmil which led to the temporary restoration of Jerusalem to Christian control, which is likely to have been the occasion of his knighting, if, that is, it really happened.[49] For the evidence about the knighting of these two Muslims is not conclusive.

I would suggest that the stories about the knighting of Saladin were used by those who wrote accounts of the Third Crusade, both in the East and in the West, not necessarily because they were historically true, but because they corresponded to experience. When judged by Western standards Saladin had many of the qualities of a good knight. His reputation for liberality was proverbial in Islam, and was proved to the Christian world by his generosity in regard to ransoms when he conquered Jerusalem. He treated Christian noblewomen with courtesy, allowing Balian of Ibelin, for example, to travel to Jerusalem in order to escort his wife to the coast before he laid siege to the city. He was also capable of generosity towards his male opponents: King Guy of Lusignan was well treated in captivity. Of course, Saladin's nobility of character was not total: he was capable of barbarities, as witness his execution of all the members of the Military Orders after the Battle of Ḥaṭṭīn, not to mention his treatment of Reynald of Châtillon.[50] But then most chivalric Western knights were not paragons either: there was only one perfect Christian knight, Galahad, and he existed only in a romance.

The crusaders seem to have formed an equally high opinion of the knightly qualities of Saladin's younger brother, al-ʿĀdil, who later became Sultan of Egypt (1200–18). The poet Ambroise, who was an eye-witness and wrote his account of the Third Crusade in c. 1195–6, reported as an example of al-ʿĀdil's courtesy how, at the Battle of Jaffa, seeing the King of England fighting on foot, he made him a present of two arab chargers. When Canon Richard of London incorporated this story in his Latin history, the *Itinerarium Regis Ricardi*, some twenty years later, he commented that al-ʿĀdil was a "man of most noble and generous character, who could stand comparison with the best of men if only he did not scorn to believe the Christian faith".[51]

Participants in the Third Crusade and those who wrote about it were wrestling with the same problem which had bothered those who went on the First Crusade: how to do justice to an enemy whose qualities they admired because they were identical with those they

---

[48] *Itinerarium . . . Regis Ricardi*, V, xii, ed. Stubbs, p. 325.

[49] Joinville, ed. de Wailly, p. 70; cited in Hague's translation p. 73, and see his note, p. 273. In an earlier passage Joinville is more cautious: "L'en disoit que li emperieres Ferris l'avoit fait chevalier". *Ibid.*, p. 73; T. C. Van Cleve, *The Emperor Frederick II of Hohenstaufen. Immutator Mundi* (Oxford, 1972), p. 203.

[50] Saladin's generosity at Jerusalem, Lyons and Jackson, *Saladin*, pp. 274–5; his liberality in general, *ibid.*, pp. 368–9; his good treatment of Guy of Lusignan, and execution of the Templars, Hospitallers and Reynald of Châtillon, *ibid.*, pp. 264–5; his courtesy to Balian of Ibelin's wife, *La Continuation de Guillaume de Tyr (1184–97)*, c. 49, ed. M. R. Morgan (Paris, 1982), p. 63.

[51] Ambroise, *L'Estoire de la guerre sainte*, ll. 11546–64, ed. G. Paris (Paris, 1897), cols. 309–10; *Itinerarium*, VI, xxii, p. 419; on the relationship between these works, Gransden, *Historical Writing*, pp. 238–42.

valued in themselves. "They have a saying that ... no men, except the Franks and themselves, are naturally born to be knights", said the author of the *Gesta Francorum*.[52] The alleged knighting of Saladin was an attempt to address the same issue. The ceremonies which are described in detail in the *Ordene de Chevalerie* are very overtly Christian in their symbolism and intention, but as Maurice Keen has pointed out, they were administered entirely by laymen, no clergy were involved at any stage.[53] By this ceremony a Muslim could become an honorary Christian knight without changing his faith.

Nevertheless, the problem remained that although Muslims might share a common form of knighthood with Christians in this life, or might be conceived as doing so, they could not share Paradise with them after death because they did not hold the Catholic faith. One solution was to assume that they had been clandestinely baptised: the collection of anecdotes compiled in c. 1260 which goes by the name of the Minstrel of Rheims relates that Saladin tried to baptise himself as he was dying, and literary examples of other Saracen leaders who embraced the Christian faith are to be found in the epic cycle of the crusades.[54] But educated Western opinion knew that these stories were born of wishful thinking, not rooted in reality.

St Thomas Aquinas considered the position of good pagans (and he defined as pagans those who had not been baptized), in his *Summa Theologica*. Unbelief, he wrote, was not in itself a sin to those who had never known true belief, and infidels were capable of performing works which were well pleasing to God.[55] Nevertheless, it remained true that baptism was the normal means of salvation, and the position of good Saracens therefore remained very doubtful, particularly as in many cases they had had the opportunity to become Christian but had not taken advantage of it.

A solution to this dilemma was expressed in literary terms by Dante. He had been born in 1265 and was therefore one of the last generation of Western people to grow up while parts of the Crusader States remained in Christian hands. He mentions Saladin twice. In the *Convivio* he numbers him with those who, like Alexander the Great, were rich but liberal and who have therefore left a blessed memory. But in the *Divine Comedy* Saladin is found in the first circle of Hell: this is Limbo, the place of those who have led good lives but are ignorant of the Christian faith and cannot enjoy the beatific vision of God. Virgil and Homer and the pagan poets live there, but Dante also finds there "a noble castle, defended with seven high walls, and moated round by a little river". Inside, he meets representatives of the good pagans: among them Electra, Hector, the elder Brutus, Cornelia, "and standing alone to one side I saw Saladin". In another part of the castle were the philosophers and scholars, who included the Muslims, Averroes and Avicenna.[56] Limbo is not a place of

---

[52] *Gesta Francorum*, Bk. III, p. 21.

[53] Keen, *Chivalry*, p. 7.

[54] *Récits d'un ménestrel de Reims au treizième siècle*, ed. N. de Wailly, c. xxi, 212 (Société de l'Histoire de France, Paris, 1876), pp. 111–12; *La Chrétienté Corbaran*, ed. P. R. Grillo, *The Old French Crusade Cycle*, vol. VII, *The Jerusalem Continuations*, Part I (University, Alabama, 1984); L. S. Crist, *Saladin: suite et fin du deuxième cycle de la croisade* (Geneva and Paris, 1972).

[55] "Infideles damnantur quidem propter alia peccata, quae sine fide remitti non possunt; non autem damnantur propter infidelitatis peccatum". *Summa Theologica, Secunda Secundae, Quaestio X, Art.* I (Paris, 1927), vol. iii, p. 63. "Unde manifestum est quod infideles non possunt operari bona opera quae sunt ex gratia ...; tamen bona opera ad quae sufficit bonum naturae, aliqualiter operari possunt". *Ibid., Art.* IV, p. 66.

[56] E. Moore and P. Toynbee, eds, *Le Opere di Dante Alighieri*, 4th edn (Oxford, 1924), *Convivio*, IV, c. xi, p. 310; *Inferno*, IV, 106–51, pp. 6–7.

torment, nor are the people who are there wicked.[57] Limbo was a spiritual state of being defined by theologians, but the Castle of Good Pagans seems to have been invented by Dante and was a complement in a way to the Saracen knights of the romances, a place where the Christian imagination might locate good Muslims after death.

When crusading was at its height some Western theologians sought to become better informed about the faith of Islam. Although they obtained a good deal of high quality information, understanding of the faith eluded them by that route. However, the greater degree of contact with Muslims and their civilization which the crusades produced resulted in a growth of respect for some individual Muslims and a widespread admiration for some aspects of their culture. An attempt was made to accommodate good Muslims in the thought-world of western Christendom as honorary knights in this world or as honorary antique pagans in the next. In a few cases a real respect for the religion in which the civilization of Islam was grounded also developed among Western observers. Ricoldo of Monte Croce, the Dominican missionary who lived for several years in Baghdad under the Mongol Īl-Khāns in the late thirteenth century, was unstinting in his praise of devout Muslims and the society that produced them:

Who will not be astounded if he carefully considers how great is the concern of these very Muslims for study, their devotion in prayer, their pity for the poor, their reverence for the name of God and the prophets and the holy places, their sobriety in manners, their hospitality to strangers, their harmony and love for each other?[58]

When all these factors are considered, one can see that the West's experience of Islam at the time of the crusades was far from being a negative one.

[57] Innocent III gave as his opinion that 'Poena originalis peccati est carentia visionis Dei", *Decretales Gregorii IX*, III, *tit.* xliii, c. 3. By placing Saracens in Limbo Dante was assuming that they were not being punished for sins they had committed, but only for original sin. A. Gaudel, "Limbes", *Dictionnaire de Théologie Catholique*, ix (I) (Paris, 1926), cols. 760–72.

[58] *Fratris Ricoldi de Monte Crucis Liber Peregrinationis*, c. xxii, ed. J. C. M. Laurent, *Peregrinatores Medii Aevi Quatuor* (Leipzig, 1864), p. 131, cited in the translation of Daniel, *Islam and the West*, p. 196. Ricoldo expanded this theme in chapters xxiii–xxix, pp. 132–5, but then found it necessary to add several chapters attacking the basis of the Muslim faith: chapters xxx–xxxvi, pp. 135–41. As U. Monneret de Villard commented about the final chapters of the work: "Siamo quindi completamente al di fuori dello studio dell'Islāmismo e del tentativo della sua compresione, ma invece entriamo in pieno nella polemica anti-islāmica. Il missionario ha preso il posto dell'osservatore e dello scienziato". *Ricoldo da Montecroce, Il Libro della peregrinazione nelle parti d'Oriente*, Institutum historicum Fratrum Praedicatorum, *Dissertationes historicae*, xiii (Rome, 1949), p. 118.

THE CATHARS AND THE SEVEN CHURCHES OF ASIA.

The Cathars claimed that theirs was the one true church and therefore denounced the Roman church as a false church which had departed from the teaching of Christ[1]. Part of the Catholic reply to this polemic was the one which had been traditional since the time of St. Irenaeus, an appeal to the apostolic succession of the Roman see, deriving from SS. Peter and Paul, which guaranteed the transmission of Christ's teaching in an unadulterated form.[2] By the middle of the thirteenth century the Cathars had developed a quite sophisticated rejoinder: while admitting that St. Paul had preached in Rome, they claimed that he and his followers had been killed in the Neronian persecution and implied that the true Roman church had come to an end at that point. They denied that St. Peter had ever been to Rome and dismissed the value of his shrine as historical evidence on the grounds that his relics had not been produced for public display until almost 300 years after his alleged death, so that there was no proof that they were the bones of the apostle at all. They accepted Catholic claims that the Emperor Constantine had given St. Sylvester of Rome temporal jurisdiction over all the western lands and admitted that the popes had ruled in

1. Th. Venckeleer, ed., 'Un recueil cathare: le Manuscrit A.6.10 de la Collection vaudoise de Dublin. I. Une Apologie', *Revue belge de philologie et d'histoire*, XXXVIII (1960), pp.815-34.
2. Irenaeus, *Adversus omnes Haereses*, III, iii, 1-3, ed. with French trans. A.Rousseau, L.Doutreleau, *Sources Chrétiennes (SC)*, 211 (1974), III (ii), pp.31-8.

unbroken succession since that time, but they stressed that the church of Sylvester bore none of the marks of the true church defined in the New Testament, whereas their own church bore all of them.[3]

Catholic theologians went to great lengths to refute the doctrinal criticisms which the Cathars made of the Roman church and to defend the Petrine claims of the holy see, but they did not make the obvious retort and ask the Cathars for proofs of their own apostolic descent. Moneta of Cremona, the most voluminous of the Catholic apologists, devoted the final book of his treatise against the Cathars and the Waldensians to a discussion about the nature of the true church. In the printed text this runs to 356 folio columns, yet only one column is concerned with Cathar origins. This brief survey says nothing whatever about Cathar history: Moneta merely identifies certain Cathar doctrines with those taught by pagan philosophers and Christian heresiarchs – Pythagoras, the Magi, the Sadducees, Mani, Tatian and Valentinus – and assumes that the Cathars must trace their descent from these heterogeneous teachers of error.[4] Most Catholic writers clearly considered it a waste of time to investigate Cathar history, since it was plain from the nature of their teaching that they had not derived their beliefs from Christ and the apostles.

Yet the Cathars themselves might have been expected to have taken a greater interest in their own history, since they believed, just as firmly as the Catholics did, that they stood in the apostolic succession. In the Provençal version of the Cathar *Ritual* the presiding elder says to the candidate who is about to be initiated:

The church of God has preserved this holy baptism, by which the

3. Moneta of Cremona, *Adversus Catharos et Valdenses libri quinque*, V, ii, 1, ed. T.A.Ricchini (Rome, 1743), pp.410-11. A.Borst, *Die Katharer, Schriften der Monumenta Germaniae Historica*, XII (Stuttgart, 1953), p.216, denied that this passage related to the Cathars, but J.Duvernoy, *Le Catharisme: La religion des Cathares* (Toulouse, 1976), p.227, has conclusively shown from southern French documents that it does. Bonacursus of Milan, *Manifestatio Haeresis Catharorum, PL*, 204, col.777, claimed that the Cathars taught that St.Sylvester was antichrist.
4. Moneta, V, ii, 2, *De Origine Catharorum, loc. cit.*, p.411.

Holy Spirit is given, from the time of the apostles until now, and it has been passed on by Good Men to Good Men until the present occasion, and this will continue to happen until the end of the world.[5]

A general statement of this kind about origins would no doubt have satisfied unsophisticated postulants, but not all consoled Cathars were simple people. Some are known from their surviving writings to have been intelligent and articulate: for example, Rainier Sacconi, who was a Cathar minister for seventeen years before becoming a Dominican, and John of Lugio, who inspired, even if he did not write, *The Book of the Two Principles,* and who was 'elder son', or co-adjutor bishop, of the Cathar church of Desenzano.[6] Such men would have needed better evidence than simple assertion that their church could trace its descent from the apostles.

In attempting to determine whether the Cathar churches had written or oral traditions about their own history, a major problem is posed by the nature of the surviving evidence. More than ninety percent of this consists either in treatises written by Catholic theologians to denounce the Cathar movement, or in depositions made by Cathars in reply to questions posed by Catholic inquisitors. Since the Catholic authorities were interested chiefly in the current faith and practice of the Cathars and scarcely at all in their origins, these records give very little information about Cathar history. The writings of the Cathars themselves, which might have contained evidence of that kind, were in large part either destroyed by their enemies[7] or lost through neglect once Catharism had ceased to be an organized movement. Nevertheless, sufficient indications survive, albeit of a fragmentary kind, to show that the Cathars did have a coherent picture of the history of their church.

One Catholic writer interested in Cathar origins was Anselm of

5. L.Clédat, *Le Nouveau Testament traduit au XIIIe siècle en langue provençale, suivi d'un Rituel Cathare* (Paris, 1887), p.xvii.
6. Rainier Sacconi, *Summa de Catharis; Liber de duobus principiis,* ed. A.Dondaine, *Un Traité néo-manichéen du XIIIe siècle. Le 'Liber de duobus principiis', suivi d'un fragment de Rituel Cathare* (Rome, 1939), pp.66, 72-6, 81-147.
7. J.Guiraud, *Histoire de l'Inquisition au moyen âge,* 2 vols (Paris, 1935-8), I, pp.xi-xv.

Alessandria. He spent more than twenty years in the service of the inquisition in Lombardy and compiled a notebook in the 1260s and 1270s which Fr. Dondaine has discovered and edited. Anselm's knowledge of Cathar history must have been gained from witnesses whom he had examined and he was able to give a detailed account of the way in which the Cathar faith had been established in Lombardy and of the reasons for the schisms which had developed in the Cathar community there. He was also able to reconstruct lists of the bishops who had ruled the Lombard Cathar churches from their inception to his own day.[8] He was even able to date the introduction of Catharism there fairly precisely. One of his notes reads:

These men introduced heresy to Lombardy from Naples: Mark, John the Jew, Joseph and Aldricus – this happened in about the year 1174.[9]

Much of the information which Anselm gives can be controlled by earlier and independent sources and can be shown to be accurate. Detailed historical knowledge of this kind, spanning a century, implies that the Cathars of Lombardy considered it important to remember the succession of bishops in their churches and may indicate that they kept records.

The southern French Cathars certainly kept records and part of this material has survived in the document often misleadingly called the Acts of the Council of Saint-Félix. This is known only in the text printed in 1660 by Guillaume Besse in his Histoire ... de Narbonne and its authenticity has been challenged.[10] I have stated elsewhere my reasons for supposing that it is genuine,[11] but I should like to draw attention to Besse's statement that he was only publishing

8. Anselm of Alessandria, Tractatus de Haereticis, ed. A.Dondaine, Archivum Fratrum Praedicatorum (AFP), XX (1950), pp.308-24.

9. Ibid., c.13, AFP, XX, p.319.

10. G.Besse, Histoire des ducs, marquis et comtes de Narbonne (Paris, 1660), pp.483-6.

11. B.Hamilton, 'The Cathar Council of Saint-Félix reconsidered', AFP, XLVIII (1978), pp.23-53. See also A.Dondaine, 'Les actes du concile albigeois de Saint-Félix de Caraman', Miscellanea Giovanni Mercati, vol. 5, Studi e Testi, 125 (Vatican City, 1946), pp.324-55.

extracts of the original source.[12] The document from which Besse made his selection was in the archive of S. Étienne at Toulouse, but it was a copy made in 1223 for the Cathar bishop of Carcassonne of a set of three documents formerly in the possession of the Cathar church of Toulouse. One was an account of the council held some fifty years earlier at Saint-Félix at which the Cathar churches of southern France had been organized; another was the text of a sermon preached to the Cathars of Toulouse by the Byzantine dualist bishop Nicetas; and the third was a record of the way in which the diocesan boundaries of the Cathar churches of Toulouse and Carcassonne had been determined.[13] The fact that the Cathars not only kept such records but also subsequently made copies of them indicates that they did have an historical awareness and that they were just as concerned as Catholics were to preserve evidence about the transmission of their faith.

But western evidence would only have been of limited help to the Cathars if they wished to prove an apostolic filiation, because the Cathar churches in western Europe were all fairly recent foundations. Even if the outbreaks of Manichaeism reported in various parts of the west in the first half of the eleventh century are regarded as evidence of Cathar activity (and I am inclined to view some of them in that way),[14] it remains true that no firm connection has been established between them and the Cathar communities of the twelfth century. There is general agreement among scholars that the earliest certain evidence for the presence of Cathars in the west during the twelfth century dates from 1143 when the Cathar bishop of Cologne and his *socius* were examined by Eberwin of Steinfeld and admitted that their faith derived from the Byzantine empire.[15] Soon after this the Cathars established a church in northern France.

---

12. 'L'Acte que ie dois donner tout entier, et dont i'employe un extraict au fond de cette Histoire, dit que...', Besse, *op. cit.*, p.325.
13. Hamilton, *op. cit.*, *AFP*, XLVIII, pp.23-53.
14. For the opposite view of alleged Manichaeism in western Europe in the eleventh century, R.I.Moore, *The Origins of European Dissent* (London, 1977), pp.23-45.
15. Eberwin of Steinfeld, *Appendix ad S.Bernardi Epistolas*, no.432, *PL*, 182, col.679.

Anselm of Alessandria was able to gather information about this because while he was inquisitor in Lombardy the north French Cathar church was living in exile in Verona.[16] The account which Anselm gives of its origins, though uncorroborated, fits in with such other facts as are known. He relates that 'Frenchmen went to Constantinople to conquer the land and found that sect'. Since he places this event before 1174 he must be referring to either the first or the second crusade and, on balance, the second crusade seems more likely, since Louis VII's army did almost attack Constantinople in 1147.[17] When they returned home, Anselm alleges, the crusaders who had become Cathars disseminated their doctrine and founded a church in northern France. Their teaching spread into southern France and northern French Cathars were also responsible for introducing the heresy into Lombardy when some of their members visited Italy.[18] Cathars were certainly present in southern France by 1165[19] and may have been there earlier[20] and when the council of Saint-Félix met the southern French already had a Cathar bishopric at Albi.[21] According to Anselm the Cathar church in Lombardy was first organized under a leader named Mark in c.1174 and this is confirmed by an independent source dating from the early thirteenth century.[22]

16. Sacconi, *op. cit.*, ed. Dondaine, p.77.
17. Odo of Deuil, *De Profectione Ludovici VII in Orientem*, IV, ed. V.G.Berry (New York, 1948), pp.68-72. Cf. C.Thouzellier, 'Hérésie et croisade', *Revue d'histoire ecclésiastique*, XLIX (1954), pp.859-62.
18. Anselm of Alessandria, *op. cit.*, ed. Dondaine, *AFP*, XX, pp.308-9.
19. *Acta Concilii Lumbariensis*, ed. M.Bouquet, *Recueil des Historiens des Gaules et de la France*, 24 vols (Paris, 1738-1904), XIV, pp.431-4.
20. The earliest certain evidence for Catharism in southern France is *Heriberti monachi epistola de haereticis Petragoricis*, *PL*, 181, cols. 1721-2, written before 1163 since it is repeated in the Annals of Margam for that year, ed. H.R.Luard, *Annales Monastici*, I, (*RS*), (London, 1864), p.15.
21. Hamilton, *op. cit.*, *AFP*, XLVIII, pp.31-5.
22. Anselm of Alessandria, *op. cit.*, ed. Dondaine, *AFP*, XX, pp.308-9. This is substantially confirmed by the anonymous *De Heresi Catharorum in Lombardia*, ed. A.Dondaine, 'L'Hiérarchie cathare en Italie, I.', *AFP*, XIX (1949), p.306, which says that Mark was consecrated a bishop in the Bulgarian *ordo*. Anselm's version is corroborated by the Saint-Félix document in which Mark is not referred to as a bishop before his consecration by Nicetas, Hamilton, *op. cit.*, *AFP*, XLVIII, pp.31-2.

From this brief survey it would appear that none of the Cathar churches in the west could trace their origins much before 1140, but that they all claimed to derive their faith from an older religious tradition in the Byzantine empire. They were therefore dependant on the information given them by eastern teachers about the earlier history of their church. The only direct knowledge that we have about the kind of historical perspective which the Cathars were given by eastern dualists is the extract from the sermon which Nicetas of Constantinople preached to the church of Toulouse in c.1175, contained in the Saint-Félix document:

> You have asked me to tell you whether the customs of the primitive churches were light or burdensome and I tell you that the seven churches of Asia were separated from each other by defined boundaries and that none of them did anything to the detriment of any of the others. And the Roman church and those of Dragometia, Melenguia, Bulgaria and Dalmatia are separated from each other by defined boundaries and they do not do anything to each other's detriment and so they live peaceably together. Do you likewise.[23]

All three sources which record Nicetas's mission refer to him as *papa*.[24] In the western church this title was reserved to the pope and its use by the Cathars confused Catholic writers, some of whom supposed that Nicetas was an heretical antipope,[25] whereas the word seems simply to have meant father and to have been given by the eastern dualists to all their prelates.[26] Anselm of Alessandria calls Nicetas 'bishop of the heretics of Constantinople'[27] and there is

23. *Ibid.*, p.52.
24. For Nicetas's mission and his influence see the excellent study of D.Obolensky, 'Papas Nicetas: A Byzantine Dualist in the Land of the Cathars', *Okeanos: Essays presented to Ihor Ševčenko, Harvard Ukrainian Studies,* VII (1983), pp.489-500.
25. E.g. 'Nempe et apostolicum cui omnes obediunt se fatentur habere', Joachim of Flora, *Expositio in Apocalypsim,* III, ix, 11 (Venice, 1527), f. 133r.
26. E.g. John Tzurillas, leader of the Bogomils in the diocese of Acmonia in the early eleventh century, was called *papa* by his followers. *Euthymii monachi coenobii Periblepthae epistula invectiva,* ed. G.Ficker, *Die Phundagiagiten* (Leipzig, 1908), p.66.
27. Anselm of Alessandria, *op. cit.,* ed. Dondaine, *AFP,* XX, pp.308-9.

no reason to doubt this description, since Hugh Etherianus, the Pisan adviser to Manuel Comnenus on western church affairs, attests the presence of a dualist community in the Byzantine capital at this time.[28]

Nicetas's reference to dualist tradition was two-fold: he appealed to the practice of the 'primitive churches' and to that of the Balkan dualist churches of his own day. In order to understand what he meant by the seven churches of Asia it is first necessary to consider his remarks about contemporary Balkan dualism. He names five churches: Rome, Dragometia, Bulgaria, Dalmatia and Melenguia. I have argued elsewhere that by Rome Nicetas meant his own church of Constantinople, the New Rome.[29] The location of the churches of Bulgaria and Dalmatia is self-explanatory and it is now generally accepted that the church of Melenguia was in the Peloponnese. Professor Obolensky's conclusion that the church of Dragometia was situated in the area of the Dragovitsa is incontrovertible[30] and it is possible that it took its name from the ancient Orthodox see of Dragovet.[31] Western writers found considerable difficulty in Latinizing the name of this church and record it in a variety of forms, of which the most common are Dragucia and Drugunthia, but in the rest of this paper it will be referred to as the church of Dragovet.

The Cathars of northern France, Languedoc and Lombardy to whom Nicetas addressed his mission had originally received their faith from the dualist church of Bulgaria.[32] When describing this filiation western writers often allude to the *ordo Bulgariae* rather than to the *ecclesia Bulgariae*.[33] By *ordo* they mean a regular,

28. A.Dondaine, 'Hugues Étérien et Léon Toscan', *Archives d'histoire doctrinale et littéraire du moyen âge*, XIX (1952), pp.109-14.
29. Hamilton, *op. cit.*, *AFP*, XLVIII, p.37.
30. D.Obolensky, *The Bogomils* (Cambridge, 1948), pp.158-62.
31. Hamilton, *op. cit.*, *AFP*. XLVIII, pp.37-8
32. *De Heresi*, ed. Dondaine, *AFP*, XIX, p.306; Anselm of Alessandria, *op. cit.*, ed. Dondaine, *AFP*, XX, pp.308-9; Hamilton, *op. cit.*, *AFP*, XLVIII, pp.23-53.
33. On this usage, W.L.Wakefield, A.P.Evans, *Heresies of the High Middle Ages* (New York-London, 1969), p.690, n.10.

sacramental succession. Nicetas came to the west specifically to denounce the Bulgarian *ordo* and at Saint-Félix near Toulouse he presided at a council at which he re-consoled all the initiated Cathars who were present and re-consecrated all their bishops in the *ordo* of the church of Dragovet.[34]

Although Nicetas succeeded in uniting all the Cathars of the west in a single *ordo*, schisms soon developed after he had returned to Constantinople. The church of Bulgaria sent an envoy named Petracius to the Cathars of Lombardy to explain that the sacraments conferred by Nicetas were invalid and subsequently some groups of Cathars returned to the Bulgarian *ordo*, others sought to have their sacraments validated by the dualist church of Dalmatia, while some, including all the churches of Languedoc, remained faithful to the *ordo* of Dragovet.[35] These schisms were never healed and Catholic observers noted that there was a major doctrinal division between those Cathars who adhered to the *ordo* of Dragovet and those who belonged to the *ordo* of Bulgaria and to the related *ordo* of Dalmatia. The Cathars of the *ordo* of Dragovet were absolute dualists, who believed in the existence of two co-eternal gods, one good and creator of the invisible cosmos, the other evil and creator of the phenomenal universe; whereas the Cathars of the Bulgarian and Dalmatian *ordines* were moderate dualists, who believed in the existence of a single god, creator of Lucifer, who had fallen from grace and become the evil demiurge who had fashioned the material universe from the four elements which the good God had made.[36]

Byzantine theologians writing in the central middle ages note similar differences between Christian dualist groups in the Balkans and refer to the moderate dualists as Bogomils and the absolute dualists as Paulicians.[37] It is therefore tempting to identify the *ordo* of Dragovet, from which the absolute dualists among the western

34. Hamilton, *op. cit., AFP*, XLVIII, pp.23-53.
35. *De Heresi*, ed. Dondaine, *AFP*, XIX, pp.306-8; Anselm of Alessandria, *op. cit.*, ed. Dondaine, *AFP*, XX, pp.309-10; Sacconi, *op. cit.*, ed. Dondaine, p.77.
36. *Ibid.*, pp.71-2, 76-7.
37. E.g. Euthymius Zigabenus, *Panoplia Dogmatica*, Tit. XXIV, XXVII, *PG*, 130, cols. 1189-1244, 1289-1332.

Cathars traced their origin, with the Paulicians, and the *ordo* of Bulgaria, which the moderate dualist Cathars regarded as their mother-church, with the Bogomils. Unfortunately a simple equation of this kind is not possible. Although the Cathars differed among themselves about certain points of theology, they all shared a common pattern of observance. They all made a rigid distinction between *credentes,* who had not been initiated and who were not bound to observe the rules of the church, and *perfecti,* who had received the Cathar baptism and who were obliged to lead very austere lives. All the Cathar churches had the same kind of organization, all used the same liturgical forms and all Cathar *perfecti* had to live in accordance with the same rules. It therefore follows that the mother churches of Bulgaria and Dragovet, from which the Cathar churches of the west traced their descent, must likewise have observed a common form of religious practice, public worship and organization, whatever doctrinal differences may have existed between them. Byzantine theologians identify the extreme asceticism which characterized the Cathar *perfecti* exclusively with the Bogomils. There is no evidence that the Paulicians made any distinction between believers and perfect, nor are they ever associated with world-renouncing forms of asceticism. It therefore follows that all the Balkan dualist churches from which the Cathars traced their descent and with which they maintained firm links in the thirteenth century were Bogomil churches.

What, then, was the issue which made necessary the western missions first of Nicetas of Constantinople and then of Petracius of Bulgaria? Obolensky has justly observed that the adoption of absolute dualist beliefs by some Cathar and Bogomil churches was of profound significance, in that whereas moderate dualism might be considered a Christian heresy, absolute dualism, which denied the first article of the Christian faith, belief in one God 'maker of all things visible and invisible', was an entirely different religion from orthodox Christianity.[38] Catholic theologians who wrote about the Cathars understandably paid particular attention to this doctrinal

38. Obolensky, *op. cit., Harvard Ukrainian Studies,* VII, pp.489-500.

innovation. Yet the Cathars themselves had no agreed statement of belief corresponding to the Nicene creed to which all their members subscribed and were therefore willing to tolerate a wide variety of doctrinal opinion within their communities.[39] There is no evidence in any of the sources that the division between the churches of Bulgaria and Dragovet was caused by doctrinal disagreements: it would appear that the schism was occasioned by a dipute about what, in Catholic terminology, would be called the validity of each other's orders.

Cathars believed that salvation was conferred by the one sacrament which Christ had given to his church, baptism in the Spirit by the laying-on of hands, which they called the *consolamentum*. Although normally administered by a bishop or his delegate, this sacrament could at need be conferred by any fully initiated Cathar of either sex. But if a Cathar committed a grave sin after his baptism, he not only lost the right to console, but all previous consolings which he had administered were *ipso facto* rendered void and had to be repeated. The reasoning behind this belief seems to have been that the *consolamentum* conferred impeccability on its recipient and that therefore any consoled Cathar who committed grave sin could not have been validly consoled and had never had the power to console others.[40] Nicetas of Constantinople, it would seem, developed doubts about the validity of sacraments conferred by the Bulgarian church and came to the west to remedy this defect, while Petracius of Bulgaria certainly cast doubt on the validity of Dragovetan sacraments.[41] Rainier Sacconi, writing some eighty years after Nicetas's mission, gave a list of fifteen Cathar churches which existed in his own day in France, Italy, the Balkans and the Byzantine empire. This ends with the words: 'the church of Bulgaria, the church of Drugunthia [Dragovet]. All took their origin from the last two named.'[42] Because of his long association

---

39. 'Item omnes ecclesiae Catharorum se recipiunt ad invicem licet habeant diversas et contrarias opiniones, praeter Albanenses et Concorrezenses qui se damnant adinvicem...'. Sacconi, *op. cit.*, ed. Dondaine, p.77.
40. This doubt was shared by Cathars of all persuasions, *ibid.*, pp.69-70.
41. *De Heresi*, ed. Dondaine, *AFP*, XIX, p.306.
42. Sacconi, *op. cit.*, ed. Dondaine, p.70.

with their church Rainier was in a position to be well-informed about Cathar history. It is sometimes supposed that he is claiming in this passage that Bulgaria and Dragovet were in origin two separate bodies and that both were sources of the Cathar movement. The rest of the evidence suggests, however, that he was making a more limited point: that in his day all the Cathars in east and west traced their orders (their line of consolings) either to the church of Bulgaria or to that of Dragovet.

The unity of organization, liturgy and dicipline which existed between the two traditions suggests that the churches of Bulgaria and Dragovet had once formed part of a single communion. Indeed, Nicetas of Constantinople's sermon to the Cathars of Toulouse implies that in his day the schism was of very recent origin, for although he had come to the west specifically to denounce the validity of the Bulgarian *ordo* he did not denounce the Bulgarian church. On the contrary, he spoke of all the Balkan churches forming part of a single communion and he evidently hoped that all Balkan dualists would come to accept the sacramental *ordo* of Dragovet and that the schism would in that way be healed. In this he proved to be over-optimistic: the schism was never healed and after 1175 there certainly were two Cathar churches, one in communion with Bulgaria, the other with Dragovet.[43] Nevertheless, any western Cathar of either church who sought to find out more about the origins of the movement would have learned about the united dualist churches of the Balkans before the schism which, as Nicetas of Constantinople had told his audience, 'have peace with each other'.

The five Balkan churches to which he referred and which existed at the time when Catharism became established in western Europe were therefore Bogomil churches. The origins of Bogomilism are reasonably well-known. It is first attested in Bulgaria in the middle of the tenth century in the reign of Tsar Peter and its foundation is attributed to *pop* Bogomil.[44] Byzantine theologians described it as a

---

43. Salvo Burci, *Liber Supra Stella*, ed. Ilarino da Milano, *Aevum*, XIX (1945), p.309.
44. For a full discussion of the growth of Bogomilism in Bulgaria see Obolensky, *Bogomils*, pp.111-67.

mixture of Manichaeism/Paulicianism and Messalianism, although this is not necessarily evidence of historical filiation so much as an attempt to classify certain heretical tenets.[45] I find it impossible to accept the view that Messalianism survived as an organized religious system in the tenth century and influenced the development of Bogomilism, although I have no doubt that certain kinds of extreme ascetic behaviour, recurrent in Byzantine monasticism, had always been labelled in that way. Paulicianism is a different matter. It was an older movement than Bogomilism and Paulician communities existed in the Balkans at a time when Bogomilism was emerging and had the opportunity of affecting its development. Constantine V had brought settlers, who included Paulicians, from eastern Asia Minor to re-people Thrace after the great plague of 748[46] and other Paulicians were settled at Philippopolis by John I Tzimisces in the third quarter of the tenth century.[47]

It is impossible to determine whether the Paulicians had any part in shaping primitive Bogomilism, but it is certain that both movements shared a common belief that the phenomenal world was not the creation of the good God: the Paulicians attributed it to an evil god and the early Bogomils to an evil demiurge who was a creature of the good God.[48] Bogomilism changed a great deal in the first century of its existence and the Paulicians certainly had some share in this. The Bulgarian Bogomils described by Cosmas the priest in the tenth century were simple-minded people of very ascetic life who do not seem to have had a liturgy or any form of structure.[49]

45. E.g. Anna Comnena, *Alexiad*, XV, viii, 1, ed. with French translation B.Leib, 4 vols (Paris, 1967-76), III, pp.218-9. Cf. Obolensky, *op. cit., Harvard Ukrainian Studies*, VII, p.500, footnote 44.
46. Theophanes, *Chronographia*, ed. C. de Boor, 2 vols (Leipzig, 1883-7), I, p.429.
47. Anna Comnena, *op. cit.*, XIV, vii, 5, ed. Leib, III, pp.179-80.
48. Peter of Sicily, *Historia Manichaeorum qui et Pauliciani dicuntur*, c.36, ed. Ch. Astruc, W.Carus-Wolska, J.Gouillard, P.Lemerle, D.Papachryssanthou, P.Paramelle, 'Les sources grecques pour l'histoire des Pauliciens d'Asie Mineure', *Travaux et Mémoires (TM)*, IV (1970), Centre de Recherche d'histoire et civilisation byzantines, pp.19-21; Zigabenus, *op. cit.*, XXVII, 7, *PG*, 130, cols. 1296-7.
49. H.-C.Puech, A.Vaillant, *Le Traité contre les Bogomiles de Cosmas le prêtre* (Paris, 1945).

When the movement spread into the Greek-speaking lands of Byzantium during the eleventh century it became much more sophisticated. The Byzantine Bogomils described by Euthymius Zigabenus in the early twelfth century are recognizably more like western Cathars than the primitive Bulgarian Bogomils had been: they distinguished between hearers and fully initiated member, they had a liturgy, a canon of scripture and a tradition of exegesis.[50]

Paulician influence is discernible at this stage for Zigabenus relates that the Bogomils of Constantinople in the reign of Alexius Comnenus

> say that the God-fearing emperors are strangers to the body of Christians ... and that the only orthodox and faithful ones were the Iconoclasts, specially Copronymus.[51]

The historical memory of the Bogomils as a religious group did not extend back as far as the Iconoclast period and in any case the adherents of a movement which originated in Bulgaria would have had little reason to revere Constantine V. The Paulicians, on the contrary, had reason to remember Constantine with kindness: he had settled their ancestors in Thrace and had not attempted to persecute them for their faith, probably because his father, Leo III, had had Gegnesius, the Paulician leader, examined by the patriarch of Constantinople who had been misled into supposing that his beliefs were orthodox.[52]

Anna Comnena attests that the Paulicians remained distinct from the Bogomils in Alexius I's reign,[53] so that Paulician influence on Bogomilism cannot be attributed to a merger between the two movements during the eleventh century. The evidence suggests rather that some Paulicians were converted to Bogomilism, that they accepted Bogomil ascetic disciplines, but that in their turn they affected the development of Bogomilism in various ways. The Bogomil cult of the Iconoclast emperors attested by Zigabenus is the earliest known example of such influence, but it became more

---

50. Zigabenus, op. cit., PG, 130, cols. 1289-1332.
51. Zigabenus, De Haeresi Bogomilorum, ed. Ficker, Die Phundagiagiten, p.99.
52. Peter of Sicily, op. cit., cc. 114-22, TM, IV, pp.47-9.
53. Anna Comnena, op. cit., XIV, viii, ed. Leib, III, pp.177-82.

pronounced in the following century. The absolute dualism of the Bogomil church of Dragovet recorded in western sources about those Cathar churches which derived their teaching from the *ordo* of Dragovet is a further sign of Paulician influence. In this connection it should be noted that Dragovet is geographically the nearest of all the Bogomil churches to Philippopolis, the centre of Balkan Paulicianism in the twelfth century, and consequently it is possible that the Bogomil church of Dragovet contained a higher proportion of Paulician converts than Bogomil churches did elsewhere. This would explain why the church of Dragovet came to accept the distinctively Paulician doctrine of absolute dualism.

But the evidence suggests that all Bogomil churches were in some measure open to Paulician influence and that Paulician converts were able to give the Bogomils an historical respectability which the Bogomils themselves lacked. The Bogomils could not trace their origins before the middle of the tenth century and although the 900-year gap which separated the *pop* Bogomil from the apostles may not have bothered the first, simple adherents of the movement, this must have troubled Byzantine Bogomils who were better educated and who had to meet the objections of learned critics. To judge from western records the Bogomils played down their Balkan origins and emphasized their Paulician antecedents when making western converts. Certainly the name of Bogomil is not mentioned in any western record relating to the Cathars, although, of course, the Cathars and their critics were aware that the proximate sources of their faith were the Bogomil churches in the Balkans. The Cathars were popularly called Bulgars, or *bougres,* a name which has enriched many western vernaculars with a new term of abuse.[54] Nevertheless, when asked by Cathars about the origins of their church the twelfth-century Bogomils would appear to have referred to the ancient traditions of their Paulician converts rather than to their own more recent Balkan tradition.

54. M.Loos has suggested that the other name commonly given to the Cathars in the west, *popelicani* (often mistakenly rendered as *publicani* by western writers), may derive from the notorious centre of Balkan heresy, Philippopolis, or Plovdiv. M.Loos, *Dualist Heresy in the Middle Ages* (Prague, 1974), p.118.

Our knowledge of the early history of the Paulicians is derived chiefly from the account of Peter of Sicily, sent as ambassador by Basil I to the Paulician state of Tephrike in 869-70. Although Mme. Garsoian has called in question the value of Peter's work as a primary source,[55] M. Lemerle has convincingly demonstrated that this is the earliest and fullest account of the Paulicians that we have.[56] Peter relates that the Paulicians could trace their origins securely from the reign of the emperor Constans II in the middle of the seventh century.[57] From then until 835 they were governed by a succession of *didaskaloi,* or religious teachers, who were assisted by *synekdemoi,* or companions.[58] When the last *didaskalos,* Sergius, was killed in 835 he had no successor, but two of the *synekdemoi* whom he had trained, Basil and Zosimus, were still alive when Peter of Sicily visited Tephrike[59] and so he had access to particularly good sources of information about Sergius' activities. Peter relates that each of the *didaskaloi* had taken the name of one of St. Paul's disciples mentioned in the New Testament and that they had also given the name of one of the churches founded by St. Paul to each of the churches which they founded themselves.[60]

The Paulicians had seven churches and I would argue that Nicetas of Constantinople was referring to them in his sermon to the Cathars of Toulouse recorded in the Saint-Félix document:

> You have asked me to tell you whether the customs of the primitive churches were light or burdensome and I tell you that the seven churches of Asia were separated from each other by defined boundaries and none of them did anything to the

---

55. N.Garsoian, *The Paulician Heresy* (The Hague-Paris, 1967), pp.27-79.
56. P.Lemerle, 'L'histoire des Pauliciens d'Asie Mineure d'après les sources grecques', *TM,* V (1973), pp.17-47.
57. Peter of Sicily, *op. cit.,* c.94, *TM,* IV, p.41. There is general agreement that 'Constantine grandson of Heraclius' in this passage refers to Constans II, Obolensky, *Bogomils,* p.32, n.3.
58. Peter of Sicily, *op. cit.,* c.183, *TM,* IV, p.67. *Synekdemos* derives from II Cor. viii, 19, where it describes the unnamed brother 'whose praise is in all the churches' whom Paul sent to Corinth as a companion to Titus. Obolensky, *Bogomils,* pp.28-37.
59. Peter of Sicily, *op. cit.,* cc. 182, 188, *TM,* IV, p.67.
60. *Ibid.,* c. 163, *TM,* IV, p.61.

detriment of any of the others.[61]

Obviously this was not a reference to the Bogomil churches in Nicetas's own day, for there are only five of them in the list which he gives and all of them were in the Balkans and Greece. He could have been referring to the seven churches of Asia named in the Apocalypse of St. John: Ephesus, Smyrna, Pergamum, Thyatira, Sardis, Philadelphia and Laodicea.[62] It is true that the Cathars held the Apocalypse in high regard and placed it immediately after the Acts of the Apostles in their canon of scripture,[63] but nothing in the text of St. John relates to church boundaries or organization, nor is there any indication in our sources that the Cathars interpreted that part of the Apocalypse in that sense.[64]

Our knowledge of the seven Paulician churches is derived from part of a letter written by the *didaskolos* Sergius which is quoted by Peter of Sicily:

I say moreover that the church of Corinth was built by Paul; that of Macedonia by Silvanus and Titus; that of Achaea was embellished by Timothy; the church of the Philippians was ministered to by Epaphroditus; the churches of the Laodiceans, the Ephesians and the Colossians were taught the faith by Tychicus.[65]

There is every reason to suppose that this letter continued to be read by the Paulicians in the twelfth century because Peter of Sicily relates that in his day the Paulicians included the letters of the *didaskalos* Sergius in their canon of the New Testament.[66] They would therefore have been made available to the Bogomils by their Paulician converts.

61. Hamilton, *op. cit.*, *AFP*, XLVIII, p.52.
62. Apoc., i-iii.
63. Clédat, *op. cit.*, pp.269-300.
64. Instances could be multiplied but the most striking is to be found in the Cathar Gloss on the Lord's Prayer: '*Adveniat regnum tuum...* Mais aquest Regne, co es lo fill de Dio, fe los sios fraires regne e preyres al sio Dio, aisicom Saint Johan dis en l'Apocalis: "Johan a las vii gleisas que son en Asia; gracia a vos e pax...".' ed. Th. Venckeleer, 'Un recueil cathare... II. Une glose sur le Pater', *Revue belge de philologie et d'histoire*, XXXIX (1961), p.768.
65. Peter of Sicily, *op. cit.*, c.163, *TM*, IV, p.61.
66. *Ibid*, c.43, pp.21-3.

XII

286

There is no evidence that the Bogomils accorded these letters canonical authority. According to Euthymius Zigabenus they accepted the New Testament in its entirety and in the Orthodox text,[67] but it is arguable that they may have treated the letters of Sergius with considerable respect. We are accustomed to read them in the text of Peter of Sicily who glossed the information about the seven churches of Asia. He tells us that six of them were founded by Paulician *didaskaloi* who took in religion the names of St. Paul's disciples and who gave to the Paulician congregations which they founded in Asia Minor the names of churches founded by St. Paul. Thus the church of Macedonia was at Kibossa and its founders, Silvanus and Titus, were really the first Paulician *didaskalos*, Constantine of Mananali, and his successor, Symeon; the church of Achaea was at Mananali and was founded by the *didaskalos* Gegnesius who took the name of Timothy; Peter did not know the location of the church of Philippi, but said that its founder, Epaphroditus, was the *didaskalos* Joseph; and he explained that the last *didaskalos*, Sergius, the writer of the letter, was known as Tychicus in religion and founded churches at Argaoun, Mopsouestia and Kynochorion, which he named Colossae, Ephesus and Laodicea respectively. Peter did not reckon the church of Corinth among the Paulician foundations, presumably because the Paulicians themselves did not claim to have established it.[68]

None of this supplementary information would have been included in the text of the letter which the Paulicians read or in that which Paulician converts made available to the Bogomils. They would have seen a letter which purported to have been written by Tychicus, one of St. Paul's most trusted assistants, to whom he refers as 'a beloved brother and faithful minister in the Lord'.[69] From what is known of their attitude to other uncanonical writings which they believed to date from early Christian or even from Old

67. Zigabenus, *op. cit.*, XXVII, 1, 21, *PG*, 130, cols. 1292, 1317.
68. Peter of Sicily, *op. cit.*, c.163, *TM*, IV, p.61.
69. Acts, XX, 4; Eph., VI, 21; Col., IV, 7; II Tim., IV, 12; Tit., III, 12. 'Calling himself Tychicus who is mentioned in the epistles of St. Paul, [Sergius] told everybody that he was the disciple of the apostle, whom he had sent to announce the word of God.' Peter of Sicily, *op. cit.*, c.152, *TM*, IV, p.57.

Testament times, it is reasonable to infer that the Bogomils would have treated an epistle of Tychicus with reverence. It is known, for example, that the Paulicians in the eleventh century accepted as genuine the apocryphal epistle of St. Paul to the Laodiceans,[70] a tradition which was transmitted by them to the Cathars, presumably through Paulicians who had been converted to Bogomilism, for the Cathars included this epistle in their New Testament.[71] Similarly the Bogomils read the *Vision of Isaiah,* a first-century Gnostic work,[72] and transmitted that to the Cathars as well.[73] Obviously Byzantine dualists sought out works which they believed to date from the apostolic age or earlier and which supported their interpretation of the Christian revelation and an alleged epistle of Tychicus would have come into that category.

There is no reason to suppose that they would have read this letter as anything more than an historical statement about the foundation of churches by St. Paul and his disciples. There is no evidence that the Paulicians attached any special symbolic value to the Pauline names which they gave to their leaders and churches. Indeed, such practices can be paralleled elsewhere in the Christian tradition in cases where it is certain that piety alone dictated the choice of names. The Paulician *didaskaloi* took the names of New Testament figures in much the same way as monks throughout the ages have taken the names of saints at their profession, while in giving their churches Biblical names the Paulicians were anticipating nineteenth-century Welsh nonconformists who called their chapels Bethesda and Salem. It is equally doubtful whether any special importance should be attached to the fact that there were seven Paulician churches, since it would appear that this number was the product of historical circumstance rather than of religious

70. 'Those of the present day recognize only the four Gospels and ... the fifteen epistles of St. Paul, because they also have an epistle to the Laodiceans.' An eleventh-century scholion on Peter of Sicily, cited by Lemerle, 'L'histoire des Pauliciens', *TM*, V, p.132.
71. Clédat, *op. cit.,* pp.432-3.
72. J.Gouillard, 'Le Synodikon de l'Orthodoxie. Edition et Commentaire', *TM*, II (1967), p.65.
73. It is quoted in the Gloss on the Lord's Prayer, Venckeleer, 'Un recueil cathare. II', *Revue belge de philologie et d'histoire*, XXXIX, p.764.

XII

symbolism: no new *didaskalos* was appointed after the death of
Sergius in 835 and therefore no new Paulician church was founded
and the number remained fixed at seven.[74]

Paulician converts to Bogomilism would therefore have interpreted this letter of Tychicus in a plain, historical sense rather than
in an esoteric way, but, to judge from Nicetas of Constantinople's
statement, they had preserved a memory that all the churches had
been situated in Asia Minor, which the names of some of them
would not lead the reader to expect. It is probably safe to assume
that they remembered the scattering of the Paulician churches
which had followed the destruction of the movement's headquarters
at Tephrike by Basil I in 878,[75] but by the twelfth century their
memory of the earlier history of those churches may have grown
rather dim and they may have supposed that the seven churches of
Asia really had been founded in the apostolic age. They may not
have supposed that all these foundations had originally been made
in Asia Minor, for the evidence of many of their names suggested
the contrary, but have thought that congregations had moved to
more remote parts of the empire during times of persecution while
retaining their original names. Such a view would be natural to
dualists of all kinds, since they had no church buildings and
understood the word church in its primary sense of assembly of the
faithful.[76] The Cathars, formed in this tradition, certainly followed
this custom when persecuted. In the thirteenth century many
French Cathars fled to Lombardy to escape the inquisition, but in
exile they continued to call themselves the church of France and the
church of Toulouse.[77]

If this argument is correct, any Cathar who wanted detailed
information about the historical transmission of his faith would have
had access to written records and oral traditions in his local church
giving details of the succession of bishops from the time of its

74. Peter of Sicily, *op. cit.*, c.183, *TM*, IV, p.67.
75. For the date see Lemerle, 'L'histoire des Pauliciens', *TM*, V, pp.103-8.
76. E.g. Zigabenus, *op. cit.*, XXVII, 18, *PG*, 130, col. 1313.
77. 'Ecclesia Franciae morantur Veronae et in Lombardia', Sacconi, *op. cit.*, ed.
    Dondaine, p.70. The church of Toulouse lived in Verona, Anselm of Alessan-
    dria, *op. cit.*, ed. Dondaine, *AFP*, XX, p.310.

foundation. He would further have been told that before that time the faith derived from churches in the Balkans and the Byzantine empire and would have been given details about them.[78] If he had met a Bogomil leader, such as Nicetas of Constantinople, travelling in the west, or if, like Nazarius, Cathar bishop of Concorezzo, he had visited his brethren in the Balkans[79] and had inquired about the more remote origins of his faith, he would, it seems, have been told the Paulician version: that before the faith reached the Balkan churches it had been practised in Asia Minor until the reign of Basil I when the churches had been scattered by persecution; that there had been seven 'primitive' churches in Asia and that they had been founded by the apostle Paul and his disciples; and that the Bogomils had proof of this in the epistle of Tychicus.

This account, supported by written evidence, would have satisfied educated and inquiring Cathars who wanted proofs about the historical transmission of their faith. It is doubtful whether the Cathar churches of the west kept any detailed records of the succession to Bogomil sees, or translated any documents relating to the Paulician churches of Asia. Certainly no trace of such records remains. The rendering of Greek and Old Slavonic names into western languages would have been an obstacle to any such undertaking, though scarcely an insuperable one, and it would seem that the Cathars saw no reason to compile such records. Once they were assured that the Bogomil churches had the necessary proofs, they could simply refer to them as the source of their own tradition. In this they resembled their Catholic contemporaries: western dioceses kept lists of their own bishops, but were not, in most cases, concerned about the proofs of apostolic succession before the foundation of their own sees, because they knew that such proofs were to be found in the archive of the apostolic see of Rome.

78. It is clear from the list of Balkan and Byzantine churches given by Rainier Sacconi that such lists were kept by the Cathar churches of the west, Sacconi, *op. cit.*, ed. Dondaine, p.70.

79. The Carcassonne manuscript of the *Interrogatio Iohannis* has a colophon which reads: 'Explicit secretum hereticorum de Concorresio portatum de Bulgaria Nazario suo episcopo plenum erroribus.' Ed. E.Bozóky, *Le Livre secret des Cathares* (Paris, 1980), p.86.

Yet the proofs in which the Cathars put their trust, proofs which ultimately derived from the Paulicians, were not authentic. The epistle of Tychicus had not been written by a disciple of St. Paul but by the *didaskalos* Sergius who died in 835, while six of the 'primitive' churches to which it refers had been founded not in the apostolic age, but by Sergius himself and his predecessors in the Paulician leadership. Indeed, the oldest of the six, that of Macedonia, had been established by Constantine of Mananali who began his ministry in the reign of Constans II. So although the Cathars in the twelfth and thirteenth centuries believed in good faith that they could trace their church back in unbroken succession to the age of the apostles, they could, in fact, only get halfway there, to about the middle of the seventh century.

This view, however, fails to take into account the first of the seven churches of Asia, that of Corinth which, according to Sergius, was 'built by Paul'.[80] Peter of Sicily makes no attempt to identify this Paul with any Paulician leader, which indicates that the Paulicians themselves believed that the church of Corinth had been founded by the apostle Paul. It is arguable that the inclusion of Corinth in Sergius's list of churches may have been no more than a device to bridge the gap which he knew to exist between the apostolic age and the lifetime of the first *didaskalos,* Constantine of Mananali. Yet in that case Sergius's choice of a Pauline foundation in southern Greece rather than of one in Asia Minor seems eccentric, if his intention was to emphasize the preservation of a Pauline tradition in Asia Minor to the time of the *didaskalos* Constantine. Moreover, the other churches to which Sergius refers all continued to exist in his own day: one of his letters is written to the second of them, the church of Macedonia, founded by Constantine and living in the ninth century at Koloneia.[81] The text of Sergius's letter suggests that the church of Corinth was also still in existence when he wrote, but that it was a pre-Paulician foundation, claiming apostolic origins, and that it had, to use modern terminology, 'entered into communion with' the Paulicians.

80. Peter of Sicily, *op. cit.,* c. 163, *TM, IV,* p.61.
81. *Ibid.,* c.158, *TM, IV,* p.59.

In Constantine of Mananali's lifetime there were various forms of what M.Gouillard has called 'Byzantine Old Catholicism' surviving in Asia Minor, groups which had broken away from the Great Church during the age of persecution, but which preserved their identity up to the time of the Iconoclast emperors, though not beyond.[82] It is possible that the early Paulicians converted a congregation of adherents of some older sect and were in turn influenced by them, just as the Bogomils later converted and were influenced by some Paulicians, and that those converts formed the church of Corinth and claimed to have been founded by St. Paul himself. A memory of some event of this kind seems to lie behind the story which Peter of Sicily learned while he was staying at Tephrike: that Constantine of Mananali had sheltered a deacon who was returning to his homeland from Arab captivity in Syria, who gave him books containing the canonical gospels and epistles which Constantine began to use as his proof-texts when he preached.[83]

Some indication of the identity of the older sect which influenced the Paulicians may perhaps be found in western sources relating to the Cathars. In the first place there is the name Cathars: this clearly derives from the Greek word *katharoi* and was the name which western dualists used of themselves. Attempts to find alternative derivations of the name have not been convincing.[84] Certainly some western writers did not understand what it meant and associated it with *cattus,* the Latin form of the German name for the *felis domesticus.*[85] No satisfactory explanation has ever been advanced about why the Cathars used this name, apart from that of Henri Grégoire who pointed out that it was the name used of themselves by the Novatians.[86] If Grégoire were right, this would

---

82. J.Gouillard, 'L'hérésie dans l'empire byzantin des origines au XIIe siècle', *TM,* I (1965), pp.300-12.
83. Peter of Sicily, *op. cit.,* c.95, *TM,* IV, p.41.
84. E.g. Duvernoy, *op. cit.,* pp.302-4.
85. Alan of Lille, *De fide Catholica contra haereticos sui temporis,* I, lxiii, *PL,* 210, col.366.
86. H.Grégoire, 'Cathares d'Asie Mineure, d'Italie et de la France', *Archives de l'Orient chrétien,* I (1948), pp.142-51.

explain why Orthodox theologians do not use the term *katharoi* to describe the Bogomils, even though the Bogomils must have used it of themselves, since the name can only have reached the west through them. *Katharoi* in Orthodox terminology was a name reserved to the Novatians and accorded to them in canon eight of the first council of Nicaea.[87] Since the Bogomils appeared to have nothing in common with the Novatians, Orthodox theologians would have thought it confusing to call them both by the same name. If the name *katharoi* derives ultimately from the Novatians, it must have been transmitted by them to the Paulicians and thence to the Bogomils, since there is no evidence to suggest that the Novatians survived as an independent sect into the tenth century when the Bogomil church was founded.

Although the Novatians and the Paulicians appear to have little in common, there is no *a priori* reason to exclude the Novatians as a possible influence on the early Paulician movement. The Novatians went into schism in the middle of the third century because they refused to accept the decision of the Great Church to reconcile those who had apostatized during the Decian persecution. They were completely orthodox in doctrine and enjoyed a wide measure of toleration under the Catholic emperors of the fourth and fifth centuries. They were found in large numbers in the eastern provinces of the empire and were particularly numerous in Phrygia and Paphlagonia, while some isolated communities survived in Asia Minor until the end of the seventh century.[88] It would therefore have been theoretically possible for Constantine of Mananali to have come into contact with a Novatian congregation when he began to teach in the reign of Constans II.

Nevertheless, this argument would merit little serious attention if the only certain facts were that both the Novatians and medieval western dualists called themselves *katharoi*, for the use of the same name by two religious groups separated from each other in time by

87. G.D.Mansi, ed., *Sacrorum Conciliorum nova et amplissima collectio*, 53 vols, (Florence-Venice-Paris, 1759-1927), III, p.671.
88. E.Amann, 'Novatien et Novatianisme', *Dictionnaire de Théologie Catholique*, XI (i), 845-9; R.Janin, 'Les Novatiens orientaux', *Echos d'Orient*, XXVIII (1929), pp.385-97.

half a millennium and in space by the eastern Mediterranean is not proof of even partial filiation. That is why Grégoire's theory has received so little serious attention. Yet there is a further piece of evidence which lends support to his view, the Cathar *Ritual*. The full text exists in a thirteenth-century Provençal version and part of the text is also preserved in a thirteenth-century Latin version.[89] Christine Thouzellier, in her edition of the Latin text, argued that the *Ritual* derived from western sources of the patristic age, but her thesis is not convincing.[90] The text for the administration of the *consolamentum* contained in both versions conforms very closely to Euthymius Zigabenus's description of Bogomil rites of initiation,[91] while certain liturgical phrases in the opening section of the Provençal *Ritual* correspond word for word with phrases which, according to Euthymius of Acmonia, the Byzantine Bogomils used in their worship in the mid-eleventh century.[92] In addition, an Old Slavonic version of the opening section of the Provençal *Ritual* is contained in a mid-fifteenth century manuscript, which some scholars consider is a transcription of a late eleventh- or early twelfth-century archetype.[93] All the available evidence therefore suggests that the Cathars obtained their service-book from the Bogomils from whom they obtained the rest of their faith.

The tenth-century Bogomils of Bulgaria described by Cosmas the priest did not use any set form of worship apart from the Lord's Prayer.[94] The *Ritual* is first attested in use among the Byzantine Bogomils in the mid-eleventh century.[95] Nevertheless, there are good reasons for thinking that the work was not composed by them. First it is extremely orthodox in sentiment and vocabulary: it is

89. Provençal text ed. Clédat, *op. cit.*, pp. ix-xxvi; Latin text ed. Dondaine, *Un Traité*, pp.151-65.
90. C.Thouzellier, *Rituel Cathare, SC,* 236 (Paris, 1977). See the critique by Duvernoy, *op. cit.*, 'Addition à la *Conclusion*', unpaginated.
91. Zigabenus, *op. cit.*, XXVII, 16, *PG*, 130, col. 1312.
92. Euthymius of Acmonia, *op. cit.*, ed. Ficker, p.77. This correspondence was pointed out by Obolensky, *Bogomils*, p.183, n.2.
93. Vatican Library, MS Borgiano Illyrico 12, ff.56r-58v, ed. C.Thouzellier, *Rituel Cathare*, pp.63-70, Table 20.
94. Puech, Vaillant, *Cosmas le prêtre*, cc. vii, xvii, xx, pp.63-4, 83, 90.
95. Euthymius of Acmonia, *op. cit.*, ed. Ficker, p.77.

difficult to detect any signs of dualism or of any other heterodox opinion in the extant versions and, as Guiraud remarked, an inquisitor could have delivered the discourses of the presiding elder to a Catholic audience without making any substantive changes in the text.[96] This suggests that it was not written by dualists, but was adapted by them from some liturgical work which had been composed for orthodox Christian use. Secondly, the *Ritual* appears to derive from very early Christian liturgical sources: Guiraud pointed this out when he examined the Provençal text[97] and Dondaine said the same in his edition of the Latin text.[98] The form of the *Ritual* therefore suggests that it antedates any Christian dualist movement except Marcionism, while its orthodox character would seem to rule out a Marcionite origin.

The Byzantine Bogomils could, of course, have adapted to their use an ancient liturgy which they had found in a manuscript collection, just as they found and used apocryphal Gnostic works like the *Vision of Isaiah*. Yet, if that is so, it is difficult to explain why they were attracted to such an orthodox text. The presiding minister in his discourse before the conferring of the *consolamentum*, for example, cites Christ's words to Nicodemus: 'Unless a man be born again of water and the Holy Spirit he cannot enter the kingdom of God,'[99] a text which flatly contradicts dualist teaching about the inefficacy of baptism by water. It seems more probable that the Bogomils inherited their liturgy from some older religious group and used it in an adapted form because they believed that it represented an ancient tradition of worship. They may have received it from the Paulicians: certainly the Bogomils are first attested as using the *Ritual* at a time when other Paulician influences, like the cult of the Iconoclast emperors, make their appearance in the movement. Yet the Paulicians clearly did not write the *Ritual* since, on liturgical grounds, its composition can be dated to a period before the mid-seventh century when their sect

96. Guiraud, *op. cit.*, I, p.126.
97. *Ibid.*, I, pp.108-42, 195-6.
98. Dondaine, *Un Traité*, pp.45-6.
99. Jn., III, 5. Clédat, *op. cit.*, p.xvi.

was founded.

The precise date of the composition of the *Ritual* can only be satisfactorily resolved by experts in early Christian liturgy and so far as I am aware the texts have not yet been examined by scholars in that field. To my inexpert eye the rite of the *consolamentum* in the *Ritual* bears a close affinity to the baptismal liturgy described in the *Apostolic Tradition* of St. Hippolytus of Rome, with the omission of baptism by water.[100] The orthodox and archaic nature of the *Ritual* certainly suggests a Novatian provenance: alone of the early schismatic groups the Novatians remained orthodox in faith, so much so that they were persecuted by the Arian emperors in the fourth century,[101] while their intense conservatism makes it likely that they preserved ancient liturgical forms into the early middle ages. I would suggest that a group of Novatians joined with the early Paulicians in the seventh century and transmitted their liturgy to them and that they are the church of Corinth, the first of the seven churches of Asia, whose foundation the Paulicians them-selves ascribed to St. Paul. Apart from a single phrase recorded by Peter of Sicily[102] nothing is known about the Paulician liturgy, but they must have had some form of public worship and some rite of initiation and I would suggest that they used the *Ritual,* which was later transmitted by them to the Bogomils and thence to the Cathars. If this argument is true, then the Cathars and the Catholics in western Europe both used a form of public worship which ultimately derived from the third-century liturgy of the Roman see. In that case, however heterodox the Cathars' understanding of the Christian faith may have been, their claim that 'the church of God has preserved this holy baptism ... from the time of the apostles until now' was not entirely without foundation.

100. B.Botte, ed., *La Tradition apostolique de Saint Hippolyte, Liturgiewissens-chaftliche Quellen und Forschungen,* 39 (Münster-Westfalen, 1963), pp.38-53.
101. Janin, 'Les Novatiens orientaux', *Échos d'Orient,* XXVIII, pp.389-92.
102. Peter of Sicily, *op. cit.,* c.156, *TM,* IV, p.59.

XIII

Wisdom from the East: the reception by the Cathars of Eastern dualist texts

Explicit secretum hereticorum de Concorresio portatum de Bulgaria Nazario suo episcopo plenum erroribus.[1]

No reputable scholar now doubts that Catharism was an offshoot of medieval eastern dualism, though it was clearly not a simple transplant but developed its own distinctive form. The Bogomils, whom the Cathars most resembled in their lifestyle and beliefs, do not seem to have had any writings of their own when they first appeared in tenth-century Bulgaria. The priest Cosmas described them as members of a rustic, pietist movement, who held dualist beliefs which they expressed in folkloristic terms. Their only book was the New Testament, which they read in the same text as the Orthodox, although they interpreted it in a heterodox way: 'Although they carry the Holy Gospel in their hands, they interpret it falsely and thus seduce men'.[2]

The older dualist church of the Paulicians, also found in the tenth-century Balkans, did have a literature of its own. While basing their teachings on the New Testament alone,[3] its members also circulated works composed by their own leaders.[4] But although the Paulicians may indirectly have influenced the development of Cath-

---

[1] 'Here endeth the secret book of the heretics of Concorrezo, brought from Bulgaria by their bishop Nazarius [and] full of errors' (*Livre secret*, p. 86). Malcolm Lambert has drawn my attention to Duvernoy's assertion that this passage should be translated 'was brought from Bulgaria to their bishop Nazarius', *La Religion*, p. 35 n. 47. This view is not convincing because Sacconi relates that Nazarius has received his teaching from the bishop of Bulgaria and his Elder Son, Sacconi, p. 58. See p. 55 below.

[2] *Le Traité contre les Bogomiles de Cosmas le Prêtre, traduction et étude*, H-C. Puech and A. Vaillant (Paris, 1945), p. 76.

[3] They may have used a slightly different canon. Peter of Sicily, *Historia Manichaeorum qui et Pauliciani dicuntur*, c.42, ed. Ch. Astruc, W. Carus-Wolska, J. Gouillard, P. Lemerle, D. Papachryssanthou and P. Paramelle, *Les Sources grecques pour l'histoire des Pauliciens d'Asie Mineure, Travaux et Mémoires* (Paris, 1970), vol. IV, p. 21.

[4] *Historia Manichaeorum*, c.43, pp. 21–3.

arism in the twelfth century,[5] there is no evidence that they penetra-
ted the West before then.

Although most recent scholarship is sceptical about the influence
of Bogomilism on Western heretical movements in the eleventh
century[6] the question seems to me to be by no means closed. If one
looks for evidence of fully fledged Bogomilism as described by
twelfth-century Byzantine writers among the alleged 'Manichees' in
western Europe in the years before 1050 it will not, of course, be
found, because it did not exist in the East either. But the 'new
Manichees' in the West were very like the Bogomilism which was
evolving in the Balkans at that time. Critics of the Bogomil hypo-
thesis draw attention to the fact that Western sources emphasise the
ascetic lifestyle of the new heretics while saying nothing about their
dualist beliefs; but a similar observation has been made about
primitive Bogomils by Sir Dmitri Obolensky: 'the exposition of the
doctrinal errors of the heretics forms a comparatively small part of
the *Sermon* of Cosmas, which is concerned above all with the moral
and social aspects of the heresy'.[7]

The development of a new heresy in Bulgaria in the second half of
the tenth century, followed by isolated outbreaks of heresy in parts
of western Europe which share many of the characteristics of the
Balkan movement, is strong presumptive evidence that the two
developments were linked. The opponents of this view claim that the
link is missing, because there is no evidence of Bogomil preachers in
the West at that time, but it seems possible that the link is being
sought in the wrong place. It is known from the writings of
Euthymius of Acmonia that at precisely the point when 'Manichee'
outbreaks are reported in the West, Bogomilism was spreading into
the Greek-speaking lands of Byzantium, and was taking root in some
monasteries there, including Euthymius's own community of the
Periblepton in Constantinople.[8] What one should perhaps be
looking for in western Europe is a correlation between the places
where outbreaks of heresy occurred and those which Orthodox
monks are known to have visited. Certainly there was no shortage of
Orthodox monks perambulating the shrines of the West at that time,

[5] B. Hamilton, 'The origins of the dualist church of Drugunthia', *Eastern Churches Review*, 6
(1974), 115–24.
[6] For example, Moore, *Origins*, pp. 23–45; M. Lambert, *Medieval Heresy*, 2nd edn (Oxford,
1992), pp. xii–xiii.
[7] D. Obolensky, *The Bogomils: a Study in Balkan Neo-Manichaeism* (Cambridge, 1948) p. 126.
[8] Euthymius of Acmonia, *Liber invectivus contra haeresim ... haereticorum qui Phundagiatae dicuntur*,
PG, 131, 48–57.

XIII

40

some of whom settled there permanently,[9] and there may have been Bogomils among them. That this was sometimes the case is suggested by a passage in the *Life* of St Simeon the Hermit of Padolirone near Mantua. Simeon was an Armenian who came to Rome in the reign of pope Benedict VIII (1012–24).[10] When he performed his devotions in the Lateran basilica he was attacked by bystanders who alleged that he was a heretic, but the pope, who had him examined by an Armenian bishop, pronounced Simeon's faith orthodox.[11] Yet the fact that this misunderstanding occurred at all suggests that some of the eastern monks who visited the West in the early eleventh century were men of heterodox views.

But if Balkan dualism did enter the West at that time it would seem to have come with no books except the New Testament. Accounts of groups which might have been influenced by dualist preachers from the East bear this out. The heretics of Monforte arrested by bishop Aribert of Milan in *c.* 1028,[12] and the followers of Gundulfo, an Italian, interrogated by Gerard of Cambrai at about the same time, both claimed parts of the bible as their sole authority.[13]

It seems improbable that either the French or the Italian groups had a vernacular version of the New Testament. The earliest partial translations of the bible into French date from the twelfth century, and into Italian from the thirteenth century, and even then only certain books were translated. It would be straining credulity to suppose that small, isolated, dissenting groups had been able to undertake major literary work of that kind a century in advance of the rest of their societies.[14] It seems likely therefore that if the missionaries were Bogomils they used a Greek or Old Slavonic text of the New Testament and paraphrased it for their followers, and

9 B. Hamilton and P. A. McNulty, '*Orientale Lumen et Magistra Latinitas*: Greek influences on Western monasticism (900–1100)', *Le Millénaire du Mont Athos, 963–1963, Etudes et mélanges* (Chevetogne, 1963), vol. I, pp. 181–216.
10 He is said to have come to Rome in the pontificate of an unnumbered pope Benedict whom the Bollandists identified with Benedict VII (974–83), but since the *Life* places Simeon's stay in the West in the reign of Arsenius, Armenian bishop of Jerusalem 1006–38, the reference would seem to be to Benedict VIII (1012–24). *De S. Simeone monacho et eremita, AASS, Jul.*, VI, 324.
11 *De S. Simeone*, c.II, 327.
12 *Landulphi senioris Mediolanensis historiae libri quatuor*, II, 27, ed. A. Cutolo, *RIS*, new edn, IV(2), 69.
13 *Acta Synodi Atrebatensis*, Fredericq, I, 2–5.
14 C. A. Robson, 'Vernacular scriptures in France', K. Foster, 'Vernacular scriptures in Italy', *Cambridge History of the Bible* (1969), vol. II, pp. 436–65.

that if they were western Europeans they paraphrased the Vulgate. But if Bogomil missions were responsible for some of the outbreaks of heresy reported in western Europe in the first half of the eleventh century, they failed to take root. Between 1051[15] and 1114 there are no reports of heresy in the West which could be considered dualist.[16]

But during the eleventh century Bogomilism spread into the Greek-speaking lands of the Byzantine Empire, where it became far more intellectually sophisticated. This is known from the treatise of Euthymius of Acmonia written *c.* 1050, and from book XXVII of the *Dogmatic Panoply* written in the early twelfth century by Euthymius Zigabenus, the private theologian of the emperor Alexius I Comnenus (1081–1118).[17] Both sources relate that the Bogomils had a service book, which seems to have been in use by the first quarter of the eleventh century.[18] The Byzantine Bogomils were developing their own theological literature. Euthymius Zigabenus cited passages from a Bogomil commentary on St Matthew's Gospel written in Greek.[19] Moreover, by the early twelfth century the Bogomils of Constantinople had extended their canon of scripture to include the Psalter and the Prophets.[20]

Between 1018 and 1186 the peoples of Thrace, Greece and Bulgaria formed part of a single state. Greek was the official language of the Byzantine Empire, but many people in the Balkans and even in mainland Greece were Slav speakers, and the Orthodox Church encouraged the use of a vernacular liturgy among them. In the ninth century Sts. Constantine and Methodius had translated the bible and the service books of the Orthodox Church into Old Slavonic, and their disciple, St Clement, founded a school of translators in the monastery of Ochrida in Macedonia. In this way the religious literature of the Greek Orthodox Church began to be rendered into Old Slavonic.[21]

[15] In 1051 Henry III hanged heretics at Goslar possibly for believing in the transmigration of souls; *Herigeri et Anselmi Gesta episcoporum jeodiensium*, II, 64, ed. R. Koepke, *MGH SS*, VII, p. 228; Lambert, *Medieval Heresy*, p. 27.

[16] For the case of Clement of Bucy in 1114 see n. 36 below.

[17] Euthymius of Acmonia's letter about Bogomilism is ed. G. Ficker, *Die Phundagiagiten: ein Beitrag zur Ketzergeschichte des byzantinischen Mittelalters* (Leipzig, 1908); see also the *Liber invectivus*. Euthymius Zigabenus, *Panoplia dogmatica*, PG, 130, cols. 1289–1332.

[18] Euthymius of Acmonia, ed. Ficker, p. 77; Euthymius Zigabenus, *Panoplia dogmatica*, XXVII, 16, PG, 130, 1312–13.

[19] *Panoplia dogmatica*, XXVII, 27–52, PG, 130, 1321–32.

[20] *Panoplia dogmatica*, XXVII, 1, PG, 130, 1292.

[21] J. M. Hussey, *The Orthodox Church in the Byzantine Empire* (Oxford, 1986), pp. 90–101; A. P. Vlasto, *The Entry of the Slavs into Christendom* (Cambridge, 1970), pp. 159–79.

42

Thus the Slav-speaking Bogomils would have had no need to translate the New Testament into the vernacular because a good, modern translation already existed. They may, however, have needed to translate the Bogomil service-book. The origins of this work are obscure and I have discussed them elsewhere.[22] It appears to have been transmitted to the Bogomils through Paulician converts, although it is not known in what language it was read by Paulicians in the Balkans. It was in use among Greek-speaking Bogomils in the first quarter of the eleventh century who may have commissioned a translation direct from an Armenian original, or from a translation into Old Slavonic made by the Paulicians. By the twelfth century both the Greek-speaking and Slav-speaking Bogomils had an identical form of service-book, although the precise wording of their liturgies may have differed. This is known because Cathars, some of whom were evangelised from Bulgaria, others from Constantinople, all shared an identical form of public worship.[23]

It is universally agreed that Catharism was present in western Europe from 1143, when a Cathar bishop and his companion were brought to trial at Cologne. These men were conscious of their eastern roots, although they themselves may not have been of eastern origin. Eberwin of Steinfeld, who conducted the trial, reports their claim that: 'hanc haeresim usque ad haec tempora occultatam fuisse a temporibus martyrum, et permansisse in Graecia et quibusdam aliis terris' (this heresy had been hidden from the time of the martyrs to the present day and had survived in Greece and certain other countries).[24] This group had evidently been living in Cologne for a while before they were arrested. Some light is shed on their origins by St Hildegard of Bingen, a friend of St Elizabeth of Schönau, whose brother Egbert led the campaign against the renewed outbreak of Catharism at Cologne in 1163.[25] In July 1163 Hildegard wrote an account of a vision she had just had about the Cathars. She saw them in an apocalyptic context as one of the consequences for the inhabitants of the earth of the unleashing of the devil, whom she describes as 'antiquus serpens cum phylacteriis

---

[22] B. Hamilton, 'The Cathars and the seven churches of Asia', in J. D. Howard-Johnstone (ed.), *Byzantium and the West c. 850 – c. 1200* (Amsterdam, 1988), pp. 291–5.
[23] Hamilton, 'Origins of the dualist church', pp. 115–24.
[24] Appendix to the Letters of St Bernard, no. CDXXXII, *PL*, 182, 679.
[25] *Sanctae Elizabeth Vita, partim ab ipsamet dictata, partim ab Eckberto fratre scripta*, PL, 195, 120–4.

vestimentorum', (the old serpent with phylacteries [amulets] on his vestments), which perhaps reflects the imagery of her vision. The sequence of future events in the Apocalypse of St John is not easy to determine, but Hildegard seems to have interpreted it in this way: after the devil had been released from the bottomless pit,[26] the four angels who had held back the four winds at the corners of the earth 'until the servants of God had been sealed',[27] unleashed them, causing evils to sweep across the world.

Hildegard gave very precise dates for those two events. Of the release of the devil she says: 'Sed tamen sexaginta anni sunt atque viginti et quatuor menses, quod antiquus serpens cum phylacteriis vestimentorum populos deludere coepit' (But sixty years and twenty and four months have passed since the ancient serpent wearing clothes decked with amulets began to lead the people astray). The year reckoning could be taken to mean either sixty-two years ago, which is how it is understood by her editor,[28] or eighty years (60 + 20) and four months ago. If the first interpretation is correct then the year in question would be 1101, whereas if the second interpretation is correct, then the passage must refer to 1083. The four months, since Hildegard was writing in July, would relate to the beginning of the christian year on Lady Day, 25 March. Of the second event, the spreading of error through the release of the four winds, she writes: 'Nam viginti et tres anni ac quatuor menses sunt, quod a perversis operibus hominum, quod ab ore nigrae bestiae efflantur, quatuor venti per quatuor angelos angulorum in magnam ruinam moti sunt (For twenty-three years and four months have passed since through the wicked works of men which are blown out from the mouth of the black beast, the four winds have been set in motion by the four angels of [the earth's] corners, causing great destruction).[29] This would give a very precise date, the beginning (in March) of 1140. It seems quite reasonable to suppose that the first appearance of Catharism in the Rhineland, which culminated in the trial of 1143, did occur at about that time, and that Hildegard is retailing information which in her day was common knowledge. But the earlier date is more problematic. If it relates to 1083, it could refer to the capture of St Peter's basilica in Rome by Henry IV,

---

[26] Rev., 9:11. Phylacteries: see Matt. 23:5.   [27] Rev. 7:1–3.

[28] St Hildegard, Ep. x, *De Catharis*, ed. J. B. Pitra, *Analecta sacra*, 8 vols. (Paris 1876–82), vol. VIII, p. 349, n. 4.

[29] *Analecta sacra*, p. 349.

which ultimately resulted in the flight of Gregory VII and the enthronement of the antipope Clement III.[30] Such a date might have seemed of apocalyptic significance to Hildegard because it witnessed the beginning of a conflict between pope and emperor which had continued intermittently for much of her lifetime. The date 1101 would have had a different kind of significance, since it marked the defeat of the new crusade sent to reinforce the christians who had remained in the Holy Land after the capture of Jerusalem in 1099.[31] If Hildegard was referring to the origins of Catharism, such a date might be more persuasive for the following reasons.

I doubt whether anybody would wish to claim that all Cathars throughout the West derived from the congregation whose leaders were brought to trial at Cologne in 1143. All the evidence suggests that Catharism entered the West by a variety of routes and that the process took quite a long time. One of the few opponents of the movement who was at all interested in its history was the inquisitor Anselm of Alessandria, who wrote in c. 1270. He tells this story: there were originally three dualist bishops in the East, in Drugunthia, Bulgaria and Philadelphia; then Greeks from Constantinople learned this faith in Bulgaria and set up a Bishop of the Greeks in Constantinople.

Postea francigene iverunt Constantinopolim ut subiugarent terram et invenerunt istam sectam, et multiplicati fecerunt episcopum, qui dicitur episcopus latinorum. [Next the bishopric of Bosnia was set up.] Postea francigene, qui iverant Constantinopolim, redierunt ad propria et predicaverunt, et multiplicati constituerunt episcopum Francie.[32] (Afterwards Frenchmen went to Constantinople to conquer land and discovered that sect and, having increased in numbers, they appointed a bishop who is called the bishop of the Latins ... Afterwards the Frenchmen who had gone to Constantinople returned to their own land and preached and, having increased in numbers, appointed a bishop of France.)

He goes on to relate that the *provinciales*, taught by preachers from France, set up four bishoprics, and how, much later, a French notary came to Lombardy and converted Mark, the first Lombard Cathar Bishop. Since Anselm dates Mark's conversion to Catharism

[30] F. Gregorovius, *History of the City of Rome in the Middle Ages*, transl. A. Hamilton (London, 1896), vol. IV (I), pp. 229–31.
[31] S. Runciman, *A History of the Crusades* (Cambridge, 1952), vol. II, pp. 18–31.
[32] Anselm of Alessandria, cap. I, p. 308.

to *c.* 1174,[33] the other events he records must be earlier. His reference to Frenchmen going to Constantinople 'to conquer the land' is usually taken to refer to the Second Crusade,[34] but there is no cogent reason for thinking this. Indeed, it could apply equally well to the First Crusade, for that had been launched partly to reconquer Asia Minor from the Turks.[35]

If this reading of the passage in Anselm is correct it would accord well with the information given by St Hildegard: that the significant date for the beginning of Catharism was the aftermath of the First Crusade. Certainly in the next fifty years Cathars begin to be recorded in many different parts of the West. 'Manichees' were reported at Soissons in *c.* 1114, although not all modern scholars would agree with Guibert of Nogent, who examined them, that they were dualists.[36] Cathars were present in the Toulousain, perhaps as early as 1145,[37] certainly by 1165 when they had their headquarters at Lombers near Albi.[38] By that time they had also established congregations in parts of northern France and the Low Countries, and had spread to Italy.[39]

Although the Bogomils who sent missions to western Europe in the first half of the twelfth century were an ethnic mixture of Byzantine Greeks and Bulgars, they were united in a common faith. But later in the century a schism occurred among them about the validity of the sacrament of salvation. This schism divided those Bogomils who were absolute dualists from those who retained the moderate dualist faith first taught by *pop* Bogomil. In broad terms, the Greek-speaking Bogomils in the churches of Constantinople and Dragovitsa (or Drugunthia) were absolute dualists, while the Slav-speaking Bogomils of Bulgaria and Bosnia (and perhaps also the

---

[33] 'Isti portaverunt heresim in Lonbardiam(sic) a Neapoli: Marchus, Iohannes Iudeus, Ioseph et Aldricus, circa tempus quo currebat Mclxxiiii' (These men brought heresy to Lombardy from Naples: Mark, John the Jew, Joseph and Aldricus, in about the year 1174). Anselm of Alessandria, cap. 13, p. 319.

[34] An opinion first suggested, I think, by C. Thouzellier, 'Hérésie et croisade au xɪɪe siècle', in Thouzellier, *Hérésie*, p. 24.

[35] Urban II's letter to Flanders, ed. H. Hagenmeyer, *Die Kreuzzugsbriefe aus den Jahren 1088–1100* (Innsbruck, 1901), pp. 136–7.

[36] Guibert of Nogent, *Histoire de sa vie*, ɪɪɪ, 17, ed. E-R. Labande (Paris, 1981), pp. 428–34.

[37] If the *Arriani* mentioned by Geoffrey of Auxerre were Cathars. M. Roquebert, *L'Epopée cathare. I, 1198–1212: L'invasion* (Toulouse, 1970), pp. 57–8. For a more cautious view, R. I. Moore, 'St. Bernard's Mission to the Languedoc in 1145', *BIHR* 47 (1974), 1–4.

[38] *Ex Actis Concilii Lumbariensis*, *RHGF*, vol. xɪv, pp. 431–4.

[39] Duvernoy, *L'Histoire*, pp. 107–12, 119–21, 129–30, 137, 165–71.

church of the Milingoi) remained moderate dualists.[40] In *c.* 1170
Nicetas, who to judge from his name and from what is known of his
teaching was bishop of the Greeks of Constantinople, that is of the
Byzantine Bogomil Church, came to the West and presided over a
council of all the French and Lombard Cathar leaders at Saint-Félix
in Languedoc.[41] For a time he succeeded in uniting all the western
Cathars in the absolute dualist *ordo*, but a division arose when a rival
mission was sent to the West by the Bulgarian Bogomils. Consequently, whereas the Cathars of Languedoc remained true to
Nicetas's teaching and held the absolute dualist faith, as did the
church of Desenzano in Italy,[42] the rest of the Cathars returned to
moderate dualism either in its Bulgarian or in its Bosnian form.[43]
This is of relevance in the present discussion, because from *c.* 1180
different Cathar churches in the West preserved links with different
Bogomil churches in the East.

It is clear from the descriptions given by their opponents and from
Inquisition records that all Cathars used a form of the same Ritual,
which would seem to have come from the Balkans, where its adoption had antedated the schism of *pop* Nicetas's day. The earliest
evidence for its use in the West comes from a sermon of Egbert of
Schönau about the Cathar community of Cologne in 1163: 'Statui-
tur in medio infelix ille qui baptizandus sive catharizandus est. Et
assistit ei archicatharus, tenens in manu libellum deputatum ad
officium hoc' (That wretch who is to be baptised, or rather to be
catharised, is stood in the middle. And the chief Cathar ministers to
him, holding in his hand the book appointed for this purpose).[44]
Egbert later says that at the point of initiation the book is placed on
the candidate's head.[45] This would mean that it included at least the
text of a Gospel, and perhaps the whole of the New Testament. It is
possible that the Cathars customarily bound their Ritual into copies
of the New Testament, as is the case with the only surviving
example, the Lyons manuscript.[46]

[40] B. Hamilton, 'The Cathar Council of Saint-Félix reconsidered', *AFP* 48, (1978), 38–9.
[41] Hamilton, 'Cathar Council', pp. 23–53; D. Obolensky, 'Papa Nicetas: a Byzantine dualist
in the land of the Cathars', *Okeanos: Essays Presented to Ihor Ševčenko, Harvard Ukrainian
Studies,* 7 (1983), 489–500.
[42] Called the Albanenses by Sacconi.   [43] Sacconi, p. 59.
[44] Egbert of Schönau, *Sermones contra Catharos,* viii, ii, *PL,* 195, 51.
[45] 'Quem imponens vertici ejus dicit benedictiones' (Placing it on his head he pronounces the
blessings); *Sermones,* viii, ii, *PL,* 195, 51.
[46] L. Clédat, *Le Nouveau Testament traduit au XIIIe siècle en langue provençale, suivi d'un Rituel
Cathare* (Paris, 1887).

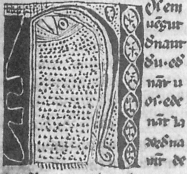

Plate 2 The beginning of the Cathar ritual, in Occitan (with some Latin), in a manuscript, possibly written between *c.* 1250 and *c.* 1280, which also contains the New Testament in Occitan. Though other texts written or used by the Cathars are known, this is the only surviving book which one can assume was itself once in the hands of Cathars in Languedoc and was used by them. Lyons, Bibliothèque Municipale, Ms. P.A.36, fol. 236r. (With permission of the Bibliothèque Municipale de Lyon.)

48

The Cathar Ritual must once have existed in a very large number of copies, but only two are known to us. An incomplete Latin text, dating from *c.* 1235–50 and written in Italy;[47] and the complete text in a Provençal version, contained in a manuscript written in the second half of the thirteenth century.[48] There are enough references in Catholic polemical writings and in inquisition depositions to show that these two examples are not eccentric but conform to the normal pattern of Cathar worship. The relationship between the Latin and Provençal Rituals was for a long time obscured by a too ready acceptance of Borst's opinion that the Latin text had been translated from Provençal.[49] As M. Roy Harris has shown, there is no evidence whatever to support this view.[50] But there is strong presumptive evidence that the Provençal Ritual had been translated from Latin, for the common forms of prayers used by the Cathars, including the Lord's Prayer and the prologue to St John's Gospel, which make up the opening section of the Ritual (see plate 2), are all in Latin, and are always cited in Latin when they occur in other, vernacular, parts of the text. It is normal practice for translated liturgies to retain certain well-known responses in the original tongue,[51] and it is reasonable to suppose that this custom was followed when the Occitan translation of the Cathar Ritual was made. The Latin Ritual of Florence and the Ritual of Lyons are not identical texts, and it is likely that they both ultimately derive from a common Latin archetype which was adapted to the use of different Cathar churches.[52]

Christine Thouzellier, who edited the Latin Ritual, while recognising common features between the descriptions of Bogomil worship in Eastern sources and the ceremonies of the Cathar Rituals, was nevertheless reluctant to assign an Eastern origin to the latter.[53] Duvernoy pointed out quite rightly that the only part of the Ritual which she was able directly to trace to a Western source is the gloss on the Lord's Prayer, but that this is the only part of the text

---

[47] *Rituel cathare.*   [48] Clédat, *Le Nouveau Testament*, pp. ix–xxvi.   [49] Borst, p. 280.

[50] M. R. Harris, 'Prolegomènes à l'histoire textuelle du Rituel cathare occitan', *Heresis* 6 (1986), 7.

[51] For example, the Coptic liturgy translated from the Greek still preserves some Greek forms. F. E. Brightman and C. E. Hammond (eds.), *Liturgies Eastern and Western* (Oxford, 1896, repr. 1965), pp. 144–88.

[52] The differences are clearly set out in the tables annexed to *Rituel cathare.*

[53] *Rituel cathare*, pp. 182–4.

which may be extemporised by the officiant.[54] The differences which she cites between the Bogomil and the Cathar rites of initiation are not significant,[55] whereas the parallels are so close that filiation seems certain. No full text of the Bogomil Ritual is known, but a mid-fifteenth century Bosnian manuscript made for Radoslav 'the Christian' (the name normally applied to Bosnian Bogomils[56]) contains an Old Slavonic version of the opening section of the Provençal Ritual, which it resembles very closely. The editors of the Radoslav manuscript argued from calligraphic evidence that it was copied from an archetype perhaps dating from the twelfth century.[57] It would appear therefore that the Radoslav manuscript preserves a part of the Bogomil Ritual, and that that Ritual was translated in its entirety into Latin in the twelfth century for the use of Western converts. It would also seem likely that the two surviving Western texts both derive from this original translation, one remaining in Latin, the other preserving some Latin forms. This would imply that the standard practice of the early Cathars had been to conduct public worship in Latin (a usage preserved in the thirteenth century by the Cathars of north and central Italy, where Latin may still have been comprehensible as an archaic form of the vernacular), and that the Cathars of Languedoc were the innovators in adopting a vernacular liturgy.

Consideration of the text of the bible used by the Cathars presents a different range of problems. Only one copy of the Cathar New Testament is known, the Occitan translation in Ms. PA 36 of the Bibliothèque Municipale of Lyons, and that was only identified because the text of the Cathar Ritual was bound in with it.[58] In addition there are numerous scriptural texts cited by Cathar writers, chiefly in Latin, but sometimes in Provençal. Despite the importance of the Lyons text, no critical edition of it has yet been made. Christine Thouzellier asserted that it was a translation from the Latin of BN Ms. Lat. 342,[59] but M. R. Harris has demonstrated that this was not so, even though the two texts are closely related. He

---

[54] Duvernoy, *La Religion*, unnumbered pages at the end of the work, 'Addition au chapitre: "Le baptême"'.
[55] Duvernoy, *La Religion*, 'Addition à la "Conclusion"'.
[56] Duvernoy, *L'Histoire*, pp. 47–76, especially pp. 69–70.
[57] The Slav text with a French translation may be found in the tables at the end of *Rituel cathare*. Thouzellier discusses the date of this manuscript with full bibliography, pp. 63–70.
[58] Ed. Clédat, *Le Nouveau Testament*.   [59] *Rituel cathare*, p. 29.

argues that the New Testament passages cited in other Cathar works, written independently of the Lyons manuscript, need to be collated to establish whether there were specific Cathar readings which diverged from the normal Vulgate tradition and were consistent throughout all the Cathar churches, an objective he describes as trying to discover whether the Cathars had an 'Authorised Version' of the bible.[60] If Duvernoy is right in his contention that some of the variants in the Lyons New Testament derive from the Greek manuscript tradition and are not found in any of the main Western Vulgate families,[61] this would suggest that the Cathars derived their text of the bible, as well as their interpretation of it, from the Bogomils.

The New Testament of Lyons contains the apocryphal Pauline Epistle to the Laodiceans. M. R. Harris has edited this, and points out that although this is the only known Occitan translation, the Epistle is found in a number of Latin and vernacular manuscripts of the Vulgate New Testament, in some of which it is placed immediately after the Epistle to the Colossians as it is in the Lyons manuscript. It is not heretical in content, being merely a catena of Pauline writings, and its use by the Cathars is not in itself a sign of heterodoxy.[62] Nevertheless, the comment of a late-eleventh- or early-twelfth-century writer, in a *scholion* on Peter of Sicily's account of the Paulicians, is worth noting: 'the Paulicians ... of the present day only recognize the four Gospels ... and the fifteen Epistles of St Paul, because they also have an Epistle to the Laodiceans'.[63] The Lyons manuscript is a product of Occitan Catharism, which was of the absolute dualist school, and it was the absolute dualists among the Cathars who had indirect links with Paulicianism.[64] It is therefore possible that the decision to include the additional Epistle was a sign of that influence, even though the text itself, as Harris has shown, was of Western provenance.

No text of the Cathar Old Testament has yet been identified, although it is known that the absolute dualists among them accepted

[60] Harris, 'Prolegomènes', p. 11.

[61] J. Duvernoy, 'A Propos de l'article de Marvin Roy Harris', *Heresis* 6 (1986), 14.

[62] M. R. Harris, 'The Occitan Epistle to the Laodiceans: towards an edition of Ms. PA 36', in A. Cornagliotti *et al.* (eds.), *Miscellanea di Studi Romanzi offerta a Giuliano Gasca Queirazza*, 2 vols. (Alessandria, 1988), vol. I, pp. 428–46.

[63] P. Lemerle, 'L'histoire des Pauliciens d'Asie Mineure d'après les sources grecques', *Travaux et mémoires* 5 (1973), 132.

[64] Hamilton, 'Origins of the dualist church', pp. 115–24.

as canonical the non-historical books, unlike the moderate dualists who would only accept the New Testament.[65] In origin this had not been a doctrinal division: the Byzantine Bogomils of the early twelfth century were moderate dualists, yet they had a scriptural canon which included substantial parts of the Old Testament.[66] This canon was adopted in a modified form by the absolute dualists among the Cathars. There are quite numerous quotations from the Old Testament in Cathar writings, and a study of these might prove worthwhile, because if a pattern of variants from the Vulgate text could be established this might make it easier to identify a Cathar text of the Old Testament, which would comprise the Psalms, the Wisdom Literature and the Prophets only.

It would not have been necessary for the Cathars to make a complete translation of their canonical scriptures from Greek into Latin, since the version they used was not significantly different from that used by all other Christians.[67] What distinguished it from the Vulgate used by Catholics were a small but significant number of variants. It is possible that further research into the Cathar use of scripture will show that there was a 'standard' Cathar text which resulted from the collation of the Vulgate with manuscripts deriving from the Septuagint tradition to produce a series of readings, like the 'manichaean' punctuation of John 1:3,[68] which were more susceptible of a dualist interpretation than the received text. A faint memory of such a process may be preserved in the gloss on the Lord's Prayer in the Cathar Ritual of Florence: '"Quoniam tuum est regnum" – hoc verbum dicitur esse in libris grecis vel hebraicis' ('For thine is the kingdom' – this phrase is said to be in the Greek and Hebrew texts).[69] If this interpretation is correct, then the Occitan version of the New Testament would have been made from the 'standard' Cathar Latin text. It is possible, as M. R. Harris has suggested, that the Cathars may not have made this translation *de novo* but have

---

[65] Sacconi, pp. 51–2, 58.

[66] Euthymius Zigabenus, *Panoplia dogmatica*, xxvii, i, *PG*, 130, 1292.

[67] Euthymius Zigabenus says that the text of the Gospel book belonging to the Bogomil leader Basil did not in any way differ from that used by the Orthodox Church; *Panoplia dogmatica*, xxvii, 20, *PG*, 130, 1317.

[68] 'Omnia per ipsum facta sunt et sine ipso factum est nichil. Quod factum est in ipso vita erat' (All things were made by Him and without Him nothing was made. That which was made in Him was life), Lyons Ritual, in Clédat, *Le Nouveau Testament*, p. 470. Augustine condemned this as a Manichaean reading, *In Johannis evangelio*, i, 1, 16, *PL*, 35, 1387.

[69] *Rituel cathare*, p. 21.

used an existing vernacular translation.[70] That could also have been collated with their 'standard' Latin text, although this cannot be known for certain until a critical edition of the New Testament of Lyons has been produced. The fact that the *incipits* of books in the New Testament of Lyons are in Latin suggests that the Cathars for whom it was made were accustomed to reading a Latin text of scripture.

All the Cathars appear to have read the apocryphal work known as *The Vision of Isaiah*. The original was a Greek Gnostic text perhaps dating from the first century AD, which is preserved in its entirety only in an Ethiopic translation. Part of the Greek text was translated into Latin in the late fifth or sixth centuries.[71] During the central middle ages a new version was made for Bogomil use, and changes were introduced in the text at places where it did not agree with Bogomil beliefs.[72] It is possible, and some scholars think likely, that this adaptation was the work of the Byzantine Bogomils and was written in Greek.[73] If so, the Greek text has not survived and the Bogomil recension is known only in an Old Slavonic version, the earliest manuscript of which dates from the late twelfth century,[74] and in a new Latin translation, which has been preserved only in a printed version made in 1522 from an unknown manuscript. It is often assumed that the Latin translation was made from Old Slavonic, but it could equally well have been made from Greek, had there been a Greek text of the dualist version.[75] Its use among the Cathars is first attested by Durand of Huesca, writing against the absolute dualist southern French Cathars in 1222–3,[76] while in *c.* 1240, the Dominican Moneta of Cremona observed that the moder-

---

[70] Harris, 'The Occitan Epistle to the Laodiceans', p. 435.

[71] *Codex rescriptus* of the Acts of Chalcedon, *Vat. Lat.* 5750; R. H. Charles, *The Ascension of Isaiah* (London, 1900), pp. xviii, 87–92, 102–8.

[72] E. Turdeanu, 'Apocryphes bogomiles et apocryphes pseudo-bogomiles', *Revue de l'histoire des religions* 138 (1950), 213–18.

[73] This was the opinion of Charles, *Ascension*, pp. xviii–xxxiii, and of E. Tisserant, *Ascension d'Isaie*, (Paris, 1909), pp. 37–8.

[74] Text in J. Ivanov, *Livres et légendes bogomiles*, transl. M. Ribeyrol (Paris, 1976), pp. 136–48.

[75] I have not been able to see a copy of the 1522 text by Antonius de Fantis, printed at Venice, and have used the reprint of it by A. Dillmann, *Ascensio Isaiae Aethiopice et Latine cum ... additis versionum Latinarum reliquiis* (Leipzig, 1877), pp. 76–83. For the view that the text was translated directly from Greek see E. Turdeanu, 'La Vision d'Isaie. Tradition orthodoxe et tradition hérétique', in I. E. Anastasiou (ed.), *Kyrillos kai Methodios* (Thessalonika, 1966–8), vol. II, p. 318. The case for a translation into Latin from Old Slavonic is made by Ivanov, *Livres*, pp. 153–60.

[76] Durand, *Liber contra Manicheos*, pp. 256–7, 287–8.

ate dualists of Lombardy held that the Prophets were evil, except for Isaiah 'cujus dicunt esse quemdam libellum, in quo habetur quod spiritus Isaiae raptus a corpore usque ad septimum caelum ductus est' (to whom they attribute a certain book, in which it is recounted that the spirit of Isaiah, being drawn out of his body, was taken up to the seventh heaven).[77] In the late thirteenth century the Cathar author of the Occitan gloss on the Lord's Prayer cited a passage from the *Vision* to illustrate his argument: 'aisicom lo angel ensegna a Ysaya profeta, e dis a luy en la soa vision: "Aici ja no es trhon ni li angel senestre mas de la vertu del seten cel an ordenament; acqui ont es lo ric fill de Dio, e tuit li cel"' (as the angel taught Isaiah the prophet and said to him in his vision: 'Here there is no Throne, nor Angels of the Left, but they are governed by the Virtue of the Seventh Heaven, where the mighty Son of God dwells, and [so are] all the heavens').[78] The fact that all Cathar churches received this book suggests that it was part of their early inheritance from the Bogomils and that its translation antedated the schisms of the late 1170s. So far as is known, the Cathars read this text in Latin and it was never translated into the vernacular.

The Cathars in general, and the moderate dualists among them in particular, were faced with difficulties because of their rejection of the accounts of creation in the Book of Genesis. This, no doubt, made them view the *Vision of Isaiah* with sympathy because it gave the authority of a canonical figure to the exposition of a dualist cosmology. Yet there is no evidence that they considered this work equal in authority to canonical scripture. Their attitude towards apocrypha seems to have been very like that of Catholic contemporaries, who would cite, for example, the *Protevangelium* for information about the life of the Blessed Virgin, while accepting that is did not possess authority as the inspired revelation of God.

After the schism the moderate dualist Cathars of Concorezzo obtained another apocryphal book from the Bogomils, but this proved more controversial. Unlike the *Vision of Isaiah*, the *Book of St John* does not seem to derive from an early Gnostic work, but to have been written by the Bogomils and attributed to St John the Divine. It is set in the framework of the Last Supper, at which St John asks

---

[77] Moneta, ii, ix, iv, p. 218.
[78] T. Venckeleer (ed.), 'Un recueil cathare: le manuscrit A.6.10. de la "Collection vaudoise" de Dublin. ii: Une glose sur le Pater', *RBPH* 39 (1961), 764.

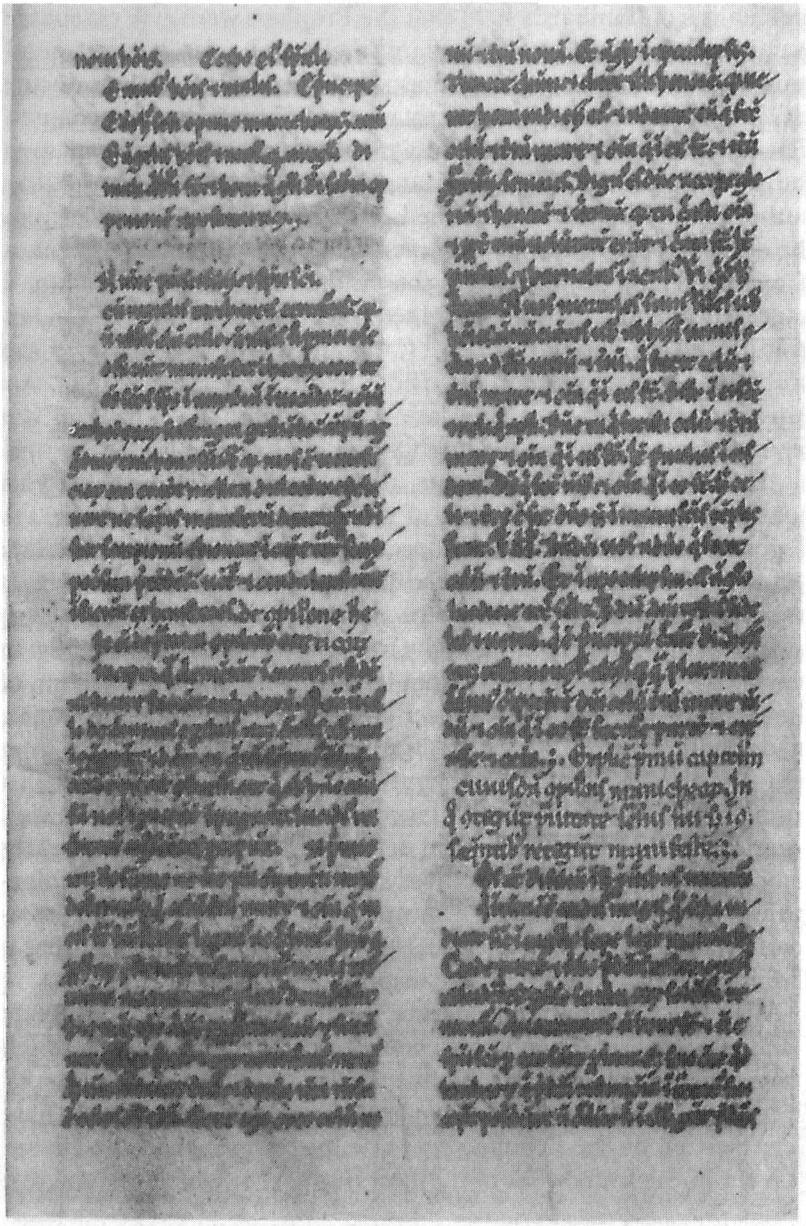

Plate 3   The beginning of an apocryphon of Bogomil origin, called the *Secretum* (Secret), which was brought from Bulgaria to the Italian Cathars in 1190. Vienna, Österreichische Nationalbibliothek Ms. Lat. 1137, fol. 158v. (With permission of the Bild-Archiv der Österreichischen Nationalbibliothek.)

the Lord to reveal to him the mysteries of the universe, and it must have fulfilled a useful function, especially for the moderate dualists, who had rejected the whole of the Old Testament and were therefore left with no coherent scriptural explanation of the nature of the creation, even though this occupied so central a place in their teaching.[79] The most recent editor of this text, Edina Bozóky, points to its strong doctrinal affinities with the Bogomilism professed by the heresiarch Basil at Constantinople in the early twelfth century as recorded by Euthymius Zigabenus, and inclines to think that the work was originally written in Greek.[80] It is difficult to be certain, because it survives only in two Latin versions: one represented by a single incomplete manuscript in Vienna (see plate 3), the other preserved in several copies which all derive from a manuscript once in the archive of the Inquisition at Carcassonne.[81]

The colophon to the Inquisition copy notes that Bishop Nazarius had brought it to the Cathar Church of Concorezzo from Bulgaria.[82] Nazarius is known from other sources. Concorezzo was the largest of the moderate dualist churches of Lombardy and derived its *Ordo* from the Bogomil Church of Bulgaria.[83] The author of the *De heresi*, writing in the early thirteenth century, names Nazarius as Elder Son of the Church of Concorezzo;[84] he had died before 1254, when Innocent IV ordered his body to be exhumed and burnt.[85] Rainier Sacconi, the convert Cathar perfect who became Inquisitor of Lombardy, writing in *c.* 1250, related how he had met Nazarius when he was a very old man, and how he asserted that Christ had an angelic nature and body received from His mother, who was an angel: 'et dixit quod habuit hunc errorem ab episcopo et filio maiore ecclesie Bulgarie iam fere elapsis annis LX' (and he said that he had been taught this error by the Bishop and Elder Son of the Church of Bulgaria almost sixty years ago).[86] This would place Nazarius's visit to Bulgaria in *c.* 1190.

Rainier does not mention *The Secret Book*, but Anselm of Alessandria, who succeeded him as inquisitor in Lombardy, recorded that through his attachment to the *Secret Book* Nazarius had caused a schism in the Church of Concorezzo, for his Elder Son Desiderius did not merely reject the book 'sed reputat illud malum' (but

[79] *Livre secret*, pp. 42–86.   [80] *Livre secret*, pp. 192–5.   [81] *Livre secret*, pp. 17–21.
[82] *Livre secret*, p. 86.   [83] Sacconi, pp. 50, 59.   [84] *De heresi catharorum*, p. 312.
[85] Potthast, no. 15492.
[86] Sacconi, p. 58.

considers it evil).[87] It is not possible to resolve the problem of the language in which this *Book* was written. There may have been a Byzantine Greek original from which the Old Slavonic translation was made for the Bogomils of Bulgaria, but that is not certain. It seems likely that the version which Nazarius brought back to Italy with him was in Old Slavonic. Anselm of Alessandria, who possessed one copy of this book, perhaps the lost Carcassonne manuscript, described it as being written in bad Latin.[88] This may reflect the fact that it had been translated from Old Slavonic and that it was more difficult to find experienced bilingual translators in that language than in Greek.

Desiderius of Concorezzo and his contemporary in the absolute dualist church of Desenzano, John of Lugio, were educated Cathars who were not interested in the mythology which had from the start formed an important part of the beliefs of the Bogomils. These young Italian coadjutor bishops wrote speculative works about dualist theology in the second quarter of the thirteenth century before persecution had begun in many parts of Lombardy.[89] Their existence suggests that there might be some truth in the letter attributed to Yvo of Narbonne, which claims that the Cathars of Como in *c.* 1214 had reported that the Cathar congregations of Lombardy and Tuscany sent believers to study logic and theology in the schools of Paris in order to strengthen their own faith and refute Catholic doctrine.[90] This story may merely be a piece of Catholic propaganda intended to make the Cathars appear menacing, but it is a fact that after *c.* 1200 the Cathars no longer sought to obtain theological writings from the Bogomils and developed a religious literature of their own.

[87] Anselm of Alessandria, cap. 1, p. 311.
[88] *'Secretum de Concorezo.* "Ego Iohannes frater vester ... etc." ... "Hoc est secretum hereticorum de Concorezo portatum de Bulgaria plenum erroribus" et etiam falsis latinis' (*The Secret of Concorezzo*. 'I John your brother ... etc.' ... 'This is the secret [book] of the heretics of Concorezzo, brought from Bulgaria [and] full or errors', and also [written in] bad Latin), Anselm of Alessandria, 319. Compare the colophon of the Carcassonne manuscript, *Livre secret*, p. 86.
[89] John of Lugio's teachings are described by Sacconi, pp. 52–7. Whether the 'quoddam volumen magnum X quaternorum' (a certain great book of ten quires) ascribed to John by Sacconi (p. 57) is the same as the *Book of the Two Principles*, or whether the latter is the work of some member of John's school, is uncertain. The teachings of Desiderius of Concorezzo are described by Anselm of Alessandria, pp. 310–12, and by Moneta of Cremona, IV, viii, i, p. 347. His work was read by St Thomas Aquinas, *Contra impugnantes Dei cultum*, c. 6, ed. P. Mandonnet, *S. Thomae Aquinatis Opuscula omnia* (Paris, 1927), vol. IV, p. 78.
[90] Matthew Paris, *Chronica majora*, ed. H. R. Luard, *RS* (London, 1877), vol. IV, p. 271.

It is possible that a great many translations of theological works were made from Greek and Old Slavonic by the Cathars and that they have not survived. I think this doubtful, because unlike the Cathars' own writings considered by Peter Biller in another chapter in this volume, there are no certain traces of such translations in the surviving sources. Scholars have looked for such materials, but have not found convincing evidence for them. Duvernoy, for example, has drawn attention to a saying attributed to the Lord in the *Gospel of the Nazarenes*, which Prepositinus of Cremona states was used by the Cathars.[91] But this is not necessarily evidence that they had a copy of the text, since the saying might have been transmitted to them orally by the Byzantine Bogomils.

Yet although the evidence suggests that a new generation of Cathar leaders tended to turn their backs on the Bogomil churches as sources of esoteric knowledge, empirical links were maintained with them throughout the thirteenth century. In 1325 Pope John XXII complained to the prince of Bosnia that 'magna haereticorum caterva de multis et variis partibus congregata ad principatum Bosnen. ... confluxit (a great crowd of heretics gathered together from many different regions has flocked to the principality of Bosnia).[92] If this report is true it would explain the sudden and apparently synchronous disappearance of organised Catharism throughout western Europe at about this time.

On a popular level 'Bulgaria' was remembered in the West as the land of marvels, from which the perfect had derived their teaching. Peter Biller has kindly drawn my attention to an inquisition deposition made between 1273–9 by Peter Perrin of Puylaurens. He had taken part in a discussion about how the weather in Languedoc was deteriorating: when the Cathar perfect were living in southern France there had been fewer storms. One person present remembered a woman saying that the perfects had a book which they would look at which enabled them to avert natural disasters of that kind, 'and this in Bulgaria'.[93]

The evidence considered in this chapter suggests that the Cathars' indebtedness to the Bogomil churches of the East in regard to books

[91] Duvernoy, *La Religion*, pp. 35–6.
[92] Ed. *Bullarium Franciscanum*, incepit J. H. Sbaralea, continuavit C. Eubel (Rome, 1898), vol. v, pp. 287–8, no. 577. Calendared, G. Mollat (ed.), *Jean XXII (1316–1324). Lettres communes, Litterae de Curia*, no. 32126 (Paris, 1909), vol. v, p. 448.
[93] Paris BN, Doat, 25 fol. 217r: *et hoc in Bulgaria*.

was very limited; that it dated chiefly from before *c.* 1170; but that nevertheless it was of great importance to the formation of Catharism. The Cathars certainly obtained their Ritual (although not the gloss on the Lord's Prayer) from the Bogomils, and the *Vision of Isaiah* came from the same source; while the argument that the Cathars collated the Vulgate text of the New Testament with a text established by the Bogomils but based on the Septuagint seems very persuasive, although in the present state of published research it must remain hypothetical.

The work of translation, I have argued, was all, in the first instance, carried out in Latin, although subsequently the Ritual and the New Testament were translated into Occitan. This ties in well with the findings about the Latinity of the Cathar perfect presented by Peter Biller in his chapter, and his observation that after the legatine council of Toulouse in 1178 the perfects were never accused of ignorance of Latin by their opponents.[94] Indeed, the evidence considered in this chapter would suggest that the Cathars initially used Latin as the language of public worship, that they read the bible in Latin, and that they translated Eastern dualist texts into Latin, and that they only used the vernacular, as the Catholic clergy at the time used it, when preaching. It was only later that the southern French Cathars adopted a vernacular liturgy and an Occitan translation of the New Testament, but there is no evidence that Cathars elsewhere ever abandoned the use of Latin as the language of worship.

So far as I am aware, little consideration has yet been given to the way in which the Cathars made translations, or, indeed, to the way in which Cathars and Bogomils communicated with each other. There were, it is true, frequent contacts between the West and the Byzantine Empire in the twelfth century, but the capacity to translate religious texts, or convey theological knowledge, requires a different kind of linguistic skill and a different range of vocabulary from that possessed by merchants or travellers. Only people resident in the Byzantine Empire for a long time were likely to develop the necessary kinds of expertise.

That some Western people living in Constantinople did become sufficiently versed in literary Greek to undertake the work of translation is known from the Latin version made in 1048–9 of the

[94] See p. 80.

Romance of Barlaam and Ioasaph. The preface tells us that this work was carried out 'in the translator's sixtieth year and the thirty-first of his residence [in Constantinople], through the encouragement of a certain nobleman, Leo, son of John ... [he] carefully rendered it in succinct language from the Greek tongue into graceful Latin, and where it was expedient he altered it and adapted it to the manners of our people'.[95] The text was thought to be a saint's life, although it was in reality a life of Prince Gautama, the Buddha, influenced by Asiatic Manichaeism.[96] Yet though it should in theory have proved attractive to Cathars, there is no certain proof that they read it. It was certainly read by Catholics for edification,[97] and I cite it here as an example, not of dualist literature, but of the conditions in which such translations were possible.

The evidence of Anselm of Alessandria is again important here. 'Postea francigene iverunt Constantinopolim ut subiugarent terram et invenerunt istam sectam, et multiplicati fecerunt episcopum, qui dicitur episcopus latinorum. ... Postea francigene, qui iverant Constantinopolim, redierunt ad propria et predicaverunt.'[98] What Anselm is saying is that the first Cathar, as distinct from Bogomil, church to be founded was the church of the Latins at Constantinople, whose members were expatriate westerners, and that it was that church which was responsible for the initial evangelisation of the West. This church survived and is recorded by Rainier Sacconi in his list of *c.* 1250 with a membership of fewer than fifty perfect.[99] But in the twelfth century it could have played a very significant role in the establishment of Catharism in western Europe. For if Anselm is correct, then there would have been westerners living in Constantinople in the twelfth century who were capable of translating Bogomil texts into Latin. It would make a good deal more sense of

---

95 Ms. viii, B. 10 of the National Library of Naples, cited and translated by D. M. Lang, 'St. Euthymius the Georgian and the *Barlaam and Ioasaph* romance', *Bulletin of the School of Oriental and African Studies* 17 (1977), 308.

96 See the introduction to the edition of the Greek text by G. R. Woodward and H. Mattingley (with new and additional introduction by D. M. Lang), *Barlaam and Ioasaph* (London 1914, repr. 1967), pp. ix–xxxii.

97 Barlaam and Ioasaph were included in the Golden Legend of James of Voragine, and Baronius added their names to the Roman Martyrology with a feast day on 27 November. A. Butler, *The Lives of the Saints*, ed. H. Thurston and D. Attwater (London, 1937), vol. xi, pp. 321–2.

98 See translation above, p. 44. Anselm of Alessandria, p. 308.

99 'Ecclesia Latinorum in Constantinopoli fere sunt L.' (There are scarcely fifty [members] of the church of the Latins in Constantinople). Sacconi, p. 50.

XIII

the origins of Catharism in the twelfth-century West to envisage that the first missions were conducted not by crusaders who had picked up some Cathar ideas while travelling through Constantinople, for their conditions of life would not have been stable enough to enable them to receive the right kind of training, nor by Greeks and Bulgars who had an imperfect command of Western vernaculars, but by members of the church of the Latins in Constantinople. Such missions would have had the opportunity to be carefully prepared, and their members would already have been using a Latin translation of the Ritual which they would have brought with them to the West. If the men who led the missions were themselves westerners who had lived for a long time in the Byzantine Empire, they would have had no difficulty in preaching their faith when they reached western Europe. They would also have been capable of undertaking a textual collation of the Vulgate with the Bogomil version of the Septuagint. This would, I suggest, help to explain the comparative ease with which Catharism spread in the West. It might also, perhaps, help to explain why Catharism became an indigenous Western movement comparatively soon.

Catholic Perceptions of East European Dualism in the Twelfth and Thirteenth Centuries*

There is no doubt that Catharism was the western branch of Bogomilism, although it is not easy to determine when it first reached the West. Sources from 1018 onwards sometimes describe dissident groups as Manichees, and this might imply a Bogomil origin for some early eleventh-century movements: I incline to think it does, but this is still a matter of considerable dispute.[1] Most medieval Catholic writers were not interested in the history of Catharism, which is one reason why so much controversy surrounds Cathar origins. One exception was Anselm of Alessandria, Dominican Inquisitor for Lombardy, who wrote in c.1266. He ascribed the origin of Christian dualism to Mani, and then made a rather surprising transition:

> He taught in the regions of Drugunthia, Bulgaria and Philadelphia, and heresy spread there so greatly that three bishops were appointed, one for Drugunthia, one for Bulgaria and one for Philadelphia. Afterwards Greeks from Constantinople ... went to trade there; and on return to their own land ... they appointed a ... bishop of the Greeks. Later Frenchmen went to Constantinople to conquer land, and discovered this sect; increasing in number they appointed a bishop ... of the Latins. Later people from Sclavonia, that is from the land called Bosnia, went to trade in Constantinople. When they returned home they ... appointed a bishop ... of Sclavonia or of Bosnia. Afterwards the French who had gone to Constantinople returned to their homeland and preached and, as their numbers grew, appointed a bishop of France.[2]

Despite his belief that Mani had visited the Balkans, Anselm deserves to be taken seriously because his account was based on the Cathars' own tradition of their origins. He places these events before the appointment of the first Cathar Bishop of Lombardy in the 1160s, and therefore the 'Frenchmen who went to Constantinople' to whom he refers cannot be members of the Fourth Crusade. Christine Thouzellier argued that this was a reference to the Second Crusade, but that seems unlikely because Balkan dualism had already entered the West before then.[3] It is a gratuitous assumption that the phrase 'intending to conquer land' meant that the Frenchmen were intending to attack the Byzantine Empire; it could equally mean that they were intending to carve out principalities in the East as a result of their expedition, and that would apply most naturally to the members of the First Crusade. I have argued elsewhere that Anselm was indeed referring to the events of 1097, and that the church of the Latins of Constantinople dates from the time of the First Crusade. This would explain how dualist missionaries from the East were able to proselytize successfully in Western Europe during the first half of the twelfth century: they knew western languages.[4]

The first secure reference to an eastern European connection in a western heresy trial dates from 1143 when Eberwin Provost of Steinfeld wrote to St Bernard of Clairvaux about a group of heretics whom he had examined at Cologne. They were undoubtedly Cathars and had a bishop of their own who informed Eberwin:

> ... this heresy has been hidden until the present day since the time of the martyrs, and has survived in Greece and certain other lands. These heretics [adds Eberwin] call themselves apostles and have their own pope.[5]

Anna Comnena reported that Basil, leader of the Bogomils of Constantinople in the early twelfth century, had twelve disciples whom he called apostles,[6] though the Byzantine sources do not describe Basil as a bishop, and so far as I am aware, the Cathar Bishop at Cologne in 1143 is the first dualist bishop to be recorded in any source.[7] The Cathars of Cologne had presumably used the word *pop*, or *papa*, at their trial when speaking of some leader of their church, or perhaps of *pop* Bogomil himself, but to western ears there was only one pope. And so with Eberwin begins the legend, which recurs periodically in Catholic writers, of the 'pope of the heretics', living somewhere in Eastern Europe and exercising the same monolithic authority over his faithful as the Pope did over the Western Church.[8]

The Cathars of Cologne were moderate dualists, but a new form of belief, absolute dualism, reached the West some twenty-five years later through the mission of *papa* Nicetas. The French dimension of his visit is described in a Cathar source known as the Saint-Félix document: I have defended its authenticity, but it does not have any bearing on the present argument, because it is not a Catholic source, and only came into the hands of the Church authorities at some unknown date in the later thirteenth century.[9] Nicetas's activities in Italy are, however, recorded in an anonymous work, the *De heresi catharorum*, written in the early thirteenth century. The author is so well informed about Catharism that it has been suggested that he may have been a perfect converted to Catholicism.[10]

Nicetas's mission occurred in about 1175.[11] He was a *papa*, a Bogomil leader; Anselm of Alessandria, who was able to draw on the independent evidence of thirteenth-century Italian Cathars whom he had examined,

2

describes him as 'bishop of the heretics in Constantinople'.[12] His name suggests that he was Bishop of the Greek Church of Constantinople rather than of the Latin Church: his mission was to introduce the western dualists to a new *ordo*. This term was used to describe the sacramental succession in the dualist churches by which, it was claimed, the rite of initiation, or *consolamentum*, had been transmitted from the apostles to the Cathar perfect. Mark of Lombardy, the *De Heresi* informs us, had been consecrated in the *ordo* of Bulgaria, but Nicetas

> began to question the validity of the Bulgarian consecration which Mark had received. Consequently Bishop Mark and his followers began to have doubts, and renouncing the Bulgarian consecration he was consecrated in the *ordo* of Drugunthia by Nicetas himself, and he remained in this *ordo* of Drugunthia for some time with all his fellow believers.[13]

Dujčev has argued that Drugunthia, or more properly Dragovitia, was in the Rhodope mountains south of Philippopolis.[14] From the *De Heresi* and all later western sources it is clear that the *ordo* of Drugunthia was considered the source of absolute dualism among the Cathars and Bogomils by Western writers, whereas the *ordo* of Bulgaria was the source of moderate dualism. Rainier Sacconi, a Cathar perfect who was converted to Catholicism, writing in about 1250, concludes his list of Cathar churches:

> ... the church of Bulgaria, the church of Druguuthia. They all trace their origin to the last two named.[15]

It is not known how long before Nicetas's mission to the West the Bogomils of Drugunthia had become absolute dualists. It is clear that the church of Drugunthia was Bogomil and not Paulician, but I have suggested that this doctrinal division among the Bogomils may have been due to the influence of Paulicians who had had a strong presence in neighbouring Philippopolis since at least the reign of John I Tzimisces.[16] By the time of Nicetas's mission, the *ordo* of Drugunthia had obviously also been adopted by the Greek Bogomil Church of Constantinople of which he was head.

The *De Heresi* tells us that Bishop Mark and all his followers accepted initiation into the *ordo* of Bulgaria at the hands of Nicetas, while the Saint Félix document shows that this change was also made by the Cathars of northern France and of Languedoc.[17] But some years after Nicetas had returned to the East, and after Bishop Mark's death, an embassy headed by Petracius was sent to the Cathars of Lombardy by the Church of Bulgaria, which reported that Bishop Simon of Drugunthia, who had consecrated *papa* Nicetas, had committed fornication, and that therefore all consolings which stemmed from him were invalid. This news led to a schism among the Cathars of Italy which was never subsequently healed. The north Italian Cathars became divided into six churches and three main doctrinal groups with different eastern affiliations. The Cathars of Desenzano, near Brescia, remained true to the absolute dualist teaching of Nicetas and sent their bishop-elect to Drugunthia to be consecrated; the Cathars of Milan, later known as the Church of Concorrezo, sent their candidate to Bulgaria to be consecrated in the moderate dualist *ordo*; while the Cathars of Mantua and Vicenza each sent their bishop-elect to Sclavonia for consecration.[18] The Church of Sclavonia is presumably the same as that of Dalmatia mentioned by *papa* Nicetas at the Council of Saint-Félix. These schisms in the Cathar churches of Lombardy must have occurred in the last quarter of the twelfth century, probably during the 1180s.[19]

Catholic writers were anxious to identify the different doctrinal strands of eastern dualism, but only in so far as they affected the development of heresy in the West. They agreed that there were three main varieties: moderate dualism, which originated in Bulgaria; absolute dualism, which originated in Drugunthia, and a new type of moderate dualism which was found in the church of Sclavonia. They were not very interested in the beliefs of the eastern communities: their normal practice was to list the beliefs of the different Cathar groups in the West and to identify their eastern affiliations. The implication is that, for example, the beliefs of the Cathars of Concorezzo and those of the Bulgarian Bogomils were identical, but this is never spelt out. Nevertheless, occasional pieces of information are given about the beliefs of the eastern dualist churches. Thus the author of the *De Heresi* relates:

> The Sclavini believe that in the time of grace the Son of God (that is Jesus Christ), John the Evangelist and Mary were three angels appearing in the flesh. They say that Christ did not in truth become incarnate, nor did he eat or drink; he was not crucified, dead, or buried; and all those things which he did as man did not really happen, but only seemed to happen ... [20]

Similarly, Rainier Sacconi tells us how:

> Nazarius, a former bishop [of Concorrezo] and a very old man, said in my hearing and in that of many others that the Blessed Virgin was an angel, and that Christ did not take human nature but angelic [nature], and a heavenly body, and he said that he had been taught this error by the bishop and elder son of the church of Bulgaria almost sixty years ago.[21]

But such information is incidental: Catholic writers were not normally concerned to give a systematic account of eastern heresy.

The most striking example of this is the fact that they say nothing about Paulician beliefs at all. Although the Paulicians must have influenced the development of absolute dualism among the Bogomils and Cathars, there is no evidence known to me of any direct Paulician influence in western Europe.[22] Western dualist movements were without exception world-renouncing: the Paulician combination of dualist belief and worldly involvement was not found in the West. The Catholic world knew about Paulicians: the army of Bohemond of Otranto during the First Crusade had attacked a Paulician village in Macedonia because its inhabitants would not venerate the Holy Cross; and groups of Paulician warriors are mentioned quite often in crusader chronicles, where they are usually labelled *Publicani*.[23] Geoffrey of Villehardouin relates that in 1205 the Paulicians had their own quarter in Philippopolis and were chiefly responsible for betraying the city to the Bulgarian Tsar because they hated the Latins.[24] Yet no Catholic writer in this period described Paulician beliefs: the doctrine of the group had no relevance to the Western Church and therefore held no interest for them.

Although a good deal is now known about the links which existed between Cathars and Bogomils in the twelfth century it does not follow that this information was generally available to the Catholic hierarchy at the time. It is perhaps significant that the earliest extant manuscript of the *De Heresi* only dates from after 1250.[25] Twelfth-century popes consistently denounced Catharism, but do not seem to have shown any interest in its origins. When their attention first turned to the Balkans in the reign of Innocent III it is perhaps unsurprising that their concern was with Bosnia. For Bosnia was part of Catholic Christendom although the Slav rite was in use there, and was under the ecclesiastical authority of the Archbishop of Dubrovnik, and the pope was thus in a position to take action about dualism there, whereas most of the rest of the Balkans and Greece at that time were under the ecclesiastical jurisdiction of the Patriarch of Constantinople.[26]

Shortly after his accession Innocent was informed by Prince Vukan of Dioclea that Ban Kulin of Bosnia and some 10,000 of his subjects had become Patarins, the name which was used in the West to describe Italian Cathars.[27] The pope does not seem to have had complete confidence in this report, but to have sought clarification from the Archbishop of Split, who confirmed that he had expelled dualists from Split and Trogir and that they had taken refuge in Bosnia, where they had been cordially received by the Ban who had wrongly supposed that they were good Christians.[28] From the account written some sixty years later by Archdeacon Thomas of Split it is known that the leaders of the Patarins whom Archbishop Bernard had brought to trial were two brothers, Matthew and Aristodius. They had grown up in Zadar and were said to have been painters and goldsmiths, who could read

Latin and Church Slavonic and who had strong connections with Bosnia. The archbishop, we are told, succeeded in persuading them to recant their heresy and with some of their followers to return to the Catholic faith.[29] There is no reason to doubt that in general terms these accounts are true. We know from the Saint-Félix document that there was a Bogomil church in Dalmatia by the early 1170s, and this is confirmed by the *De Heresi* written in Innocent III's reign, which recounts how some of the Italian Cathars had links with that church. It is not at all surprising that if it was persecuted some of its adherents should have taken refuge in nearby Bosnia, or that the Prince of Dioclea should have tried to make political capital out of this.

Innocent III asked King Emerich of Hungary to persuade Ban Kulin to expel the heretics from his lands.[30] The Ban responded by sending an embassy to the Pope, led by the Archbishop of Dubrovnik and some of those accused of heresy, asking that a legate be sent to investigate the charges.[31] Innocent delegated this work to his chaplain, John of Casamaris, and the consequence of his mission was the document known as the Agreement of Bilino Polje. This was signed on 30 April 1203 by the legate, Ban Kulin, the archdeacon of Dubrovnik, and 'the priors of those men who until now have alone had the right to be called Christians in the land of Bosnia'. There were seven of them: Dragite, Lubin, Drageta, Pribis, Luben, Rados and Bladosius. The Agreement explains in some detail how they promised to make their communities into orthodox, single-sex monastic groups within the Catholic church. They would have chapels in each community, furnished with altars and crosses and with texts of the Old and New Testaments, in which they would recite the canonical hours; and they would appoint chaplains to say Mass on Sundays and holy days, and would receive holy communion seven times a year. They undertook not to call themselves Christians any more, but brethren, so that they would not seem to be arrogating the name of Christian exclusively to themselves. Except by implication there is no indication what their heresy had been, although they were required to make the specific commitment: 'henceforth we will not receive any known Manichaean or other heretic to live with us'. 'Manichee' in official Catholic usage at that time certainly meant Cathar.[32]

It is often assumed that these heretics were dualists. Their exclusive use of the name Christian would suggest this, as would the fact that they were organized in communities, which was also a feature of western Catharism.[33] The specification in the Agreement that they should recite the Divine Office and hear Mass suggests that they had not previously been doing so, and the insistence that they should have chapels with altars, crosses and copies of the canonical scriptures in the full text might imply that they had previously had none of these things, all of which would be characteristic features of Cathar communities. But in the absence of further information it is possible to argue at they were heterodox groups of a non-dualist kind. Innocent III's ,eatment of them is in accordance with his general policy towards dissidents in the early years of his reign; he was anxious to reconcile them to the Church whenever possible and to allow them to continue to live in community: he licensed arrangements of this kind for the Waldensian followers of Bernard Prim and Durand of Huesca, who became Poor Catholics, and also for the Humiliati.[34]

Later in his reign Innocent found himself in the unusual position of being recognized as canonical head of large parts of the Byzantine patriarchate. In 1202 Kalojan, ruler of Bulgaria, wishing to secure independence of Byzantium, opened negotiations with Rome which led to Innocent's conferring a pallium on the Archbishop of Trnovo, and to the coronation of Kalojan by a papal legate in 1204. In that same year as a result of the Fourth Crusade most of the European lands of Byzantium came to form part either of the Latin Empire, or of the Venetian dominions, and thus passed under the ecclesiastical authority of the Latin Patriarch of Constantinople.[35] Innocent therefore had the opportunity of dealing simultaneously with dualism in East and West.

It is possible, but by no means certain, that he was responsible for inducing Tsar Boril of Bulgaria to convene a Synod at Trnovo in 1211 at which Bogomilism was condemned. The Synodikon which was then issued contains the most detailed account that we possess of the beliefs of the Bogomils in the thirteenth century.[36] It cannot be proved that the Pope had any hand in this, but the fact that the Synod was held in the middle of the Albigensian Crusade and at a time when the Bulgarian Church was in communion with the Holy See suggests that there was a connection. As is known from western sources, the moderate dualists of western Europe, who made up the largest Cathar church in Italy,[37] traced their descent from the Bogomil church of Bulgaria. Its leader, Peter the *dyed* of Sofia, was among those whom the Synod of Trnovo condemned.[38]

The absolute dualist Cathars, who constituted a sizable group in Lombardy and comprised all the churches of the Cathars in southern France, were a more serious challenge to Catholic orthodoxy than the moderate dualists, since they did not accept belief in a single creator.[39] Their headquarters was at Dragovitia near Philippopolis, and the Bogomils of Constantinople shared their beliefs, as is known from the western sources considered above. It is therefore astonishing that Innocent III did not attempt to take any action against them, since both churches formed part of the Latin Empire of Constantinople. It is, I think, possible that Innocent was unaware of the existence of these churches, because the evidence which is available to us was not known to him. I know of no reference to Bogomils in any western source written in the Latin Empire of Constantinople[40] and this suggests that the leaders of the Catholic Church there were not at this time aware of the presence of dualism in their territories, but considered that Bulgaria was the home of eastern dualism. This view was shared by popular opinion in France in the early thirteenth century when the term *bougre* began to be used to describe perfected Cathars.[41] It presumably derived from the account which the Cathars themselves had given of their own origins.

The belief that in some sense dualism was an international conspiracy designed to subvert the Catholic religion was first voiced at curial level by Conrad Cardinal of Porto, the legate of Pope Honorius III in southern France. In June 1223 he convoked a council of the French church to meet at Sens, and reported that an antipope had arisen 'on the frontiers of Bulgaria, Croatia and Dalmatia, next to Hungary', to whom the Cathars of Albi were turning for advice. He continued:

> This satan has appointed ... a certain Bartholomew of Carcassonne ... as his vicar in the diocese of Agen ... Vigouroux de Bathona, bishop of the heretics, has shown sinful reverence to him, and has ceded to him his office and his see in the place called Pujols, and has himself gone to the region of Toulouse. This Bartholomew sends letters everywhere styling himself: 'Bartholomew servant of the servants of the Hospital of Sound Faith greeting'. He ... is consecrating bishops and trying to set up churches of error.[42]

There is no doubt that Vigouroux de Bathona should be identified with Vigouroux de la Bacone, who was Cathar bishop of Agen in 1223: this is confirmed by Durand of Huesca, writing at precisely that time.[43] Yves Dossat in his study of Vigouroux, cites the evidence of two Inquisition witnesses (one of whom was Raimond of Perelha, Lord of Montségur), that in c.1229 Vigouroux was consecrated Elder Son (i.e. coadjutor bishop) of the church of Agen by the Cathar Bishop of Toulouse. Dossat has also assembled evidence about Bartholomew of Carcassonne, who was active among the Cathars of Languedoc from c.1210 to c.1227, but he nevertheless inclines to think that there is no substance in Conrad of Porto's report.[44] But as I have argued elsewhere, Conrad's information helps to elucidate the otherwise inexplicable anomalies of Vigouroux' career.[45]

This evidence suggests that during the peace which followed the collapse of the first stage of the Albigensian Crusade in 1219, when the Cathar churches of Languedoc were trying to reconstitute themselves after ten years of sporadic persecution, an attempt was made to reintroduce there the moderate dualism which had been in abeyance since the mission of 'papa' Nicetas in c.1172. Whether the initiative came from the Balkan or the Southern French side it is impossible to know: but it would appear that Bartholomew of Carcassonne was consecrated Bishop by a Bogomil prelate and persuaded the Cathar Bishop Vigouroux of Agen to abdicate in his favour. That a schism did develop among the southern French Cathars in the mid-1220s is known from the deposition of Raimond Arrufat, made to the Inquisition of Toulouse in 1245. He recalled how in 1225 he and other men from Castelnaudry had been held as hostages in Narbonne, where one of them who had Cathar sympathies fell gravely ill. But when two local *perfecti* came to console him, he refused their ministrations because they 'were not of the faith of the heretics of Toulouse', and died unconsoled.[46] The Cathars of Toulouse were absolute dualists, and it is known from Inquisition sources that absolute dualists did not regard the sacraments of any of the moderate dualist groups as valid.[47] The two perfect at Narbonne in 1225 were therefore presumably followers of the moderate dualist revival of Bartholomew of Carcassonne. This schism, which might seriously have weakened the southern French Cathar movement, did not last. Bartholomew died in c.1227, and as the inquisition records show, Vigouroux was reconciled to the absolute dualists of Toulouse and was consecrated Elder Son, that is coadjutor bishop, of his old see of Agen by them in c.1229.[48] This whole episode had little long-term consequence, but it represents the last known intervention by the Balkan dualists in the affairs of the western Cathar churches in the period with which I am concerned in this paper.

Cardinal Conrad's description of the location of the Balkan 'antipope' who had encouraged this moderate dualist revival is vague. He could have been the bishop of either the Bulgarian or the Bosnian Bogomils, for both were moderate dualist communities. Conrad, of course, misunderstood the use of the term *pop*, or *papa*, to describe the Bogomil bishop, just as Eberwin of Steinfeld had done eighty years before, and so the myth of the antipope of the heretics persisted in Catholic circles.[49]

Meanwhile Honorius III was troubled by fresh reports of heresy in Bosnia. In 1221 he wrote to his legate in Hungary, Mgr. Accontius, urging him to exhort the king to take action against the heretics in Bosnia; and in 1225 he transferred the Bosnian Church to the jurisdiction of the Hungarian Archbishop of Kolocza because he alleged that Bosnia was 'infected with heretical wickedness'.[50] These actions were very parallel to the measures which Innocent III had taken in regard to Languedoc and which Honorius III was in process of repeating at this time: to call on the principal lord to discipline a prince who refused to co-operate with the Church in its fight against heresy. In the case of Bosnia the principal lord at first took no action.

Gregory IX, who succeeded Honorius in 1227, was concerned to stamp out dualism everywhere. He had no jurisdiction over the lands which remained in Byzantine control, although Bogomils were present in some of them,[51] and seems to have been unaware of the presence of Bogomils in the Latin Empire of Constantinople. That presence is not in any doubt, because the Orthodox Patriarch Germanus II (1222-40), living in exile at Nicaea, was sufficiently worried to write an encyclical to the faithful of Constantinople warning them against the Bogomils.[52] Gregory IX instituted proceedings against the Catholic Bishop of Bosnia, accusing him of being ignorant of the rudiments of the faith, and of tolerating heresy to the extent that his own brother was an heretical leader. It was not alleged that the bishop himself was a heretic, but in 1233 he was removed from office by the pope's legate, Cardinal James of Palestrina.[53] Ban Ninoslav undertook to uphold the Catholic faith and was placed under papal protection, but this did not last and in 1234 Pope Gregory licensed the Duke of Croatia to make war on Bosnia with crusading privileges.[54] Gregory was also concerned about the presence of Bogomils in Bulgaria. Papal influence had ended there in c.1232 when the Bulgarian Church returned to the communion of the Orthodox Patriarch at Nicaea.[55] In 1238 Gregory IX incited King Bela IV of Hungary to crusade against Tsar John Asen II, but nothing came of this because of the Mongol invasion of Hungary in 1241-2, which also put an end to the prolonged crusade against Bosnia.[56] Gregory was implementing the decrees of the Fourth Lateran Council in regard to Bosnia and Bulgaria: if secular rulers failed to co-operate with the Church in enforcing heresy laws, their lands should be exposed to crusades led by Catholic princes.[57]

Gregory IX set up the papal Inquisition to combat Catharism and an important, though not exclusive, part in its work was undertaken by the Dominican Order. Although the medieval Inquisition lacked any central organization, its officials being personally responsible to the pope alone, the Dominican inquisitors, who were well-educated men, trained in the scholastic tradition, began to collect information about dualism in a systematic way and to make it available to the whole western Church. Cathar perfect converted to Catholicism through the work of the friars were often very well-informed about the movement, men like Rainier Sacconi, who had been a Cathar minister for seventeen years before his conversion by St Peter Martyr.[58] Rainier joined the Dominican Order and succeeded Peter as Inquisitor in Lombardy, and his *Summa* about heresy written in c.1250 is considered one of the best sources for the study of thirteenth-century Catharism, because Rainier was not concered with polemic, but sought only to give information about the dualists which an inquisitor would find useful. This is what he has to say about eastern dualism:

> There are sixteen churches of the Cathars [ten in France and Italy]. The Church of Sclavonia. The Church of the Latins of Constantinople. The Church of the Greeks in the same place. The Church of Philadelphia in Romania. The Church of Bulgaria. The Church of Druguuthia [sic]. And they all trace their origin to the last two named. ... The Church of the Latins in Constantinople has

about fifty members. The Churches of Sclavonia and Philadelphia and of the Greeks [of Constantinople] and of Bulgaria and of Druguuthia have in total about 500 members.[59]

The figures which Sacconi gives are presumably those of fully-initiated members, whom the Cathars called the perfect, and the number of unconsoled adherents would have been far greater. Now Sacconi is, of course, trying for propaganda purposes to minimize the threat posed by organized dualism to orthodox Christianity in East and West. Even so, if one takes a multiplier of 100 to estimate the proportion of believers to perfect, this only produces a figure of 50,500 dualist adherents scattered throughout the Balkan lands and the Greek and Latin Empires of Constantinople. If this conjecture is true, then Bogomilism must have been a substantial movement in the thirteenth century, but not so dominant a one as Catharism was in parts of western Europe at that time.

Although King Bela IV of Hungary in 1254 asked Innocent IV for help against his heretical Bosnian and Bulgarian neighbours[60] he received none, and no later western writer makes any reference to contemporary dualist movements in Bulgaria or the Byzantine lands. In 1261 the Latin Empire, and with it the Latin Patriarchate of Constantinople, came to an end, although parts of mainland Greece and most of the islands remained under Catholic rule for far longer. In this late period some western theologians did develop an interest in the origins of Catharism and in its links with Balkan dualist movements of the twelfth century. It is from the second half of the thirteenth century that Anselm of Alessandria's account comes, and it was during the same period that the surviving manuscript of the *De Heresi* was copied, giving details of the links between the Italian Cathar churches and the Balkan dualist movements.[61]

The papacy lost interest in eastern dualism in the second half of the thirteenth century except in the case of the western Balkans which were near to Italy and also part of the Western Church. When the Mongol threat receded and Innocent IV attempted once more to make the Catholic Church of Bosnia subject to the Church of Hungary, it seceded from his obedience in 1252. Scholars agree that there was a dualist church in Bosnia after that date, but there are diverging views about whether it was a small dissenting group, tolerated by the rulers, or whether it became the established religion of the whole country.[62] The thirteenth-century evidence with which I am concerned does not help to address this problem: the sources simply speak of the presence of heresy there and in the neighbouring regions. Nicholas IV in 1291 ordered the Franciscan Provincial Minister of Sclavonia to delegate two of his brethren to work as inquisitors in Bosnia,[63] and in 1298 Boniface VIII extended their brief to include Serbia, Croatia, Dalmatia, Rascia and Istria as

11

well.[64] It would appear that they achieved very little because they received no adequate support from the secular authorities.

In western eyes Bosnia appeared the Balkan territory most sympathetic to Cathars in the early fourteenth century. Pope John XXII in 1325 complained to Prince Stefan Kotromanić that 'a great crowd of heretics from many different regions has gathered together and migrated to Bosnia'.[65] There is certainly a degree of hyperbole in this description: all the Inquisition sources suggest that there were no longer enough Cathars left in Western Europe to constitute 'a great crowd'. Nevertheless, the Pope's letter may be a true, though exaggerated account, because there are virtually no reports of any Cathar perfect in the West after that date. A strategic withdrawal to Bosnia, where dualism had been tolerated since the late twelfth century, may have seemed the best solution to the Cathars of Western Europe after ninety years of persecution, if, that is, they had retained enough organization to make concerted plans.

In conclusion the evidence suggests that there was a generally held belief in Western Europe throughout this period that Bulgaria was the seat of dualist heresy, an opinion reflected in the popular use of the term *bougre* to describe male Cathar perfect, which presumably reflected the Cathars' account of their own origins. Gradually, as they examined Cathar suspects, the Church authorities came to learn more about their links with the eastern dualist churches, the organization of those churches and their different belief systems. The latter did not interest them very much: they were more concerned to find out what western Cathars believed than to trace the origins of those beliefs. The papacy became directly involved with Balkaan dualism in Innocent III's reign, but he and his successors directed their attention chiefly to Bosnia and Bulgaria, and this suggests that they were not aware of the presence of Bogomils elsewhere in eastern Europe. Moreover, Conrad of Porto's alarmist report about the existence of a pope of the heretics in the region of Bulgaria, Dalmatia and Croatia may have led later popes to concentrate their energies on those areas. Even when papal concern about heresy in other parts of eastern Europe had waned, belief in the presence of an active dualist community in Bosnia persisted in the curia. The watchfulness of the Inquisition in this regard, long after Catharism had disappeared from the West, suggests that the Catholic authorities may have feared a return of dualist missions to the West, and that it was from Bosnia that they were expected to come.[66]

Endnotes

* This paper was given at a Conference on 'Heresy in Eastern Europe' held at the School of Slavonic and East European Studies of the University of London in July 1994.

1 c.1018, 'exorti sunt per Aquitaniam Manichei'; 1022, 'apud Tolosam inventi sunt Manichei'; c.1028, 'concilium adgregavit ... dux Willelmus apud sanctum Carrofum pro extinguendas haereses, quae vulgo a Manicheis disseminabantur.' Adémar de Chabannes, *Chronique*, cc. 49, 59, 69 ed., J. Chavanon (Paris, 1897), pp. 173, 185, 194; 1043-8, Roger II of Cambrai, 'Aiebat enim in quadam parte diocesis suae quosdam rusticos esse ... perversum Manicheorum dochma [sic] sectantes ...', *Herigeri et Anselmi Gesta Episcoporum Leodiensium*, II, c. 62, ed. R. Koepke, *Monumenta Germaniae Historica Scriptores* [henceforth *MGH SS*], VIII, p. 226. Current debate about the nature of early eleventh-century western heresies is accurately summarised by M. Lambert, *Medieval Heresy*, 2nd edn (Oxford, 1992), pp. 9-32.

2 'Et docuit in partibus Drugontie et Bulgarie et Filadelfie; et multiplicata est ibi heresis ita quod fecerunt tres episcopos: Drugontie, alius Bulgarie, alius Filadelfie. Postmodum greci de Constantinopolim ... iverunt causa mercacionis illuc, et reversi ad terram suam ... ibi fecerunt episcopum ... grecorum. Postea francigene iverunt Constantinopolim ut subiugarent terram et invenerunt istam secta, et multiplicati fecerunt episcopum ... latinorum. Postea quidam de Sclavonia, scilicet de terra que dicitur Bossona, iverunt Constantinopolim causa mercacionis; reversi ad terram suam ... constituerunt episcopum ... Sclavonie sive Bossone. Postea francigene, qui iverant Constantinopolim, redierunt ad propria et predicaverunt et, multiplicati constituerunt episcopum Francie.' Anselm of Alessandria, *Tractatus de hereticis*, c. 1, ed. A. Dondaine, 'La hiérarchie cathare en Italie. II', *Archivum Fratrum Praedicatorum* [henceforth *AFP*], XXIV (1959), p. 308 (Reprinted, A. Dondaine, *Les Hérésies et l'Inquisition XIIe-XIIIe siecles* (Variorum, London, 1990), No. IV).

3 C. Thouzellier, *Hérésie et hérétiques. Vaudois, Cathares, Patarins, Albigeois*, Storia e Letteratura, Raccolta di Studi e Testi, 116 (Rome, 1969), p. 24. All scholars agree that Cathars were present in Cologne in 1143, see n. 5 below.

4 B. Hamilton, 'Wisdom from the East: the reception by the Cathars of Eastern dualist texts', in P. Biller and A. Hudson, eds., *Heresy and Literacy. 1000-1530* (Cambridge, 1994), pp. 38-60.

5 'Hanc haeresim usque ad haec tempora occultatam fuisse a temporibus martyrum, et permanisse in Graecia, et quibusdam aliis terris. Et hi sunt illi haeretici, qui se dicunt apostolos, et suum papam habent.' Appendix to the Letters of St. Bernard, no. CDXXXII, J.P. Migne, ed., *Patrologia ... Latina* [henceforth *PL*], 182, 679.

6 Anna Comnena, *Alexiad*, XV, viii, 3, ed., B. Leib, 3 vols (Paris, 1937-45), III, p. 219.

7 The first Bogomil bishop to be named in any source is Simon of Drugunthia, the consecrator of *papa* Nicetas of Constantinople, *De Heresi Catharorum in Lombardia*, ed. Dondaine, 'Hiérarchie. I', *AFP*, XIX (1949), p. 306. (Reprinted, Dondaine, op. cit., No. III).

8 A. Borst, *Die Katharer, Schriften der Monumenta Germaniae Historica*, 12 (Stuttgart, 1953), pp. 209-10.

9 The surviving witness is a seventeenth-century printed text of a copy made in 1223 for Peter Isarn, Cathar Bishop of Carcassonne. The source presumably came into Catholic hands through the work of a papal or episcopal inquisitor in the later thirteenth century. B. Hamilton, 'The Cathar Council of Saint-Félix reconsidered', *AFP*, XLVIII (1978), pp. 25-53. (Reprinted, Hamilton, *Monastic Reform, Catharism and the Crusades (900-1300)* (Variorum, London, 1979), No. IX).

10 Ed. Dondaine, *AFP*, XIX, pp. 280-312; Borst, op. cit., pp. 10-11.

[11] The St. Félix document is dated 1167, but mistakes might have occurred in the copying; Anselm of Alessandria states that Catharism first entered Lombardy, 'circa tempus quo currebat Mclxxiiii', and that Nicetas's mission took place after that, *Tractatus*, c.13, ed. Dondaine, *AFP*, XX, p. 319. The Council of St. Félix must have been held before 1177 when Raymond V of Toulouse complained that absolute dualism was being preached in Languedoc. Gervase of Canterbury, *Chronica*, ed. W. Stubbs, Rolls Series [henceforth RS], 2 vols (London, 1879-80), I, p. 270.

[12] '...episcopus erat illorum de Constantinopolim', *Tractatus*, 1, ed. Dondaine, *AFP*, XX, p. 309.

[13] 'cepit causari ordinem bulgarie, quem marcus habebat. Unde marcus episcopus cum suis subditis hesitare incipiens, relicto ordine bulgarie, suscepit ab ipso Nicheta ordinem drugonthie. Et in illo ordine drugonthie aliquibus temporibus cum suis omnibus complicibus commoratus est.' *De Heresi*, ed. Dondaine, *AFP*, XIX, p. 306.

[14] I. Dujčev, 'Dragvista-Dragovitia', *Revue des études byzantines*, 22 (1964), pp. 215-21.

[15] 'Ecclesia Bulgarie. Ecclesia Duguuithie. Et omnes habuerunt originem a duabus ultimis.' Raynerius Sacconi, *Summa de Catharis*, ed. F. Sanjek, *AFP*, XLIV (1974), p. 50.

[16] Anna Comnena, *Alexiad*, XIV, vii, 5, ed. Leib, III, pp. 179-80.

[17] *De Heresi*, ed. Dondaine, *AFP*, XIX, p. 306; the St. Félix document was printed by G. Besse, *Histoire des ducs, marquis et comtes de Narbonne* (Paris, 1660), pp. 483-6, and I have reprinted it, op. cit., *AFP*, XLVIII, pp. 51-3.

[18] *De Heresi*, ed. Dondaine, *AFP*, XIX, p. 308.

[19] See the list of Italian Cathar bishops in Dondaine, *AFP*, XX, p. 306.

[20] 'Sclavini tempore gratie credunt quod filius dei, scilicet ihesus christus, et Johannes ewangelista [sic] et maria fuerunt tres angeli apparentes in carne. Et dicunt quod christus non in veritate carnem suscepit, nec comedit, nec bibit, nec crucifixus, nec mortuus, nec sepultus est, et omnia que secundum humanitatem fecit, non erant in veritate set [sic] in apparencia...', *De Heresi*, ed. Dondaine, *AFP*, XIX, p. 311.

[21] 'Nazarius vero quondam eorum episcopus et antiquissimus coram me et aliis multis dixit quod beata Virgo fuit angelus, et quod Christus non assumpsit naturam humanam sed angelicam, sive corpus celeste, et dixit quod habuit hunc errorem ab episcopo et filio maiore ecclesie Bulgarie iam fere elapsis annis LX.', Sacconi, *Summa, AFP*, XLIV, p. 58.

[22] Paulicians are distinguished from all other Christian dualists in not being ascetic and world renouncing. P. Lemerle, 'L'histoire des Pauliciens d'Asie Mineure d'après les sources grecques', *Travaux et Mémoires* [henceforth *TM*], 5 (1973), pp. 1-145. No western group shares this distinctive combination of dualist belief and worldly behaviour and J. Duvernoy is almost certainly correct in interpreting the term *Publicani*, used in some twelfth-century sources to describe western heretics, as cognate with the word used in the Vulgate to describe tax-collectors (*publicani*), *Le Catharisme: la religion des Cathares* (Toulouse, 1976), pp. 306-7.

[23] E.g. *Gesta Francorum et aliorum Hierosolymitanorum*, I, iii, ed. with English trans. R. Hill (London, 1962), p. 8; Robert the Monk, *Historia Iherosolimitana*, III, xiv, *Recueil des Historiens des Croisades, Historiens Occidentaux* [henceforth *RHC Occ.*], III, p. 763; Baldric of Dol, *Historia Jerosolimitana*, II, vii (MS G), *RHC Occ.*, IV, p. 39, n. 16.

[24] Geoffroi de Villehardouin, *La Conquête de Constantinople*, 399, ed. E. Faral (Paris, 1938-9), II, p. 210.

[25] Dondaine, ed., *De Heresi*, *AFP*, XIX, pp. 283-4.

[26] J.V.A. Fine, *The Late Medieval Balkans* (Michigan, 1987), p. 18.

[27] Innocent III, *Regesta*, II, CLXXVI, *PL*, 214, 725-6; cited in part in *Pontificia Commissio ad redigendum Codicem Iuris Canonici Orientalis: Fontes* [henceforth *CICO*],

ser. 3, vol. II. *Acta Innocentii papae III (1198-1216)*, ed. T. Haluščynski (Vatican City, 1944), p. 68.

[28] *Idem*, no. 19, p. 209; Bogomils may have been present in Split in 1186 when Archbishop Peter forbade conventicles to be held there, a decision confirmed by Pope Urban III, *Epistolae et Privilegia*, LXVI, PL, 202, 1446-9.

[29] Thomas archidiaconus, *Historia Salonitanorum Pontificum ... usque ad Rogerium*, c. xxiii, ed. F. Rački, *Monumenta spectantia Historiam Slavorum Meridionalium*, 26 (Zagreb, 1894), p. 80.

[30] *CICO*, ser. III, vol. II, no. 19, p. 209.

[31] *Ibid.*, no. 28, pp. 224-5.

[32] 'Nos priores illorum hominum, qui hactenus singulariter Christiani nominis praerogativa vocati sumus in territorio Bosnae'; 'et nullum deinceps ex certa scientia Manichaeum, vel alium haereticum ad habitandum nobiscum recipiemus'. *Ibid.*, no. 36, pp. 235-7.

[33] E.g. The Cathar Latin *Ritual*, which was in use in Tuscany, contains this rubric about the rite of *consolamentum*: 'tunc ipse credens debet venire cum illo qui ancianus est de hospicio illius' ['then the believer should come accompanied by the man who is the Elder in charge of his hospice'], ed. C. Thouzellier, *Rituel Cathare, Sources chrétiennes*, 236 (Paris, 1977), p. 222.

[34] C. Thouzellier, *Catharisme et Valdéisme en Languedoc à la fin du XIIe et au début du XIIIe siècle*, Publications de la Faculté des Lettres et Sciences humaines de Paris, Series "Recherches", XXVII (Paris, 1966), pp. 215-99; Frances Andrews, 'The early Humiliati. The development of an Order c.1176-c.1270', unpublished Ph.D. thesis (University of London, 1994).

[35] On Bulgaria, A. Luchaire, *Innocent III : les royautés vassales du Saint-Siège* (Paris, 1908), pp. 96-116; on Byzantium, J.M. Husssey, *The Orthodox Church in the Byzantine Empire* (Oxford, 1986), pp. 184-219.

[36] M.G. Popruzhenko, ed., 'Sinodik carja Borila', *Bălgarski Starini*, VIII (Sofia, 1928); the anathemas against the Bogomils have been excerpted and translated into French, H-C. Puech and A. Vaillant, *Le Traité contre les Bogomiles de Cosmas le prêtre*, Travaux publiés par l'Institut d'Etudes slaves, XXI (Paris, 1945), pp. 344-6. Papal intervention, though possible, cannot be proved: the fact that a cardinal was sent to Bulgaria by Innocent III five years earlier in 1206 does not seem conclusive, *Chronicon Alberici monachi Trium Fontium*, ed. P. Scheffer-Boichorst, *MGH SS*, XXIII, p. 886

[37] Raynerius Sacconi, the Cathar perfect who became Inquisitor for Lombardy, writing in c.1250, provides the only set of comparative statistics for membership of Bogomil and Cathar churches. He computes the total number of perfect, or full members, at c.4,000, of whom 'MD et plures' belong to the church of Concorrezo, *Summa, AFP*, XLIV, p. 50.

[38] Synodikon of Tsar Boril, ed., Popruzhenko, *Bălgarski Starini*, VIII, p. 68; trans. Puech and Vaillant, op. cit., p. 346. On the use of the title *dyed*, D. Obolensky, *The Bogomils. A Study in Balkan Neo-Manichaeism* (Cambridge, 1948), pp. 242-4.

[39] Sacconi estimates the absolute dualists of Lombardy, the Albanenses, at c.500, *Summa, AFP*, XLIV, p. 50. There are no accurate statistics for the numbers of Cathar perfect in Languedoc before the Albigensian Crusade, but since the crusaders are known to have massacred at least 1,000 of them, they must have numbered several thousand. On the challenge which absolute dualism posed to traditional Christianity, D. Obolensky, 'Papa Nicetas. A Byzantine dualist in the land of the Cathars', *Harvard Ukrainian Studies*, VII (1983), pp. 489-500.

[40] In the twelfth century Hugh Etherianus, the Pisan adviser to Manuel I Comnenus, had written a (still unpublished) tract against the Patarenes: A. Dondaine, 'Hugues Éthérien et Léon Toscan', *Archives d'histoire littéraire et doctrinale du moyen âge*,

19 (1952), pp. 109-14; Sacconi, writing in Lombardy, attests the presence of dualists in the Latin Empire in c.1250: 'Ecclesia Latinorum de Constantinopoli. Ecclesia Grecorum ibidem.' *Summa, AFP,* XLIV, p. 50.

[41] Duvernoy, *La religion des Cathares,* pp. 309-11.

[42] '... in finbus Brunarum [sic], Croatiae et Dalmatiae, juxta Hungariam nationem ...'; 'Iste satanas quemdam ... hominem usque in Agenum dioecesim diffamavit, nomine Bartholomaeum Carcensem ... Cui Bartholomaeo Vigorosus de Bathona haereticorum episcopus funestam exhibendo reverentiam, sedem et locum suum concessit in villa quae dicitur Pojors, et seipsum transtulit in partes Tholosanas. Iste Bartholomaeus qui litterarum suarum undique discurrentium prius salutationis alloquio seipsum intitulat in hunc modum, *Bartholomaeus servus servorum hospitalis sanae fidei tali salutem:* ipse etiam ... creat episcopos et ecclesias perfidiae ordinare contendit.' J-D. Mansi, *Sacrorum Conciliorum nova et amplissima collectio,* 31 vols (Florence-Venice, 1795-98), XXII, 1204. There is a variant text of this letter ed. C-L. Hugo, *Sacrae antiquitatis monumenta historica, dogmatica, diplomatica* (Étival, 1725), I, pp. 115-17.

[43] His treatise is datable 1222/3, C. Thouzellier, ed., *Une Somme anti-cathare: le 'Liber contra Manicheos' de Durand de Huesca.* Spicilegium Sacrum Lovaniense. Etudes et documents, 32 (1964), p. 78.

[44] Y. Dossat, 'Un évêque cathare originaire de l'Agenais, Vigouroux de la Bacone', *Bulletin philologique et historique (jusqu'à 1610),* année 1965 (1968), pp. 623-39, [consecration of Vigouroux, pp. 633-4; evidence about Bartholomew, pp. 638-9]; reprinted, Y. Dossat, *Église et hérésie en France au XIIIe siècle* (Variorum, London, 1982), No. XIII.

[45] Hamilton, 'Cathar Council', AFP, 48, pp. 44-9.

[46] '... Petrus de Gibel non fuit tunc hereticatus in morte, quia noluit hereticari a predictis hereticis, quia non erant de fide hereticorum de Tholosano ...', ed., C. Douais, 'L'Albigéisme et les Frères Prêcheurs à Narbonne', *Bulletin de la commission archéologique de Narbonne,* III (1894), p. 358.

[47] 'Item omnes ecclesie Catharorum recipiunt se ad invicem licet habeant diversas et contrarias opiniones, preter Albanenses et Concorrenses, qui se dampnant ad invicem...', Sacconi, *Summa, AFP,* XLIV, p. 59. The Albanenses were Lombard absolute dualists who held the same beliefs as the southern French Cathars, while the Cathars of Concorrezo were Lombard moderate dualists of the Bulgarian *ordo.*

[48] See the deposition of Raymond of Perelha, lord of Montségur, cited by Dossat, 'Un évêque', p. 634, n. 1.

[49] Conrad located the antipope 'in finibus Brunarum, Croatiae et Dalmatiae, juxta Hungariam nationem', Mansi, XXII, col. 1204. This almost certainly refers to the Bishop of the dualist church of Bosnia, see Y. Stoyanov, *The Hidden Tradition in Europe* (London, 1994), pp. 190-1.

[50] *CICO,* ser. III, vol. III, A.L. Tautu, ed., *Acta Honorii III et Gregorii IX (1216-41)* (Vatican City, 1950), no. 83, pp. 111-112; '... terras ... infectas haeretica pravitate ...', *ibid.,* no. 136, p. 183.

[51] E.g. 'Ecclesia Philadelfie, in Romania.' Sacconi, *Summa, AFP,* XLIV, p.50. This church was in the Byzantine Empire of Nicaea.

[52] G. Ficker, *Die Phundagiagiten: Ein Beitrag zur Ketzergeschichte des byzantinischen Mittelalters* (Leipzig, 1908), pp. 114-25.

[53] *CICO,* ser. III, vol. III, nos. 177, 194, pp. 233-4, 268-9.

[54] *Ibid.,* nos. 197, 198, 207, pp. 271-2, 283; A. Theiner, ed., *Vetera Monumenta Historica Hungariam Sacram Illustrantia* (Rome, 1859-60), I, pp. 129-30, nos. 221-2.

[55] J. Gill. *Byzantium and the Papacy 1198-1400* (New Brunswick, 1979), pp. 63-4.

[56] *CICO,* ser. III, vol. III, nos. 229, 248, 248a, 248b, pp. 308-10, 325-8

[57]   Canon III, ed. Mansi, XXII, cols 987-8.

[58]   'Ego autem frater Rainerius olim heresiarcha...' 'Preterea dico indubitanter quod in annis XVII, quibus conversatus sum cum eis ...' Sacconi, *Summa, AFP*, XLIV, pp. 44, 45.

[59]   'sunt autem XVI omnes ecclesie Catharorum. ... Ecclesia Sclavonie. Ecclesia Latinorum de Constantinopoli. Ecclesia Grecorum ibidem. Ecclesia Philadelfie, in Romania. Ecclesia Bulgarie. Ecclesia Duguuithie [sic]. Et omnes habuerunt originem a duabus ultimis. ... Ecclesia Latinorum in Constantinopoli fere sunt L. Item ecclesia Sclavonie et Philadelphie et Grecorum, Bulgarie et Duguuithie omnes simul fere D. Sacconi, *Summa, AFP*, XLIV, pp. 49-50.

[60]   *CICO*, ser. III, vol. IV(I), ed. T. Haluščynski and M.M. Wojnar, *Acta Innocentii papae IV (1243-54)* (Rome, 1966), no. 112, pp. 191-4.

[61]   Dondaine, *AFP*, 19, pp. 283-4.

[62]   The former view was propounded by J.V. Fine, *The Bosnian Church. A New Interpretation* (New York, London, 1975), but has not met with wide acceptance.

[63]   *CICO*, ser. III, vol. V(II), ed. F.M. Delorme and A.L. Tautu, *Acta Romanorum Pontificum ab Innocentio V ad Benedictum XI (1276-1304)* (Vatican City, 1954), Nos. 76, 77, 102, 105, pp. 137-40, 173-5, 176-80.

[64]   *Ibid.*, no. 123, pp. 202-3.

[65]   '... magna haereticorum caterva de multis et variis partibus congregata ad principatum Bosnensem ... confluxit...', *CICO*, ser. III, vol. VII(ii), ed., A.L. Tautu (Vatican City, 1952), no. 78, p. 160.

[66]   See the evidence given to the Inquisition by Giacomo Bech of Chieri near Turin in 1387 about contacts with the Cathars of Bosnia, ed. G. Amati, 'Processus contra Valdenses in Lombardia superiori anno 1387', *Archivio storico italiano*, ser. III, I(ii) (1865), pp. 16-52, II(i) (1865), pp. 3-61.

XV

THE IMPACT OF CRUSADER JERUSALEM
ON WESTERN CHRISTENDOM

Ever since St. Paul wrote to the Galatians describing the Christian dispensation as "Jerusalem which is above . . . which is the mother of us all," the name Jerusalem has had a double significance for Christians. It is the heavenly city to which they are all journeying, but it is also the city in Palestine where their faith began. When pilgrimages to the earthly Jerusalem were first made in the fourth century, some people questioned their religious value. Supporters argued that to visit the places of Christ's earthly life was a powerful stimulus to devotion, but their critics replied that since all Christians were citizens of the heavenly Jerusalem there was no need for them to cross the world to reach a place in which, spiritually, they ought to be living already. St. Jerome summed up the latter view in a phrase which opponents of pilgrimage frequently quoted: "It is not praiseworthy to have been to Jerusalem, but it is praiseworthy to have lived the good life in the [new] Jerusalem." This does not sound very memorable in English, but the Latin

is more snappy: "Non Hierosolymis fuisse, sed Hierosolymis bene vix-
isse laudandum est."[1]

This view never won universal approval: there were always some
Christians who considered that it was spiritually valuable for citizens
of the new Jerusalem to visit the old Jerusalem. Pilgrimage persisted
even though the Arabs conquered Jerusalem in 638 and it became a
Muslim city, but the number of Western pilgrims to the Holy Land increased greatly in the eleventh century. There are a variety of reasons for
this: the conversion of Hungary to Catholicism, and the extension of Byzantine power in the Balkans and north Syria meant that most of the journey could be made through Christian territory, while on a religious
level there was a greater awareness of the humanity of Christ. This is
exemplified in many eleventh-century devotional writings, but particularly in those of St. Anselm. Moreover, monastic reformers were inspired by the ideal of the *vita apostolica*, the desire to return to the
kind of life lived by Christ and his apostles. This was an ascetic ideal
which sought Christian perfection through renunciation of the world
and self-sacrifice. Pilgrimage to the Holy Land was not a necessary part
of this type of spirituality, but many of the reformers were sympathetic
to such journeys as penitential and devotional acts. Consequently, large
numbers of people made the Jerusalem journey; in 1064, for example,
7,000 Germans, led by four bishops, set out to keep Easter there.[2]

There can be no doubt of the fervor which this pilgrimage inspired
in those who undertook it. The places made holy by Christ's presence
were regarded as spiritual powerhouses. This sentiment was closely connected to the cult of relics, and Jerusalem was the greatest relic in Christendom, for no other place on earth was more hallowed by God's
presence than the city where his Son had been crucified and had risen
from the dead. Yet the impact of Jerusalem on eleventh-century pilgrims was spiritual rather than visual. It was a Muslim city, physically
dominated by two great Islamic shrines, the Dome of the Rock and
the al-Aksar mosque. Christians were tolerated there, but were treated
as second-class citizens, and were only free to practise their cult inside
their own churches. But in the eleventh century these were few in number. In 1009 the Caliph al-Hakim had ordered the destruction of the
church of the Holy Sepulchre, and four years later commanded that

---

[1]St. Jerome, *Epistola ad Paulinum*, ed. Isidor Hilberg, *Corpus Scriptorum Eccle-
siasticorum Latinorum* (Vienna, 1866–   ), LIV, *Ep.* LVIII, p. 529.
[2]Einar Joranson, "The Great German Pilgrimage of 1064–5," in Louis J. Paetow (ed.),
The Crusades and other Historical Essays presented to Dana C. Munro (New York,
1928), pp. 3–43.

all Christian churches in his empire should be demolished.[3] Although the latter order was not systematically carried out, it is probable that the great shrine churches around Jerusalem were ruined at that time: they were certainly in ruins when the First Crusade reached the city.[4] al-Hakim's successors allowed the Byzantine Emperor to sponsor the rebuilding of the Holy Sepulchre and the work was completed in 1048;[5] but the other great shrine churches remained unrestored, while the Holy Sepulchre was administered by Greek Orthodox clergy who celebrated the liturgy in a form unfamiliar to Western pilgrims.

I had expected to find that the increase in pilgrimage to Jerusalem in the eleventh century would have influenced the mainstream of Western piety. There is no evidence that it did so. The scholars who wrote biblical commentaries were not knowledgeable about, or indeed very interested in, the circumstances of Christ's earthly life, even though they could talk to people who had visited the Holy Land. St. Bruno of Segni, for example, who completed his commentaries on the Gospels in ca 1089, has this to say about John 20:1: "Early on the first day of the week, while it was still dark, Mary Magdalene came to the tomb and saw that the stone had been removed from the tomb."

> On a literal level [we must understand] that great love drove this woman to seek the Lord at the tomb while it was still dark. But the spiritual sense of the passage is that she was still enveloped in darkness because she had not yet received enlightenment within herself.[6]

There is no evidence here that Bruno, who had certainly met men who had been to Jerusalem, had learned anything from them about the layout of the city which helped him to comment on this text. Such examples could be multiplied.

Although there was no abatement in the desire to make the Jeru-

[3]Marius Canard, "La destruction de l'église de la Résurrection par le calife Hakim et l'histoire de la descente du feu sacré," *Byzantion*, 35 (1965), 16–43.

[4]Saewulf, *Certa Relatio de Situ Jerusalem*, cc. 21, 22, ed. with Italian translation, Sabino de Sandoli, *Itinera Hierosolymitana Crucesignatorum (saec. XII–XIII)* ("Pubblicazioni dello Studium Biblicum Franciscanum," Collectio Maior, No. 24 [3 vols.; Jerusalem, 1981–1983]), II, 22.

[5]Virgilio C. Corbo, *Il Santo Sepolcro a Gerusalemme* ("Pubblicazioni dello Studium Biblicum Franciscanum," Collectio Maior, No. 29 [3 vols.; Jerusalem, 1981–1982]), I, 139–181; II, pl. 4, 5.

[6]*S. Brunonis Episcopi Signiensis Commentaria in Joannem*, III, XX, ed. Jacques-Paul Migne, *Patrologia Latina* [henceforth *PL*], Vol. 165, col. 590. On the dating, Beryl Smalley, "Peter Comestor on the Gospels and his sources," *Recherches de Théologie ancienne et médiévale* [henceforth *RTAM*], 46 (1979), 93.

XV

salem journey in the late eleventh century, fewer people went after
the Turkish invasions of the Near East in the 1070's made the roads
unsafe.[7] So when the First Crusade was preached in 1095 it owed its
appeal in part to the fact that a generation had grown up who wanted
to go to Jerusalem but had found difficulty in doing so. The chief aim
of the Crusade in the view of the participants was to "liberate the
church of God in Jerusalem," and against all probability they succeeded
and on July 15, 1099, entered the city in triumph. They made it an entirely Christian city by the simple expedient of slaughtering all non-
Christians whom they found there, and refusing to allow any Muslims
to return there later. They also made it a Catholic city. Before 1099
Eastern Christianity in its various forms had dominated the church life
of Jerusalem, and the only Catholic presence had been the small monastery of St. Mary of the Latins, with its adjacent hospital, founded to
care for western pilgrims.[8] Pope Urban II wished the Orthodox Patriarch to remain in charge, but the crusaders would have none of
this.[9] They found the idea of owing religious obedience to an alien
Greek hierarchy repugnant, and established the Western Catholic
Church throughout their dominions, run by a patriarch and bishops
who spoke their language and shared their cultural and social values.
Eastern Christians in all their bewildering variety were given religious
freedom by the crusaders and were allowed to run their own churches
in their own traditional ways, but the Catholic Church enjoyed a
specially privileged status because it was the church of the rulers, and
all the chief shrines were entrusted to it.[10]

[7]Steven Runciman,"The Pilgrimages to Palestine before 1095," in Kenneth M. Setton
(gen. ed.), A History of the Crusades, Vol. I, Marshall W. Baldwin (ed.), The First Hundred Years (Philadelphia, 1958), pp. 68–78.

[8]Willelmi Tyrensis Archiepiscopi Chronicon, XVIII, 5, ed. Robert B. C. Huygens,
Corpus Christianorum Continuatio Mediaevalis, LXIII, LXIIIA (Turnholt, 1986)
[henceforth cited as WT], II, 815–816.

[9]This seems clear from the fact that his legate, Adhémar of Le Puy, had treated the
Orthodox Patriarch, Symeon II of Jerusalem, as the canonical authority; Heinrich Hag-
enmeyer, Epistulae et chartae ad historiam primi belli sacri spectantes (Innsbruck,
1901, reprinted Hildesheim, New York, 1973), nos. VI, IX, pp. 141–142, 146–149.
Symeon died at the time the Franks took Jerusalem, and they elected a Latin Patriarch
without reference to the Orthodox clergy; Albert of Aix, Liber Christianae Expeditionis,
VI, xxxix, Recueil des Historiens des Croisades, Historiens Occidentaux (5 vols.; Paris,
Académie des Inscriptions et Belles Lettres, 1844–1895) [henceforth RHC Occ], IV,
489. Urban II had died on July 29, 1099, and none of his successors challenged the
appointment of Latins to the patriarchal see of Jerusalem.

[10]Orthodox Eastern Christians were allowed to keep their own churches and rites
but were made subject to the Catholic hierarchy, whereas the separated Eastern Christians were allowed virtual autonomy; Bernard Hamilton, The Latin Church in the Crusader States: the Secular Church (London, 1980), pp. 159–211.

Historians of the crusades have concentrated on these negative aspects of the religious policy of the Frankish rulers and have written comparatively little about their attempt to make the city which they had liberated into a religious center for the Christian world. This was more ambitious than any comparable piece of religious town planning undertaken in the Middle Ages, and resembled the policy of the first humanist pope, Nicholas V, who wished to rebuild Rome as a great Renaissance city, symbolizing the power of the Church on earth.[11] The Catholic clergy in the Holy Land in the twelfth century had a quite clear aim, that of making the earthly Jerusalem a symbol of the heavenly city, and in this endeavor they had the full support of the Frankish laity. When Rorgo Fretellus, archdeacon of Nazareth, wrote a guidebook to the Holy Places in 1137, he considered that this aim had been achieved, and he was able to exhort his readers to "ponder upon the holy city of Jerusalem ... which is an allegory for us of the heavenly paradise."[12]

In 1099 the western conquerors had found a great deal which needed to be done in order to turn a Muslim city, full of ruined Christian shrines, into a Christian city where all the sacred sites were duly honored. Special attention was paid to the church of the Holy Sepulchre. This, the greatest of all the shrines in the city, included three cult centers: the rock pinnacle of Calvary, scene of the Crucifixion; Christ's burial chamber, scene of the Resurrection; and the cave in which St. Helena had found the True Cross. Constantine the Great had built a complex of sanctuaries to connect the three sites, but the new church of 1048 which the crusaders inherited had separated them. This was a circular church with a pillared gallery and an apse at the west end. As in the Pantheon at Rome, there was a circular opening in the roof, beneath which stood the shrine of the Holy Sepulchre encased in a marble aedicule. The Calvary Chapel was in a corner of the courtyard to the west of the rotunda, while the St. Helena crypt was not included in the complex at all.[13] The crusaders completely redesigned the site. The apse of the rotunda was demolished, as was the courtyard and its chapels, and a Gothic cathedral was built on to the west end of the rotunda. The Calvary chapel was incorporated in the cathedral; it was built over a pillar of natural rock and was approached by a staircase from the south aisle. Another staircase,

[11]Paolo Portoghesi, *Rome of the Renaissance* (London and New York, 1972), p. 11.

[12]". . . considera sanctam Iherusalem, contemplare et ipsam Syon, que celestem para-dysum allegorice nobis figurat." *Rorgo Fretellus et sa description de la Terre Sainte. Histoire et édition du texte*, Petrus C. Boeren (Amsterdam, 1980), p. 6.

[13]Corbo, *Il Santo Sepolcro*, I, 139–181; II, pl. 4, 5.

pierced in the wall of the ambulatory, gave access to the St. Helena crypt. The Catholic Patriarch's throne, which stood behind the high altar in the new choir, thus faced down the whole length of the cathedral toward the entrance to the Holy Sepulchre in the center of the rotunda.[14] The Crusaders had obtained from the native Christians of Jerusalem a relic which they believed was a substantial portion of the True Cross. They encased this in a golden reliquary studded with cabuchon jewels, and it was permanently on view for the veneration of the faithful in a chapel of the new apse.[15]

It took fifty years to complete the crusader cathedral,[16] and much other work was carried out concurrently. The Franks converted the great Muslim shrine, the Dome of the Rock, which stood on the platform of the Temple of Herod, into a church which they called the Temple of the Lord. The crescent which surmounted it was taken down and replaced by a great golden cross, visible from a considerable distance, a symbol that Jerusalem was now indeed a Christian city. The Franks covered the rock, round which the shrine is built and which gives it its name, with a marble floor, and surrounded this with an octagonal iron grill. This central space became the sanctuary of the Christian church and was venerated as the site of the presentation of Christ.[17]

The Franks also rebuilt the other ruined shrines in and around the city. The most important of these was the church of Mount Sion, just outside the medieval walls. This was believed to stand on the site of the house in whose upper room Christ had celebrated the Last Supper, and where also the Holy Spirit had descended on the faithful at Pentecost. The Franks rebuilt this as a two-storey church, in which the upper church represented the upper room.[18] On the Mount of Olives to the east of the city stood the ruins of the church of the Ascension:

[14]*Ibid.*, I, 183–209; II, pl. 6, 7.

[15]Theodoric, *De Locis Sanctis*, c. ix, ed. de Sandoli, *Itinera*, II, 328.

[16]The dedication inscription was recorded by John of Würzburg, *Descriptio Terrae Sanctae*, c. xiii, ed. de Sandoli, *Itinera*, II, 262.

[17]Fulcher of Chartres, *Gesta Francorum Iherusalem peregrinantium*, I, c. 26, vii, ed. Heinrich Hagenmeyer (Heidelberg, 1913), pp. 287–288; Austin Canons had been given this shrine by 1112, Joseph Delaville Le Roulx, *Cartulaire générale de l'Ordre des Hospitaliers de St. Jean de Jérusalem (1100–1310)* (4 vols.; Paris, 1894–1906) [henceforth *CGOH*], I, 26, no. 25; WT, VIII, 3, ed. Huygens, I, 387; John of Würzburg, *Descriptio*, c. iv, ed. de Sandoli, *Itinera*, II, 236–244; Theodoric, *De Locis*, cc. xiv, xv, *ibid.*, II, 334–340; photographs of the grill in Camille Enlart, *Les monuments des croisés dans le royaume de Jérusalem. Architecture religieuse et civile* (2 vols.; Paris, 1925–1928), Album I, pl. 40, figs. 132–133.

[18]Initially they repaired the ruined Byzantine church, *Vie et pèlerinage du Daniel, bégoumène russe, 1106–1107*, c. xli, trans. B. de Khitrowo, *Itinéraires russes en Orient*,

the crusaders rebuilt this as a circular church. The high altar stood on the supposed site of Christ's Ascension; it was sheltered by a marble canopy, but the roof of the church was open to the sky.[19]

There were also the shrines associated with the life of the Blessed Virgin Mary which had to be restored and maintained. Near the Temple was the reputed site of her parents' house, and there the Franks built the church of St. Anne, one of the most simple and beautiful early Gothic churches in the world.[20] Near the foot of the Mount of Olives was the site of the tomb in which Mary had been buried for forty days prior to her assumption, and this was rebuilt by the Franks, who refashioned the old crypt as a subterranean basilica, which was entered from ground level through a Gothic portico opening on to a wide ceremonial staircase.[21] Other sacred sites in the hinterland of Jerusalem needed to be maintained. Bethlehem, where Christ was born, is only a few miles to the south of the city: the basilica, a modification of that built by Constantine the Great, still stands there, but the Franks raised it to the dignity of a bishopric and appointed a chapter of Catholic canons.[22] A few miles east of the Mount of Olives is Bethany, the home of Jesus's friends Mary and Martha, where Lazarus was raised from the dead. In 1138 Queen Melisende founded a Benedictine convent there to care for this complex of shrines.[23] The same queen built a house of Premonstratensian Canons to serve the shrine of St. Samuel on

---

I (i) (Geneva, 1889), pp. 36–37. By 1112 it had been entrusted to a community of Austin Canons, *CGOH*, I, 26, no. 25, who rebuilt it with a stone vault, Enlart, *op. cit.*, II, 248; Theodoric, *De Locis*, c. 22, ed. de Sandoli, II, 348.

[19]Ralph of Caen, *Gesta Tancredi in expeditione Hierosolymitana*, c. 113, *RHC Occ*, III, 685; entrusted to Austin Canons by 1112, *CGOH*, I, 26, no. 25; Saewulf, *Peregrinatio ad Hierosolymam et Terram Sanctam*, c. 18, ed. de Sandoli, II, 20; John of Würzburg, *Descriptio*, c. 14, *ibid.*, II, 264–266; Theodoric, *De Locis*, c. 27, *ibid.*, II, 356.

[20]Saewulf, *Peregrinatio*, c. 16, ed. de Sandoli, II, 18; John of Würzburg, c. 16, *ibid.*, II, 268–270; Paul Deschamps, *Terre Sainte romane* (La Pierre-qui-vire, 1964), pp. 163–221.

[21]Daniel, *Pèlerinage*, c. xxii, ed. de Khitrowo, *op. cit.*, I (i), 23; Saewulf, *Peregrinatio*, c. 5, ed. de Sandoli, II, 118; John of Würzburg, *Descriptio*, c. 17, *ibid.*, II, 272–276; Theodoric, *De Locis*, c. 23, *ibid.*, II, 350–352.

[22]Denys Pringle, *The Churches of the Crusader Kingdom of Jerusalem. A Corpus*, Volume I: *A-K (excluding Acre and Jerusalem)* (Cambridge, 1993), pp. 137–156; Gustav Kühnel, *Wall Painting in the Latin Kingdom of Jerusalem* (Berlin, 1988), p. 3; Hans-Eberhard Mayer, *Bistümer, Klöster und Stifte im Königreich Jerusalem, Schriften der Monumenta Germaniae Historica*, 26 (Stuttgart, 1977), pp. 44–80; Hamilton, *Latin Church*, p. 59.

[23]Saewulf, *Peregrinatio*, c. 23, ed. de Sandoli, II, 24; John of Würzburg, *Descriptio*, c. 6, *ibid.*, II, 246; Theodoric, *De Locis*, c. 28, *ibid.*, II, 358; Pringle, *op. cit.*, I, 122–

Mountjoy, the hill from which pilgrims obtained their first sight of Jerusalem as they came up from the coast.[24] In the reign of Melisende's son Amalric the Cistercians came to the Holy Land and built an abbey at Ain Karim, near Jerusalem, the birthplace of St. John the Baptist.[25]

All these great shrines were served by religious communities. Austin Canons had charge of the Holy Sepulchre, Mount Sion, the Mount of Olives, and the Temple of the Lord; Benedictine monks served Our Lady of Josaphat; Benedictine nuns held the church of St. Anne and the convent of Bethany.[26] Their chief function was to ensure that the liturgy was performed in these churches, and every day and night, without intermission, throughout the period of Frankish rule, the eight services of the Divine Office were sung and the Eucharist celebrated daily with full ceremonial at all these shrines.

There were also numerous lesser sacred sites in and around the city, and the communities of the great churches took charge of many of them. For example, the canons of Mount Sion maintained the chapel of the *lithostrotos*, the pavement where according to St. John's Gospel Pilate sat in judgment;[27] the Benedictines of Our Lady of Josaphat had the garden of Gethsemani in their grounds, and maintained two chapels there to commemorate Christ's Agony in the Garden and the Sleep of the Apostles;[28] the nuns of St. Anne's, who had charge of the adjacent pool of Bethesda, built a chapel to honor Christ's healing of a paralytic man there;[29] while the canons of the Mount of Olives administered a church built on the site where Christ had first taught the Lord's

---

137; B. Hamilton, "Rebuilding Zion: The Holy Places of Jerusalem in the Twelfth Century," in Derek Baker (ed.), *Studies in Church History* [henceforth *SCH*], 15 (Oxford, 1977), p. 113.

[24]Mayer, "Sankt Samuel auf dem Freudenberge und sein Besitz nach einem unbekannten Diplom König Balduins V," *Quellen und Forschungen aus italienischen Archiven und Bibliotheken* [henceforth *QFIAB*], 44 (1964), 35–71.

[25]Leopold Janauschek, *Originum Cisterciensium*, I (Vienna, 1877), p. 158, no. 405; Theodoric, *De Locis*, c. 38, ed. de Sandoli, II, 368; Pringle, "Cistercian Houses in the Kingdom of Jerusalem," in Michael Gervers (ed.), *The Second Crusade and the Cistercians* (New York, 1992), pp. 183–198; Pringle, *Churches of the Crusader Kingdom*, I, 38–47.

[26]Hamilton, "Rebuilding Zion," *SCH*, 15 (1977), 105–116.

[27]Theodoric, *De Locis*, c. 25, ed. de Sandoli, II, 354.

[28]Saewulf, *Peregrinatio*, c. 5, ed. de Sandoli, II, 18; Theodoric, *De Locis*, c. 24, *ibid.*, II, 352.

[29]Theodoric, c. 26, *ibid.*, II, 356.

Prayer.[30] The Knights of St. John built a church at Abu Ghosh because they believed it was the village of Emmaus.[31]

The construction of this large number of shrine churches and of the abbeys and priories for the communities which served them, the fortification of those which were outside the city walls and needed protection from enemy raids, and the endowment of all these institutions with adequate lands to maintain their fabric and clergy, proved extremely expensive. The whole of western Christendom contributed to this work, and the communities which administered the holy places were given property throughout Catholic Europe, but the collection and transmission of rents was often difficult; so a specially heavy burden fell on the local Catholic population. The Frankish nobility were extremely generous patrons of the Church. Moreover, in the Kingdom of Jerusalem Muslims and eastern-rite Christians, who made up the bulk of the rural population, were not required to pay tithes. These were levied normally only on the Frankish lord's share of the crops. Thus almost the entire burden of supporting the Catholic establishment and the elaborate church building program was borne by the Franks.[32] This shows the Frankish settlers in the Levant in a rather different light from that in which they are customarily portrayed. They are often described as men who had come to the East in search of a fortune, as brave warriors, or political intriguers, and no doubt there is some truth in such views, but they also had a strong commitment to the care of the Holy Places which were in their charge. They were concerned that God should be fittingly honored by professional clergy in the land which was peculiarly His own, and they were prepared to spend large sums of money for that purpose. Although Palestine is described in the Old Testament as "a land flowing with milk and honey," that is the view of desert nomads: seen through the eyes of men coming from the West, it did not appear a rich country. Good farmland was limited, and much of the region was suitable only for grazing sheep and goats. Moreover, the Crusader Kingdom was almost constantly at war with its Islamic neighbors, and a high proportion of

[30]Saewulf, *Peregrinatio*, c. 18, ed. de Sandoli, II, 20 (reports it destroyed); Theodoric, c. 27, *ibid.*, II, 356 (on the new church).

[31]Louis-Hugues Vincent and F. M. Abel, *Emmaus, sa basilique et son histoire* (Paris, 1932); Pringle, *Churches of the Crusader Kingdom*, I, 7–17.

[32]Hamilton, *Latin Church*, pp. 145–151; Jean Richard, "Le paiement des dîmes dans les états des croisés," *Bibliothèque de l'École des Chartes* [henceforth *BEC*], 150 (1992), 71–83.

its revenues was spent on defense. Yet the Franks did not stint in their giving to the Holy Places, and a substantial proportion of good agricultural land was devoted to the upkeep of the shrines.[33]

Twelfth-century Jerusalem became the most important pilgrimage center in the Christian world. Western pilgrims found the journey much easier than before, because as soon as the coastal cities of Syria and Palestine had come into Christian hands the fleets of the great Italian maritime republics, Genoa, Pisa, and Venice, began to trade with the Crusader States and to bring pilgrims there. Two main sailings took place each year, one in March, the other in late July.[34] Such voyages were not without danger; ships sank, or sometimes were driven ashore on the African coast where their passengers might be enslaved, but the journey was far quicker than it was by land,[35] and did not involve traveling through Muslim territory at all.

In the early days of Frankish settlement pilgrims found that the roads of the kingdom were more unsafe than the sea-lanes; brigandage was rife, and parties of raiders from Egyptian-held Ascalon attacked travelers. The road from the coast to Jerusalem was littered with their corpses.[36] In 1119 Hugh of Payens, a Burgundian nobleman, gathered a band of fellow knights who took religious vows to keep the roads safe for pilgrims. This small band of men grew within twenty years to be the first of the great international Military Orders, the Knights Templar, but its members remained mindful of their original vocation and built small towers to guard the main pilgrim routes of the kingdom, which came to have some of the safest roads in the Christian world.[37]

There were other problems connected with pilgrimage. Many pilgrims arrived in Jerusalem destitute, having spent all their resources on the journey; some were old people who had set out with the intention of dying in the Holy City; while many others fell sick because they were exposed to diseases to which they had no immunity. Before the First Crusade there had been a small hospital in the city to care for western pilgrims, but after 1099 this grew in size and wealth, and the community who served it was given the status of an independent

[33]Hamilton, *Latin Church*, pp. 137–158.

[34]John H. Pryor, *Geography, Technology and War, Studies in the Maritime History of the Mediterranean, 649–1571* (Cambridge, 1988), pp. 3–4.

[35]An average spring passage to Acre from the West took "about four to six weeks," *ibid.*, p. 3.

[36]Saewulf, *Peregrinatio*, c. 3, ed. de Sandoli, II, 12.

[37]WT, XII, vii, ed. Huygens, I, 553–555; Malcolm Barber, *The New Knighthood* (Cambridge, 1994), pp. 1–114.

religious Order by Paschal II in 1113, that of the Hospitallers of St. John of Jerusalem. This Order soon developed a military wing which, like the Knights Templar, played an important role in the defense of the kingdom,[38] but the Hospitallers never neglected their charitable work. The hospital of St. John in Jerusalem was the biggest in the Christian world. It had several hundred beds,[39] and the standards of care were high. The statutes of 1182 state:

> And the brethren of the Hospital shall without charge look after the sick by day and by night as if they were their lords ...; in every ward of the house where the sick are lying, nine servants shall be appointed to look after them, who on the orders of the brethren shall humbly wash the heads and feet of the patients, and launder their clothes, and make their beds, and prepare their food, and give them drinks, and minister to the needs of the sick in every way.[40]

In the maternity ward each bed was supplied with a separate cradle to prevent overlying. In addition the hospital cared for the healthy but destitute; warm clothing and shoes were regularly distributed to the poor, and on three days a week the brethren offered bread, wine, and a cooked meal to "all the poor who came to ask for it."[41]

Conditions, therefore, were as good for pilgrims as they could be made in twelfth-century Jerusalem. There are no reliable statistics of the number of people from the West who visited the city during the years of crusader occupation, nor, I think, does the information exist from which any but minimum figures could be computed, but they were clearly very numerous. Perhaps the best indicator is the fact that the Frankish population of the Kingdom has been reliably calculated at some 140,000 people in 1180,[42] and there must have been almost as many in the northern states of Tripoli and Antioch. The Frankish population in all these states had been recruited chiefly from pilgrims over the space of eighty years, but the number of pilgrims who stayed in the Holy Land was never more than a fraction of the total; the majority returned to the West.

[38]WT, XVIII, 5, ed. Huygens, II, 815–817; Paschal II's bull *Pie postulatio pietatis, CGOH*, no. 30, I, 29–30; Jonathan Riley-Smith, *The Knights of St. John in Jerusalem and Cyprus, 1050–1310* (London, 1967), pp. 32–84.

[39]Two thousand, according to John of Würzburg, *Descriptio*, c. 15, ed. de Sandoli, II, 266; one thousand, according to Theodoric, *De Locis*, c. 13, *ibid.*, II, 334. Both figures are almost certainly notional.

[40]The Rule of Roger des Moulins of March 14, 1182, *CGOH*, no. 627, I, 427.

[41]*Ibid.*, I, 425–429.

[42]Joshua Prawer, "The Sources and Composition of the *Livre des Assises des Bourgeois,*" in *Crusader Institutions* (Oxford, 1980), pp. 380–381 and n. 38.

The city which these pilgrims visited was very different from that which their predecessors had seen before the First Crusade. Although it was eastern and exotic, there was also much about it which was reassuringly familiar; the ruling classes talked French and dressed in western fashions.[43] The dominant religion was Catholicism, and the familiar Mass of the Latin rite was celebrated in almost all the shrines which the pilgrims wanted to visit. There were, of course, eastern Christians there as well, for Jerusalem was the center of the entire Christian world, and pilgrims came there from all the eastern churches. Western pilgrims met the native Greek and Syrian Orthodox, Maronites from Lebanon, Armenians, Georgians from the Caucasus, Russians from the far north, Nestorians from Persia and Iraq, St. Thomas's Christians from the Malabar coast of India, and Syrian Jacobites who acted as hosts to Egyptian Copts and to Christian pilgrims from Nubia and perhaps from Ethiopia as well.[44] Most of them had their own churches, some of which were very fine, like the Armenian cathedral of St. James built in the crusader period,[45] and together they formed a microcosm of the universal Church, a reminder to western visitors that however strong Islam might seem, the apostolic preaching had reached all parts of the known world and had borne fruit.

But it was the Catholic churches which the pilgrims from the West chiefly wished to see because these were the principal shrines. By the second half of the twelfth century many of them had been embellished with frescoes, mosaics, and bas-reliefs, illustrating the biblical incidents with which the shrines were connected, accompanied by appropriate texts. I am inclined to be skeptical about Ruskin's view that the stained glass and wall paintings in medieval cathedrals were the Bible of the poor, because unless the poor had exceptionally keen sight, much of the detail was not readable from ground level, while the learned symbolism which the artists used was not readily accessible to the simple. But in twelfth-century Jerusalem the situation was quite different. Visual images were not used so often to demonstrate theological truths as to illustrate matters of fact connected with particular sites. The representations, therefore, were for the most part straightforward, not allegorical, and although

---

[43]Prawer, *The World of the Crusaders* (Jerusalem, 1972), p. 87.

[44]John of Würzburg, *Descriptio*, c. 27, ed. de Sandoli, II, 290; Enrico Cerulli, *Etiopi in Palestina. Storia della comunità etiopica di Gerusalemme* (2 vols.; Rome, 1943), I, 8–19.

[45]It is first recorded in *ca* 1170 by John of Würzburg, *Descriptio*, c. 15, ed. de Sandoli, *Itinera*, II, 268; Kevork Hintlian, *History of the Armenians in the Holy Land* (Jerusalem, 1976), pp. 51–56.

most lay pilgrims could not read the Latin texts, the guides who conducted them round the holy places, who were often priests, could do so. Few of these decorations have survived, but they were described in some detail by contemporaries. Thus round the cornice of the shrine of the Holy Sepulchre, which was at the heart of the pilgrimage, was written in letters of gold the passage from the Epistle to the Romans: "Christ, being raised from the dead, will never die again; death no longer has dominion over him"; while over the entrance to the tomb itself was a mosaic showing both the laying of Christ's body in the tomb, and also the three Maries coming to the Sepulchre to be greeted by an angel who told them that the tomb was empty.[46] In the apse of the new cathedral was a fresco of Christ's resurrection. I quote the description of a pilgrim who saw it in *ca.* 1170:

> In his left hand Christ carries the Cross and in his right hand Adam [freed from Hell]. He looks imperially toward heaven and enters heaven with an enormous stride, his left foot raised and his right foot still on the ground. He is surrounded by his Mother and St. John the Baptist and all the Apostles . . . [and] this text is written . . . right the way round the apse: "Christ ascending on high led captivity captive and gave gifts unto men."[47]

But pilgrims were not tourists: they did not simply go on guided tours of these churches to admire the works of art: their chief concern was to worship God there. When celebrated chorally and with full ceremonial, the liturgy of the medieval Western Church was magnificent, and it was celebrated in that way daily in all the chief churches of Jerusalem. The purpose of the liturgy everywhere was to show forth the mysteries of the Christian faith, but in Jerusalem symbol and reality met. This is best seen by examining the liturgy of Holy Week, which pilgrims were particularly anxious to keep in the Holy City.

A number of liturgical texts survive from crusader Jerusalem, but they have not received a great deal of attention from historians and few have been properly edited.[48] Among them is the Ritual of the Holy Sepulchre, which contains this rubric for Palm Sunday:

---

[46]Theodoric, *De Locis Sanctis*, c. 5, ed. de Sandoli, *Itinera*, II, 320–322.

[47]*Ibid.*, c. 7, II, 324–326; Alan Borg, "The Lost Apse Mosaic of the Holy Sepulchre, Jerusalem," in Alan Borg and Andrew Martindale (eds.), *The Vanishing Past. Studies of Medieval Art, Liturgy and Metrology presented to C. Hohler*, BAR International Series III (1981), pp. 7–12.

[48]E.g., Victor Leroquais, *Sacramentaires et missels manuscrits des bibliothèques publiques de France* (Paris, 1924), I, 301–303; V. Leroquais, *Bréviaires manuscrits des Bibliothèques publiques de France* (Paris, 1934), I, 265–267; II, 387–388; III, 189–192.

> After matins have been said and before sunrise the lord patriarch, accompanied by the treasurer of the church of the Holy Sepulchre carrying with him the wood of the life-giving cross, together with the prior of Mount Sion and the prior of the Mount of Olives and the abbot of Our Lady of Josaphat and their communities, shall go to Bethany where Our Lord raised Lazarus from the dead.[49]

Meanwhile, the canons of the Holy Sepulchre, the brethren of the Hospital of St. John, the canons of the Temple of the Lord, and the monks of St. Mary of the Latins shall assemble with the people of Jerusalem near the garden of Gethsemani, where they shall bless and distribute branches of palm and of olive. The patriarch and his company will dress in white vestments at Bethany, and will walk to Jerusalem led by the patriarch carrying the golden reliquary of the cross, symbolizing Christ. As the patriarch's procession reaches the Mount of Olives, the people of Jerusalem shall come to meet it bearing branches in their hands and singing "Hosanna in the highest," and, led by the patriarch, the entire crowd shall climb the steps to the Golden Gate of the Temple (which is opened only on that one day of the year), the gate, as the rubric says, "through which the Lord Jesus entered in." There prayers would be said, before the crowd dispersed to their different churches for the Mass of the day.[50]

And so the week went on. On Maundy Thursday the patriarch led clergy and people to the abbey of Mount Sion, and in the upper room, where Christ had breathed on the Apostles and said, "If you forgive the sins of any, they are forgiven them," he absolved penitents, while the choir sang the seven penitential psalms. This was a very important ceremony, for those who had committed grave and public sins, like willful murder, often had the Jerusalem journey imposed on them as a penance, and at this point they were restored to the communion of the Church.[51]

Holy Week ended with events which centered round the shrines inside the church of the Holy Sepulchre. On Good Friday while it was still dark and lauds was being sung in the choir, the Holy Cross was taken from its chapel and carried up the stairs to the chapel of Calvary.

---

[49]Charles Kohler, "Un Rituel et un bréviaire du Saint-Sépulcre de Jérusalem," *Revue de l'Orient latin* [henceforth *ROL*], VIII (1900–1901), 412.

[50]*Ibid.*, pp. 412–413.

[51]"... et finito sermone archidiaconus, introductis penitentibus, adducet ad patriarcham. Tunc incipiet septem psalmos penitentiales sine letania, et faciet absolutionem." ["... and when the sermon has ended, the archdeacon, having brought the penitents into [the church], shall present them to the patriarch. Then he will begin [to sing] the seven penitential psalms and shall pronounce the absolution."], *ibid.*, pp. 414–415.

The patriarch and his canons then took off their shoes and climbed barefoot to Calvary to venerate the cross, and were followed by a long procession of lay people and pilgrims. At about midday the cross was carried back to its chapel and the patriarch celebrated the solemn Good Friday liturgy in the Calvary chapel, the very place, as it was thought, where Christ had been crucified. There the St. John Passion was chanted, the Good Friday reproaches sung, and Holy Communion distributed.[52]

On Holy Saturday the focus of worship shifted to the shrine of the Holy Sepulchre, scene of the Resurrection. The patriarch sat enthroned in the new choir, facing down the length of the cathedral toward the Sepulchre and flanked by his canons. The whole church was packed with worshipers; Catholic residents, western pilgrims, and eastern Christians of all kinds, for in the Middle Ages most of the churches of east and west observed the Julian calendar and kept Easter on the same day. All the congregation, clergy and people alike, held unlighted candles. Twelve very long Old Testament lessons were sung, showing how Christ's Incarnation had been prefigured since the creation of the world. During the last of them the patriarch chose four pilgrims from among those present, usually men of eminence, to fetch the Holy Cross from its chapel. Barefooted, and preceded by acolytes with unlighted tapers and a thurifer swinging a censer, they passed through the choir carrying the cross to the shrine of the Holy Sepulchre. All the lights in the church had been extinguished, and the faithful were awaiting the coming of the new fire. In accordance with an Orthodox tradition, which the Catholic clergy continued to observe, one of the lamps in the Holy Sepulchre was lighted, apparently spontaneously, at this service on Easter Eve. How this was done is not known; it was intended to symbolize the risen Christ, but it was regarded as miraculous by the more simple-minded pilgrims.[53] It was an impressive ceremony. The party with the cross approached the Sepulchre, and the leader knelt and looked in to see whether a flame had yet appeared; if it had not, then he and his party slowly circled the shrine while tension mounted and the assembled pilgrims prayed aloud and wept. This process was repeated up to six or seven times in some years, by which time the church was growing dark. When the light appeared the cross-bearer entered the Sepulchre and lit his candle from it, and he then took his lighted candle to the patriarch who lit his own candle

---

[52]*Ibid.*, pp. 418–420.
[53]The full Easter ceremonies are described *ibid.*, pp. 420–423; Alistair J. MacGregor, *Fire and Light in the Western Church* (Alcuin Club Collection, 71 [Collegeville, 1992]), pp. 154–247.

from it, and gradually the light passed to all those present, so that the whole cathedral became a sea of light as candles passed up into the gallery of the rotunda, the Calvary chapel, and the clerestory of the new cathedral, while a deacon sang the *Exultet*, "Let the company of angels now rejoice." The patriarch then came down the choir and blessed the waters of the font, and parents brought their children, born during Holy Week, to be baptized. The patriarch baptized the first, and then another priest took over from him as he moved back to his throne and began to sing the Mass of Easter. The Gospel appointed was that of St. Matthew:

> After the sabbath, as the first day of the week was dawning, Mary Magdalene and the other Mary went to see the tomb.[54]

This was sung by a priest who faced down the choir to the very Sepulchre from which the light of the Risen Christ had just come, while behind him the congregation could see reflected in the light of thousands of candles the fresco in the apse of Christ striding into heaven carrying in his right hand Adam, the father and type of all men.[55]

A number of accounts written by twelfth-century pilgrims convey something of the impression which the crusader city of Jerusalem made on them. One of the most vivid is the memorial dictated in old age by Abbot Nicholas of Thvera in Iceland, who had made the pilgrimage in *ca.* 1140:

> Jorsalaborg is the most splendid of all the cities of the world, and is celebrated in song everywhere throughout all Christendom because wondrous signs of Christ's Passion are still to be seen there. There . . . is the church . . . [of] the Lord's Sepulchre and the place where the Lord's cross stood, where one can clearly see Christ's blood on the stone as if it were newly bled, and so it will always be until doomsday.[56]

These accounts were intended to be read by those who stayed at home. John of Würzburg, writing in the 1160's, dedicated his book about the Holy Land to his friend Dietrich and added:

> . . . I have tried to collect . . . information about the holy places and specially about the holy city of Jerusalem, and to record it as carefully and clearly as I can. I think this description will be welcomed by you . . . for if you do not happen to come here and see these places for yourself, yet

---

[54]Mt. 28:1.
[55]Theodoric, *De Locis Sanctis*, c. 7, ed. de Sandoli, *Itinera*, II, 324–326.
[56]John Wilkinson, with Joyce Hill and William F. Ryan (eds.), *Jerusalem Pilgrimage 1099–1185* (Hakluyt Society, 2nd series, Vol. 167 [London, 1988]), p. 217.

by reading my account and meditating about it you will learn to reverence their holiness much more.[57]

These descriptions of Jerusalem were written by educated men, chiefly clergy, and we do not know how other pilgrims responded, though we are sometimes given a glimpse of them at second hand. The German Theodoric, who visited Jerusalem in about 1170, relates how in the Calvary chapel he saw a great heap of wooden crosses which travelers had brought there from their own countries.[58] This laconic statement draws attention to a whole range of lay piety: the desire of pilgrims to comply literally with Christ's advice to each of his followers to "take up his cross daily and follow me."

It is important not to make too rigid a dichotomy in twelfth-century society between the learned and literate, and the simple and illiterate. Accounts of the shrines were written in Latin by clergy, but some of them were translated into the vernacular and reached a wider and different reading public, while then, as now, learned guides, who had read the literature, shared that knowledge with pilgrims who had not. Non-literate pilgrims likewise shared their experiences of the Holy Land with their acquaintance in the West. The nobility presented relics which they had obtained there to their local churches,[59] while poor pilgrims shared their experiences in more modest ways by bringing home phials of holy oil and holy water, bearing representations of the Lord's Sepulchre.[60] And, of course, the western priories of the great shrine churches of Jerusalem and of the Military Orders which had their headquarters there, sometimes built replicas of the holy places, which acted as focuses of devotion to people who could not travel to the holy city, like the Holy Sepulchre at Barletta in Apulia, or the Temple Church in London, consecrated by the patriarch of Jerusalem in 1185.[61]

The opportunity to visit a western, Catholic Jerusalem ended in 1187 when the city was lost to the Christians once more. Saladin's first act was to remove the great gold cross from the Dome of the Rock and to

[57]John of Würzburg, *Epistola*, ed. de Sandoli, *Itinera*, II, 228.

[58]Theodoric, *De Locis Sanctis*, c. 12, ed. de Sandoli, II, 332.

[59]E.g., Maurice lord of Craon brought back from the Holy Land in 1169 a variety of relics for local churches, including fragments of the Cross, a chip of the rock of Calvary, a splinter of the stone of the Holy Sepulchre, part of the column of the flagellation of Christ, filings from the hammer and a nail of the Passion, a piece of our Lady's dress, and relics of the three Patriarchs of Hebron and of St. Catherine of Alexandria; Bertrand de Brousillon, *La Maison de Craon, 1050–1480. Étude historique accompagnée du cartulaire de Craon* (2 vols.; Paris, 1893), I, 100–105, nos. 137–146.

[60]André Grabar, *Ampoules de Terre-Sainte* (Monza-Bobbio, Paris, 1958).

[61]Damiano Neri, *Il S. Sepolcro riprodotto in Occidente* (Jerusalem, 1971).

712THE IMPACT OF CRUSADER JERUSALEM ON WESTERN CHRISTENDOM

reconsecrate the Temple Mount to the worship of Islam.[62] Jerusalem became once again a Muslim city, where Christians might indeed still go as pilgrims, but where they might only worship inside their churches.

But eighty-eight years of pilgrimage had had a lasting effect on the religious awareness of the Christian West. It is possible to document its impact on the world of scholarship. Beryl Smalley has drawn attention to the lectures which Peter Comestor, chancellor of Notre Dame, gave on the Gospels in the theology schools of Paris in the 1160's and '70's. Unlike his immediate predecessors, Peter was primarily interested in the literal meaning of the Gospels, rather than in their moral or mystical sense, and Beryl Smalley was struck by the knowledge he had of the topography and antiquities of the Holy Land, which is not found in eleventh-century writers.[63] This is evidence of the impact which pilgrimage to the Christian Kingdom of Jerusalem was making. In this instance the impact proved long-lasting, for Peter's lectures formed the basis for the section on the life of Christ in his major work, the *Historia Scholastica*. This is an account of the history of the world from the creation to the death of SS. Peter and Paul; in other words it is an historical companion to the Old and New Testaments, and it became a set text in the theology schools of Paris during the later Middle Ages.[64] In that way the kinds of knowledge about the background to the Gospels made available as a result of the Frankish occupation of the Holy Land became part of the intellectual heritage of learned western churchmen.

But I should like to suggest that pilgrimage to Jerusalem in the twelfth century affected a far larger section of the population of the West than the theology faculty of Paris. A new kind of piety is certainly evident in thirteenth-century Western Europe which for convenience' sake one might label Franciscan. Its hallmark was a devotional interest in the lives of Christ and the Apostles as described in the Gospels, and an attempt

[62]Baha ad-Din, *Life of Saladin*, tr. C. R. Conder (Palestine Pilgrims Texts Society [London, 1897]), p. 120.
[63]Beryl Smalley, "Some Gospel Commentaries of the Early Twelfth Century," *Recherches de Théologie ancienne et médiévale [RTAM]*, 45 (1978), 147–180. Peter Comestor's lectures on the Gospels are still in manuscript; in her study of them Beryl Smalley was struck by his knowledge of the topography of the Holy Land, which was not available in older works, and suggests as sources for some of this information "guidebooks for pilgrims, and visitors to the Holy Land on their return." Smalley, "Peter Comestor on the Gospels and his Sources," *RTAM*, 46 (1979), 84–129 (quotation p. 122).
[64]Peter Comestor, *Historia Scholastica, PL*, Vol. 198, cols. 1053–1722; Smalley, "The Gospels in the Paris Schools in the Late Twelfth and Early Thirteenth Century," *Franciscan Studies*, 39 (1979), 230–254.

by the believer to identify with them and to share in their feelings.[65] Typical of this kind of spirituality is the story told of how in 1223 St. Francis arranged for the midnight Mass of Christmas to be celebrated at Greccio in a stable, in the presence of farm animals, in order to re-enact the circumstances of Christ's birth as described by St. Luke and to make the congregation aware of how the Lord had shared their every-day life.[66] Equally typical is the Franciscan cult of Mary as the Sorrow-ing Mother, with whom the Christian was urged to identify as she stood at the foot of the cross contemplating the sufferings of Christ.[67]

This affective piety, which stresses Christ's human weaknesses rather than his superhuman strengths, is very different from the eleventh-century quest for the perfection of the Apostolic Life. I would suggest that this change in Western religious sensibility occurred at least in part because throughout most of the twelfth century Jerusalem had been a western, Catholic city and it had been possible for the pilgrims who visited it to appreciate the Gospel narratives on a literal level because the whole ethos gave them every encouragement to do so.

The new piety was influential and enduring. It passed from the Franciscans to the Brethren of the Common Life, whose teaching, the *Devotio Moderna*, was influential in shaping the thought both of Luther and of Ignatius Loyola, and which came to form part of the devotional traditions of Catholics and Protestants alike.[68] If I am right, this shift in Western religious sensibility has proved to be one of the most enduring achievements of the crusading movement.

[65]The literature on this subject is huge. For a recent survey with bibliographical guidance see Simon Tugwell, "The Spirituality of the Dominicans"; J. A. Wayne Hellmann, "The Spirituality of the Franciscans"; Keith J. Egan, "The Spirituality of the Carmelites"; Adolar Zumkeller, "The Spirituality of the Augustinians"; Richard Kieckhefer, "Major Currents in Late Medieval Devotion," in Jill Raitt (ed.), *Christian Spirituality*, Vol. II: *High Middle Ages and Reformation* (New York, 1988), pp. 15–108.

[66]Thomas of Celano, *The First Life of St. Francis*, Bk. I, c. XXX, trans. Placid Hermann, in Marion A. Habig (ed.), *St. Francis of Assisi. Writings and Early Biographies. English Omnibus of the Sources for the Life of St. Francis*, 3rd ed. (London, 1979), pp. 299–302.

[67]This found its classic expression in the *Stabat Mater*. Frederic J. E. Raby, *A History of Christian Latin Poetry from the Beginnings to the Close of the Middle Ages*, 2nd ed. (Oxford, 1953), pp. 415–443. John Moorman, *A History of the Franciscan Order from its Origins to the year 1517* (Oxford, 1968), pp. 266–272.

[68]Regnerus R. Post, *The Modern Devotion* (Leiden, 1968).

XVI

Ideals of Holiness:
Crusaders, Contemplatives, and Mendicants

EW IDEALS APPEAR more incompatible than that of the crusader vowed to religious violence and that of the monk vowed to contemplative prayer. Some people at the time of the First Crusade, such as St Anselm, certainly took this view.[1] But such an attitude was not common, because monks took a leading part in launching the crusade movement and in perpetuating it. Urban II, who preached the First Crusade, was a former prior of Cluny, while the Second Crusade would never have been viable without the enthusiastic preaching of St Bernard of Clairvaux. During the first hundred years of the movement, crusading and the contemplative life were very closely linked. This was inevitable, because the religious ideal to which Western Christians aspired at that time was a monastic one: the highest form of the Christian life was considered to be that of the monk who renounced the world in order to devote himself to a life of prayer, and the highest form of the monastic life was thought to be that of the hermit, who was seen as part of the spiritual élite, defending the ramparts of the city of God against the forces of supernatural evil.[2] This vocabulary, Pauline in origin, is also evidence of the common purpose that inspired crusaders and monks, both of whom fought against the enemies of the faith. The ideal of Christian holiness to which the late eleventh-century Western church aspired was exemplified in St Peter Damian, cardinal bishop of Ostia, who had set aside his dignity, second only to that of the pope in the Catholic hierarchy, and retired to live as a hermit at Fonte Avellana.[3]

The crusade movement marked the first major shift in medieval Western religious thinking away from an ideal of world renunciation to one of world affirmation for lay people. However mistaken the crusading ideal may appear to modern religious sensibilities, the First

---

1 St Anselm, *Epistolae*, ii. 19, *P[atrologiae cursus completus, series] L[atina]*, ed. J.-P. Migne (Paris, 1844–64), clviii. 1,167–70.
2 St Peter Damian, *Liber qui appellatur 'Dominus vobiscum'*, 19, *PL*, cxlv. 248.
3 J. Leclercq, *S Pierre Damien, ermite et homme de l'Église* (Rome, 1960).

Crusade was designed to offer the fighting men of western Europe an opportunity to use their aggressive instincts in the service of God and his church, so that they could live the Christian life not by renouncing the world and becoming monks, but by dedicating their everyday skills to a religious purpose. Yet, when contemporaries analysed the crusade, they still thought in traditional ways: Jonathan Riley-Smith argues that the armies of the First Crusade were regarded as a kind of monastery on the march for the duration of the campaign.[1] In other words, all attempts to live the Christian life fully, even if they were made by laymen, were conceptualized at that time in monastic terms.

The crusade had been launched, at least in part, to free the holy places and, contrary to all rational expectation, it succeeded. On 15 July 1099, Jerusalem came into Christian hands for the first time in 461 years; during the next decade, a great arc of territory stretching from the middle Euphrates to the Sinai desert was brought under Western control. The crusader kingdom had been born, with its capital in Jerusalem, flanked by the three partially autonomous, northern states of Tripoli, Antioch, and Edessa. Having conquered the holy places, it was now the warriors' task to defend them. They were not qualified, however, to perform the religious cult in them: that required professionally trained clergy.

Those clergy need not have been Western; there were many native Christians in the crusader kingdom, representing to the newcomers a bewildering variety of confessions, but among them there was a substantial number of Orthodox Christians. Urban II had sought to restore full communion with the Orthodox churches and had intended that the crusade should further that aim. He seems to have envisaged a settlement in which the Orthodox church would be established and would administer the holy places, while the crusaders formed a military governing class with their own Catholic chaplains. But this solution was not acceptable to the crusaders, and Urban II's death in 1099 deprived the scheme of its chief proponent.[2] The crusaders, with the ready assent of Urban II's successors, established a Catholic hierarchy throughout the lands which they ruled, and although they tolerated the diversity of confession among the native Christians, and allowed the Orthodox at least to place altars in some of the principal churches, they confided all the great pilgrim shrines to the Catholic clergy.[3]

---

[1] J. Riley-Smith, *The First Crusade and the Idea of Crusading* (London, 1986), 147-52.
[2] B. Hamilton, *The Latin Church in the Crusader States* (London, 1980), 1-17.
[3] Ibid., 18-85, 159-211.

The focus of the First Crusade was the chief shrine of the Christian world – the Church of the Holy Sepulchre. This site incorporated what were believed to be the rock of Calvary and the tomb of Christ. The old basilica had been demolished by the fanatically anti-Christian Caliph Hakim in 1009; the church that the crusaders took over had been built in 1048 under the patronage of the Byzantine Emperor Constantine IX. This rotunda, built around the Holy Sepulchre, was linked to an enclosed courtyard containing the Calvary chapel.[1]

The Holy Sepulchre and the basilica of Bethlehem were the only important shrines that the Franks found in working order. Most of the other churches were in ruins: this was true of most of the churches outside the walls of Jerusalem and of the Orthodox cathedral of Nazareth.[2] The Franks, therefore, embarked on an extensive building programme: by 1109, a new cathedral had been built at Nazareth,[3] and the shrine churches outside the walls of Jerusalem were restored at about the same time. The Church of Mount Zion, venerated as the site of the upper room where Christ had celebrated the Last Supper and the Holy Spirit had descended at Pentecost, was also completely rebuilt,[4] as was the Church of the Ascension on the Mount of Olives.[5] The crusaders turned Jerusalem into an exclusively Christian city, and its chief Muslim shrine, the Dome of the Rock, was converted into a Christian church known as the Temple of the Lord, because it was thought to stand on the site of the Presentation of Christ. The living

---

1 There is a huge literature on the Holy Sepulchre, but a good, brief guide to the phases of development to the twelfth century is provided by C. Couäsnon, *The Church of the Holy Sepulchre Jerusalem*, The Schweich Lectures, 1972 (London, 1974).
2 The English pilgrim Saewulf, who visited the Holy Land in 1101-3 and was the first pilgrim to leave an account of his journey after the crusader conquest, wrote of Bethlehem: 'Nothing habitable is left there by the Saracens [except for the church of the Holy Nativity], but it is all ruined, exactly as it is in all the other places outside the walls of Jerusalem'; and of Nazareth: 'But the city of Nazareth is wholly ruined and all pulled down by the Saracens': *Jerusalem Pilgrimage, 1099-1185*, trans. J. Wilkinson, J. Hill, and W. F. Ryan, The Hakluyt Society, 2nd series, clxvii (London, 1988), 108, 111.
3 The Russian Abbot Daniel who visited Nazareth in Baldwin I's reign reports: '[The shrine of] the Holy Annunciation ... was once laid waste but now the Franks have taken it and rebuilt it thoroughly': ibid., 164. The first Latin bishop of Nazareth is recorded in 1109: Kohler, 'Chartes de l'abbaye de Notre-Dame de la vallée de Josaphat en Terre Sainte (1108-1291): Analyses et extraits', *Revue de l'Orient Latin*, vii (1899), 113-14, no. 2.
4 A Latin prior of Mount Zion had been appointed by 1112 when he took part in the election of the Patriarch Arnulf: *Le Cartulaire du Chapître du Saint-Sépulcre de Jérusalem*, ed. G. Bresc-Bautier, *Documents relatifs à l'histoire des croisades publiés par l'Académie des Inscriptions et Belles-Lettres*, xv (Paris, 1984), 207, no. 91. On the architecture of the crusader church of Mount Zion, see C. Enlart, *Les monuments des croisés dans le royaume de Jérusalem: architecture religieuse et civile* (Paris, 1925-8), ii. 248.
5 A shrine had been built by the time of Saewulf's visit in 1101-3: 'The place [of the Ascension] is defended by a wall ... and there is an altar inside over the place itself': *Jerusalem Pilgrimage*, 107.

rock in the centre of the mosque was covered with a marble pavement and surrounded by an ironwork screen to form the sanctuary in the Christian shrine. The conversion of the mosque into a church was completed in 1114.[1]

All these new Jerusalem shrine churches were entrusted to Austin canons.[2] It was no doubt the presence of these communities in the Holy City which led the Patriarch Gibelin, when he was dying in 1112, to exhort Baldwin I to introduce canons regular into the Holy Sepulchre as well: thus, the chapter of secular canons set up there in 1099 were, in 1114, offered the choice of living under a rule or surrendering their benefices. Thereafter, the Sepulchre became a house of Austin canons,[3] who began to rebuild the church because the Byzantine rotunda was not large enough to hold the great crowds of pilgrims flocking there each year, now that the city was in Christian hands. The rotunda and the Calvary chapel were incorporated in a new romanesque cathedral, not completed until 1149 and, substantially, the church which is there today.[4] Austin canons also formed the chapters of the new Catholic cathedral of Nazareth and of the basilica of Bethlehem,[5] which, in 1108, was raised to a cathedral at the request of Baldwin I.[6] A community of Austin canons was also founded in his reign to serve the important shrine of Hebron, the alleged burial place of the patriarchs Abraham, Isaac, and Jacob.[7]

Like the crusade movement, the Austin canons owed much to the patronage of Urban II and, as J. C. Dickinson points out, their religious aims were inspired by the eremitical movement of the eleventh century;[8] St Peter Damian, the paradigm of sanctity at the time of the First Crusade, had been one of their chief supporters.[9] They were no doubt chosen to administer the holy places because

---

[1] William of Tyre, *Chronicon*, ed. R. B. C. Huygens, viii. 3, *Corpus Christianorum, continuatio mediaevalis*, lxiii, lxiiiA (Turnhout, 1986), i. 387.

[2] The priors of Mount Zion, the Mount of Olives, and the Temple of the Lord are all first recorded in 1112: *Cartulaire générale de l'Ordre des Hospitaliers de St Jean de Jérusalem (1100-1310)*, ed. J. Delaville Le Roulx (Paris, 1894-1906), i. 26-8, nos. 25, 28.

[3] *Le Cartulaire du Chapître du Saint-Sépulcre*, 74-7, no. 20; 85-6, no. 25.

[4] Couäsnon, *Holy Sepulchre*, 57-62.

[5] Hamilton, *Latin Church*, 116.

[6] H.-E. Mayer, 'Die Gründung der Bistümer Askalon und Bethlehem', in *Bistümer, Klöster und Stifte im Königreich Jerusalem*, Schriften der Monumenta Germaniae Historica, xxvi (Stuttgart, 1977), 44-80.

[7] D. Pringle, *The Churches of the Crusader Kingdom of Jerusalem: A Corpus* (Cambridge, 1992), i. 224-39.

[8] J. C. Dickinson, *The Origins of the Austin Canons and Their Introduction into England* (London, 1950), 38.

[9] St Peter Damian, *De communi vita canonicorum*, PL, cxlv. 503-12.

they lived in community and were thus able to sing the whole of the Divine Office in the shrines – this was the pattern in those great basilicas of Rome that were served by monastic communities at the time of the First Crusade.[1] Secular canons tended to be more lax about their liturgical duties and were under no obligation to recite the night office publicly.

The Benedictine presence in Jerusalem antedated the Latin conquest. There had been a Western monastic community there in the ninth century, but that had died out; a new start was made around 1070, when a group of merchants from Amalfi founded a monastery known as St Mary of the Latins to care for Western pilgrims. Sometime before 1099, an adjacent convent of nuns, dedicated to St Mary Magdalene, was set up to care for women pilgrims, together with a hospital under the jurisdiction of the abbot of St Mary's to look after the sick and destitute.[2] After 1099, these three institutions developed separately: the hospital became independent in 1113 and from it grew the Military Order of St John of Jerusalem,[3] while the convent became autonomous and was known as Great St Mary's.[4] The monastery of St Mary of the Latins was unusual among the Catholic foundations in crusader Jerusalem in that it was not a shrine church and was therefore of no great interest to pilgrims; but it enjoyed status as the oldest Catholic community in the city. Pope Paschal II placed it immediately under the protection of the Holy See and directed that the brethren should observe the Benedictine Rule according to the use of Monte Cassino and sing the psalms to the same chant as that used in the Roman Church.[5] In other words, it was to represent Roman liturgical norms in a kingdom whose ruling class came chiefly from northern Europe.

A group of Benedictine monks was said to have accompanied Duke Godfrey from Lorraine on the First Crusade and to have taken charge of the Church of Our Lady in the valley of Jehosaphat[6] – the chief Marian shrine in Jerusalem, believed to be the site of her burial and

1 G. Ferrari, *Early Roman Monasteries*, Pontificio Istituto di Archeologia Cristiana, Studi di Antichità Cristiana, xxiii (Vatican City, 1957), 365-75.
2 William of Tyre, *Chronicon*, xviii. 5, *Corpus Christianorum, continuatio mediaevalis*, lxiiiA. 815-17.
3 The bull *Pie postulatio voluntatis*, in *Cartulaire générale*, i. 29-30, no. 30; J. Riley-Smith, *The Knights of St John in Jerusalem and Cyprus, 1050-1310* (London, 1967), 32-59.
4 B. Hamilton, 'Rebuilding Zion: The Holy Places of Jerusalem in the Twelfth Century', in *Studies in Church History*, xiv (Oxford, 1977), 112-13.
5 W. Holtzmann, 'Papst- Kaiser- und Normannenurkunden aus Unteritalien', *Quellen und Forschungen aus italienischen Archiven und Bibliotheken*, xxxv (1955), 50-3, no. 1.
6 William of Tyre, *Chronicon*, ix. 9, *Corpus Christianorum, continuatio mediaevalis*, lxiii. 431. Certainly a monastery had been founded there by 1101-3: *Jerusalem Pilgrimage*, 106.

assumption into heaven. A third Benedictine monastery was founded on Mount Tabor in 1100 by Tancred, prince of Galilee. This was the site of the Transfiguration of Christ, and although Tabor enjoyed a less popular cult in the Western church than Nazareth, the monastery was, in the early years of the Latin Kingdom, the focus for pilgrims to Galilee, because the church of Nazareth was still in ruins. In 1103, Paschal II made Abbot Gerald of Tabor the Catholic archbishop of Galilee, and although he lost those powers in the ecclesiastical reorganization in 1109 when the diocese of Nazareth was set up,[1] Tabor remained an important Catholic pilgrimage centre in the crusader kingdom.[2]

Communities of women were also founded in the kingdom, all of which followed the Benedictine Rule. The convent of St Mary Magdalene at Jerusalem, which had existed before the First Crusade, flourished under Latin rule: its buildings had to be extended and, by the second half of the twelfth century, the abbess, Stephanie of Courtenay, was a member of the royal family and the house had become known as Great St Mary's. The convent of St Anne to the north of the Temple Mount served the shrine of Mary's birthplace, the alleged site of the house of St Joachim and St Anne. It was probably a community of Eastern-rite nuns in 1099 but, by the 1130s, had become a Catholic foundation and Baldwin II's youngest daughter, Yveta, made her profession there.[3] As his eldest daughter, Melisende, who became queen of Jerusalem in her own right, did not think it proper (so William of Tyre relates) that her younger sister should be a mere nun, Melisende founded the convent of Bethany in 1138 so that her sister could become abbess there when she had completed her religious training. The shrine of Bethany incorporated the home of Christ's friends Mary and Martha, and the tomb of their brother Lazarus whom he had raised from the dead. When the nuns went there, the shrine chapels, previously administered by the canons of the Holy Sepulchre, were completely rebuilt and the whole complex of convent buildings ringed by fortifications, one massive ruined tower of which may still be seen.[4] (Bethany was in the open countryside on the very edge of the Judaean desert, and the danger of raids by Muslim marauders and armed bandits was very real.)

---

[1] Hamilton, *Latin Church*, 60.

[2] Theoderic [Account of the Holy Places], *Jerusalem Pilgrimage*, 312.

[3] Hamilton, 'Rebuilding Zion', 111.

[4] William of Tyre, *Chronicon*, xv. 26, *Corpus Christianorum, continuatio mediaevalis*, lxiiiA. 709-10; S. J. Saller, *Excavations at Bethany (1949-53)*, Publications of the Studium Biblicum Franciscanum, xii (Jerusalem, 1957).

It is unlikely that these convents depended solely on the vocations of the native Franks. The professed sisters were of noble birth, yet the number of noble families in the entire Frankish East at that time was not large and, because women enjoyed considerable social freedom there, the religious life was less attractive than it was in the West. No doubt some of the nuns were women pilgrims who had decided to stay in the Holy Land, such as Sibyl, the wife of Count Thierry of Flanders and aunt of Henry II of England, who refused to return to the West with her husband when their pilgrimage ended in 1158 but, much against his will, was professed in the convent of Bethany.[1]

In the Holy Land, there were far more sacred sites than there were communities to serve them. The older houses accepted the care of nearby shrines: thus, the monks of Josaphat administered the adjacent Garden of Gethsemane and built chapels there to commemorate the Agony in the Garden and the Sleep of the Apostles.[2] Sometimes, communities took over quite distant shrines: the canons of the Holy Sepulchre maintained a priory at Quarantena, the site of Christ's temptation in the wilderness, in the hills above Jericho.[3] But many holy places remained unattended and the kings of Jerusalem were eager to attract new monastic communities to undertake their care.

Baldwin II (1118-31), in an attempt to bring Cistercians to the Holy Land, offered the hill of Mountjoy to St Bernard of Clairvaux. Although Bernard declined the gift for his own order, he persuaded Baldwin II to give it instead to the newly founded Premonstratensian canons, who were very like the Austin canons but with a special vocation to preaching and parish work.[4] Mountjoy, the hill from which pilgrims obtained their first sight of Jerusalem, and which was believed to be the burial place of the prophet Samuel, had a house of canons before 1131.[5] In that year, Innocent II appointed another Premonstratensian named Amalric as official preacher both to pagans and Christians in the Holy Land; he took up this work in 1136 and was given as a base a shrine church near Lydda, believed to be the

---

1 Robert of Torigni, 'Chronicle', ed. R. Howlett, *Chronicles of the Reigns of Stephen, Henry II, and Richard I*, Rolls Series, lxxxii, pt. 4 (London, 1889), 205.
2 Hamilton, 'Rebuilding Zion', 108-9.
3 'Ecclesiam Quarantene cum pertinentiis suis', listed in Celestine II's confirmation of the Holy Sepulchre's possessions: *Cartulaire du Chapître du Saint-Sépulcre*, 56, no. 12.
4 *Epistola ad Abbatem Praemonstratensem, S. Bernardi Opera: Epistolae*, ed. J. Leclercq and H. Rochais (Rome, 1977), viii. 149-50, no. 253.
5 H.-E. Mayer, 'Sankt Samuel auf dem Freudenberge und sein besitz nach einem unbekannt Diplom König Balduins V', *Quellen und Forschungen aus italienischen Archiven und Bibliotheken*, xliv (1964), 35-71.

burial place of the prophet Habakkuk and of St Joseph of Arimathea.[1]
The two communities of canons living under the rule of Premontré
recruited quite well but, as far as is known, they did not evangelize the
Muslim rural population as Innocent II had hoped they would.[2]

Although St Bernard could not be induced to make a foundation in
the crusader states, shortly after his death the first Cistercians settled at
Belmont in the Lebanon in 1157. This was a daughter-house of
Morimond, and the land on which it stood was given by the counts of
Tripoli. Four years later, another daughter-house of Morimond was
founded, the abbey of Salvatio near Jerusalem.[3] Neither of these communities served shrines, for it was the Cistercian ideal to live in the
eremum, remote from human habitation. But in 1169, Belmont
founded a daughter-house at St John *in nemore*, or St John in the
Woods, within walking distance of Jerusalem, supposedly on the site
of the cave where John the Baptist had grown up in seclusion – that
association may have made the custody of this shrine acceptable to the
order.[4]

The Holy Land under Latin rule also attracted hermits, the highest
ideal of the Christian life to which Catholic piety in the twelfth
century aspired. Thanks to the discovery by B. Z. Kedar in the
Centuriators of Magdeburg of extracts from the lost works of Gerard of
Nazareth, we can flesh out the meagre evidence we previously had
about the twelfth-century hermits in the crusader states.[5] Some were
what St Bruno of Querfurt had called 'rational hermits, those who live
in accordance with a rule',[6] such as those who clustered round the
monastery of Jubin near Antioch.[7] But others were true solitaries, and
they were sufficiently numerous for the Catholic patriarch of Antioch,
Aimery of Limoges, to find it necessary to legislate that no anchorite
should live on the Black Mountain unless he had a spiritual director.[8]
Many of these hermits practised extreme forms of asceticism, wearing
sackcloth, going barefoot, fasting rigorously, and undertaking various

[1] N. Backmund, *Monasticon Praemonstratense* (2nd ed., Berlin, 1983), i, pt. 2. 498, 507.
[2] Hamilton, *Latin Church*, 101-2.
[3] L. Janauschek, *Origines Cisterciensium* (Vienna, 1877), i. 139, no. ccciv; 144, no. ccclxv; B.
Hamilton, 'The Cistercians in the Crusader States', in *One Yet Two: Monastic Tradition East and
West*, ed. M. B. Pennington (Kalamazoo, 1976), 405-7.
[4] Janauschek, *Origines Cisterciensium*, i. 158, no. ccccv; Theoderic, *Jerusalem Pilgrimage*, 308.
[5] B. Z. Kedar, 'Gerard of Nazareth, a Neglected Twelfth-Century Writer in the Latin East',
Dumbarton Oaks Papers, xxxvii (1983), 55-77.
[6] *Brunonis Vita Quinque Fratrum*, ed. R. Kade, 2, M[onumenta] G[ermaniae] H[istorica] S[criptores],
xv. 718.
[7] Kedar, 'Gerard of Nazareth', 66.
[8] Ibid., 74, citing Gerard of Nazareth's *De conversatione virorum Dei*, 33.

forms of corporal mortification, notably self-flagellation. In the kingdom of Jerusalem, they were found in three main areas: in the valley of Jehosaphat outside the walls of Jerusalem; on the slopes of Mount Tabor in Galilee;[1] and, towards the end of the First Kingdom, on the slopes of Mount Carmel near Haifa.[2] The hermits of Jerusalem seem to have been loosely supervised by the abbot of Our Lady of Josaphat,[3] and those in Galilee may have been under the general direction of the abbot of the Mount Tabor monastery. But there were also some true recluses, such as Cosmas the Hungarian who, in King Fulk's reign (1131-43), lived with his companion Boniface 'enclosed in a narrow cell on the walls of Jerusalem [and] was always intent on murmuring prayers'.[4] Of course, the eremitical life was an important part of the Eastern Christian tradition as well, and hermits were no novelty in the Holy Land, but Catholic hermits could only live freely there when it was under crusader rule.

The Frankish settlers in the East could not have borne the cost of building so many new churches and monasteries and endowing communities to serve them without outside help. For their states were not rich: good agricultural land was at a premium, while the costs of defence were high. But the entire Catholic world recognized its obligation to support the great shrines of the Holy Land. I cite as an example, which could be multiplied many times, the opening words of a deed of gift made to the Holy Sepulchre in 1137 by Count Rodrigo of Traba:

> Our fathers have told us, as they have learned from the Gospels, that the holy church of the Resurrection of the Lord should be held in greater esteem than all others because Our Lord Jesus Christ consecrated it, not through the witness of the prophets, nor through the blood of the martyrs, but he dedicated it to himself through his own presence and by the shedding of his own blood and by the glory of his Resurrection.[5]

Although none of the other shrines could compete in dignity with the Holy Sepulchre, they all in some measure attracted benefactions from the Christian West. These most often took the form of grants of land, but the shrine churches of the East also received gifts of

---

1 B. Z. Kedar, 'Palmarée, abbaye clunisienne du xiie siècle en Galilée', *Revue Bénédictine*, xciii (1983), 261-2.

2 James of Vitry, *Historia Orientalis*, 52 (Douai, 1597, republished Farnborough, 1971), fo. 86.

3 Kedar, 'Gerard of Nazareth', 75.

4 Ibid., 72. 'Chosmas, Ungaricus heremita; Bonefatius, socius ejus', witnessed a charter in 1135: *Cartulaire du Chapître du Saint-Sépulcre*, 220, no. 101.

5 Ibid., 170-1, no. 72.

churches, and of rents, as well as some commercial privileges, from all parts of western Europe. The communities of the Latin East normally established priories in the West to administer their endowments and collect their revenues, and on paper some of the eastern foundations were very rich.[1] Nevertheless, a substantial part of the cost of maintaining the holy places continued to be borne by the Franks living in the East, and it says much for their religious commitment that, despite the paucity of their lands and the high costs of defence, they were generous benefactors of the Catholic church.

The crusade movement had had a particular appeal for the devout members of the warrior class and, within a generation of the establishment of the crusader states, that range of piety found institutional expression in the foundation of three military orders: the Knights Templar, the Knights of St John, and the Knights of St Lazarus.[2] Yet, although the religious ideal which the military orders represented was attractive to the society of the twelfth-century West and to that of the crusader states, their work was regarded as ancillary to the custody of the holy places: the Templars saw it as an important part of their vocation to police the pilgrim roads of the kingdom,[3] while the Knights of St John and St Lazarus spent a considerable part of their income in running hospitals for the care of sick and poor pilgrims and of lepers respectively.[4] All three orders dedicated their military resources to the defence of the Holy Land. But at the heart of the kingdom were the holy places, served by regular clergy, canons, monks, and nuns, who sang the eightfold office day and night, without a day's intermission, throughout the eighty-eight years of Frankish rule.

The monastic witness to belief in a divinely ordered cosmos

---

[1] See, e.g., G. Bresc-Bautier, 'Les possessions des Églises de Terre-Sainte en Italie du Sud', in *Roberto il Guiscardo e il suo tempo* (Rome, 1975), 13-34.

[2] For a brief and up-to-date survey of the work of all three orders, see A. Forey, *The Military Orders from the Twelfth Century to the Early Fourteenth Century* (London, 1992). For detailed work on the Knights of St John, see J. Riley-Smith, *Knights of St John*; for the Knights Templar, M. C. Barber, *The New Knighthood: A History of the Order of the Temple* (Cambridge, 1994); for the Knights of St Lazarus, M. C. Barber, 'The Order of Saint Lazarus and the Crusades', *Catholic Historical Review*, lxxx (1994), 439-56, repr. Barber, *Crusaders and Heretics, 12th-14th Centuries* (Aldershot, 1995).

[3] That was their initial function: William of Tyre, *Chronicon*, xii. 7, *Corpus Christianorum, continuatio mediaevalis*, lxiii. 553-5.

[4] John of Würzburg (c. 1170) gives a vivid account of the work of the Hospital of St John in Jerusalem, in *Jerusalem Pilgrimage*, 266-7. On the medical work of the order, see T. S. Miller, 'The Knights of St John and the Hospitals of the Latin West', *Speculum*, liii (1978), 709-33; S. Shahar, 'Les lépreux pas comme les autres: L'Ordre de Saint-Lazare dans le royaume latin de Jérusalem', *Revue Historique*, cclxvii (1982), 19-41.

expressed in the symbolism of the Divine Office is impressive. Every year, thousands of pilgrims came to the Holy Land from the West and were able to follow the liturgy in the very places to which it referred: to walk to Bethlehem on Christmas Eve like the shepherds and, like them, to kneel at the site of the manger during the Midnight Mass; to follow in the Lord's own footsteps through Jerusalem during Holy Week, from his triumphal entry down the Mount of Olives on Palm Sunday to his Resurrection in the Holy Sepulchre on Easter Day.[1] But the liturgy performed at the holy places was not primarily intended to edify the pilgrims, who were only present in any numbers for a few weeks in the year, but was a perpetual act of worship offered to God in those places specially hallowed by the presence of his incarnate Son on behalf of the entire Frankish community, and, indeed, of the whole Catholic world.

* * *

When the Franks were defeated at Hattin in 1187, they lost most of their lands to Saladin. As a result of Western intervention in the Third Crusade, and especially through the determination of Richard I of England, peace was agreed with the Sultan in 1192 whereby the Franks retained a long, thin strip of coastline stretching, with some gaps, from Jaffa in the south to Antioch in the north. However, the majority of the holy places remained in Muslim hands. At the request of the bishop of Salisbury, Hubert Walter, Saladin allowed Catholic priests to be attached to the Holy Sepulchre and the cathedrals of Nazareth and Bethlehem in order to say mass in the Latin rite for the benefit of Western pilgrims,[2] but the presence of Catholic religious communities in the shrine churches came to an end and they reverted once more to the control of Eastern-rite Christians.

Those religious communities of the kingdom of Jerusalem that had enough endowments either in western Europe or in the newly constituted kingdom of Acre survived in the troubled years after 1187, while those that lacked them did not. The Austin canons of Hebron are not found after 1187, nor are the new Cistercian communities at Salvatio and St John *in nemore.* But all the other foundations mentioned here continued to exist, in exile, in the new crusader capital of Acre, which must have suffered from extreme ecclesiastical overcrowding. Apart from having its own cathedral and parish

---

1 Kohler, 'Un Rituel et un Bréviaire du Saint-Sépulcre de Jérusalem (xiie-xiiie siècle)', *Revue de l'Orient Latin,* viii (1900-1), 383-500.

2 *Itinerarium Peregrinorum et Gesta Regis Ricardi,* ed. W. Stubbs, vi. 34, Rolls Series, xxxviii, pt. 1 (London, 1864), 438.

churches, and chapels for various groups of Western merchants, it was also the headquarters of the three military orders. The patriarch of Jerusalem and the canons of the Holy Sepulchre also made their home there, as did the canons of Mount Zion, the Mount of Olives, and the Temple of the Lord; the Premonstratensians of St Samuel's; the Benedictine monks of Our Lady of Josaphat, St Mary of the Latins, and Mount Tabor; the Benedictine nuns of Great St Mary's, St Anne's, and Bethany; while the bishop of Bethlehem and the archbishop of Nazareth, accompanied by their chapters of Austin canons, fixed their pro-cathedrals there.[1]

These arrangements were only intended to be temporary. It was hoped that the kingdom of Jerusalem would soon be restored to Christian rule and that the regular clergy would be able to return to their shrine churches. That this took longer to achieve than had been hoped was not through any lack of crusading zeal, for new crusades to liberate Jerusalem were launched at the rate of one a decade. Yet they did not meet with success. The Imperial crusade of 1197 was abandoned because of the premature death of Henry VI; the Fourth Crusade of 1203–4 was diverted to Constantinople; and the Fifth Crusade of 1219–21, having rejected Sultan al-Kamil of Egypt's offer to restore the Holy Land, was outmanoeuvred and forced to surrender. But when Emperor Frederick II came on crusade in 1228 and was offered similar terms by al-Kamil, he accepted them. Frederick II's position was unusual: he was not only the leader of a crusade, but was also the king of Jerusalem and, at the time of his crusade, excommunicate.

Under the terms of the treaty of Jaffa, al-Kamil made a ten-year truce with Frederick II and restored to him Jerusalem, Bethlehem, Nazareth, and some other parts of the former crusader kingdom, together with narrow corridors connecting them to the Frankish lands on the coast. Nobody was pleased by this settlement: the Islamic establishment was scandalized that Saladin's nephew should have returned their third holy city to the Christians without a fight, while Catholic opinion was outraged that the Temple Mount in Jerusalem should have been left in Muslim hands, and that the Muslim population of the city should have been guaranteed freedom of worship by the excommunicate emperor. The Knights Templar were particularly annoyed because their headquarters in the former mosque of al-Aksar remained in Muslim control.[2] On 17 March 1229,

---

1 Hamilton, *Latin Church*, 299–300.
2 For Frederick's Crusade, see T. C. van Cleve, 'The Crusade of Frederick II', in *A History of the*

Frederick II entered Jerusalem and performed a solemn crown-wearing in the Church of the Holy Sepulchre; the following day, the Catholic patriarch placed the city under an interdict.[1]

Despite this unpropitious beginning, Jerusalem remained in Christian control for fifteen years. In 1230, Frederick II made his peace with the pope and was reconciled to the church, so there was no longer any need for the Catholic authorities in the Holy Land to remain hostile to the terms of the peace of Jaffa.[2] Yet the religious communities living in exile in Acre showed little enthusiasm to return to the liberated holy places. There were many practical reasons for this: first, there was civil war in the kingdom between the representatives of Frederick II and the barons of the high court led by John of Ibelin – the Emperor's men controlled Jerusalem and Tyre, while the Ibelins had their headquarters in Acre.[3] Second, none of the holy places was defensible: Bethlehem and Nazareth were unwalled, while the walls of Jerusalem had been demolished by Prince al-Muazzam of Damascus during the Fifth Crusade.[4] As the Franks did not control the hinterland of any of these cities, they were vulnerable to enemy attack. Yet these problems were more apparent than real: no barrier was put in the way of churchmen who wished to return to Jerusalem by either faction in the civil war, while the Sultan was scrupulous about observing the terms of the truce.

There were also problems specific to individual communities. Saladin had turned the patriarch's palace into a Sufi mosque and the convent of St Anne into a *madrasa*;[5] he had also demolished the monastery of Our Lady of Josaphat and the upper church, though not the crypt church, and had used the stone to repair the walls of the city.[6] Probably before 1229, the complex on Mount Zion also was

Crusades: II: *The Later Crusades, 1189-1311*, ed. R. L. Wolff and H. W. Hazard (Philadelphia, 1962), 429-62; D. Abulafia, *Frederick II* (London, 1988), 164-201.
1 On the significance of Frederick's coronation, see H.-E. Mayer, 'Das Pontifikale von Tyrus und die Krönung der lateinischen Könige von Jerusalem', *Dumbarton Oaks Papers*, xxi (1967), 200-10.
2 Abulafia, *Frederick II*, 200-1.
3 Philip of Novara, *The Wars of Frederick II against the Ibelins in Syria and Cyprus*, trans. J. L. Lamonte (New York, 1936), with historical introduction.
4 Oliver of Paderborn, *Historia Damiatina*, ed. J. Hoogeweg, 24, in *Die Schriften des ... Oliverus, Bibliothek des litterarischen Vereins in Stuttgart*, ccii (1894), 203.
5 H. Vincent and F. M. Abel, *Jérusalem*: II: *Jérusalem Nouvelle* (Paris, 1914-26), 291, 679.
6 Ernoul, 'L'estat de la cité de Iherusalem [v. 1231]', 24, *Itinéraires à Jérusalem: Publications de la Société de l'Orient Latin, série géographique*: III: *Itinéraires français*, ed. H. Michelant and G. Raynaud (Paris, 1882, repr. Osnabrück, 1966), 50-1; C. N. Johns, 'The Abbey of St Mary in the Valley of Jehosaphat, Jerusalem', *Quarterly of the Department of Antiquities in Palestine*, viii (1938), 117-36.

partly destroyed.[1] Moreover, all the churches and monasteries that had remained in Christian hands had been restored to Eastern-rite Christians, chiefly Orthodox, and would need to be adapted once more for the Catholic liturgy. But again these were not serious problems, and all the difficulties combined were negligible compared with those that had confronted the first settlers in 1099.

Because their houses had not been returned to Christian rule, four communities – the convent of Bethany, the canons of Mountjoy, the Benedictines of Mount Tabor, and the canons of the Temple of the Lord – had no alternative but to stay in Acre. The others were reluctant to return, partly because the Catholic patriarch, Gerold of Lausanne, refused to accept the conditions of Frederick II's settlement with the Sultan whereby the practice of Islam was tolerated in Jerusalem. He would not return to live there, but continued to rule from Acre and merely sent the abbot of the Mount of Olives and the dean of Jaffa to act as his legal representatives.[2]

After Gerold's death in 1240, there was a long interregnum, and his successor, Robert of Nantes, only reached the East a few months before the final loss of Jerusalem in 1244.[3] Although Charles Kohler argues that the prior and canons of the Holy Sepulchre returned to Jerusalem in 1230, the evidence is inconclusive.[4] It seems more likely that only a small group of them may have done so, and that the Holy Sepulchre became, as it were, a kind of daughter-house of the Holy Sepulchre at Acre. There is no evidence that any attempt was made by the community of Josaphat to return to Jerusalem and restore their mother-house; nor is there any indication that the monks of St Mary of the Latins went back. Because Gerold spoke of 'sending' the abbot of the Mount of Olives to Jerusalem, one may infer that most of that community had not returned to live there. Indeed, the only community that may have returned, although the evidence is un-certain, was that of Great St Mary's.[5] In all other cases, the churches

---

[1] Perhaps by al-Muazzam in 1219, and certainly by the Khwarismians in 1244, though the chapel of the Cenaculum remained intact: Vincent and Abel, *Jérusalem*, ii. 463-4.
[2] *Le Cartulaire du Chapître du Saint-Sépulcre*, 341-2, no. 184.
[3] Hamilton, *Latin Church*, 261-3.
[4] Kohler, 'Un rituel et un Bréviaire', 448-50.
[5] The eighteenth-century Raybaud inventory of Hospitaller charters, many of which have not come down to us, contains this entry for 16 Aug. 1233: 'Bail passé par Mabile, abesse du monastère de Nostre-Dame Majeure en Hierusalem, à Pons de Cisternaty et Raymonde, sa femme, d'une maison au quartier du Patriarche, sous la cense de 3 besans': 'Inventaire de pièces de Terre-sainte de l'Ordre de l'Hôpital', ed. J. Delaville Le Roulx, *Revue de l'Orient Latin*, iii (1895), 83, no. 243. But although the leased property was in Jerusalem, the nuns might not have returned there. Cf. Vincent and Abel: 'Dès le début du xiiie siècle … l'église Ste Marie la Grande était exploitée en carrière, tandis que ses dépendances claustrales annexées à l'Hôpital

were restored in 1229 to the Catholic cult and a few clergy were seconded to minister to pilgrims and maintain the shrines,[1] but most members of those communities continued to live in the safety of Acre.

The church of Nazareth also experienced similar difficulties when it was restored to Frankish rule in 1229. This is known from the constitution which Archbishop Henry drew up in 1251 for the canons of his church, in which he explains that:

> Although ... sixty-four years or more have passed since the victory of Saladin over the Christians, yet since then, because of the war against the Saracens and their attacks on the Christians, the holy places of the kingdom of Jerusalem, and especially Nazareth, have been neglected and left without clergy, and have suffered grave and irreparable damage on both a spiritual and a material level through the neglect and indeed the total absence of canons, for so far scarcely anyone, or no one suitable, could be found who was prepared to devote his life there to the service of God.[2]

All was not well at Bethlehem either, although the canons did return there. Innocent IV complained that John the Roman, bishop-elect between 1238 and 1245, had alienated the property of the see and even pledged the Hammer and a Nail, two of the instruments of Christ's Passion, and the arm of St Thomas, as collateral for a loan of 1,500 bezants.[3] Moreover, the communities who, for whatever reason, stayed at Acre did not live in an exemplary way. In 1238, Pope Gregory IX appointed a commission to investigate reports that the abbots of St Mary of the Latins, the Mount Tabor monastery, and Our Lady of Josaphat 'had put aside the observance of the [Benedictine] Rule, and were wastefully spending the assets of their monasteries by living lives of luxury and indulging the desires of the flesh'.[4]

Of course, there are lax clergy in any age: complaints had been made about the scandalous lives of some Catholic churchmen in Jerusalem before 1187.[5] But between that date and 1229, people in the Frankish East, and for that matter in the Catholic West as well, had radically changed their attitudes towards the role of religious communities in the Holy Land. In the First Kingdom, it was considered that the regular clergy fulfilled an essential function on behalf of the whole

---

devenaient le bimarestan de Saladin': *Jerusalem*, ii. 963.

1 'Les Pelerinaiges por aler en Iherusalem (v. 1231)', *Itinéraires à Jerusalem*, 93-8.
2 *Les Registres d'Innocent IV*, ed. E. Berger (Paris, 1884-1921), no. 5,538.
3 Ibid., nos. 1,531-2.
4 L. Auvray, *Les Registres de Grégoire IX* (Paris, 1896-1955), no. 4,140.
5 E.g., Heraclius, Patriarch of Jerusalem, *La Continuation de Guillaume de Tyr (1184-1197)*, ed. M. R. Morgan, 38-9, in *Documents relatifs à l'Histoire des Croisades* (Paris, 1982), xiv. 50-1.

community, and in some sense on behalf of the whole Catholic world, by performing the liturgy in the holy places, the protection of which was the kingdom's *raison d'être*. By 1229, people no longer thought about the work of those communities in the same way; although there were practical reasons why the monks and canons might have found it difficult to return to Jerusalem, these were not insuperable, and it is clear that no pressure was put on them to do so. How are we to explain this change in religious attitudes?

* * *

The change may reflect a broader one in Catholic spirituality that occurred in the crucial years between the loss of Jerusalem in 1187 and its recovery in 1229. During that time, two new religious orders were founded that made a revolutionary and extremely rapid impact on the Western church: the Dominican and Franciscan friars. The friars were monks, but their vocation was to a life of active ministry rather than to one of contemplative prayer. And they taught that lay people might strive for perfection not by renouncing the world, but by seeking to consecrate their daily lives to the service of God. They tried, in accordance with the legislation of the Fourth Lateran Council of 1215, to encourage lay people to take a more active part in the worshipping life of the church by regular attendance at mass and by receiving the sacraments. As a result, lay piety became far more eucharist-centred than it had been for centuries.

A new ideal of holiness developed. St Peter Damian, the hermit cardinal, was replaced by St Francis and St Dominic as the model of the Christian life, the cult of Francis enjoying particularly strong popular support. It is true that in his last years Francis largely withdrew from the world to live in contemplation on Mount Alvernia, but this was neither how he was remembered nor how he had spent the greater part of his life, which was in ministering to ordinary people. The older model of holiness – the Peter Damian model – had implied that the only way to lead a truly Christian life was by withdrawing from the world; the new model, that of Francis and Dominic, implied that involvement in the world was, if rightly practised, an equally sure path to salvation.[1]

The mendicant orders influenced the crusade movement. Although, in an ideal world, the friars would have wished to convert everybody

---

1 The literature on the two orders is vast. I would draw attention to S. Tugwell, 'The Spirituality of the Dominicans' and J. A. Wayne Hellmann, 'The Spirituality of the Franciscans', in *Christian Spirituality*: II: *High Middle Ages and Reformation*, ed. J. Raitt et al. (New York, 1988), 15-50.

to Christianity by peaceful persuasion, they were prepared to sanction the use of force against rulers who would not allow evangelization in their lands. That, in practice, meant most Islamic rulers, as in Muslim states it was considered blasphemous to criticize the revelation given to the Prophet, and to do so was normally punishable by death.[1] The friars, who were used throughout the thirteenth century as crusade preachers, thus influenced the way in which a new generation of crusaders understood their role.[2]

The Franks living in the crusader states were influenced by the new orders almost from the start. The Franciscans established a province there in 1217 with its headquarters at Acre, where St Francis stayed during the Fifth Crusade,[3] and other communities were founded before 1250 at Antioch and Tripoli.[4] At some time before 1228, the Dominicans also set up a province in the Holy Land, almost certainly with its headquarters at Acre.[5] The new ideals of Christian perfection propagated by the mendicant orders probably affected the ways in which pilgrims, crusaders, and the Catholic inhabitants of the Frankish East came to regard the holy places by the time they were restored to Christian rule in 1229. But it must be recognized that the new spirituality did not lead to any decline in crusading fervour; even though the crusade was becoming increasingly diversified in the thirteenth century, there was still a very strong response in western Europe to appeals for the Holy Land. When Frederick II's ten-year truce with the sultan of Egypt expired in 1239, a new crusade came to the East led by Theobald of Navarre, reinforced a year later by an independent expedition led by the brother of Henry III of England, Richard of Cornwall. Between them, they succeeded in preserving and improving the Frankish *status quo*.[6] When Jerusalem fell to the Muslims again in 1244, Louis IX of France took the cross and led a host against Egypt in an unsuccessful attempt to recover it: it was important to Christian esteem that the holy places should remain in Western hands, and it was also important that pilgrims should be able to visit them freely.

But thirteenth-century lay people who visited the holy places,

---

1 B. Z. Kedar, *Crusade and Mission: European Approaches towards the Muslims* (Princeton, 1984), 136-203.

2 E.g., S. Lloyd, *English Society and the Crusade, 1216-1307* (Oxford, 1988), 45-57.

3 M. Roncaglia, *Biblioteca bio-bibliografica della Terra Santa* ser. IV, tom. I: *Storia della Provincia di Terra Santa* I: *I Francescani in Oriente durante le crociate (sec. xiii)* (Cairo, 1954), 32-3, 53.

4 Ibid., 53-4, 56.

5 W. A. Hinnebusch, *History of the Dominican Order* (New York, 1965-73), i. 173.

6 P. Jackson, 'The Crusades of 1239-41 and Their Aftermath', *Bulletin of the School of Oriental and African Studies*, l (1987), 32-60.

whether they were crusaders, pilgrims, or the Catholic inhabitants of the crusader states, were more conscious of their own role in the worshipping life of the church than earlier generations had been. When they visited the shrine churches of Jerusalem, Bethlehem, and Nazareth, they expected to be able to assist at mass in them, and the more devout among them wanted to make their confessions and receive Holy Communion. This eucharist-centred piety necessitated the presence of priests in those churches to lead the faithful in worship, but it did not entail the presence there of monastic clergy to sing the Divine Office on behalf of the whole Christian community. The mendicant orders had, of course, no *locus standi* in the shrine churches, which remained the property of the twelfth-century foundations; nevertheless, when Jerusalem returned to Christian rule in 1229, both orders established their own foundations there. The Franciscan house was near the Via Dolorosa,[1] and the Dominicans may even have made Jerusalem their headquarters for a time; for it was there that, in 1236, Prior Philip reconciled the Jacobite patriarch of Antioch, Ignatius, to the Roman Church and clothed him in the habit of the Dominican order. He also reconciled the Coptic archbishop of Jerusalem and opened negotiations about church unity with the Nestorian patriarch of Baghdad, as he informed Pope Gregory IX.[2]

The mendicant orders never claimed that the active life was the only valid type of Christian vocation. They recognized the importance of the contemplative vocation in the church, and, indeed, in some of their own brethren. The dominance of these new forms of spirituality in the thirteenth-century Frankish East was not, therefore, in any sense inimical to the eremitical life; indeed, hermits continued to flourish there. Driven from Jerusalem and Galilee as a result of the conquests of Saladin, in the thirteenth century they were found chiefly on the Black Mountain of Antioch, and on the slopes of Mount Carmel in the kingdom of Acre.[3] Those on the Black Mountain did not survive the Mameluke conquest of 1268, but those in the southern kingdom had a different fate. In the early thirteenth century, the prior of the hermits of Carmel, St Brocard, asked the patriarch of Jerusalem, St Albert, to draw up a rule for his brethren, which was later ratified by Honorius III. Later in the century, the Carmelites began, with papal license, to found houses in western Europe as their security in the

---

1 Roncaglia, *I Francescani in Oriente*, 41-4.
2 Matthew Paris, *Chronica Maiora*, ed. H. R. Luard, Rolls Series, lvii, pt. 3 (London, 1872-83), 396-8; the text in *MGHS*, xxiii. 941-2; and J. Richard, *La papauté et les missions d'Orient au moyen age: Collection de l'École française de Rome*, xxxiii (Rome, 1977), 57-8.
3 James of Vitry, *Historia Orientalis*, 32, 52, pp. 63, 86.

Holy Land was threatened. In the West, the order was reorganized and became more like the other orders of mendicant friars, but the tradition of contemplative prayer was never lost among them, and was revived in the sixteenth century with the formation of the discalced Carmelites led by St Teresa of Avila and St John of the Cross. This, perhaps, was one of the least predictable consequences of the crusades for the religious life of the West.[1]

Jerusalem and Bethlehem fell once more to the Muslims in 1244, as did Nazareth in 1265, never to be regained. In 1291, the last remaining cities and fortresses on the Syrian mainland were lost to the Franks and the survivors retreated to Cyprus and the West. Among them were members of the communities who had administered the holy places in the First Kingdom, who retired to their European priories, in many cases taking with them the title deeds to the Palestinian properties which they hoped one day to reclaim.

* * *

As Norman Housley shows in *The Later Crusades*, the crusading movement still had almost three hundred years of active life before it after the fall of Acre in 1291.[2] Although the Western powers were never strong enough to drive the Mamelukes from the Holy Land, a Catholic presence was restored there within a generation. In 1332-3, King Robert of Naples bought the chapel of the *cenaculum*, the Upper Room on Mount Zion, from the sultan of Egypt. It was entrusted to the Franciscans and became the headquarters of the Franciscan Custodia Terrae Sanctae in 1336. In that year, the order was allowed to found a convent at the Holy Sepulchre and, about 1345, at Bethlehem.[3] However, the Austin canons of Mount Zion, living at St Samson's Orleans;[4] those of Bethlehem, living at Clamécy near Auxerre; and the canons of the Holy Sepulchre, living at Perugia and other Western priories, were not asked to return to the Holy Land.[5] Though it is true that the new arrangements for the presence of

1 On eremitism in the Holy Land and the growth of the Carmelite order, see A. Jotischky, *The Perfection of Solitude: Hermits and Monks in the Crusader States* (University Park, 1995); L. Saggi et al., 'Carmelitani', *Dizionario degli Istituti di Perfezione* (Rome, 1975), ii. 460-521.

2 N. Housley, *The Later Crusades: From Lyons to Alcazar, 1274-1580* (Oxford, 1992).

3 L. Lemmens, *Die Franziskaner im Heiligen Lande*: 1: *Die Franziskaner auf dem Sion (1335-1552)* (2nd ed., Münster, 1925).

4 E. Rey, 'Chartes de l'abbaye du Mont-Sion', *Mémoires de la Société nationale des antiquaires de France*, 5th series, viii (1887), 31-6.

5 Comte Riant, 'Les archives des établissements latins d'Orient', *Archives de l'Orient Latin* (Paris, 1881), i. 707.

Catholic clergy at the holy places were by permission of the sultan, he must have been guided by the advice of the king of Naples, who appears to have considered friars better suited to represent Catholic interests in the Holy Land and to minister to Western pilgrims there than the older communities of canons. The Franciscans have continued to do this work ever since.

XVII

THE OTTOMANS, THE HUMANISTS AND THE
HOLY HOUSE OF LORETO

In the summer of 1464 Pope Pius II journeyed slowly from Rome to Ancona which he had named as the assembly point for a new crusade against the Ottoman Turks. Pius was already very ill and he turned aside to visit the shrine of Our Lady of Loreto near Recanati.[1] The chapel dated from the late twelfth century and contained a miracle-working image of the Blessed Virgin which was believed to have been carried there by angels.[2] This shrine was an important local pilgrimage centre: it had a hostel, it was served by several priests and administered by a guardian.[3] When he had completed his devotions the Pope presented the chapel with a golden chalice and paten[4] and then went on to Ancona. His visit to Loreto did not confer any visible benefits on him for his projected crusade did not receive adequate support and within a month he was dead.

The lack of good fortune experienced by this distinguished pilgrim might have discouraged others from following his example and prevented Loreto from ever becoming a major shrine had not the new pope, Paul II, fared better when he had visited it while still a cardinal. One of the first acts of his pontificate was to grant a partial indulgence to all pilgrims who went to Loreto on Sundays and on the feasts of Candlemas, the Assumption and the Nativity of the Virgin, 'on account of the great and marvellous and almost innumerable miracles which there are made manifest as works of the same gracious Virgin, and which we most plainly have experienced in our own person'.[5]

Pilgrimage was stimulated by papal patronage, and because the chapel was tiny, just thirty-one feet long by thirteen wide, a new basilica began to be built in 1468. Paul II encouraged this work by offering a plenary indulgence in 1471 to all

---

[1] See the letter of S. Nardini of 14 July 1464 cited by L. Pastor, *The History of the Popes from the Close of the Middle Ages*, trans. F. I. Antrobus (London, 1894), III, 357.
[2] The church of St Mary 'in fundo Laureti' is first mentioned in a charter of 1193-4, U. Chevalier, *Notre-Dame de Lorette. Étude historique sur l'authenticité de la Santa Casa* (Paris, 1906), pp. 141-3; Paul II in 1471 spoke of this church 'in qua, sicut fidedignorum habebat assertio, ipsius Virginis gloriose ymago angelico comitante cetu mira Dei clementia collocata existebat', *ibid.*, p. 207.
[3] *Ibid.*, pp. 156-84
[4] The text of the inscription in H. Tursellinus, *Lauretanae Historiae, Libri Quinque*, I, xxvi (Rome, 1597), pp. 56-7.
[5] Chevalier, *op.cit.*, pp. 201-2.

those who visited the shrine on certain days and contributed to the building fund.[6] The old chapel was left standing and became a church within a church, like the wooden chapel of Portiuncula in the Franciscan basilica near Assisi.

The guardian of Loreto at that time was Pietro di Giorgio Tolomei, usually called Teramano, the man from Teramo. He wrote a brief guide to the shrine for the benefit of pilgrims, which was in the form of a pancarte and hung on the wall of the old chapel. This told a surprising story: that the chapel of Loreto was part of the Holy House of Nazareth, being the room in which

> the Blessed Virgin Mary was born, and grew up, and where she was greeted by the Archangel Gabriel. Afterwards she reared her Son, Jesus Christ, in the same room until he was twelve years old. Finally, after the Ascension of the Lord...the Apostles...seeing that many divine mysteries had taken place in that room, ordered that it should be made a church in honour...of the Blessed Virgin Mary...and they celebrated divine worship there. And the evangelist St Luke made there with his own hands an image and likeness of the Blessed Virgin Mary which has remained there until the present day...

Teramano then went on to relate the later history of the Holy House which had remained at Nazareth until the local population became converted to Islam, when it embarked on a series of peregrinations. First angels carried it through the air to 'Sclavonia' and placed it near 'a certain city called Fiume', but because it was not sufficiently honoured there the angels subsequently carried it across the sea to a wood near Recanati. This belonged to a noblewoman named Loreta, and consequently the House became known as Our Lady of Loreto (sic). However, the new site was not entirely satisfactory: pilgrims who wished to visit the house were attacked by robbers in the wood, and so angels came and moved the shrine to a nearby hill. This belonged to two brothers, who saw the House as a tourist attraction, began to charge entrance fees, and then quarrelled about the takings. Our Lady of Loreto was displeased and so once more the angels moved the House, this time to stand beside the highway, where it was freely accessible to everybody and where it had remained ever since. It was seemingly only at this point that local people began to be worried that the House had no foundations, so they built a wall around it and laid strong foundations beneath the wall, thereby, it might be thought, obscuring the evidence of the House's miraculous character.

Teramano gave no precise dates for the various translations of the Holy House, but went on to explain that they had all occurred before 1296, for in that year the Virgin appeared in a dream to a certain holy man living nearby and told him the whole story. Hitherto, it is implied, the people of Recanati did not know where this mysterious House had come from. The holy man told the city council about his dream and they took steps to check its veracity by taking the measurements of the Holy House and then sending sixteen commissioners to Nazareth to find whether these dimensions corresponded with those of the original site. Not only did the investigators find that the Loreto and Nazareth measurements were a perfect match, they also found an inscription at Nazareth which said that the Holy House used to be there but had since gone away.

---

[6] *Ibid.*, pp. 207-8.

As Chevalier has shown in his meticulous examination of the sources for the history of Loreto, Teramano's is the first account to identify the shrine with the Holy House of Nazareth or to describe its miraculous translation. [7] There was, of course, already a tradition in the West, dating from the time of the crusades, of building shrines which were intended to symbolize some of the Holy Places. Their purpose was to foster devotion to the true Holy Places and to serve as substitute pilgrimage centres for people who were unable to visit the Holy Land. Some of them, like the Holy Sepulchre at Barletta in Apulia, were western dependencies of Holy Land shrines, dating from the time of the Latin Kingdom of Jerusalem,[8] but others were simply founded as acts of piety by returning pilgrims. This was true of the shrine of Our Lady of Walsingham in Norfolk, built by a local noblewoman whose son had been to the Holy Land in the twelfth century. It represented the shrine of Nazareth, and the claim was later made that the Virgin had appeared in a dream to the foundress and shown her a model of the Holy House of Nazareth as a blueprint for the design of the East Anglian shrine.[9] Yet none of these earlier foundations claimed to be one of the Holy Places transplanted: that distinction was reserved to Loreto.

Teramano attempted to substantiate his claim, but the testimony which he adduced was not very impressive: he cited no earlier documentary evidence and did not even appeal to a well-established local tradition preserved orally. He said that Paolo Renalducio of Loreto had told him that his grandfather's grandfather had seen the angels bring the Holy House across the sea and set it down in the wood; and that another local man, named Francesco, who was 120 years old, had said that his grandfather's grandfather had lived in the wood of Loreto and had watched while the House was moved by angels from that wood to the hill of the two brothers.[10] Teramano was a simple man and his account was intended to appeal to simple people. Evidence of a parallel kind continues to be cited by authors of popular works about the paranormal and, seemingly, to be accepted as satisfactory by many of their readers.[11] What is unusual about Teramano's story is that it came to be accepted by educated Catholic opinion and by the papal curia within a comparatively short time of being written.

In theological terms the story was unexceptionable. The Church could not deny that God sometimes caused physical objects to be moved by the ministry of angels, because Holy Scripture relates how the prophet Habakkuk, while holding a dish of pottage in his hands, was carried by an angel (who seized him by the hair of his head), from Judaea to Babylon in order to feed Daniel in the lion's den.[12]

---

[7] Text of Teramano, *ibid.*, pp. 210-12; Chevalier's analysis of it *ibid.*, pp. 212-32.

[8] F. Bonnard, 'Barletta', *Dictionnaire d'Histoire et de Géographie Ecclésiastiques* (= *DHGE*), VI (1932), 837-41.

[9] The earliest evidence for the Marian dream is the Pynson Ballad of the late fifteenth century, J. C. Dickinson, *The Shrine of Our Lady of Walsingham* (Cambridge, 1956), pp. 124-30.

[10] Chevalier, *op.cit.*, p. 212.

[11] e.g. The archaeological remains from Atlantis, including a mummified body in a stone coffin, found on a 'new island' south of the Azores by a British sea-captain and reported in a New Orleans newspaper, for which all the material evidence, including the ship's log, has been lost. C. Berlitz, *Atlantis* (London, 1984), pp. 78-9.

[12] This story, found only in the Septuagint text of the Book of Daniel, was part of the Vul-

Similar stories were told, although rarely, in the lives of the saints, like that of the angels who carried the martyred body of St Catherine of Alexandria to the top of Mount Sinai.[13]

Nevertheless, there is a great difference between agreeing that God is able to perform a particular miracle and conceding that He has done so. The humanist popes who reigned in the second half of the fifteenth century and the scholars, mostly trained in the Renaissance tradition, who staffed the curia can have had little natural sympathy with the simple pieties of Teramano, which rested on no surer evidence than the hearsay of his oldest parishioners. For although the Holy Places were *in partibus infidelium*, the popes did not rely on travellers' tales for news of them, but could check Teramano's story with their official representatives in the Holy Land.

The Mamluk Sultans of Egypt, who had swept away the remnants of the Crusader States in 1291, were nevertheless inclined to be well-disposed towards Catholic pilgrims because an important part of their income was derived from trade with the western powers. In 1332-3 the Sultan an-Nasir allowed King Robert of Naples to buy the Cenaculum on Mount Sion, believed to be the site of the house of St John, and this became the headquarters of the Franciscan Custodia Terrae Sanctae. The friars were responsible for celebrating Mass in the Latin rite at the church of the Holy Sepulchre and in the church of the Holy Nativity at Bethlehem and they were also placed in charge of all Catholic pilgrims to the Holy Land and were required to organize their tours and ensure that they observed the law.[14] Itineraries sometimes included Nazareth, although the friars had no church there and the former Latin cathedral of the Annunciation had not been rebuilt after its destruction by the Sultan Baibars in 1263.[15]

Francesco Suriano (1450-c.1528), who was successively guardian of the Franciscan convent in Beirut, member of the community of the Custodia in Jerusalem and twice superior-general of the Franciscans in the Holy Land and papal legate to the Maronites (1514-15), protested vigorously in his writings that the Holy House of Loreto was not that of Nazareth. He pointed out that the true Holy House had been carved out of the rock of the hillside of Nazareth and was therefore of its nature immovable.[16] His was, however, virtually a lone voice. The

---

gate canon of the Old Testament, Daniel, XIV, 32-8. In the Authorized Version it is printed as part of the apocryphal book, Bel and the Dragon (vv 33-9), 'cut off from the last chapter of the Book of Daniel'.

[13] Symeon Metaphrastes, *Martyrium sanctae...Aecaterinae*, J. P. Migne, *Patrologia Graeca* (= *PG*), CXVI, 302.

[14] L. Lemmens, *Die Franziskaner im Heiligen Lande. I Die Franziskaner auf dem Sion (1335-1552)*, 2nd edn (Münster, 1925). See also H. F. M. Prescott, *Jerusalem Journey* (London, 1954) and *Once to Sinai* (London, 1957) on pilgrimage to the Holy Land in the later fifteenth century.

[15] 'Annales de Terre Sainte', ed. R. Röhricht, *Archives de l'Orient Latin*, II (1884), 451; H. Leclercq, 'Nazareth. VII. L'Église de l'Annonciation'. *Dictionnaire d'Archéologie chrétienne et de Liturgie* (= *DACL*), XII(I) (1935), 1039-53.

[16] Francesco Suriano, *Il Trattato di Terrasanta e dell'Oriente* ed. G. Gulobovich (Milan, 1900), p. 146. For his life see B. Bagatti's preface to T. Bellorini, E. Hoade, trans, *Fra Francesco Suriano. Treatise on the Holy Land.* Publications of the Studium Biblicum

fame of Loreto spread unchecked by any word of caution from the curia. On the contrary, it was the papal governor of Bologna, Vicenzo Casale, who arranged for Teramano's account to be translated into Greek, Spanish, French, German, Slavonic, Italian and even Arabic for the use of pilgrims, a sure sign that the shrine was already beginning to obtain an international reputation. Then in 1488 the Bishop of Recanati gave Loreto to the reformed Carmelites of Mantua who, through the contacts available to their Order, were able to diffuse the legend still more widely.[17]

Pilgrims spread the cult in their own countries. In the early sixteenth century the Bakers' Guild of Rome commissioned Bramante and Antonio di Sangallo the younger to build a church for them near the Piazza Venezia, which they dedicated to S. Maria di Loreto.[18] Richard Bere, Abbot of Glastonbury (1494-1524), as Leland relates, 'cumming from his embassadrie out of Italie made a chapelle of Our Lady de Loretta, joining to the north side of the body of the chirch';[19] while in 1533 a Scotsman, Thomas Doughty, established a hermitage at Musselburgh dedicated to Our Lady of Loreto and modelled on the Italian shrine.[20]

The popes, while continuing to grant privileges to Loreto, made no reference to its claim to be the Holy House of Nazareth until 1507, when Julius II, issuing a confirmation of the privileges of the shrine, stated that it was 'commonly believed as a matter of pious opinion' (*ut pie creditur et fama est*) that the shrine really was that room in which

> the most blessed Virgin was conceived, where she grew up, where being greeted by an angel she by a word conceived the Saviour of the ages; where she...brought up her first-born son; where she fell asleep while praying when she was taken up from this wicked world to the worlds above; and which the holy apostles consecrated as the first church in honour of God and of the same blessed Virgin, where the Mass was first celebrated.
>
> It was first carried in the hands of angels from Bethlehem (sic) to the regions of Sclavonia and the place called Fiume, and then by the same angels to the wood of the woman Laureta, who had a special devotion to the...Virgin Mary, and next was taken from that wood...to the hill of the two brothers, and finally, because of the strife which arose between them, it was translated to the public highway in the district of Recanati.[21]

The papal notaries who drafted this document showed a proper caution: they do not say that the shrine of Loreto is the Holy House of Nazareth, only that it is thought by some devout people to be so. Yet they do claim that the shrine has many sacred associations which had never traditionally been assigned to the Holy House of Nazareth. It had for centuries been believed that the Virgin had been born and had grown up in her parents' house in Jerusalem, on the site of which the

Franciscanum, 8 (Jerusalem, 1949).

[17] Chevalier, *op.cit.*, p. 238.

[18] P. Partner, *Renaissance Rome, 1500-1559. Portrait of a Society* (London, 1976), p. 104.

[19] J. Leland, *The Itinerary*, ed. L. Toulmin-Smith (London, 1907), I, 90; cited D. Knowles, *The Religious Orders in England* (Cambridge, 1959), III, 23.

[20] A. Macquarrie, *Scotland and the Crusades, 1095-1560* (Edinburgh, 1984), p. 113.

[21] Chevalier, *op.cit.*, p. 262.

church of St Anne had been built.[22] The Annunciation and the childhood of Christ had indeed always been associated with Nazareth on the authority of St Luke's Gospel,[23] but it was believed that after the Crucifixion the Virgin did not return to Nazareth, but was taken into the house of St John[24] which was associated with the *Cenaculum* in Jerusalem, the shrine of the upper room, where the Eucharist had first been celebrated by the Lord himself on Maundy Thursday. Pilgrims were shown in the Cenaculum the site of the room in which the Virgin died,[25] but her assumption into heaven was associated with the place of her burial, the church of our Lady of Josaphat near the garden of Gethsemani.[26] None of these shrines, of course, was identifiable with Bethlehem, the place of the Lord's birth, the name which by a strange oversight was inserted in Julius II's bull in place of Nazareth. The papal chancery in 1507 was clearly not concerned with giving historically accurate information about the various Marian shrines in the Holy Land, but with fostering religious devotion among the pilgrims who flocked to the Holy House of Loreto, who were encouraged to meditate in that place about all the major events in the life of Mary.

This bull gave official papal approval to the cult of the Holy House of Loreto although it did not endorse the claim that it had been moved there from Nazareth by the ministry of angels, which was regarded merely as a pious opinion. Julius II himself held Loreto in great respect and went there twice, once in 1510 and again in the following year to give thanks for his preservation from danger at the siege of Mirandola.[27] Yet perhaps the most striking evidence of the way in which the cult of Loreto had come to be accepted at all levels of Catholic society in the early sixteenth century is the fact that Erasmus wrote a liturgy for the shrine in 1524, for few Catholics who remained faithful to the old religion at the time of the Protestant Reformation were more critical of the legends of the saints than the author of *In Praise of Folly*.

In his introit for the Mass Erasmus puns on the Latin form of Loreto, *lauretum*, 'the laurel grove':

> Laurus odore juvat, speciosa virore perenni,
> Sic tua, Virgo parens, laus omne virebit in aevo.

---

[22] Legends about the Virgin's early life ultimately derive from the apocryphal Book of James (or Protevangelium), trans. M. R. James, *The Apocryphal New Testament* (Oxford, 1924), pp. 38-49. For their localization in Jerusalem see J. Wilkinson, *Jerusalem Pilgrims before the Crusades* (Warminster, 1977), p. 170.

[23] Luke, I, 26, II, 39, 51.

[24] John, XIX, 27.

[25] Wilkinson, *op.cit.*, p. 172; for the shrine in the crusader church of Sion see *Theoderich's description of the Holy Places, circa 1172 A.D.*, translated A. Stewart, Palestine Pilgrims' Texts Society (= *PPTS*) (London, 1891), pp. 36-7.

[26] Wilkinson, *op.cit.*, p. 158; T. S. R. Boase, 'Ecclesiastical Art in the Crusader States in Palestine and Syria. A. Architecture and Sculpture', in K. M. Setton, gen. ed., *History of the Crusades*, vol IV, ed. H. W. Hazard, *The Art and Architecture of the Crusader States* (Madison, WI., 1977), pp. 96-7.

[27] Chevalier, *op.cit.*, p. 270-1.

This theme is taken up again in the liturgical sequence to be sung between the Epistle and the Gospel. The Gospel is St John's account of the wedding at Cana of Galilee[28] and is followed by a long homily in which Erasmus considers the Virgin in her role as wife of St Joseph and as an exemplar of married life.[29] Throughout the liturgy Erasmus makes no reference to the translation of the Holy House, and no doubt this omission was deliberate,[30] nevertheless, by writing this liturgy he was helping to diffuse the cult which was based on the popular belief that the shrine of Nazareth had been brought to Loreto.

A cult which could, within a generation, gain widespread popularity among all sections of the Western Church and come to be viewed with benevolent tolerance by learned humanists both inside and outside the curia evidently spoke in some profound way to the needs of the age. In order to understand why this was so it is necessary to examine the religious and political context in which the legend grew, for it is arguable that belief in the translation of the Holy House helped to solve a religious dilemma which confronted the West in the later fifteenth century.

The liberation of the Holy Places had been one of the chief aims of the crusading movement since its inception in the eleventh century. Although Acre, the last Frankish stronghold in the Holy Land, was lost in 1291, hope of recovering these shrines was still very much alive throughout much of the fifteenth century. Palestine was still ruled by the Mamluk Sultans of Egypt, one of the most formidable military powers in the known world[31], who had driven the Franks out in the thirteenth century. Their strength did not in itself deter western crusading zeal: throughout much of the fourteenth century fresh crusades to the Holy Land were planned by the popes at Avignon,[32] while in 1365 Peter of Lusignan, King of Cyprus, attacked Egypt, the centre of Mamluk power, and sacked Alexandria.[33]

That was to prove the last serious western attempt to wage war on the Mamluks, for in the second half of the fourteenth century a new Islamic power, that of the Ottoman Turks, began to wrest the Balkans from Christian control. This alarmed the Catholic powers of Europe and the last of the great traditional crusades, composed of contingents from most of the western lands, set out to attack the Ottomans in 1396, led by John, count of Nevers, eldest son of the Duke of Burgundy. The two armies met at Nicopolis on 26 September, where the

---

[28] John, II, 1-10.
[29] *Liturgia Virginis Lauretanae, Desiderii Erasmi...Opera Omnia*, ed. A. Vander, 10 vols (Lugduni Batavorum, 1703-6), V, 1327-34; H. Krivatsy, 'Erasmus and his Mass for the Virgin of Loreto', *Erasmus in English*, 4 (Univ. of Toronto, 1972), p. 2. I am indebted to Dr T. W. O'Reilly of University College, Cork, for this reference and also for the reference in n. 74 below.
[30] This is the opinion of Chevalier, *op.cit.*, p. 311.
[31] D. Ayalon, *The Mamluk Military Society* (London, 1979).
[32] N. J. Housley, *The Avignon Papacy and the Crusades, 1305-78* (Oxford, 1986).
[33] P. W. Ebury, 'The Crusading Policy of King Peter I of Cyprus', in P. M. Holt, ed., *The Eastern Mediterranean Lands in the Period of the Crusades* (Warminster, 1977), pp. 90-105; R. Irwin, *The Middle East in the Middle Ages. The Early Mamluk Sultanate, 1250-1382* (London, 1986), pp. 145-7.

superiority of the Ottomans was proved beyond doubt and the chivalry of the west was cut to pieces.[34]

The growth of Ottoman power at first seemed to preclude the possibility of any new crusade against Egypt, but the political situation in the Eastern Mediterranean was drastically changed by the intervention of Timur-i-Leng, better known to Englishmen as Tamburlaine, who from his capital at Samarkand sought to reconstitute the Mongol Empire. In 1402 he invaded Asia Minor, defeated the Ottoman army and took the Sultan Bajezid captive; but although Timur died in 1405 and his empire did not long survive him,[35] the Ottomans did not speedily recover their pre-eminence in the Balkans. Bajezid died in captivity and this led to a civil war among his sons which lasted for more than a decade, enabling the other Turkish princes of Asia Minor to free themselves from Ottoman suzerainty and the independent Christian rulers in the Balkans to recoup their strength.[36]

It seemed to some western observers that it might be possible to exploit this situation by launching a new crusade which would crush the demoralized Ottoman army in the Balkans and then link up with the independent Christian powers there, notably the Byzantine emperor. Since the Aegean islands, Crete and Cyprus were all ruled by western powers it should then prove possible for the crusade to liaise with a western fleet at Constantinople, launch an attack on the Mamluks in Palestine and recover the Holy Places. The western ruler who had greatest faith in a policy of this kind was Philip the Good, Duke of Burgundy (1419-67), the son of John the Fearless who had led the ill-fated crusade of Nicopolis. He was not alone among the rulers of the west in this regard, for in 1421 Henry V of England joined with him in sending Gillebert de Lannoy on an espionage mission to the Eastern Mediterranean.[37] De Lannoy spent two years there, travelling to Constantinople, to Rhodes, headquarters of the Knights of St John, to Jerusalem, to the Mamluk capital of Cairo and to Crete, the chief province of the Venetian empire. The detailed report which he wrote contains a wealth of tactical information which would be needed by anybody planning a combined campaign against the Ottomans and the Mamluks.[38]

Philip's belief in the feasibility of a crusade of this kind apparently remained unaffected by the defeat of the combined armies of Poland, Hungary, Transylvania and Serbia, led by a papal legate, Cardinal Cesarini, at Varna in 1444, where the Ottomans showed that they had fully recovered their military pre-eminence.[39] As though this defeat had never happened, Philip sent an embassy to the French court in 1452 to urge Charles VII to take the cross. It was led by Jean Germain, Bishop of Chalon-sur-Saône, who tried to persuade the King that he should campaign

---

[34] A. S. Atiya, *The Crusade of Nicopolis* (London, 1934).

[35] M. M. Alexandrescu-Dersca, *La Campagne de Timur en Anatolie (1402)* (Bucharest, 1942; reprint London, 1977).

[36] H. Inalčik, *The Ottoman Empire* (London, 1973), pp. 17ff; J. W. Barker, *Manuel II Palaeologus, 1391-1425* (New Brunswick, 1969), pp. 200-89.

[37] R. Vaughan, *Philip the Good* (London, 1970), pp. 268-9.

[38] G. de Lannoy,*Oeuvres*, ed. C. Potvin (Louvain, 1878), pp. 51-162; A. S. Atiya, *The Crusade in the Later Middle Ages* (London, 1938), pp. 190-7.

[39] O. Halecki, *The Crusade of Varna* (New York, 1943).

XVII

against the Ottomans as a preliminary to marching to the Holy Land and recovering Jerusalem from the Mamluks.[40] The simplicity of this solution to the Eastern Question, although it might have appealed to St Louis, proved less attractive to his Valois successor. Nevertheless, news of the fall of Constantinople in the following year did profoundly shock the entire Christian West and at the Diet of Frankfurt in 1454 a new crusade against the Ottomans was planned by representatives of the Emperor Frederick III and of Pope Nicholas V.[41]

For various reasons preparations for this war were delayed until the pontificate of Pius II (1458-64) who was a zealous proponent of the crusade. This attracted considerable support: Philip of Burgundy had already taken a conditional crusading vow; the Pope took the cross himself in 1462 and in the next year both Cristoforo Moro, the new Doge of Venice, and Matthias Corvinus, King of Hungary, offered Pius their support. In his bull *Ezechielis* of October 1463 the Pope summoned the faithful of the west to join him at Ancona in the following summer for a crusade against the Ottomans. The expedition could, moreover, be financed without the Pope's having to tax the clergy, since in 1462 an alum mine had been discovered at Tolfa in the Papal States. This was the only substantial source of the mineral, essential in the manufacture of textiles, known in western Europe: previously all supplies had come from Ottoman-controlled Phocaea in Asia Minor. Within a year the papal enterprise was employing 8,000 operatives.[42] Yet despite these good auguries the crusade did not prosper. Louis XI of France persuaded Philip of Burgundy, the most committed of all the potential leaders, to withdraw his support,[43] and although many poor people took the cross there was virtually no response from the rulers and the great nobility of the west. Pius II died at Ancona in 1464, perhaps not fully aware that the crusade to which he had devoted so much of his reign would not take place.[44]

There is no suggestion in any source that Pius II had envisaged that his crusade would, after defeating the Ottomans, sweep on to recover Jerusalem from the Mamluks. Such a strategy was no longer conceived as being practical, for from his new capital of Constantinople the Sultan Mehmet the Conqueror had established control over the Balkans far more firmly than any of his predecessors had succeeded in doing. He had also begun systematically to annexe independent states which might provide a Christian army with bases and make common cause with it. Thus in 1456 he had conquered Athens, last successor-state of the Latin Empire of Constantinople, and in 1460 had annexed the Byzantine despotate of Mistra; in 1461 he took over the independent Turkish Candarid principality in northern Asia Minor, and then conquered the neighbouring Greek Empire of

[40]Ch. Schefer, 'Le discours du voyage d'Oultremer au très victorieux roi Charles VII, prononcé, en 1452, par Jean Germain, évêque de Chalon', *Revue de l'Orient Latin*, III (1895), 303-42.
[41]The German princes showed no great enthusiasm for the project, Pastor, *op.cit.*, II, 302-4.
[42]R. J. Mitchell, *The Laurels and the Tiara. Pope Pius II, 1458-1464* (London, 1962), p. 193 n.
[43]Vaughan, *op.cit.*, pp. 369-72.
[44]C. M. Ady, *Pius II* (London, 1913), pp. 304-48; Pastor, *op.cit.*, III, 311-74; Atiya, *Crusade in Later Middle Ages*, pp. 226-30.

Trebizond on the Black Sea coast; in 1462 he expelled the Genoese from Lesbos and in 1463 annexed Bosnia.[45] By Pius II's reign it was no longer realistic to suppose that the Turks could be dislodged from power in a single campaign, and the Pope aimed in the first instance to restore Constantinople to Christian control. The future recovery of the Holy Places had become only a theoretical possibility.

Pius's successor, Paul II, was a Venetian, and perhaps for that reason had a more realistic conception of how best to counter the Ottoman threat. Pius II had shown conclusively that there was no longer any possibility of raising a pan-European crusade, and since that was so the Catholic West needed an effective system of defence to halt the Ottoman advance. Venice, with its powerful fleet and string of fortresses and islands in the Adriatic and the Aegean, afforded the best naval protection to the west, while Hungary held the Danube frontier against an Ottoman advance by land.[46] The new Pope therefore gave these two powers the money which his predecessor had raised for the crusade to enable them to make war on the Ottomans, and throughout his reign he continued to subsidize the defences of Hungary with the profits of the alum-mine of Tolfa.[47]

Although these measures may have helped to check the Ottoman advance they did not halt it. In 1470 the Sultan captured Euboea from the Venetians; in 1473 he incorporated the last independent Turkish principality in Asia Minor into his empire; in 1475 he annexed the Genoese port of Kaffa in the Crimea; and in 1479 his forces occupied Cephalonia, the oldest of all the western possessions in the Greek islands.[48] In the same year the Venetians ended their sixteen-year war against the Ottomans and conceded the loss of all the territories which the Sultan had annexed during that time.[49]

Venetian neutrality deprived the Italian states of their chief naval protection and on 11 August 1480 an Ottoman naval force captured Otranto in the kingdom of Naples. Public opinion throughout Italy was profoundly shocked, partly by the barbarous way in which the Turks treated the civilian population of the city, but chiefly because this was the first time for 500 years that a Muslim army had held a town on the Italian mainland. Pope Sixtus IV (1471-84) preached a crusade and raised a fleet with the help of the Italian powers. Attempts to raise money for this war outside the peninsula met with a mixed response: Edward IV of England, for example, declined to contribute.[50] Nevertheless, the crusade was an unqualified success and the Ottomans surrendered Otranto to this Christian army on 10 September 1481.[51]

---

[45] F. Babinger, *Mehmed the Conqueror and his Time*, trans. R. Manheim, ed. W. C. Hickman (Princeton, 1978), pp. 129-224.
[46] The Hungarians inflicted a severe defeat on the Ottomans at Belgrade in 1456, *ibid*, pp. 136-44; on the strength of Venice, M. E. Mallett and J. R. Hale, *The Military Organization of a Renaissance State, Venice, c.1400-1617* (Cambridge, 1984), pp. 45-50.
[47] Pastor, *op.cit.*, IV, 79-84; Atiya, *Crusade in Later Middle Ages*, p. 230.
[48] Cephalonia had been captured by the Normans of Sicily in 1185 and was never subsequently restored to Byzantine rule, W. Miller, *The Latins in the Levant* (London, 1908), p. 2.
[49] Babinger, *op.cit.*, pp. 279-384.
[50] He alleged that the Scottish peril precluded his doing so, C. A. Scofield, *The Life and Reign of Edward IV*, 2 vols (London, 1923), II, 389-90.
[51] Pastor, *op.cit.*, IV, 334-47.

Yet it was clear to everybody that the Ottomans might attack Italy again at any time, and in such circumstances it would have been irresponsible of the Holy See to consider preaching a new crusade against the neutral power of Mamluk Egypt in order to recover the Holy Places. That inveterate globe-trotter, Friar Felix Fabri, who made the Jerusalem journey twice, once in 1480 and again in 1483, devotes a long section of his memoirs to an account of the early crusades and of the establishment of Frankish rule in the Holy Places, but concludes:

> the Holy Land has been so utterly lost to us that now no one so much as thinks about recovering it, and there is no longer any way to recover it, unless it should please God to work some miracle to that end.[52]

In the early sixteenth century the prospect for crusading deteriorated still further, for in 1517 the Ottoman Sultan, Selim the Grim, annexed the Mamluk Empire thus becoming ruler of the Holy Land. The Ottoman Empire remained immensely powerful throughout the sixteenth century and although popes continued to offer the crusade indulgence from time to time to those who were prepared to aid the rulers of Catholic Europe to withstand Turkish attacks, the conception of launching a traditional crusade to recover the Holy Places was abandoned as totally impractical.[53]

This was the political context in which the Catholic West became aware, through Teramano's publicity, that one holy place at least had been safely translated to the Italian marches and that there was no need to fight a new crusade to wrest the Holy House of Nazareth from infidel control. This must certainly have reflected what many people would have liked to believe: it absolved them from any obligation to plan an ideological war to which they were committed by four centuries of tradition but which there was no longer any possibility of winning. Indeed, because of the Ottoman seizure of Otranto, the shrine of Loreto itself seemed to be in need of protection against infidel attack and Pope Innocent VIII (1484-92) ordered Baccio Pontelli to fortify the new basilica and its piazza so that it could be defended in time of war.[54] In this way the defence of Italy could be regarded as a kind of crusading activity designed to preserve the Holy House.

Western opinion may also have been sympathetic to Teramano's simple fantasy because it conformed to an observable phenomenon, the flight to the west, and particularly to Italy, during the second half of the fiteenth century of Christian refugees from Islamic lands, many of whom brought relics with them. For the first time in 700 years there were two eastern-rite members of the Sacred College. John Bessarion, former Orthodox Archbishop of Nicaea, had been one of the chief architects of the act of union between the Catholic and Orthodox churches achieved at the Council of Florence in 1439. Pope Eugenius IV had created him a cardinal and, when the majority of the Orthodox faithful repudiated the union, Bessarion returned to Italy in 1440 and remained there for the rest of his life.[55] His

---

[52] *The Wanderings of Felix Fabri*, trans. A. Stewart, *PPTS* (London, 1892-7), II(ii), 377.

[53] 'It is still not possible to decide when the crusades came to an end'. J. Riley-Smith, *What were the Crusades?* (London, 1977), p. 76.

[54] G. Capadoglio, 'Loreto', *Enciclopedia Italiana di Scienze, Lettere ed Arti* (Rome, 1949), XXI, 505.

[55] J. Gill, *Personalities of the Council of Florence* (Oxford, 1964), pp. 45-54.

Greek fellow cardinal was Isidore, metropolitan of Kiev and head of the Russian Church, who had been born in the Morea. He was driven from Russia because of his loyalty to the union of Florence, was made a cardinal, like Bessarion, and was employed on various diplomatic missions by the Papacy. At the time of the Ottoman conquest in 1453 he was papal legate in Constantinople, but he succeeded in escaping and returning to Rome which he made his permanent home.[56]

These uniate clergy were soon followed by a distinguished group of aristocratic refugees seeking asylum from the Ottomans, many of whom sought assistance from the popes. The most eminent of them was Thomas Palaeologus, Despot of Mistra, brother of the last Byzantine Emperor, Constantine XI, who reached Rome in 1461.[57] Two years later Giovanni Asan Zaccaria, claimant to the extinct Frankish principality of the Morea, also became a papal pensioner. In 1466 Catherine, the Queen-mother of Bosnia, left Ragusa where she had been living in exile and came to Rome, followed in 1467 by Stephen Brankovič, Despot of Serbia, who had previously been living at the court of Scanderbeg, the chief opponent of the Ottomans in the western Balkans. Finally in 1480 the exiled Leonardo Tocco, Count-palatine of Cephalonia, came to live in Naples.[58]

Some of these exiles were Catholics by birth, others, like the Despot Thomas, were members of the Orthodox Church who were loyal to the union of Florence; while Catherine of Bosnia had the rare distinction of being a convert to Catholicism of many years' standing from the Bogomil heresy, the Balkan form of Catharism.[59] Thus in most cases there was no confessional barrier separating these refugees from their western hosts and they therefore had no reservations about committing to the care of the western Church the religious relics which they had brought with them. Giovanni Asan, titular prince of the Morea, is thought to have brought the cross of the Zaccarias to his ancestral city of Genoa. This was a reliquary which had come into the possession of the Genoese lords of Chios, which was believed to contain a portion of the True Cross that had once belonged to St John the Evangelist and had been brought by him to Ephesus where he had ended his life as bishop.[60] Leonardo Tocco certainly brought the foot of St Anne, mother of the Virgin, from Cephalonia to Naples and placed it in his private chapel, and it was so highly regarded that his residence became known as the Palazzo del Santo Piede.[61] But the relic which was treated with the greatest honour was the head of the Apostle Andrew which the Despot Thomas brought with him from Patras.

Its arrival in the States of the Church was viewed as highly significant by Pius II, for Andrew was St Peter's brother[62] and was believed to have founded the

[56] Ibid., pp. 65-78.
[57] S. Runciman, Mistra, Byzantine Capital of the Peloponnese (London, 1980), pp. 82-93.
[58] W. Miller, 'Balkan exiles in Rome', in Essays on the Latin Orient (London, 1921), pp. 497-515
[59] M. Loos, Dualist Heresy in the Middle Ages (Prague, 1974), p.317; J. V. Fine, The Bosnian Church. A New Interpretation (New York, 1975), p. 302, does not think that the Bosnian heretics were dualists.
[60] Miller, Essays, pp. 500-1.
[61] Ibid., p. 513.
[62] John, I, 40.

church of New Rome, Constantinople, just as Peter was believed to have founded that of Old Rome.[63] Although the union of Florence had been repudiated by the mass of the Orthodox faithful the western church remained committed to it, and the arrival in Italy of Thomas, himself a uniate Catholic, bringing the head of St Andrew and seeking the protection of St Peter's Vicar, moved Pius to stage one of those great symbolic spectacles at which the Renaissance popes excelled.

Thomas reached Rome early in 1461 and at papal high Mass on *Laetare* Sunday, the fourth Sunday in Lent, was presented with the Golden Rose, the jewel which was awarded each year by the pope to the most distinguished Catholic ruler.[64] Its presentation to an exiled Byzantine prince was an indication of the importance which Pius attached to Thomas's arrival, for in the Pope's view he was the true Catholic heir to the ancient Christian Empire of the East. The relic of St Andrew meanwhile was lodged in the citadel of Narni until preparations had been completed to receive it in Rome with solemnity. The Pope offered a plenary indulgence to any Catholic who attended the translation in Holy Week 1462 and this had the desired effect, for at the appointed time a large number of pilgrims swelled the population of the city.

The reliquary containing the Apostle's head was brought to the tower of the Ponte Molle outside Rome on Palm Sunday 1462 by an escort led by the Greek Cardinal Bessarion. On the following day the Pope and the Sacred College went to welcome the Apostle. The reception took place at an altar erected in the fields beside the Via Flaminia: there the reliquary was opened and the Pope knelt and addressed a prayer to St Andrew. In a macabre oratorical flourish Pius likened the Apostle's skull to a shrine, and he apostrophized pilgrims to the Holy Places:

> O ye who journey to Jerusalem out of reverence for the Saviour, to see the places his feet have trod, behold the abode of the Holy Spirit, the throne of divinity. Here, here the Spirit of God alighted [at Pentecost]... here were the eyes that often beheld God in the flesh. This mouth often spoke to Christ...Behold, a mighty shrine![65]

A solemn Te Deum was then sung, followed by a hymn in sapphics composed by the Bishop of Ancona, and the reliquary was then taken just inside the walls of Rome to the church of S. Maria del Popolo where it remained overnight.

On the following day the Pope, seated in a golden chair and holding the reliquary in his hands, was carried in procession to St Peter's by bearers, while members of the diplomatic corps walked beside him holding a baldachino over his head. Pius could not walk because he had severe gout, but the rest of the Roman clergy, led by the College of Cardinals and dressed in festal robes, followed on foot out of reverence for the Apostle and the long route proved a marathon for the elderly and unathletic among them.[66] When they reached St Peter's the Pope

---

[63] F. Dvornik, *The Idea of Apostolicity in Byzantium and the Legend of the Apostle Andrew* (Cambridge, Mass., 1958).

[64] C. Cartari, *La Rosa d'oro pontificia* (Rome, 1681) p. 87.

[65] *Memoirs of a Renaissance Pope. The Commentaries of Pius II. An Abridgement.* Trans. F. A. Gragg, ed. L. C. Gabel (London, 1960), p. 246.

Pius commented: 'Some who had been reared in luxury and had scarcely been able to go a hundred feet except on horseback, on that day, weighed down as they were with their sacred robes, easily accomplished two miles through mud and water'. *Ibid.*, p. 250.

dismounted and carried the reliquary into the basilica. He wept as they passed the statue of St Peter in the vestibule, who seemed to be welcoming his brother Andrew after a separation of 1400 years. The Pope placed the reliquary on the high altar, built over St Peter's tomb, and the cardinals came forward to venerate it. The spectators were specially moved by the sight of the aged Cardinal Isidore of Kiev, who had had a stroke which had deprived him of his speech, but who nevertheless made the effort to pay his respects to the Apostle, for he had been born at Monemvasia in southern Greece quite near to St Andrew's shrine at Patras.[67]

The translation of the relic reached its climax in a dialogue between the two Apostles: Cardinal Bessarion spoke on behalf of Andrew, imploring aid for the Peloponnese against the Turks, while Pius replied in the person of Peter, promising to meet his brother's request. When the ceremony was ended the relic was lodged in the security of the Castel Sant'Angelo until the special chapel which the Pope had ordered to be built in St Peter's was ready to receive it. The importance which Pius attached to the reception of the Apostle's head may be gauged from the fact that he chose to be buried in St Andrew's chapel in the Vatican.[68]

The later fifteenth century was thus a time when many relics of the apostolic age were brought to the west by refugees and were for the most part accepted with reverence by the highest ecclesiastical authorities. The normal authentication procedures could not be applied in the case of these relics, because it was not practical to take depositions from witnesses in their places of origin, and western churchmen had therefore to rely on the good faith of those who presented the relics to them. The only way of testing whether these relics were genuine was to observe whether miracles were performed at the shrines where they were housed. This situation created a climate of popular opinion which was sympathetic to the legend of Loreto. In theological terms it was no more difficult to accept that God's angels had moved the Holy House from Nazareth to Loreto than that God had moved the heart of Thomas Palaeologus to bring the head of St Andrew from Patras to Rome. In any case, the Holy House passed the empirical test of being a genuine relic because it was generally agreed that many miracles were wrought there.

Nevertheless, the fact that educated Catholic opinion was prepared to accept so improbable a legend, unsupported by any evidence worthy of consideration, indicates that the late medieval western church was less interested in the historical provenance of relics than in the devotional uses to which they were put. Francesco Suriano's reasoned objections to the claims of Loreto, to which reference has been made above,[69] were not refuted by the numerous supporters of

---

[67] Gill, op.cit., pp. 65, 76.
[68] The fullest account of the translation is that given by Pius himself, Memoirs, ed. Gabel, pp. 244-59. The St Andrew's chapel was demolished in 1610 by Paul V to make way for new buildings at the Vatican. Pius was later re-buried in S. Andrea della Valle, which stood on the site of his family's Roman house, the Palazzo di Siena, Ady, op.cit., pp. 339-40.
[69] See n. 16 above.

the Italian shrine, but were ignored, even though he wrote with authority as Guardian of the Holy Places and papal representative in the east.

The attitude of the popes and their advisers to Loreto had, paradoxically, far more in common with that of the Protestant reformers than with that of isolated Catholic critics. Protestants held that the veneration of relics and pilgrimages to thaumaturgic shrines, even if these were associated with Christ himself, and irrespective of whether they were authentic, were not merely unnecessary but also undesirable acts, because they detracted from the cultivation of God's presence in the interior life. The Catholic Church, on the contrary, continued to teach that material symbols, like relics and shrines, could be used by God as channels of grace and help men to focus their experience of the divine. Nevertheless, the church held that a symbolic shrine was as effective a means of grace as the historical shrine which it represented. In the fifteenth century, for example, the devotion of Stations of the Cross was introduced in many parts of western Europe. This consisted of a set of representations, at that time varying in number, portraying Christ's journey from the judgment hall of Pilate to Calvary, and this made it possible for any Christian to accompany Christ on the Via Dolorosa in his meditations without making the pilgrimage to Jerusalem. Protestant and Catholic attitudes to relics and pilgrimages were thus mirror images of each other, for both were more concerned with the cultivation of interior piety than with the performance of external acts of devotion. This was inevitable since both traditions were profoundly influenced by the same late medieval forms of spirituality, notably the *Devotio Moderna*.

The prevalence of such religious attitudes helps to explain why the Holy See appears to have thought it unimportant whether the shrine of Loreto was really the Holy House of Nazareth, as it was popularly supposed to be, or whether it was merely a symbol of that shrine, just as Stations of the Cross were symbols of the Via Dolorosa. Certainly the identification of the Holy House of Loreto with all the Marian shrines, not simply with that of Nazareth, made in Julius II's bull of 1507 as noted above,[70] suggests that the curia was more concerned to promote religious devotion than to authenticate the Loreto legend as historically accurate. For pilgrims visiting Loreto were encouraged by Julius II to meditate about the entire life of the Virgin and her place in the economy of salvation, and Loreto in this way became a symbol not only of Nazareth but also of all the Marian shrines of the Holy Land.

Since alternative shrines existed in western Europe it was no longer so important an expression of Christian commitment for Catholics to visit the Holy Land and thereby, as one participant in the First Crusade had expressed it, 'to follow in the footsteps of Christ, by whom they had been redeemed from the power of hell'.[71] It was, of course, still possible to visit Palestine, for when the Ottomans conquered it in 1517 they allowed the Franciscans of the Custodia Terrae Sanctae to continue to minister at some of the shrines there and to conduct

---

[70] See n. 21 above.
[71] *Gesta Francorum et Aliorum Hierosolimitanorum*, ed. & trans. R. Hill (London, 1962), p. 2.

parties of western pilgrims round them. One of the first western visitors after the Ottoman conquest was the young Ignatius Loyola who went in 1523.[72] His experience there impressed him so profoundly that when in 1534 he and six companions took religious vows at Montmartre, which marked the foundation of the Society of Jesus, their preferred intention was to go to the Holy Land and to restore it to Christian control by inaugurating a spiritual crusade which would lead to the conversion of the people there by peaceful means.[73] This did not happen, since the Pope, to whose authority Ignatius and his friends committed themselves, had other uses for the new Society. In his *Spiritual Exercises* Ignatius interiorized the crusading experience: the Christian was no longer urged to fight for the recovery of the Holy Land, not even, as Ignatius had himself first envisaged, with spiritual weapons alone, but to range himself on the Lord's side in the spiritual combat described by St Paul. [74] This is a striking example of the way in which the Catholic reformers shared with their Protestant opponents a desire to emphasize the importance of cultivating interior piety rather than of performing external acts of devotion.

The total lack of interest which the humanist popes and scholars of the late fifteenth and early sixteenth centuries showed in the historical authenticity of the Loreto legend led to its being generally accepted in the Catholic world of the post-Tridentine period. This was not only true of the unsophisticated. Matteo Ricci, the Jesuit who was responsible almost single-handed for opening up China to Catholic missions, had been born at Macerata, some twenty miles southwest of Loreto, in 1552.[75] He did not question the truth of the legend and was able to impress his Chinese catachumens with the validity of evidence for the Incarnation by stating that he had himself been born near the house of the Mother of the Lord of Heaven.[76]

The cult of Loreto was, of course, repudiated in Protestant countries. As Knowles remarked of the new buildings erected at Glastonbury by Abbot Bere, among which was the Loreto chapel:

> Some of those who worked as young men on the masonry of these edifices may well have earned good wages for pulling them down.[77]

Among the English recusant community, however, the Holy House retained its popularity, and in Charles I's reign a translation of Teramano's guide was printed for English visitors to Loreto, with the ingenuous title, 'The Wondrus Flittinge of the Kirk of Our B.Ledy of Loreto'.[78]

---

[72] J. Brodrick, *Saint Ignatius Loyola. The Pilgrim Years* (London, 1956), pp. 118-46.
[73] *Monumenta Historica Societatis Jesu*, I (Matriti, 1894), *Vita Ignatii Loiolae ... auctore J. A. de Polanco*, p. 50.
[74] The Meditation of the Two Banners, for the fourth day of the second week, *Obras Completas de San Ignacio*, ed. I. Ipparraguirre (Madrid, 1963), pp. 225-7. See n. 29 above.
[75] V. Cronin, *The Wise Man from the West* (London, 1955), p. 8.
[76] J. D. Spence, *The Memory Palace of Matteo Ricci* (London, 1985), pp. 232-3.
[77] Knowles, *Religious Orders*, III, 23.
[78] *English Recusant Literature, 1558-1640*, selected and edited D. M. Rogers, vol 108 (1972), facsimile endpaper.

The building of the new church of Loreto continued throughout the period of the Reformation controversies. Although work on the basilica started in 1468, the façade was not finished until 1587 while the bronze doors were only completed in 1610. Many of the artists of the high Renaissance had some share in the work: Bramante, Sansovino and Giuliano and Antonio di Sangallo the Younger among them. The Holy House was enclosed on the outside with an elaborate marble casing covered with bas-reliefs, the work of Andrea Sansovino, Aurelio and Girolamo Lombardi, Raffaello da Montelupo, Baccio Bandinelli and Simone Mosca.[79]

While it would not be true to say that the legend of Loreto grew in the sixteenth century, since no substantial additions were made to Teramano's account of the origins of the House, nevertheless, some matters of detail, left vague in the earlier account, were filled in by Girolamo Angelita. He was an official of the commune of Recanati, and his *Lauretanae Virginis Historia*, published in 1531, was the first history of the shrine to be printed. He presented a copy to Pope Clement VII who had visited Loreto in the previous year immediately after the coronation of Charles V at Bologna.[80] Whereas Teramano had dated the translations of the Holy House to some unspecified period before 1296, Angelita gave exact dates. He relates that the House reached Dalmatia on 10 May 1291, and we may reflect that it is fortunate that this vote of divine no-confidence was unknown to the crusader garrison of Acre which at that time was still fighting spiritedly against the Mamluk army.[81] On 10 December 1294, Angelita continues, the House arrived in the wood of Loreto and in the following July or August it was translated to the hill of the two brothers, although he gives no date for its final removal to its present site.[82]

Loreto continued to be a popular place of pilgrimage, so much so that other churches wanted some share in its attraction. Arguably the most idiosyncratic instance of this is that remarked upon by the Maurist, Dom Michel Germain, who visited the Benedictine abbey of Farfa in the Papal States in 1685 and wrote to a colleague:

> On garde avec religion une clé qu'on tache de croire qu'elle ait été celle de la maison de Notre-Dame de Nazareth, transferée à Lorette.[83]

It was not until the nineteenth century that people became informedly interested in the historical basis of the Loreto legend. It did not prove difficult to adduce literary and archaeological evidence which showed that the Holy House could not have formed part of the sanctuary of Nazareth before 1291. This tempted some devout people to defend the authenticity of the shrine of Loreto and the most ingenious attempt must surely be that of Count Monaldo Leopardi. He conceded that his opponents' arguments about the differences between the Holy House of Loreto and the Holy House of Nazareth, as it had been described by

[79] Capadoglio, 'Loreto', *Enciclopedia Italiana*, XXI, 504-5.
[80] H. Leclercq, 'Lorette', *DACL*. IX(II), 2495-6.
[81] Acre fell on 18 May 1291, S. Runciman, *A History of the Crusades*, (Cambridge, 1954), III, 417-21.
[82] [H. Angelita], *Lauretanae Virginis Historia* (no date, no place).
[83] Cited, Leclercq, 'Lorette', *DACL*, IX(II), 2506.

pilgrims who visited the site before 1291 and whose testimony was confirmed by recent excavations, was irrefutable. He nevertheless argued that the Loreto legend was true, because the angels had removed the real Holy House from Nazareth in sub-apostolic times, had concealed it in an unknown place for centuries, and then had brought it to Dalmatia in 1291 as a consolation prize, one must suppose, to the Catholic west which was about to lose control of the Holy Land forever. It therefore followed that the House of Loreto was the true Holy House, whereas the one which pilgrims to Nazareth had visited in the middle ages and whose vestiges archaeologists had uncovered was merely a later building erected on the empty site.[84]

Loreto is important to the historian in its own right, not simply, or even chiefly as an example of religious credulity. The desire for thaumaturgic shrines, places where human beings may directly experience the Divine presence, is a very deep-rooted part of human experience. Loreto was such a place long before the legend of the Holy House became attached to it, for pilgrimages had been made to the miracle-working image of the Virgin in the old church since at least the early fourteenth century.[85] Had Teramano not told his story Loreto would no doubt have remained like the Marian shrines at Walsingham or Rocamadour, held in great veneration, but only attracting pilgrims from a restricted area. The story of the translation of the Holy House brought Loreto to the attention of all Catholic Europe and made the shrine famous because it spoke to the needs of a generation.

Loreto is not a unique example of a local shrine which achieved international recognition because a totally unhistorical legend became associated with it, for an analogue is provided by the old church at Glastonbury. This wooden church, which predated the Saxon conquest of Somerset in the seventh century, was held in such esteem that it was preserved after the Saxons had built a new stone church, and it survived until it was destroyed by fire in 1184. Because of this wooden church, the monks of Glastonbury claimed that theirs was the oldest church in Britain, and their sceptical colleague, William of Malmesbury, who investigated this claim, wrote in his *Antiquities of Glastonbury* in 1125 that the church was indeed very old, and speculated whether it might have been founded by some mission sent to Britain in the first century by the Apostle Philip, who was traditionally credited with having evangelized Gaul. When a new edition of William's work was prepared at Glastonbury some hundred years later a passage was interpolated stating as a fact that such a British mission had been led by St Joseph of Arimathea. The fourteenth-century historian, John of Glastonbury, gave a more elaborate version of this story, relating how Joseph and his son Josephes had accompanied St Philip to Gaul and then travelled across to Britain miraculously on Josephes' shirt, spread out on the sea, bringing with them two silver cruets, containing the blood and sweat of the Lord, and how they had founded the wooden church of St Mary at Yniswitrin, the glass island of Glastonbury, in the year A.D.63.[86]

[84] M. Leopardi, *La Santa Casa di Loreto, discussioni istoriche e critiche* (Lugano, 1841). See the comments of Ch. de Smedt, 'La Santa Casa de Lorette', *Analecta Bollandiana*, 25 (1906), 491-2.
[85] Chevalier, *op.cit.*, pp. 156-7.
[86] J. Armitage Robinson, *Two Glastonbury Legends: King Arthur and St Joseph of*

These stories helped to transform Glastonbury from a local shrine into a great international pilgrimage centre. Joseph of Arimathea had glamour in the later middle ages because in the *Grand Saint-Graal*, the first volume of the Prose Vulgate Cycle of Arthurian romances dating from the early thirteenth century, he is credited with being the first guardian of the Holy Grail and with having brought the sacred vessel to England. The monastic writers of Glastonbury did not claim that their abbey possessed the Grail, but valued Joseph because he was a link with the apostolic age whom no other people had appropriated in their account of their own Christian origins. The English church could, through Joseph, claim that it had been founded in the lifetime of the Apostles. Nor was this simply a harmless affectation: the English delegation at the Council of Constance (1414-17) claimed precedence because their country had become Christian before any other nation represented there.[87]

Judged by historical criteria the Glastonbury legends have as slender a claim to belief as those of Loreto; yet despite this both shrines have remained vigorous pilgrimage centres to the present day. In the case of Loreto this indicates that its religious vitality was not simply the product of the particular circumstances prevalent in western Europe in the late fifteenth century when the legend of the Holy House first became known. The shrine already had a numinous and thaumaturgic character as a local pilgrimage centre long before it became internationally famous. It was a place where pilgrims claimed to experience God's grace, and some observers in the Renaissance period argued that this was the only function which really mattered. Antoine de Vergy, the humanist bishop of Besançon, who licensed Erasmus's liturgy of Loreto for use in his diocese on Marian feast days, has this to say about the cult:

> It is not our business to discuss how God, in this place or in that, manifests his power and glory in his saints, whereas it is our religious duty at all times to worship the Divine Majesty and to give thanks for his beneficence however it has been conferred.[88]

Arimathea (Cambridge, 1926).
[87] *Ibid.*, pp. 40-1.
[88] *Erasmi...Opera*, ed. Vander, V, 1335.

ADDENDA

A good deal of new work has been published since some of these articles first appeared: in some cases it has amplified points which I have made, in others it has challenged my opinions or in some cases led me to change them. I give details below of the principal works of this kind.

In the case of all articles relating to the Latin Kingdom of Jerusalem reference should be made to the examination of records by H.E. Mayer, *Die Kanzlei der lateinischen Könige von Jerusalem*, 2 vols., Monumenta Germaniae Historica Schriften, 40 (in two parts) (Hanover, 1996).

Our understanding of the place of the Latin Church in the Kingdom of Jerusalem has been revolutionized by the magisterial work of D. Pringle, *The Churches of the Crusader Kingdom of Jerusalem. A Corpus*, 2 vols. (Cambridge, 1993, 1998). A third volume, dealing with the churches of Jerusalem, Acre and Tyre is in preparation. Reference to the entries in this work should be made for all churches in the Crusader Kingdom referred to in my articles, which are too numerous to list separately.

I.

pp.144–7. Baldwin I's marriages have been discussed from a new perspective by H.E. Mayer, 'Etudes sur l'histoire du Baudouin Ier roi de Jérusalem', in his *Mélanges sur l'histoire du royaume latin de Jérusalem*, Mémoires de l'Académie des Inscriptions et Belles-Lettres, n.s. V (Paris, 1984), pp. 10–91.

p.156. Queen Melisende's role as a patron of the arts and the production of the Psalter which bears her name are discussed by J. Folda, *The Art of the Crusaders in the Holy Land, 1098–1187* (Cambridge, 1995), pp. 119–328 (Psalter, pp. 137–58).

p.163. The problem of the sources relating to Agnes of Courtenay's marriage to Reynald of Sidon has been elegantly solved by R. Hiestand, 'Die Herren von Sidon und die Thronfolgekrise des Jahres 1163 im Königreich Jerusalem', in B.Z. Kedar, J. Riley-Smith and R. Hiestand, eds., *Montjoie. Studies in Crusade History in Honour of Hans Eberhard Mayer* (Aldershot, 1997), pp. 77–90.

p.168. See the full discussion by P.W. Edbury and J.G. Rowe, 'William of Tyre and the Patriarchal Election of 1180, *English Historical Review*, 93 (1978), pp. 1–25.

p.169. n.132. See B. Hamilton, 'The Elephant of Christ: Reynald of

Châtillon', *Studies in Church History*, 15 (London, 1978), p.105.

p.170. Mayer argues plausibly that Agnes of Courtenay died before Baldwin IV, H.E. Mayer, 'Die Legitimität Balduins IV von Jerusalem und das Testament der Agnes von Courtenay', *Historisches Jahrbuch*, 108 (1988), pp. 88–9.

p.171. On Sibyl's coronation see B.Z. Kedar, 'The Patriarch Eraclius', in B.Z. Kedar, H.E. Mayer, R.C. Smail, eds., *Outremer. Studies in the History of the Crusading Kingdom of Jerusalem* (Jerusalem, 1982), pp. 177–204.

II.

Much new information relvant to this article is contained in Peter Edbury's important book, *John of Ibelin and the Kingdom of Jerusalem* (Woodbridge, 1997).

III.

The transmission of the fief of Transjordan between 1166 and 1174 is discussed in detail by H.E. Mayer, who also rightly points out that King Amalric forced Walter III to exchange Beirut for a money fief, and that Walter is not recorded as Lord of Blanchegarde until 1174: *Die Kreuzfahrerherrschaft Montréal (Šobak)*, Abhandlungen des deutschen Palästinavereins, 14 (Wiesbaden, 1990), pp. 215–28.

IV.

p.199. Agnes's marriage to Reynald of Sidon, see Hiestand's article, cited at I, p.163 above.

p.201. On the date or Agnes's death see Mayer's article cited at I, p.170 above.

V.

There is an important new study of Manuel's reign by Paul Magdalino, *The Empire of Manuel I Komnenos 1143–1180* (Cambridge, 1993).

p.354. The Bethlehem mosaics: see Folda, *Art of the Crusaders*, pp. 347–64; Pringle, *Churches*, I, pp. 137–56; A. Jotischky, 'Manuel Comnenus and the Reunion of the Churches: . . . the Conciliar Mosaics . . . in Bethlehem', *Levant*, XXVI (1994), pp. 207–23.

p.354. Stephen Lay has argued that Baldwin IV's leprosy had not been diagnosed at the time of his coronation, 'A Leper in Purple: the Coronation of Baldwin IV of Jerusalem', *Journal of Medieval History*, 23 (1997), pp. 317–34.

p.362. On Baldwin IV's leprosy see Piers D. Mitchell: 'Leprosy and the case of King Baldwin IV of Jerusalem', *International Journal of Leprosy*, 61 (1993), pp. 283–91.

p.365. There is a new edition of Leontios' *Life*: D. Tsougarakis, ed. with commentary and English translation, *The Life of Leontios Patriarch of Jerusalem* (Leiden, 1993).

VII.

On the legatine Council of 1140 see R. Hiestand, 'Ein neuer Bericht über das Konzil von Antiochia, 1140', *Annuarium Historiae Conciliorum*, 20 (1988), pp. 314–50.

VIII.

p.272. See Hiestand's article cited in VII above.

p. 276. On the Patriarch Athanasius see: A. Failler, 'Le patriarche d'Antioche Athanase Ier Manassès', *Revue des études Byzantines*, 51 (1993), pp. 63–75, who points out that this Patriarch has traditionally been wrongly numbered Athanasius III.

p.290. n.80, On the value of the Lyons text of the Eracles see the important new work of P. Edbury, 'The Lyon *Eracles* and the Old French Continuations of William of Tyre', in Kedar *et al*, eds., *Montjoie*, pp. 139–153.

IX.

p.14, n.80. See the new edition of the Life of St. Leontios, cited at V. p. 365 above.

p.17, n.98. See the works cited at V, p. 354 above.

X.

Of general importance for this topic is the work of R. Ellenblum, *Frankish Rural Settlement in the Latin Kingdom of Jerusalem* (Cambridge, 1998). Moreover, as Pringle has shown in his *Churches of the Crusader Kingdom*, the number of Frankish churches and chapels in rural areas of the Latin Kingdom was far greater than I have suggested here.

p.163. Tithes; see the important discussion by J. Richard, 'Le paiement des dîmes dans les états des Croisés', *Bibliothèque de l'Ecole des Chartes*, 150 (1992), pp. 71–83.

p.165. On the Templars in the Holy Land see, M. Barber, *The New Knighthood. A History of the Order of the Temple* (Cambridge, 1994); on the Italians in the Latin Kingdom: M. Favreau-Lilie, *Die Italiener im Heiligen Land vom ersten Kreuzzug bis zum Tod Heinrichs von Champagne (1098–1197)* (Amsterdam, 1988).

XI.

p.382. The discussion of the textual problems of the *Itinerarium peregrinorum* should also include: H. Möhring, 'Eine Chronik aus Zeit des dritten Kreuzzugs: das sogennante *Itinerarium Peregrinorum I*', *Innsbrucker Historische Studien*, 5 (1982), pp. 149–67.

p.387. There is a new edition of the travels and letters of Riccoldo of Monte Croce, ed. R. Kappler, with French translation, Riccold de Monte Croce, *Pérégrination et Lettres* (Paris, 1997).

XII.

This topic is treated more fully in Y. Stoyanov, *The Hidden Tradition in Europe* (London, 1994) and also in B. and J. Hamilton, *Christian Dualist Heresies in the Byzantine World c. 650–1450* (Manchester, 1998).

p.276. On the location of Dragometia see: J. Dujčev, 'Dragvitsa-Dragovitia', *Revue des Etudes Byzantines*, 22 (1964), pp. 215–21.

pp.279–80. The evidence for the Church of Drugunthia is considered by M. Angold, *Church and. Society in Byzantium under the Comneni 1081–1261.* (Cambridge, 1995), pp. 492–5.

XIII.

p.40. On the presence and influence of eastern Christian holy men in Western Europe in the first half of the eleventh century see the discussion of St. Gregory of Nicopolis in T. Head, *Hagiography and the Cult of Saints. The Diocese of Orleans 800–1200* (Cambridge, 1990), pp. 257–81.

p.51. On the Cathar text of the New Testament see also: S. Westley, 'Quelques observations sur les variantes présentées par le Nouveau Testament Cathare Occitan, le MS de Lyon (PA.36)', *Heresis*, 1996, pp. 7–21.

XIV.

p.5. Crusaders became familiar with Paulician contingents serving in the Byzantine and Muslim armies, whom they described as *publicani*. The sources for this are listed in N.G. Garsoian, *The Paulician Heresy* (The Hague, Paris, 1967), pp. 15–16.

p.10. For the Balkan Crusades see Stoyanov, *Hidden Tradition*, pp. 184–7.

p.15, n.40. A translation of Hugh Eterianus's tract against the Bogomils will be found in Hamilton and Hamilton, *Christian Dualist Heresies*, pp. 234–50. Janet Hamilton is preparing an edition of the Latin text.

XV.

p.697. On the restoration of the Holy Sepulchre after 1009 see M. Biddle, *The Tomb of Christ* (Phoenix Mill, 1999).

p.704. On Templar patrolling of pilgrim roads see D. Pringle, 'Templar Castles on the road to the Jordan', in M. Barber ed., *The Military Orders. Fighting for the Faith and Caring for the Sick* (Aldershot, 1994), pp. 148–66.

p.711. On western replicas of the Holy Places see G. Bresc-Bautier, 'Les imitations du Saint-Sépulcre de Jérusalem (IXe – XVe s.)', *Revue d'histoire de la spiritualité*, 50 (1974), pp. 319–42.

XVII.

Some of my conclusions are criticised by Norman Housley in 'Holy Land or holy lands? Sanctified space in the late Middle Ages and the Renaissance', which will appear in vol. 36 of *Studies in Church History* ed. R. Swanson (in preparation). On the Ottoman threat to Western Europe in the fifteenth century see N. Housley, *The Later Crusades. From Lyons to Alcazar 1274–1580* (Oxford, 1992), pp. 80–117.

p.6. n.22 The Protevangelium should be read in the text of O. Cullmann, in *New Testament Apocrypha*, ed. W. Schneemelcher, English trans. R. McL. Wilson, 2 vols. (Revised edn., Westminster, 1991–92), I., pp. 421–38.

INDEX

The following abbreviations are used to indicate to which Orders religious communities belonged. AC Austin Canons; B Benedictines; C Cistercians; D Dominicans; F Franciscans; H Hospitallers; P Praemonstratensian Canons; T Knights Templar.

Fulcher, Latin Patriarch of Jerusalem: I 153,
155, 159; IV 198
Fulk V of Anjou, King of Jerusalem:
I 149–52; III 140; V 362 n.49; VII 2–5,
7–8, 10, 13, 17; VIII 288 n.28; XVI 701

Garnier l'Aleman: II 19
Gautama the Buddha: XIII 59
Gawain of Cheneché: II 16
Geoffrey of Lusignan, Count of Jaffa: II 14
Geoffrey of Villehardouin, Marshal of
Romania: II 17–18; XIV 5
Georgian Church: XV 706
Gerald of Nazareth: VII 18; VIII 283; XVI 700
Gerald, Lord of Sidon: I 163–4; IV 199–200,
203 n.36
Gerard, Bishop of Cambrai: XIII 40
Germanus II, Orthodox Patriarch of
Constantinople: XIV 10
Gerold of Lausanne, Latin Patriarch of
Jerusalem: IX 19 n.105; XVI 706
Giacomo Bech of Chieri: XIV 17 n.66
Gibelin, Latin Patriarch of Jerusalem:
XVI 696
Glastonbury abbey: XVII 5, 16, 18–19
Godfrey of Bouillon: I 143; XVI 697
Godvera, first wife of Baldwin I of Jerusalem:
I 144
Gospel of the Nazarenes, perhaps read by
Cathars: XIII 57
Gregory III, Armenian Catholicus: VIII 280
Gregory IV, Armenian Catholicus: VIII 281;
IX 13
Gregory VII, Pope: VII 5; IX 1; XI 373, 378,
380; XIII 44
Gregory IX, Pope: VIII 283; XIV 9–10;
XVI 707, 710
Gregory X, Pope: VI 99, 101
Guibert of Nogent: XI 374; XIII 45
Guy Brisebarre 'of Beirut': II 15 n.7;
III 141–6
Gundulfo, Italian heretic: XIII 40
Guy of Lusignan, King of Jerusalem, Lord of
Cyprus: I 167–72; II 13–16, 24; III 139;
IV 203 n.49; V 371–2; XI 385
Guy of Montfort, bailli of Sidon: II 17, 21

al-Hakim, Fatimid Caliph: XV 696–7;
XVI 695
Hattin, Battle of, 1187: I 171; VIII 284; IX 18;
X 166; XI 382, 385; XVI 703
Hebron, Latin bishopric of: X 161 n.15, 162
n.17, 167 n.41
cathedral of (AC): IX 9; XV 711 n.59;
XVI 696, 703

Helena, St, Empress: XV 699
Helena of Milly, Lady of Transjordan: III 141
Helvis of Ibelin: I 173; II 17
Henry VI, Holy Roman Emperor: II 16–17;
XVI 704
Henry of Castile, son of Ferdinand III: VI 101
Henry I, King of Cyprus: II 16 n.21, 22–4
Henry I, King of England: VII 3, 8 n.28
Henry II, King of England: III 136; VIII 284
Henry III, King of England. VI 92–4, 101
Henry of Bethsan, constable of Cyprus: II 17
Henry I, Count of Troyes: V 369
Henry II of Troyes, lord of Jerusalem:
II 14–20; VIII 285
Heraclius, Latin Patriarch of Jerusalem: I 168,
170–71; IV 200, 203 n.21, n.41; VIII 277
Herman of Carinthia, translator: XI 375
Hermits in the Latin East. XVI 700–1
Hierapolis, Latin archbishopric of: VII 18;
VIII 278; X 162 n.17
Hildegard of Bingen, St: XIII 42–5
Hippolytus of Rome, St, Apostoilic Tradition
of: XII 295
Hodierna, Countess of Tripoli: I 147, 151,
154–6; III 140 n.27; VIII 273
Holy Cross, relics of: XV 700; XVII 12
Honorius III, Pope: II 21; VI 93; X 161;
XIV 8–9; XVI 710
Hospitallers:
Order of St John of Jerusalem: I 156; VI 98;
VII 3; VIII 284–5; IX 15; X 163 n.21,
165, 168 n.47, 169; XV 703, 705;
XVI 697, 702; XVII 8
hospitals: at Constantinople, V 374
at Jerusalem: IX 1; XV 704–5, 708;
XVI 697
Masters of: Gilbert d'Assailly: III 139
Jobert: III 139
Roger des Moulins: V 366; VIII 277;
XV 705 n.40
Hubert Walter, Bishop of Salisbury: IX 18;
XVI 703
Hugh III, Duke of Burgundy: V 368–72
Hugh Eteriano, theologian: V 360;
VIII 282–3; IX 12; XII 276; XIV 15 n.40
Hugh II of Le Puiset, Count of Jaffa:
I 149–50; VII 7
Hugh I of Lusignan, King of Cyprus: I 173;
II 16 n.17, 18, 20–1
Hugh of Ibelin, Lord of Ramla: I 160, 163;
IV 198–200; V 358
Hugh Martin: II 13–14, 16
Hugh of Tiberias: I 173; XI 383
Humphrey II of Toron, Constable of
Jerusalem: I 165; III 138–9; XI 382–3

Humphrey III of Toron: III 142–3; XI 383 n.39
Humphrey IV of Toron: I 167, 169, 171–3;
II 14, 20; III 143; IV 203 n.47; XI 383
n.39

Ignatius II, Jacobite Patriarch of Antioch:
XVI 710
Ignatius Loyola, St: XVII 16
Ilkhanate of Persia, Catholic missions to:
XI 376
Innocent II, Pope: VII 6–7, 10–12, 14–18;
VIII 271; IX 7; X 160 n.8; XVI 699–700
Innocent III, Pope: II 20 n.52, 21 n.57;
VI 94–5; XI, 387 n.57; XIV 5–7, 9. 12,
15 n.36
Innocent IV, Pope: II 24; VI 93; X 163 n.24,
168; XIII 55; XIV 11; XVI 707
Innocent VIII, Pope: XVII 11
Inquisition, papal: XIV 10–12
Irenaeus, St: XII 269
Isabella I, Queen of Jerusalem: I 163, 165,
167–9, 171–3; II 13–14, 16–18, 20–21;
III 141; IV 203 n.47; VI 358, 363
Isabel II, Queen of Jerusalem, Holy Roman
Empress: I 173; II 13, 20–22
Isabella or Toron: II 22 n.66; III 143
Isidore, Metropolitan of Kiev, cardinal:
XVII 12, 14
Islamic religion, medieval western views of:
XI 373–87
Prophet Muhammad: XI 374–6
Shi'ites: XI 376–7
Italian churches in Crusader States: X 165–6,
168 n.46

Jabala, Latin bishopric of: VIII 278, 284;
X 162 n.17
Bishop Hugh of: VII 18–20; VIII 272
Jacobite Church: VIII 278–80; IX 10–13;
X 160, 169; XV 706
Jaffa, Latin church of: IX 19 n.105; X 162,
n.18,19, XVI 706
James of Durnai, Marshal of Jerusalem: II 20
James of Vitry: X 166, 168
Jerome, St: XV 695
Jerusalem
Church of the Holy Sepulchre (AC): I 149,
151 n.46, 156; V 354, 365, 368;
VII 15–16, 18; IX 8, 10, 16–17, 19;
X 163 n.22,25; XV 696–7, 699–700,
702, 707–11; XVI 695–6, 698–9, 701,
703–6. 711; XVII 4; ceremony of New
Fire at: IX 15–16; XV 709–10;
Orthodox clergy of: V 368; IX 8, 14,
16; XV 697; *Ritual* of: XV 707–10

Latin Patriarchate of: IX 5–6; X 162–3,
166–8; XVI 694, 704, 711
hermits of: XVI 701
Orthodox community of: IX 5, 8, 16, 20;
X 161–2, 169; XV 698 n.10, 706;
XVI 694
Religious houses of: *Cenaculum, see* Our
Lady of Sion; Church of the
Ascension, Mount of Olives (AC):
IX 9, 19 n.105; X 167 n.43; XV 700,
702, 708; XVI 695, 704, 706;
Dominican priory: XVI 710;
Franciscan priory: XVI 710; Our Lady
of Josaphat (B): I 148, 156; IX 9,
15–16; X 164 nn.29, 31, 33, 167 n.43;
XV 701–2, 708; XVI 697, 699, 701.
704–7; XVII 6; Our Lady of Sion
(AC): IX 9, 17; X 167 n.43; XV 700,
702, 708; XVI 695, 704–5, 711;
XVII 6; St. Anne's (B): X 167 n.,43,
XV 701–2; XVI 698, 704–5; XVII 6;
St John *in nemore* (C): XV 15; XV 702;
XVI 700, 703; St Mary's the Great
(B): I 160; X 167 n.43; XV1, 697–8,
704, 706; St Mary of the Latins: IX 1;
X 164 n.30, 167 n.43; XV 698, 708;
XVI: 697, 704, 706–7; St Mary
Magdalen (B). IX 1; St. Samuel's
Mountjoy (P): 1, 156; IX 15; X 167
n.43; XV 701–2; XVI 699, 704, 706;
Salvatio (C): XVI 700, 703; *Templum
Domini*: I 156; IX 9; X 167 n.43;
XV 700, 702, 708, 712; XVI 695, 704,
706
Jesus (Isa) in the Koran: XI 378
Joachim of Fiore: XI 381–2
Joan of Acre, daughter of Edward I of
England: VI 100
John of Brienne, King of Jerusalem: II 19–21,
24; VI 92
John of Casamaris, papal legate: XIV 6
John Chrysostom, St: VIII 273, 283
John the Roman, Latin bishop-elect of
Bethlehem: XVI 707
John I Tzimisces, Byzantine Emperor:
XII 281; XIV 3
John II Comnenus, Byzantine Emperor: V 353;
VII 3–4, 7–13, 17; VIII 275, 278, 280
John of Damascus, St: XI 376
John of Ibelin, 'old lord' of Beirut: I 173;
II 15, 18–22; III 141; XVI 705
John of Ibelin, Count of Jaffa, *Livre des
Assises* of: III 136, 145
John IV, Orthodox Patriarch of Antioch:
VII 2; IX 1–4